Carole,
A Lucky Little Rabbit

By Carole Markarian

Copyright © 2007 **Carole Markarian**

All rights reserved by the author. No part of this publication may be reproduced, stored in a retrieval system or transmitted in any form or by any means electronic, mechanical, photocopying, recording or otherwise, without the prior written permission of the author.

ISBN: 978-0-6151-8292-6

Acknowledgments

    Yasue Nakamoto will always be the most meaningful person in my life. She's been my loyal domestic partner for nearly thirty years. Without her help through good and bad times, God knows where I'd be, what I'd be doing, or even if I'd still be alive. My tiny princess doesn't complain, her constant love, pleasant attitude, patience, and absolution, comforts me as I write this bittersweet autobiography.

    We are pleased to enjoy a loving pet business brimming with amazing clients. Early on we befriended Bruce and Regina, who trusted us with their dogs for many years. While we prayed for a miracle to buy our first home, the kindhearted couple readily helped us; we'll always cherish their goodwill.

    Through our popular shop K-9 Tubs, Yasue and I have been privileged to serve many wonderful pets, and patrons, besides being part of a caring neighborhood. Supporters are always near to bear our dreams or dilemmas. Countless friends deserve credit for being with us from the outset, including Diane Frolov, Andy Schneider, Michael and Kathy Tucci, Susan and Brian Wakil, Cal Meeder, James MacDonald, and Victor De Foe. I am grateful to Bill Condon and Nicole Conn for being my pals, likewise for blazing controversial trails while producing great films. Mom, Dad, and Nana are no longer here, but will live in my heart eternally, I think of them each day in prayer. "Peace, be with you."

    It is important to thank my constant benefactor, and guardian, the Infant of Prague for manifesting his promise. "The more you honor me, the more I will bless you." He's kept his word, I've been granted a better life than I anticipated. Twice a month for nine consecutive days, I meditate at my altar, and devote a personal novena to him. By sharing love and grace, I am indeed, 'A Lucky Little Rabbit.'

Table of Contents

Part One...1
My early years were not much fun.

Part Two...90
Change was inevitable. Soon I would be in another zip code.

Part Three...147
I assembled a new circle of interesting friends in Los Angeles.

Part Four...238
Both my parents passed away before we bought our first house.

Part Five...325
Our pets, great friends and celebrities are discussed.

Writing a book is actually harder than doing housework. While this has taken six years things may have changed a bit. This true story has taken my mind off health problems stemming from my prior wild life. I can't believe that I reached this age. Guilt about whatever I've done is minimal and I don't have many regrets, so I hope you don't judge me harshly.

Introduction

I was born to dysfunctional parents in Massachusetts in September of 1939. At age thirteen I proudly confessed my feelings for women to the family and quit school in the tenth grade. The only guy I ever became intimate with was Phillip Mahoney. We enjoyed each other, but usually held personal agendas. Predictably I went to work in a filthy shoe factory, which accepted my active gay lifestyle.

Gentle, charming accents attracted me. I've always been enchanted with foreign ladies. My first true love was a beautiful young Greek Goddess, Niki. We were completely happy together until her controlling father decided it was time for Niki to marry a rich man. She obeyed, and I lost my mind.

Provincetown on Cape Cod was my beloved home for eight years, the background of my addiction to heavy drugs in the turbulent sixties. The insanity of losing Niki brought about recklessness in behavior. Within a short time I became a big, moneymaking dope dealer, amused myself with different lovers, struggled through various rehab programs, and ultimately moved to California. Serendipity, or destiny, guided me to a bizarre pet grooming school where I glanced at Yasue Nakamoto and immediately fell in love.

The government paid for my school enrollment in 'Bark 'N' Purr', introducing me to a whole new world. Yasue didn't speak much English and I understood no Japanese, yet it never mattered. We shared meager lunches as we grew quite fond of each other. Soon she became my devoted partner and encouraged our business, which has provided a good living, in addition to beautiful friends.

Nicole Conn, a famous writer, took precious time to examine my first shitty draft. She viewed my life as quite fascinating, but not without difficulties, I overcame some rather dark phases which were hard to openly admit. People will understand and forgive. Everything is temporary, and nothing is ever perfect.

My pal the author expected to read more about the pain involved, and said the disturbing incidents were glossed over. I avoid dwelling on the past and prefer to discuss a productive journey to inner peace. This story is not intended to dishearten anyone, simply to share hope through an honest account of my life.

As a teen I thought about journalism, folks noticed I had a nose for the news, but I couldn't stay in school for an education. My second language, astrology, is often used as a reference to certain characters or events within. Though I didn't graduate high school, I attended L.A. City College for computer science classes in the late eighties. I realized people would come to rely on their PCs, even before our obsession with the Internet. I couldn't have written this book without a computer and a word-processing program.

As a ring-around-the-collar Catholic, I'm disciplined to respect tradition, but I refuse to feel guilty about my sexual preference. I choose to live a simple life, I don't follow or lead, it's safer to be in the middle. Today there are no urgencies. I enjoy quiet moments in the yard, listening to birds or gazing at flowers. Luck is timing and opportunity, so be careful what you wish for; anything is possible.

Peace and Love,

Carole, a Lucky Little Rabbit.

Carole,
A Lucky Little Rabbit

Part One

"Greet all human beings with positive and charitable thoughts. Be kind to individuals, with a desire toward self-improvement. Encourage, nurture and activate their valiant souls."

    Laura Swan, a French-speaking American Indian from Webster Massachusetts was my dad's mother. She was royalty within the Nipmuc Tribe; a nomadic group called 'Huguenots' also lived in Webster. This very old quaint country town is surrounded by a large peaceful body of water known as 'Lake Chargoggagoggmanchauggagoggchaubunagungamaugg'. Its long rambling name, translated by local Indians, meant: "You fish on your side, I'll fish on my side, and no one will fish in the middle." The vast pristine loch possessed an imaginary central boundary, which allegedly kept the peace. According to guides from the bordering towns of Oxford or Dudley, there are literally fifteen G's in the spelling. Now they simply call it Webster Lake, the ancestral home of two dissident clans.

    My grandfather was christened Aram Markarian. At the turn of the century, he fled from Armenia to Constantinople with his younger brother. It was rumored that my handsome grandpa robbed a stagecoach in Turkey and made his way to France with a lot of gold. They didn't speak English, but eventually came to America by working on a cargo ship, sailing from Paris to Boston. While hedging the law, they learned to speak French. The fugitive lads arrived here before the atrocious genocide. In Bean Town they boarded a truck full of destitute laborers on their way to harvest crops in the town of Webster.

Grandmother Laura was very beautiful, smart, even a member of the city council. What could two exotic people from completely different worlds have in common? By chance they both spoke French! Saturday night dances were held regularly at rural town halls, which is how Aram and Laura met. They quickly fell in love, married, and relocated to the big city of Worcester. Aram was fearlessly confident about finding work; he heard through the grapevine that unskilled foreign men were hired every day at the American Steel and Wire Company. That's when he changed the family name to Johnson.

My grandfather stood in a long line to meet the hiring boss; however, the guy couldn't understand his broken English. A Swedish man named 'Johnson' was in front and got hired at once. After several hopeless attempts, Aram decided to say his name was Johnson too. There were no Social Security statistics then, and formal identifications were seldom requested. He finally got a steady job at the steel mill, worked hard, and proudly handed the money to Laura in a clean pay envelope every Friday night.

Dad had a sister named Millie and a younger brother, named Larry. Millie married a wealthy guy who owned the Guarantee Bank in Worcester. Though we never actually met, she was a snob who disliked my father. His aristocratic sister denied any attachment to our family.

When Laura Swan died of Jaundice, Dad was in jail for stealing a car, but they allowed him to attend his young mother's funeral in handcuffs. Aram subsequently suffered a massive heart attack on the way home from his tiny farm. I barely knew Uncle Larry, his wife, or his kids. Dad used to take me to their house to watch the Friday night fights in black and white. Larry had a sudden aneurysm at the mill, and we soon lost touch with his family.

People drank a lot of bathtub gin, and other homemade concoctions during the thirties. Stills were common to people throughout the post depression. My Uncle Leo even tried to pass off green tea as real marijuana. Neighborhood folks secured well-stocked cellars, but my father knew his way around everyone's private basement storerooms. Thanksgiving time gave him an excuse to steal turkeys off neighbors' back porches. He usually delivered them home to our chagrined family. He robbed the poor to give to the poorer. Brawling in street fights later turned him into a lightweight boxing champion in the army. If you talked with the women in his life, they'd say he was a lover not a fighter; no matter what, he was still my charismatic father. Right or wrong, I admired his winning attitude and confidence.

Mary Margaret O'Callahan, my mother's mom, came from County Cork. She married the philandering Cornelius Fitzpatick Jones, a Welsh-Irishman, who stuck poor Nana with eight kids and no money.

Mom and Dad were married in spite of folks' objections. She was seventeen and pregnant, he was five years older and wildly attractive with a pearly white smile. My sister Anne came along shortly after, but their beautiful tiny cherub only lived for three months. She was born with an upside-down stomach.

In the Year of the Rabbit, Theresa Margaret Jones and Harry Earl Johnson became my natural parents. Dad was attracted to Carole Lombard so they named me Carole Ann. My brother arrived on Sunday, August 23 1942. Earl Anthony was three years old before he spoke; the doctor said he was just lazy. Mothers usually dote on their sons, and Mom truly did, but I was favored in other ways.

Dad missed Anne's passing, just like other family crises. He was either drunk, in jail, or fishing with friends. The rogue was always in trouble so a tough judge sentenced him to the army, which wasn't a good option. He shipped off to France and discovered soldiers earned gold medals for injuries. Everyone who really knew the truth claimed Dad shot a small piece of his own forefinger off and landed in an English hospital. Somehow the quixotic hero received the Purple Heart and gave it to me several years later.

After a short hitch in the military, he went to work at the American Steel and Wire Company, the same career as Aram. The big boss often sent a black limo to pick him up when they needed certain expertise. He was popular, amusing, drank a lot, and slept deeply. Once, in the early hours, a yellow parakeet woke him when the house was on fire and saved his life. As a Scorpio-Phoenix, he defied some close calls.

While Dad was overseas, my lonely young mother began drinking heavily to become more sociable. He returned from the service sooner than expected and found her at home passed out cold. After I told him where she hung out, he clasped my hand as we jogged around the corner to visit Mom's recent companion.

Eddy Durkin was a puny creep who constantly shook from too much booze, or perhaps not enough. Dad placed a sharp butcher knife to her friend's throat while wearing a violent facial expression. "Eddy, I'm back, if you ever go near my wife again, I'll kill you. Do you understand? Enough said."

Divorce was inevitable. Nana tried guilt-tripping me about loyalty to Mom, which didn't matter because I always favored Dad. The judge took my brother and me into a private room to ask which parent we preferred. Earl chose Mom, but I picked my father at once; he was lively and fun, while she was too strict and critical. Dad moved my stuff to his immaculate bachelors' hotel room and everyone wept when it was over.

He gave me his bed and slept in a chair; Dad was a gentleman in spite of his rough façade. That colorless chamber wasn't like a real home, and it just didn't seem right to eat all our meals in restaurants. Besides, I felt uneasy about putting a crimp in his female companionship. We decided it was best if I lived with Aunt Emily, Uncle Leo, and Nana. For ten bucks a week, I remained their star boarder for a while.

Number one Pakachoag Street was the last house on an unpaved, dead-end road. It was a loving home as long as Nana was there for me. She always saved the really big leftover cigarette butts when I was a teen and handed me two dollars each time her Social Security check arrived. Nana was a generous Taurus, who loved wearing a flashy collection of junk jewelry. Of all the grandchildren, it appeared she liked me best. When school was over for summer, she treated me to long train rides in the fancy coach.

Uncle Leo bought his dream cottage for two thousand dollars during the mid-thirties. The modest home had a small living room, a family-type kitchen, den, one master bedroom, and a tub-less lavatory for everyone to use. I shared an upstairs garret with Nana, while my cousin Barbara enjoyed the largest loft. Dad brought me lots of toy army weapons, but it wasn't really fun to play alone in the empty room. Mom tried to make a lady out of me; she purchased a beautiful ceramic doll when times were tough. In protest of her constant nagging, I sawed the doll's head off shortly after my father delivered a miniature tool chest.

There were only four houses on the dead-end road, only a few blocks away from Holy Cross College. My best friend, Mary Walsh, and I adopted that whole campus as our personal playground.

My uncle's small cheerful cottage sat behind the huge wooden back gate of Whittal's Yarn Company. Every housewife within miles labored at the enormous brick factory, the pay was small, but the work was steady, with good benefits. Aunt Emily, Leo's wife, worked in the old-fashioned dusty mill for over forty years. At precisely four o'clock a screeching whistle blew, and amidst a sea of weary co-workers she'd race out of the broad portal with a Camel dangling from her lips, balancing a thermos bottle and lunch pail. My gossip-loving relative appeared committed to watching *Dark Shadows* and *The Liberace Show* five days a week on a black and white TV.

She was second-generation English, and smoked like a sailor. The tiny lady sat in a rocking chair constantly crocheting handkerchiefs, and doilies with a cigarette butt flapping. Designing delicate things and planting pansies in spring was her absolute therapy. As the coughing exacerbated, she spit up nasty smokers' mucus which probably ruined plenty of pretty lace hankies. Em was a Sagittarius, money matters were important, but she always had a little cash tucked away for rainy days. I used to wonder if they took me in because of Dad's liberal compensation each Friday night, or did she actually like me.

After divorcing Dad in the early forties Mom decided life might be better in New York City, so she packed a few things, and we left on a Greyhound with two suitcases. Her older sister Aggie lived in the Bronx section with five spoiled kids and her cheerful husband Sam Weirauch.

Aggie was rude and cruel the moment we showed up at her door. Sam drove a cab, smoked cheap cigars, and worshiped his children. We went there hoping for temporary shelter, instead, Aggie sarcastically advised Mom to get rid of us. She claimed it was hopeless to find work in the city with two youngsters. I never forgot our cross-eyed, buck-toothed aunt's insensitive rejection. Revenge on that hateful woman wasn't deliberate, although twenty years later I had a love affair with her married daughter Joy, arousing many family animosities.

Aggie flatly refused to help, but other relatives lived in the big city. Mom called her sister Jennie, and her marvelous husband Bill offered us a haven in their large one room Manhattan place. The childless couple drank a lot; they probably went through a quart of whiskey every night, while a steady debate continued as to where Mom might find everyday waitress work. Sometimes Uncle Bill took my brother and me shopping at Woolworth's, which seemed like Disneyland to us. Suddenly, Jennie turned into another bitchy sibling; she was lucky to have a good guy like Bill, even if he was a hillbilly from Arkansas.

Mom settled for some hard jobs during that period, and usually made her way to a sleazy bar after work. She met Pete Perez when I was around six, and little Earl was three. One Sunday Pete noticed us feasting on a complimentary saloon buffet. I'm sure we looked down on our luck. The courteous sweet-talking gentleman asked to join us. In a short time Mom was charmed into marriage; while my brother and I despised the creep, he became our wicked stepfather anyway. Pete arranged our move to a fifth-floor walk-up, cold-water flat, on W. 99th Street. At least we got away from Jenny and Bill's constant bickering.

Pete insisted that Mom become the building manager, a.k.a. the janitor, to earn free rent. She had to scrub five flights of marble hallway floors with lye soap on her hands and knees. The huge structure was across the street from Pete's radio shop. Our colorless unit, sparsely furnished with high ceilings, was always very cold.

Unsettling circumstances ensued; I'm blessed with being mercurial, and bounce back by letting go of negative stuff without delay. No matter what, I tried to keep a smile and a sunny disposition. Cheerful days at that madhouse were few and far between. Whenever Mom could, she'd treat us to a one-cent shaved ice from a roving street cart, nonetheless it was hard to act carefree like other kids. We did have fun standing on the curb as the street cleaner drove by, and especially when someone opened up a fire hydrant on hot summer days. I also enjoyed watching big kids play stickball in the alley. One time a friend's parents took me to see the Botanical Gardens and Zoo; this was my happiest childhood memory of New York.

Pete Perez, a Taurus, was a dark complexioned Puerto Rican mean-spirited short man. Possessions meant everything, including his only daughter, Helen. I was filled with resentment and we didn't speak much. He owned two radio repair shops with old parts like speakers, tubes, etc. The creep was in a good mood one day and actually showed me how to build a crystal radio in a cigar box.

He kept rolls of cash in small tin cups, but I never took paper money. Pete caught me stealing a dime once and dragged me through the streets in the pouring rain, paddling my butt all the way to a police station. Luckily a nice Irish cop gave me a lecture and invited me to join the PAL. I never stole again, not even for my favorite ten-cent cherry pie.

I constantly felt abandoned and missed my father desperately; I prayed he would save us from that wretched stepfather. Though Dad never came to New York, I loved him anyway.

Pete was insightful enough to see the television industry rising in the near future so he began to study it. Maybe that's why he had two stores, one for radios and one for TVs. Our country was at war during the forties and folks couldn't live without radios, so he made a lot of money selling vacuum tubes etc. For some odd reason, I thought he was up to no good; he always skulked around late at night. In time I assumed he was dealing dope in those dinky stores. He was a clever guy when it came to electronics, but he didn't realize how impressionable children were. God, forgive me, but I really hated him then.

I met his ex-wife, Stella, a few times, she was a Nordic type woman, blonde, chiseled face, but taller than Pete, and wore her hair pulled straight back in a bun. One night after dark, I happened to look across the street at the shop and saw Pete kissing her, but no one ever believed me. Perez assured my mother in the beginning that he had no feelings for his ex. Pete and Stella had two offspring, Helen and Richard. When I was thirteen years old, their daughter, Helen, had to go on welfare, her first junky husband Jimmy went to jail for a while. To escape his low-life family, their son, Richard, joined the army at a young age. After the service he became a professional jazz trumpet player well known for melancholy music.

Our fat, cynical, negative, Capricorn cousin Barbara came from Worcester to visit us on W. 99th Street once. Jenny, the aunt we first stayed with in New York, was Barbara's mother, but she didn't raise her. Before sweet Uncle Bill Page, Jenny was married to a wealthy lawyer, William Serawitz. When Barbara was born, she was immediately given to, and fostered by, Aunt Emily and Uncle Leo. Little Emily became her stepsister, and they were raised Catholic. Hardhearted Jenny had no problem giving her baby away; the rich attorney never wanted children, while she fancied her cushy Park Avenue lifestyle. Their marriage ended abruptly, but Jenny got nothing to show for it except a hateful, embittered daughter.

My mother was only twenty-nine years old when she went through menopause. Her behavior was extreme; she'd sit in the rocking chair for hours bellowing, "I'm an old, old woman."

Barbara came to visit us at the time and was unaffected by my mother's breakdown. Our cousin took a lot of hot bathes, and pranced around the large chilly apartment naked, overweight, and ugly. She always had to belittle everyone; perhaps it made her feel superior. I didn't know what was going on, and Earl was too young. Finally Mom had a complete hysterectomy, but not before she sought out every Puerto Rican mystic healer in New York City. Throughout her quest, she took me to some dark, creepy areas, which might have scared other kids my age, but the eerie places filled with strange illustrations and exotic aromas, actually fascinated me. At eight years old I began to think about creating my own altar.

She got well after the surgery and became a very energetic person. Pete knew he couldn't hold on to her much longer now that she was thinking straight again. He bought a tiny candy store right around the corner to keep her busy. The creep had plenty of cash for what was needed; yet certain things were still hard to come by during those war years, like cigars and cigarettes. My first ever job, was selling Camels across a sticky counter for a penny apiece while I stood on a heavy Coca-Cola box. Mom battled fervently over the rights to carry major newspapers with other storeowners, but eventually got what she needed.

It was a stressful business and the hours were long. Mom often made a bed for Earl and me by placing a couple of old blankets on stacked wooden soda cases, but we never really slept well.

Some of the toughest characters on the Westside frequented our friendly little candy store, and they were always perfect gentlemen. I had a steady job at Mom's sweet shop selling cigarettes until it was time to start school in September. Mom could only endure the little place for a year so Pete sold it for a profit.

Every poor neighborhood breeds its own bully, a twelve-year-old psychopath who lived across the street, Johnny Coyne, was a real menace on our block. He was a tall blond, always yelling at someone, he even screamed obscenities at his own mother; something I would never think of doing.

When Mom sold the candy store, she had a little money, and bought me a brand-new pair of metal roller skates, the kind that you had to tighten up on your feet with a key. I was supposed to stay close to our big brick apartment house, but these skates were magical, I felt like I could fly to Mars whenever I put them on.

At seven years old, my second job was running errands for Mrs. Carr, a southern woman who lived up on the fifth floor of Johnny's building; I went to the market for her several times a week. Her stuffy apartment smelled like honeysuckle, and she was very nice. Each time I went for her buttermilk, she paid with a lady dime. When I finished the chores, I'd put on my shiny skates and turn into a sidewalk aviator with Mercury at my heels.

Johnny Coyne couldn't bear to watch me showing off speed or precision, and would go out of his way to trip me. He finally brought me down onto the hard cement ground one afternoon, but he wasn't satisfied that I only took a fall, so he pushed my head onto the stoop and broke my nose. Pete insisted I pay for my own emergency hospital visit with the little money I'd saved up. Mom went right to Johnny's house to tell them about their hateful son and hold his parents responsible for the bill.

*****

It was time to begin my elementary education, but the schools in New York City were overcrowded and understaffed because of the war. Lessons came easily to me however. I was an astute Virgo, blessed with an excellent memory. On the first day, I met with designated staff members who seemed impressed and put me directly into the second grade. I skipped the first grade and never went to kindergarten. The rundown school, P.S. 101, caused endless anxieties and apprehensions, and I was miserable there.

My homeroom had a long narrow coat closet, where a fat sweaty black boy called Walter repeatedly tried to accost me for a dry hump. He was obsessed with trying to make body contact with me, but I always fought him off. There was never a teacher around when I needed one; his intimidation persisted without any ramifications. Each day I ran all the way home because that pathetic lad would be right behind me. One of the few good things about Pete the creep was that he owned a huge white German shepherd dog called Johnson, he was a loyal friend. He enjoyed chasing the dumb kid all the way up our tall iron gate to bite him on the buttocks. Eventually Walter finally stopped following me home from school.

That kind of drama went on until we moved to Bridgeport, Connecticut, which was Pete's idea of the perfect place to bring up kids. It was a wretched, smelly, industrial metropolis. There were some nice beaches and parks available if you had enough money to get to there. Pete made a few trips before we finally relocated, then he rented a big apartment on Berkshire Avenue. He also chose the furniture, which in my opinion was rather gaudy. Our new sofa and armchair were very rough and scratchy, made of a blue velvet faux material; I didn't care to sit on it much. The long coffee table had a pretentious blue glass mirror top where Mom and Pete spilled plenty of cheap red wine on Saturday nights.

We never socialized with any neighbors around there. Mrs. Hart was a mean old widowed woman who lived downstairs, and she was always antagonistic toward Pete. The rummy-faced wasp just didn't like Puerto Ricans. She tried to make friends with me to learn something about our family, but one day she gave me a piece of old chocolate which poisoned me. As soon as I got sick, my mother went berserk and had a huge altercation with her, though I honestly don't know if she did it on purpose. Mom had a quick Irish temper and a habit of raising hell about issues concerning prejudice, regardless of where we moved.

Berkshire Avenue was in a very nice residential neighborhood, and my mother was anxious to work in the garden. The large Victorian house had a charming backyard, but Mrs. Hart didn't want Mom to even be in it, so they fought even more. Luckily the shrew didn't have the final say in the matter.

My brother attracted animals, and he was responsible for finding a dog named 'Fuzzy'. Sometimes he deliberately carried an ice-cream cone behind his back so a pet would follow him home like the Pied Piper. Finally Pete agreed to let the cute little mixed terrier live with us. Mom used to boil several buckets of hot water on the stove for our Saturday night bath. I always got to soak first in fresh clean hot water, next it was my brother's turn. Afterward Earl had to bathe Fuzzy in our dirty water.

We noticed something wrong when the dog started to dig a large hole in the ground next to the house. Every day I'd fill up the opening and Fuzzy would dig it up again. I came home from school one afternoon to find the poor helpless animal lying dead in the hollowed out space. At first we thought it was just cooler for him to lie in the dirt, later Mom told us he was trying to bury himself because he realized he was dying. We never knew for sure, but could it be that Mrs. Hart poisoned him too?

Schools in Connecticut seemed more advanced than those in New York, and I began to enjoy studying every day. When I was in the fourth grade there was a contest involving music. I don't remember the guidelines, but my teacher told me to listen to distinct sounds with special earphones and explain why certain sounds impressed me. She said my answers were insightful, and I actually won a scholarship for music education. The instructor told me to choose any musical instrument I'd like to play and the school would provide free lessons. It sounds silly, but I chose the clarinet. Sadly I had to decline that wonderful grant. Asking Pete to buy me an instrument was a ridiculous idea, he would have only laughed.

In another life, Mrs. Evangeline Hart could have easily been related to Archie Bunker. She taught me and a few other neighborhood kids a bigoted rhyme. 'Chinky, Chinky Chinaman, sitting on a fence, is trying to turn a nickel into fifty cents.' She even gave us a scary explanation as to how the Chinese people got their rice. "When Caucasian children walk past their houses, the Chinks carry them away silently, and grind them into rice, that's why it's white." Out of concern I asked how they got rid of the blood, she replied, "Their race can perform many strange and magical tricks on foolish children."

For reasons known only to him, sneaky Pete had a profound fear of the law, which is why he always tried to act like a well-respected citizen. My mother's final feud with the old biddy downstairs brought the cops to our door and Pete was really furious. Their quarrel involved Fuzzy. Mom confronted Evangeline fiercely about poisoning the dog, and she denied it emphatically. Now that my screwy family had caused the scene of the century in that very ticky-tacky neighborhood, it was time for us to move elsewhere. There was never any question about who had to leave. Mrs. Hart was the landlord's sister.

This time we relocated to a dump on East Main Street near Pete's Radio and TV shop. I became best friends with Shirley James, a zany girl my age who lived nearby and went to the same public school. She was one grade behind me, and not too smart. Mae James, her widowed mom, always collected welfare. Mae was very poor, but she seemed like a happy person. She was short, toothless, and kept a fresh pot of hot soup on the stove regularly, in addition to batches of thick bread with fresh creamy butter. Their tiny apartment was delightful, it smelled great, and radiated love. Mary Ellen, a tall geeky-looking spinster was Shirley's passive older sister. Archie, the youngest child, was my brother's age, and Don, the first born, wasn't home much. Mae shouted at them a lot; in many ways I admired the closeness of this Polish family.

An attractive seventeen-year-old girl called Beverly lived right across the hall with her young, hip single mother. I spent a lot of time at Shirley's house. The ladies were all good friends and practiced how to act sexy when they danced together to impress boys if they could attract a date. It stimulated me to watch their sleazy gestures. This was our only source of entertainment then. There was limited dance space in their tiny places so everyone worked up a sweat. Bev's mom took me aside once to tell me politely that I needed to wear an underarm deodorant. I was mortified and stayed away from there until a daily essence became part of my routine. My mother had never mentioned it because she didn't use any.

Nelson Novatni was an available charming teen whom I dated occasionally, and the lad followed me everywhere. He was sweet, very handsome, and now that I think about it, had obvious gay tendencies. Once in a while we'd have a soda, or see a movie, although I couldn't keep my mind off the seductive Beverly. I felt happier and more comfortable being around girls, even though males are much easier to please. Shirley didn't turn me on. She was kind of homely, and not really my type. We were good friends, and never thought of ourselves any other way. I can remember music from those lighthearted days, and the latest raunchy dance song *The Cow*, Cow Blues aroused our female hormones each Friday night. We were also hung up on an erotic tune called *Marie*, and played that worn-out vinyl repeatedly.

My colorful best friend Shirley James was no genius, but lots of fun and made me laugh constantly. My mother really couldn't stand her, nevertheless the hypocrite pretended to and bought us matching pajamas every Christmas. Mom was a narrow-minded, judgmental person; she only needed one good reason to forbid me from hanging out with my bird-brained Polish pal Shirley. Suddenly something happened, which gave her plenty of cause to discontinue our adventuresome friendship.

One very cold New Year's Eve, Mom, Pete and Mae James, went out to celebrate. They drank together often, and I knew they would be out late that night. Shirley, Archie, Earl and I, were left at home in Nonni's care, the woman downstairs. She was only supposed to check on us if we got loud or rowdy. The ocean, or actually the filthy bay of Bridgeport, was about three blocks away. After ten o'clock I got restless, and asked the kids if they wanted to go for a boat ride to finish the old year with some fun. They always went along with my ideas so we tiptoed down the stairs holding our breath. We walked briskly through those frigid empty streets until we got to the place where I'd stashed a hefty pair of oars. I'd explored the area beforehand to learn where useful things were kept in case I ever needed to borrow something.

A string of dinghies were gathered in a neighborhood boatyard, and we picked a sturdy one to carry us out to the harbor. I rowed like crazy, heading for the sea, and we traveled a long distance very quickly. Suddenly, a colossal ship was coming right at us. The waves became enormous, the kids were frightened, and blaring horns continued to blow behind us. Fortunately, we got out of the ship's way just in time, but the U.S. Coast Guard soon caught up with us. They'd been following us for a while, shouting through a bullhorn, but I just kept paddling. The headline the next day read: 'Two thirteen-year-olds, and two ten-year-old youths were arrested New Year's Day for taking an ocean voyage. This was really a big oops.

Several misdemeanor charges were filed. We'd stolen the boat, a pair of oars, and trespassed, besides endangering other vessels in the harbor. The greatest embarrassment from my prank was being escorted home at five in the morning by staunch officers in crisp white uniforms. Now we had to face Mom and the others. They took turns screaming, but relinquishing our precious cigarettes was the worst penalty. When the court case concluded, our only punishment was enduring a harsh lecture from the judge.

*****

While living in Bridgeport, we took one-week vacations at Myrtle Beach, which was only a short drive up the coast. I dreaded these occasions. Pete usually booked a small, dank, mildewed cabin way across from the ocean; he invited every friend or relative who could get there. Mr. Perez wanted people to think of him as a well-respected man about town, doing all the right things. Sometimes my Nana would come down from Worcester by bus to visit, she loved to see us, but she also enjoyed gambling and playing amusement park games. That 'Pitch Till you Win' booth yielded her plenty of little blue Jesus statues. Nana was a marvelous person to be with. Typically she wore funny hats, along with several articles of cheap jewelry, which highlighted a gaudy broach in the center of her long floral dresses.

We were taking another humdrum vacation at the beach one summer when someone started a bogus rumor that young girls got pregnant from swimming out too far in the ocean. I wonder how many adults screwed kids up with that absurdity, they couldn't fool me for an instant; I always enjoyed swimming, and never had a baby.

Dilapidated dives on the boardwalk served up some delicious food. Mom wasn't a great cook, therefore giant heroes, and fried eggplant sandwiches from seaside cafés tasted luscious. Nana brought me lots of goodies when she came to visit. As I said before, I was the favorite out of all her grandchildren. Years later she told me how much I meant to her just before she passed away.

My brother was an amusing con artist. He started a shoeshine business directly in front of an illustrious local pool hall patronized by Mafia members. The kid worked hard polishing footwear for some bloated, tough, burly, cigar-smoking guys, who seemed fond of him. Earl actually sang pieces from the opera *Pagliacci* to his favorite customers, though I have no idea where he learned it. Vinny, the owner of the pool hall, had one son, Giorgio, who subsequently married our seductive stepsister Helen.

Mom taught us to work hard, it was the only way to get the extra essentials we required at this age, earning our own money was mandatory. We were trained to be more ambitious than other kids. Vinny, the Italian boss man really liked us, and he gave me a job sweeping out his chalky smoke-filled pool hall, which allowed me to learn how to play billiards. The mob guys were generous, but Earl and I did other things for quick cash, like running errands. Generally we shopped at a local grocery store for a few old folks; I even cut Mrs. Lamb's overgrown green toenails once in a while, which was pretty gross.

Earl and I routinely visited an alley called 'Niggers' Lane', scrounging for surplus coins. I presumed the habitat got its name because black people were the only race living down there. I'm ashamed of using the 'N' word in my story, but this was a very real place. The deteriorating oppressive block was a large single integral wooden structure, and there were twenty small ground-floor units within the complex. I visited the place when I befriended a young black girl whose name I can't remember now. From the outside it smelled horrible, but if you went into her place, it was immaculate, warm, and welcoming.

Fistfights commonly took place in the notorious alley behind her cozy apartment, and plenty of loose pocket change spilled onto the dirt from drunken brawlers. After the Saturday night skirmishes, my brother and I did well, picking up coins each Sunday morning. Sometimes we found more than twenty dollars in silver.

Earl was running down that hill very fast one day, and got a huge gash in his leg from falling on the bottom part of a thick broken Coca-Cola bottle. The gaping hole was deep, and it sickened me to see raw flesh. I vomited before lugging him up the hill to our house. Pete drove him to get stitched at the hospital, but the poor kid couldn't go swimming until the next summer. Then the following June my clumsy brother fell out of a tree and broke his arm two days before our school vacation started.

My mother knew of two distant crackpot relatives who were living in Bridgeport, so she began a friendship with them. Edie was Emily's sibling, Mom's sister-in-law. Paul Bachand, her husband, was a robust Frenchman with a deep loud abrasive voice. Edie was only about 4' 9". She wore petite flowery printed housedresses, with tiny size three shoes imported from the famous Cinderella Store. They met in Worcester, and shortly after marrying Paul was assigned to a good job in Bridgeport with a big railroad company and stayed until he retired. These characters never had children, which was probably just as well.

Fishing was the only sporty activity my mother ever took part in. The Bachands lived just a few blocks from the ocean. Our happy-go-lucky aunt was quite an experienced fisherman and eagerly taught Mom. Edie was the butchest little straight lady I ever met. The dwarfed psychotic would be fine for a while, and start taking huge doses of prescription drugs which she'd saved up. Schizophrenia caused her to land in the state hospital. Narcotic cough medicines and paregoric were her favorites, but nesting at the asylum would only cure her insanity temporarily. Edie really enjoyed being in a sanitarium, she felt safe, happy, and very popular with inmates at a comfortable institution. She could actually laugh at her own lunacy once she got home as she'd begin to accumulate additional drugs for the next breakdown.

Their snug apartment was on the third floor of an old wooden corner building. Paul frequented the outside bathroom down the hall so he could drink his daily booze, whatever he guzzled smelled horrible. Prior to our arrival in Connecticut, he'd been arrested for declaring their cocker spaniel, Molly, as his child on income tax returns. In between their stupors, I'd stay over on Fridays to watch late night spooky movies featuring John Carradine. It was an amusing escape from the Perez chaos, even though they were insane. The Bachands may have lived in their own worlds, but they always treated me kindly.

Helen, my attractive stepsister, relocated from New York to Bridgeport shortly after we got there. Pete helped support her four small kids, but he was also needed for other reasons. Her young life was difficult, and she moved right into a project where welfare folks just sat around on benches all night singing in A cappella.

Baby Gladys had arrived first before Helen was even sixteen, after that she conceived three more. Jimmy, the drug-addicted husband, was back in jail, so she opted to date his playful brother Joey.

He came from the city under the guise of helping her with the kids, but Joey was actually in love with Helen. Before I turned fourteen, the same charming Puerto Rican guy dispensed my first shot of heroin in the bedroom when she wasn't home. It's apparent now that rape was on his mind. The man smooth talked me into getting an injection and made it sound like I'd be going to heaven. He said I'd feel totally free of pain. After I finally agreed, he gave me a small dose. The needle was barely out of my vein when I vomited all over him, putting a huge crimp in his naughty plans. Once again I was a lucky little rabbit. Men simply can't resist a cute teenage virgin, no matter how much in love they are.

My twenty-one-year-old stepsister with silky smooth white skin and petite body was hot. I enjoyed staying at her place whenever I could. Helen was the first woman I ever had erogenous feelings for, though she flirted with everyone. There were always errands to do, and I babysat whenever she needed me. She acted more like a passionate Puerto Rican than a cold Swede who usually attracted generous escorts. We slept together in a small bed, and I felt more excited each time I was near her. We did a lot of heavy petting, which you really couldn't call lovemaking, then she dumped me for the first useful male caller. Pete's promiscuous daughter was indeed fortunate to end up marrying a sweet guy like Giorgio Guccione, who treated her well. He was an active Good Fellow, well connected with plenty of money.

During school vacations in Bridgeport, I spent a lot of time at public community playgrounds, which I found enjoyable; it also got me out of the house. Each small park had a few councilors to teach kids arts and crafts, and occasionally they even took us on fun outings. Beardsley Park was my favorite, there were beautiful lush green areas for picnicking, a lake for swimming, and the pristine setting went on for miles. The enormous park had gazebos, a bandstand, and many enigmatic crisp, rolling streams. Mitzi Buchwalder, the friendly playground leader took us there but had no idea she was my summer fantasy. In the fall I sent a note stating my feelings, it was no surprise that she never responded.

I was raised to be independent, and I never wanted to affiliate with or follow any particular group. My mother decided it might be good for me to join the Girl Scouts of America, so she signed me right up. A fight ensued between her and Pete over the high cost of a uniform, in addition to the required accessories. The idea of looking like a nerdy freak in an awful green dress didn't thrill me at all. Mom finally scraped up enough money for the gear, and I was outfitted appropriately for my first Girl Scout meeting.

The group met in the basement of an old church, an extremely tough-looking woman named Angie was the leader of this troupe. After I'd only gone there twice, the bully began to insult my hair.

Angie was a heavyset Italian with a hard mean face; she was obnoxious, and reeked of garlic. From the moment I walked in that hall she was on my case for one thing or another. The bitch should have tended to her own appearance, including excess facial and nostril hair. She said I looked like a dirty greaser, yet I wore the latest Tony Curtis hairstyle. Without hesitation I gave her the finger. That gesture was the end of my scouting career, the ugly drab uniform, and the expensive gear Pete resented so much. 'Be Prepared'. The scout's motto never prepared me to feel humiliated, how could anyone respect a leader like her?

Pete was embarrassed, even angry, if I got into trouble for rebellious behavior or personality issues; Mom had to handle him. When we lived on Berkshire Avenue, we had a large living room where Pete first taught my mother how to dance the Tango. I despised him because he wasn't really a nice person, but the creep knew how to dance. His moves were smooth, and he always managed to make Mom look great as they performed together. She asked him to go out dancing soon after the girl scouts fiasco, and maybe it would take his mind off the consummate nuisance in his life, me.

Their favorite dance bar was in a slummy commercial part of East Main Street, right across from Shirley James' house. It was a tiny beer and wine tavern which reeked of pickled eggs and kielbasa. The floor was covered with dirty sawdust for lazy slobs to spit on. The filth in their hangout never stopped Mom and Pete from drawing a crowd to show off those passionate Spanish moves. They put on a grand show, and drunken admirers inflated Pete's ego enough to give him chance to forget about our quarrels.

In between their awful fights, we traveled from Bridgeport to

Worcester. Mom would wake us in the middle of the night to say: "Come on, kids, we're leaving this son of a bitch." She never warned us when she was leaving him, but we didn't own much so it was easy to get away quickly and quietly.

We continued to go back and forth from Bridgeport to Worcester by Greyhound for the next few years. Each time she deserted the jerk, she'd always retreat to her mother, but I felt happy whenever we went back to Worcester. Dad, Nana, and my old friend Mary Walsh (Walshie) were constantly there for me. We wanted a stable home life, which was something Mom couldn't give us then; we were frequently on the move and seldom relaxed. I do hate change, nowadays I stay close to home; it's my secure lifeline to peace of mind.

We had a few amusing moments in Bridgeport, like the time Mom took my brother and me fishing on the shores of Pleasure Beach with Aunt Edie. Suddenly my mother hooked a giant eel. She got very nervous, dropped the pole, and screamed bloody murder while running from that monstrosity of a catch. She decided then and there that fishing was not for her, but Earl adopted it as his favorite sport.

There used to be a huge circular German beer garden further down the beach in the amusement park area. In spite of continuous glass windows open all around, the boisterous place still reeked of stale beer and cigarettes. Almost every Sunday during the summer Mom and Pete took Edie and Paul to spend the day there. They ate, drank and carried on absurd conversations about nothing. This dull-witted group acted crude, even embarrassing. I thought the Lord's Day was intended for people to love each other, instead, I felt resentful about watching meaningless drunken gatherings. My brother and I tried to stretch what little money they gave us for rides and games while they sat at a crowded table indulging.

It was a good day for kids whenever a wedding reception was held at the big social hall on Elm Street. We enjoyed ourselves when the Italians rented the enormous room. They served the best food and treats. People seemed happy and more generous at wedding celebrations. My pals and I would wash our faces, slither into the function, unnoticed, then head straight for the food. With plenty of good music, folks were busy dancing or kissing and hardly ever looked at us. We were uninvited waifs, but if someone were to see through us, they would probably wink to let us know it was okay.

Italians danced to the Tarantella, Polish revered the Polka, but to us any genre of a live band was entertaining. With full bellies, and little boxes of Italian candies bulging from our pockets, we always left the party beaming. To express our gratitude for what they shared, we'd always kiss the new bride and groom on the way out.

Pete kept a tight rein on my mother's house money. He expected her to budget all the meals on three dollars a day. She shopped at the butcher's shop to buy meaty soup bones and say they were for the dog, only we didn't have one. Then we went by the grocery store to pick up bread, a few fresh vegetables, and a giant package of egg noodles. She did her best with what she had, if we ate enough bread to absorb the watery soup we could get quite full. Pete made excuses for not eating with us, he would rush over to his daughter Helen's for spicy hot rice and beans, and he went there often. They seldom acted cordially to each other, but now, it was nice to see my mother and Helen cooking together. Mom learned to make a few Puerto Rican dishes, though I always hated that type of food, especially rice and gandules.

Mom taught me how to mend old clothing, something I didn't mind doing. First I learned to sew a button on. Then I'd turn up hems, which required common pins. Our tiny apartment wasn't well lit, and I dropped a couple of needles on the floor. One morning Pete got out of bed, and walked into the living room barefoot, he stepped right on a tiny pin I might have missed. He yelled and screamed about my carelessness, but later his big toe actually swelled way up. He went to a local doctor for some antibiotics and a tetanus shot and had to pay twenty dollars. Pete said I should start saving money for the bill; his discomfort was completely my fault. The disparaging creep never said a kind word to me.

Our sadistic stepfather was particularly mean to my little brother, which put me in agony. Pete may have picked on him a lot because he looked like Dad. Though they never met, Perez was jealous; he hated our natural father for absolutely no reason. If they ever came face to face, I could have started trouble. I used to fantasize that someday Dad would come to New York and murder him with his bare hands. Our lives were certainly unpleasant, and we weren't happy children. Earl could easily let things go, but I was more high-strung.

On Sunday afternoons when the weather was cold, they sent us to a movie, which was eighteen cents, but we always got a quarter and spent the rest on a box of candy which cost seven cents. Perez always cooked Sunday dinner before we went to the show; he was no Wolfgang Puck. Mom was drunk and passed out in bed by noon, exactly where and how he wanted her to be, inebriated and passive.

Whatever food he wanted to get rid of first went directly onto our dishes. One Sunday he made roast pork, which wasn't really cooked enough. His rule was that no one could leave the table until all the food was gone from our plates. While Pete was glaring at my brother to see if he had finished, I stuffed my unwanted food into the kitchen table drawer above my lap. As soon as he left the room, I disposed of my meal by dropping it down the dumbwaiter in the hall. Earl refused to eat the fatty part of the greasy uncooked meat so Pete locked him in a closet until he finished that disgusting pork.

Other than criticizing him, which he hated, we were defenseless and afraid of Pete's abusive behavior. It was time to go to the movies that afternoon, and I wasn't going anywhere without my brother, who was still being held a prisoner in the closet. Our nondescript apartment was on the eighth floor of an ugly concrete building. I went out into the cold drab hallway, where I knew people usually hung around, and began to make a big scene by shouting to Earl, "We really have to leave. Tell your cruel stepfather you must get out of the closet right now. Come on, let's go or we'll miss the weekly serial."

I continued screaming, but the neighbors didn't know what to think so I told them the reason my brother was locked up. Pete overheard this conversation and let him out at once, then gave me one of his dirty looks. Earl and I finally left together for the movies, with a whole quarter in our pocket.

When I was around thirteen, I saved money for trips to the famous Apollo Theater in New York City. Two dollars took me straight to the city by train, where I hoped to see my favorite rhythm and blues artists like Ruth Brown, The Cadillacs and

Johnny Ace. I attended several concerts starring famous entertainers of the fifties. Those dazzling performers released auras of soulful energy which inspired everyone to dance. African-American music turned me on. It was great for dancing, and it appealed to the essence of my teenage spirit. Mom didn't like or appreciate my taste at all. Could she have been prejudiced?

I dated a beautiful chocolate-colored young man named Tyrone Emmanuel. In a way he resembled Prince, the singer who stopped using that name for a while, except Tyrone was much more handsome, chic, and intelligent for his age. We were never sexual, but kissed a lot and enjoyed being close while listening to music. However, one very seductive hit song called *Night Owl* always aroused us.

Tyrone lived with his sweet old grandmother on South Street. Whenever I went there to visit, she greeted me with genuine honest affection. Granny always smelled delightful, and she had the nicest smile I ever saw. Their building was ordinary from the outside, yet once you got down to their subterranean quarters it was a different world. The furniture looked incredibly modern, they had an abundance of electronic sound equipment, and thick bright red carpeting covered every inch of their enormous living room floor.

His parents were hardly ever home, but Tyrone usually had plenty of money for those 45-speed records. Sometimes we shopped at lively black music stores, I think his wealthy folks were connected with the recording industry. I only dated this amazing guy for a brief time, but Mom decided to leave Pete again. Ty's family subsequently moved to an undisclosed place when we finally got back to Bridgeport.

Wayne Parsell was another of my good-looking boyfriends in Bridgeport, an actual toe-to-head blond. He kept a small live monkey as a pet; the rascal bit my finger hard once while I was trying to feed him. His father owned a popular nautical marina; they rented boats, sold them, dispensed live bait, night crawlers, and carried everything a salt-water fisherman could possibly need. Wayne was a kind person, he even shared some earnings with me, but his father, the big macho dick, was awfully tough on this only son. Each time he screamed at Wayne, I felt repulsed and angry, but he told me not to be concerned.

Many people needed Parsell's to rent boats for weekends, and always paid in cash. Some backtracked for extra fuel, or bait, it put additional money in Wayne's pocket. He grinned each time he got the chance to rip his father off. When I was there, he shared kickbacks with me which seemed to gratify him. My suntanned love appreciated being with me; we laughed a great deal which may have eased some of his hurt. If ever a kid could justify murdering a parent, Wayne had the appropriate grounds. We spent that entire jubilant summer together, sailing off at sunset, smoking Lucky Strike cigarettes, and feeling blissful.

*****

There was a huge sewer treatment plant located at the end of East Main Street. Some local kids dove right off the pier into the polluted Atlantic Ocean. I jumped in a couple of times until I found out we were swimming in human waste. Directly across the street, a place called The Pipes was our regular hangout. It was a square city block with countless rows of concrete sewer pipes. There were mazes of tunnels within these cylinders; you could easily lose someone if you chose to. This was where I first learned the fine art of inhaling cigarettes.

Francis Ferrence, an American-Czech boy, tried to get my hand down his pants, but I twisted his arm till he yelled. Acting courageous and being independent came naturally. Wing cigarettes were fifteen cents a pack and cashing in soda bottles paid for my smokes, I owed no one.

My brother and I received a weekly allowance of twenty-five cents for doing odd chores around the house, but I made an extra dime when I took our rent money over to the landlord once a month. We cashed in soda bottles if we're lucky enough to find any and earned a little recreation money. Earl had recently joined The Boy Scouts of America, but he needed extra cash for furnishings. Therefore, I bribed him with two whole dollars to take me and Shirley along on one of their overnight camping trips.

Shirley's younger brother, Archie, was a scout in Earl's troop. There was also a really great-looking lad called Stanley Kowalski whose foster parent Joe was the group leader. It was hard to get approval for Shirley and me to camp out with boys for one night, but eventually we went on their outing. Before I left the house,

Mom handed me a thick blanket, one large raw potato, and an uncooked chicken breast.

It was cold and windy that night as we were nested right next to the ocean. I started to cook my own food on the giant campfire when Shirley decided the outdoors was too messy for her, so she left about midnight. Shortly after she walked home, I likewise abandoned the place. Stanley came over while I was getting ready to disappear and told me if I stayed for a while, he would keep me warm, but he meant it in a courteous way. We smoked a cigarette, chatted for a bit, then agreed to go for a bike ride together the next day. Mom wasn't surprised when I came home in the middle of the night freezing and smelling of smoke. I was still carting the half-baked potato and piece of burnt and bloody chicken.

My mother trusted me later that same week to take the final payment for our television set to an appliance store. When I got there, I swung hard on the outside awning, causing a whole plate glass window to come crashing down. I really fouled up, and even lost Mom's money in all the confusion. That was an awful week.

Riding alongside Stanley Kowalski was exciting, clean, healthy fun. He literally had the same name as the character in *Streetcar*; otherwise there wasn't the slightest likeness between them. Each day we pedaled our bicycles one or two blocks further, than the day before. He conditioned me not to be afraid of whatever we might find ahead.

Stanley and his brother John were wards of the state. They lived with their delightful stepfather Joe, and worked for him on Saturdays. Joe was in waste management and drove a huge garbage truck. The boys usually rode on the back to pick up trash at specific stops.

Bridgeport had endless viaducts, and one icy Saturday without warning, Stanley stood up in the truck, cracking his head open on a low bridge. He fell from the rig and died instantly.

Shirley and I were forced to attend the wake, but the thought of it was daunting. I'd never seen a dead person before; Stanley looked so unnatural. We were annoyed and sickened while viewing his body. Our friendship was much too brief. I cared for him, more than anyone in the world then. After that morbid physical display, we loitered at a soda shop with the dollar Mom had donated. I don't know why, but we played Ruth Brown's song *Mama, He*

Treats Your Daughter Mean. My beautiful Stanley wouldn't mistreat anyone; he was the most considerate young man I ever knew. The jukebox consoled us until our nickels ran out.

*****

Bruce, a fine-looking, affluent Italian fellow who befriended me, was definitely gay. I don't know how our peculiar rapport began, but we both attended Central High School. He was a senior while I was only a sophomore. Once he arranged a spontaneous excursion to New York City for a Saturday night with a couple of teens I'd never met before. This unexpected invitation suddenly made me realize I had to dress up like a girl. Yipes! The only garments I chose to wear then were old Levis, or Wranglers, with simple Madras cotton shirts. I always felt uncomfortable and awkward wearing ladylike apparel.

When she wasn't pregnant, my feminine stepsister Helen was rather small and petite. She lent me a basic black dress, but finding the right shoes was a problem. Mom and Helen wore a half-size smaller, but I squeezed into a snug pair of black heels regardless. After days of anxiety, Bruce and the eager couple picked me up in his imported German car, and we hit the road for The Big Apple. We strolled endlessly through the streets of Greenwich Village and by midnight my feet were so blistered I had to walk barefoot for the rest of the night. Putting on Helen's tiny stiletto heels was a very bad idea.

It only took a couple of hours to get to the city by way the turnpike filled with well-lit tollbooths. Bruce said this whole occasion would be his treat, so the rest of us had very little money. He seemed to really know where he was going once we arrived in the Village. Our first stop was to a trashy upstairs bar on W. 4th Street, where several queens were presumably hoping to cruise him. None of us really knew if he was gay or not, teenagers can be very naïve. Having my first underage drink in a public place was a bit unnerving, but the breezy waiter served me a tall, cold, bright red 'Singapore Sling anyway.

We hit a few blasé bars first, then around twelve thirty; we reached a famous Drag Queen Show. Bruce definitely wanted to see this extravaganza, but it took our last penny to get inside. The place featured an amazing exhibit of makeup, outrageous costumes, and chic drag queens.

When the show was over Bruce realized he didn't have enough money to go through all the tollbooths on the way home. He suggested we panhandle for instant cash, which wasn't easy at four a.m. People are suspicious by nature, but more so in New York City. Mom waited up for me all night; eventually we scrounged enough change to get back to Bridgeport. I hardly ever saw my gay chum after our trip, and in time I found my own way back to that colorful district. Something felt right whenever I was around homosexuals.

*****

Mom taught us to work hard for what we wanted, and I really wanted to get out of Bridgeport. By doing odd jobs or running errands, I was able to earn the few dollars I needed to run away from home. I left Perez's insanity several times to go back to Worcester by bus. I would depart from the Greyhound depot like a seasoned traveler and always brought along a paperback to show off my intellect. During one of my runaway commutes, the best seller of the week happened to be *The Power of Positive Thinking*, by Norman Vincent Peale. I analyzed the book and considered the lessons, which might even prove useful. For instance, if a weird creep sitting way in the back of the coach ever approached me, I'd keep a positive attitude, and try to exercise good judgment, but not before I kicked him squarely in the crotch.

This time I returned to Worcester as a sophomore in high school and paired up at once with Mary Walsh, my best friend. We used to skip school regularly to see Brigitte Bardot movies, or other foreign films that played at the Fine Arts Theater around ten a.m. After a while Mr. Chaugnassy, the local truant officer, recognized us on sight and escorted us back to our chagrined families.

Mary's mother was a very attractive Assyrian lady, quite a large woman, and her cheerful dad was purely Irish, but rather short. My mother used to have a crush on Walshie's father, while my dad really fancied her mother, Peg.

When we were young, and hung around Holy Cross College, we enjoyed having fun at the campus radio station; we also rode on corrugated toboggans through the snowy hills of this choice Catholic academy. If it were extra cold outside, the guys at the radio station would permit us come in. Then we could express our opinions about recent movies, music or dance fads over live broadcasts. Our choices were simple, rock and roll for dancing, and films that featured Brigitte Bardot or Marilyn Monroe. When they asked about trendy fashions, we said: "Everyone needs to own a fluorescent chartreuse or fuchsia jacket."

My best friend and confidant, Walshie, was a year and a half older, yet we were in the same grade at school together. She was a naturally gifted athlete whom I greatly admired. Whether it was field hockey, basketball, or softball, she was amazing in any sport. I noticed she applied a ballet rhythm while playing, so I studied her confident, systematic, graceful, and flexible moves. Jeannie Allen, managed our Amateur Athletic Union women's softball-team, and Corky Callahan the coach, appeared to be her lover. They insisted on picking us up before games or practices since we didn't drive. Out of the entire squad of rookies, we were their favorites, two lowly kids from the bosom of South Worcester.

Jeannie chose me as her assistant team manager; my Virgo efficiency became a valuable asset to our club. I kept schedules on track, made lists for everyone to follow, and served as the group's chief motivator. Our team, The Rockets, played all around New England; we headlined in competitions, and proudly earned several coveted trophies. It was my responsibility to rev up the gals before each game, so I gave them a brief pep talk: "Think positively! We can beat these bums; you can't lose if you play as one collective team, just stay focused." Walshie was the fiery short stop who never missed a ball. I was the svelte high-strung pitcher, always ready to intimidate the big butch slugger at home plate.

We had sharp reflexes and worked very well together, but I always felt awkward wearing those baggy uniforms which the team provided. I liked all my clothing altered to fit my body correctly. Hats were the main annoyance, my head is small, and most of them were much too large for me. In the good old days, women were required to keep something on their heads when Walshie and I used to attend Sunday mass. It didn't seem fair that we were never permitted to wear our boyish softball caps at church, although neither of us ever had the nerve to try. Was fashion decorum or

Catholic guilt holding us back?

Dad took me out once a week when I was younger. We went to ball games, or bowled a few strings, but always ended up in a saloon trying to escape from one of his blonde bimbos. I aimed to get favorable grades on report cards to earn rewards or blessings, but I didn't have to study very hard for high marks, I simply remembered key words or phrases the teacher paraphrased relative to an assignment.

When I finished with my homework, I tackled my cousin Peter's lessons for a small amount of cash, he never complained about paying since my compositions usually got him A+. On the other hand, Walshie didn't like anything about school, she only wanted to play sports, go to parties or have fun with the girls. She was always my most significant, and loyal, friend, we were downright honest about everything.

The coach took Jeannie right home to study after a game, and drove us back. She dropped Walshie off first, which made me the last passenger, and I realized Corky intended for us to be alone, which really scared me. She was twelve years older and very charismatic, while I was shy. Some heavy petting began in her car late one night when we were parked at the end of Pakachoag Street. She awakened feelings I didn't know existed. Later I described my experience to a friend who I thought might relate. Walshie was actually my only lesbian sister. We tried to make out once, but ended up laughing in each other's faces.

Clandestine affairs at drive-in movies were thrilling. Corky had a persona like no other woman I'd ever been enchanted with. We were steady lovers until I had to leave abruptly for Connecticut, which broke her Irish heart. I needed to help Mom during a family crisis. She invited me to join her later for a free vacation at Hampton Beach, but I didn't have the right clothes, so I made up lame excuses. She was a hot-blooded Pisces, it could have been a great holiday, but, regretfully, I forfeited her tempting offer.

Walshie's younger sister, Nancy, began to blossom in the chest, but she got teased a lot. Walshie would walk up to that poor conscientious adolescent and place her fingers over the kid's nipples, saying with a giggle: "I'm calling Berlin, come in, come in." She'd gently twist and turn them as though they were radio dials; she constantly referred to breasts as 'knobbies'. "Check out those incredible knobbies."

Getting good seats for the traditional Holy Cross football game on Thanksgiving Day was a great gift, Dad always brought his pal Duckeye along, while I wouldn't go anywhere without Walshie. The two crazy steel workers usually got drunk together at games. One time he fell backwards off the top row of the bleachers. A gentleman seated high in the stands told us he saw him plunge, land on the ground, get up, then dust himself off. Duckeye was a rugged Polish guy who couldn't be embarrassed or insulted, he wasn't very bright, which is probably why Dad liked him. After that plunge, however, he seemed to vanish.

We were dedicated to sports, and always needed cash to keep up with fads. Walshie decided to quit school and find a job, so I did the same. She went to work at a plastics company, which was quite a new industry at the time. I was promptly hired at the H. & H. Brown Shoe Company, even though I was only fifteen. Inspecting shoes turned out to be a steady job, and I survived the place off and on for nearly eight years.

Working came easy, but playing softball and falling in love were my main teenage anxieties. I needed someone to be romantic with every single day, or at least be involved with a feminine person. Without being aware, Walshie and I were dating the same young lady, Joyce LeTurneau. I secretly made love with my buddy's girl to prove she was really just a jezebel. Walshie deserved much better. Later we had a huge fight because of Joyce, it hurt very much when she stopped being my best friend for a while.

I was happy to gain access to a 1949 Ford which belonged to Herbert Brindley the third, a.k.a. Pooky, a definitive nerd. Perhaps the guy thought he was my boyfriend because I paid attention to his every blasé word. Pooky trusted me enough to let me teach myself how to drive without him being in the car. Uncle Leo always kept him distracted in the cellar by showing off an awesome collection of antique gramophones and scratchy cylinder-type records. While they amused themselves cranking up old music players, I drove his car all around our neighborhood. One night I plowed through old Mrs. Flemming's fence on Pakachoag Street, but my driving skills improved after much practice.

One fine Sunday morning I 'borrowed' his coupe, put some gas in it, and picked Walshie up without delay. We blazed the trail to Connecticut in his shinny black Ford and felt like moonshiners on the run.

Perez had acquired custody of his daughter Helen's baby by then, whom he'd actually fathered. Walshie and I began conspiring to abduct little Pete shortly after I found out who had him and where they lived.

The three-year-old was alone with big Pete, who was lying next to several empty jugs and saturated in wine. We entered through an open back door and carried the kid out of their dingy pigsty. We quickly bundled him in a filthy blanket, then crept out quietly, lucky for us Pete never woke up. His frail body reeked of death as we slithered past. He might have even died in that rat-infested shack outside Bridgeport.

This sweet vulnerable child needed to be rescued, regardless of the trouble ahead, and we knew the law would be waiting for us. Walshie and I could be facing serious kidnapping charges, in addition to not having a driver's license.

Pooky was beaming when we finally waltzed in, and relieved to see his car intact. He never complained, and said I could continue driving the Ford if I got a legal permit.

Kidnapping the neglected helpless child and taking him home to Nana felt great, but what was I thinking? We really couldn't keep him. All I wanted to do was feed the youngster a few good meals and love him.

Several changes had taken place since the last time I ran away from Bridgeport. Helen had married Giorgio and moved to the high-class suburbs; Pete had sold the shop and worked out of his house. He adopted the baby when my mother finally left him and moved to New Haven with a cross-eyed creep named Chris.

Helen came all the way to Worcester with her new husband to claim her own baby from my family. Fortunately, she refused to press charges against us after she realized the abominable conditions her father kept him in. Little Pete assumed my mother's married name at birth, so Helen wouldn't get in trouble with Giorgio at the time, but her ugly secret of incest was now on public record. For doing the right thing, Walshie and I were basically considered heroes by our friends. Once again my luck was good; we barely got a slap on the wrist from the authorities for our rebellious crusade. Amen to that.

*****

Before I had a car, I bought an old Triumph motorcycle for fifty bucks, which was noisy, but in good working order. One evening I took my Uncle Leo for a wild ride on the back of my bike beyond the hills of Holy Cross, which scared him into lending me money to buy Pooky's old Ford, which I adored. Herbert Brindley the third was from a wealthy family and replaced the coupe with a new convertible.

Paying my uncle back meant I had to drive him to Hopkinton every Friday night after work to his rustic summer camp. The cabin was only a block away from North Pond. It had a well for water, very little electricity, no indoor plumbing, and a smelly outhouse. He bought a whole acre for eight hundred dollars in 1954. It was just above the starting location for the annual twenty-six-mile Boston Marathon.

Uncle Leo lived for fishing; it was his greatest love and favorite recreation. The sweet man was colorblind; he never drove a car so I became 'The Hopkinton Express'. On Sunday evenings, I went an extra eighteen miles to bring him home from camp, then my own adventures could begin. He was my dearest uncle, and took care of my mother through the years; therefore, I never resented transporting him.

Grafton was a rural town with a huge foundry on the slope of a picturesque New England valley. The guards were always off duty on Sunday nights and left a few tow trucks open. Several winding dirt roads behind the plant turned into our personal obstacle course for driving competitions. A gang of crazy biker boys owned some antique cars and rented them to us for playing chicken on weekends. Those banged up old Fords were taller than most cars, and stood high above the ground. Except for jeeps or trucks, they were the only vehicles that could make it over the bumpy boulder-covered paths. Many dangerous trails surrounded a small deep pond, if you overshot a specific curve, you could end up in the drink. The tow trucks came in handy for hauling people out of the lagoon, but luckily I never missed a turn.

Walshie and I decided to bum around the dark streets down by the brewery instead of going to a dance or the diner one Friday night. Someone foolish, who apparently worked there, left a whole case of bottled beer on an empty loading dock and probably intended to pick it up later. Without hesitation, we whipped that heavy wooden box around the corner and over to the Sacred Heart Schoolhouse. We jimmied a window open, then partied for hours in a sheltered Catholic classroom. On the way home we tried washing the beer smell from our mouths by devouring handfuls of pungent grapes from a cousin's yard. Aunt Emily couldn't really tell if I was drunk, the whole family was involved in a red-hot poker game every Friday. I went straight to bed feeling no pain and avoided the relatives in the kitchen.

Our team was scheduled for softball practice the next morning, but my hangover was awful. Walshie suggested having an ice-cold coke, so we stopped at Ponya's Spa, where I used to work. The gruff Polish woman taught me all about cleaning, besides taking care of her store. Ponya really liked me, but I was fired when she discovered me giving away free cigarettes and sodas to friends.

Ammello's Diner was our hangout; we even chose the music that went into the jukebox weekly. The back of the place had a few square feet of open floor where we danced for hours, sipping coffee. These were our *Happy Days*. Walshie acted like Potsy, and I dressed like Fonzie long before the TV show.

I was followed down Southbridge Street one night after I left the diner by a couple of young guys in a Chevy. They asked politely if I wanted a ride home and I said, "Sure why not?" The first clue about their bad intentions dawned on me when they turned around and went the wrong way. It was really scary, so I began babbling nervously and fast, they kept telling me to shut up, but I couldn't.

We drove far away from my neighborhood to an obscure rock quarry where they began to get aggressive. They soon booted me out of the car because of my drama. I kicked, screamed and carried on, while those animalistic creeps got nothing for their desperate attempt, except a headache. It was a long walk home, and I was in trouble again for being late, but I couldn't talk about it to anyone other than Mary Walsh. This wasn't the first or last situation that my absurd chattering spared me from something terrible.

For savage amusement some of the kids shot bats and rats late at night down by the river near Whittal's Mill. My cousin Peter was an excellent shot, and a great guy, but always the typical horny teenager.

A huge carnival, *The World of Mirth*, arrived in August; I was Aunt Emily's star boarder then. It sprawled out by the railroad tracks on Southbridge Street for a week with all the freak shows one could possibly bear. My car was having problems, and I parked it on our dead-end dirt road until I saved enough money to fix it. Each day after work, I took a shower, dressed up neatly, and walked a mile to cruise the extravaganza. There were gambling booths, cotton candy, hot dogs, and many eccentric characters.

One graphic act held my interest, a performance which featured sexy black girls dancing to risqué vaudeville arrangements. Soon I became intimate with the leading lady, Dee. Every night I gazed tenderly at the twenty-five-year-old beauty, assured that she was singing only to me. Most of the carnival arrived by train, and some of the crew lived on board, including Dee. After her last number we went to her berth, drank cheap wine, and fooled around. By the end of that week I was in love. I packed a few things and left a farewell note to my family. Then I got on the filthy train with some sleazy carnival folks, and headed for their next stop, Bangor, Maine. Sleepless nights, drunks, freaks, and bedbugs quickly caused me to phone home for bus money. My life seemed ideal, even beautiful, after living in their world.

*****

There is a tattoo on my upper left arm which was done by an American Indian pal called Lucky; unfortunately, she didn't quite live up to her name. She was a large girl with a huge appetite. Each lunch hour at the shoe shop, we'd sit on the back stairs of an empty section, while she pricked Indian ink into my arm and penned the word 'Gypsy'. It was the name I gave my first car, but now it belonged to me because I did move around a lot. My butch pal actually robbed a grocery store once, and got busted immediately. First she helped herself to something to eat, then sat down and fell asleep on the floor right in the middle of the burglary. I never saw poor Lucky after that, but my crude tattoo is a permanent reminder of her.

*****

After another exciting rendezvous on our private street with Corky Callahan, I sat on the splintered porch steps until dawn agonizing over how to confess my unnatural feelings to my family. At last I admitted being a homosexual in the middle of Sunday breakfast, and I told them I decided to live an openly gay life. Nana went silent, my bold announcement broke her heart, and so it was time to leave Pakachoag Street for good.

Shortly after dropping that bomb I moved into a working-class rooming house on Main Street. I already knew a few gay residents who lived there. Flo Maine was a very tall, husky, powerful, butch woman, but enjoyed wearing dainty, lacy undies. My regular job was at the shoe shop, but on Saturdays I worked at The Minute Car Wash with Flo Maine and her girlfriend Helen for extra money. We shared things at my new communal abode, besides the bathrooms and kitchen. Once in a while we even divvied up food and drink, and everyone got along well. I remained a carefree bachelor at the crowded homestead until a woman named Belle entered my life. I relocated to a cold-water flat on Irving Street.

I developed a close friendship with Phil Mahoney when I worked at Brown's. He was a delightful Scorpio Irishman, but married with three kids. The short adorable guy walked past my workbench frequently to make small talk; one day I took him up an offer to visit the upstairs discount store. Phil ran the entire return department and lavished me with the finest samples of size-four, stylish boys' shoes.

He began taking me out to fine restaurants, and we bonded. I was positively gay, so why was I having an affair with a married man? Our dates were limited, which left additional time for my women companions. During our liaison he was cautioned not to ever get me pregnant or I'd be forced to meet with his wife. I literally passed for a male then and didn't quite understand his obsessive desire for me.

Phil was kind, generous, and a cheerful guy, who I sincerely liked; however, we probably seemed like an odd couple since we were both comparatively short and masculine. He embezzled an incredible amount of money from our company, but I felt no guilt about sharing the proceeds since he was the actual thief. He always tossed an empty chewing gum package stuffed with two or three twenty-dollar bills when he passed my bench after making a sale. The figure depended on how much he earned from various bargain hunters seeking damaged shoes. His clients bought rejects by the case; he even sweetened the deal if they paid cash. Most of his steady customers owned cheap army and navy stores. Brown's didn't see half their profits, which was none of my business while he was putting cash in my pocket.

Sometimes on Saturday he took me along to shop at a huge smelly, wholesale meat distributor. The graphic impression of dead cow carcasses hanging from hooks and walking on bloody sawdust floors gave me nightmares. Phil bought plenty of meat for his own family, and sent me home with some for my hungry friends on Main Street. They figured he was a chump and could only think of him as a gold mine. He loved me, and I cared for him in a way they would never understand. It wasn't my intention to use or take advantage of him; he was just a charitable guy who made it difficult to refuse gifts.

Phil enjoyed trading in cars, though I never cared for his family-style taste in them. Unlike our usual Saturday activities, we didn't go shopping; instead, he drove to a used foreign sports car dealer in the boondocks. I dreamed about those tiny seductive autos, and my fantasy was to take Brigitte Bardot for a ride through the most breathtaking places in Massachusetts. Without a blink, he bought me a pre-owned 1957 black MGA; this gift may have been the beginning of the end to our relationship. He wouldn't see much of me once it was registered. The following year, I upgraded to a 1960 black MGA.

Several of my trendy sidekicks from a Boston gay bar, expected me to show up every Friday night in my shiny sports car. I liked to dress sharp, and carousing with a hip Bean Town entourage felt special. Before driving there, I took black beauty diet pills to get me through eighty-six miles of highway, back and forth to Worcester. Ignorant truckers thought it was entertaining to use my open convertible for an ashtray, but I'd just smile, and extend my middle finger as I sped past the buffoons.

Gays generally congregated in a centrally located comfort zone. I became aware of Arbela Hotchkiss through Flo Maine and Helen.

She was living on a predominantly gay street with her lover Rose LaValle, a heavyset butch woman. I was embarrassed when Rose made a brazen pass at me; I assumed that aging dykes simply enjoyed hitting on young ones, hoping to get lucky. Rose finally tried to persuade me to join them as a third party for lovemaking, I said no way. Belle, however, had a different agenda and wanted me all to herself. She graciously broke up with Rose after we began dating, soon we moved to a small apartment in a gay-friendly building on Irving Street which cost ten dollars a week.

Belle was an attentive selfless Virgo with a heart of gold, and she took good care of me. She wasn't particularly attractive, or even the stylish type of woman I usually chased, yet she had a pleasant appeal. Her teeth protruded a bit when she smiled, and after a few drinks she performed sexy dances, attempting to turn me on. I pretended to admire her clumsy erotic gestures, which made her happy anyway.

Single attractive young ladies thought I was a good catch back in the day. Worthy females were mine whenever I chose to flash my seductive bedroom eyes. It was easy to satisfy fresh gay virgins; I even pleased experienced women, though I could never relax enough to let anyone reciprocate physically.

I made a few rules clear with Belle from the start concerning our open relationship. Being twelve years older helped her to accept the fact that I would only stay if she allowed me to see other people, including Phil Mahoney. When I dated other women, Belle was very accommodating; she prepared a hearty meal and ironed my clean starched shirt. The apartment was immaculate, we had plenty of food, and the laundry was always caught up, once in a while I changed outfits several times a day. Our landlord, Eric Olson, lived across the hall with Phyllis, his sex-starved wife, who later became one of my lovers.

In the two years we were together, I didn't display much affection towards Belle until we went to visit her son David in Maine one summer. Belle's parents lived on the outskirts of Portland; they raised her boy from shortly after he was born. The old couple worried about him inheriting her gay tendencies, and she never admitted who his father was. Behaving like silly teens, Belle and I made passionate love as soon as they went out. Maybe it just seemed more exciting because we were doing taboo things in their moral Protestant home. She was amazing, I regret not appreciating her sooner, but I was always too absorbed with someone else.

Almost two years later, while I was living in New Jersey with my lover cousin Joy, Walshie called from Worcester to tell me Belle just died of emphysema at the age of thirty-six. She was upset, and couldn't stop crying. Belle's devoted lover, Reggie, a young black woman, took good care of her until the end.

Walshie said she suffered a lot, and I began to sob uncontrollably. It felt gratifying to know we shared something special, if only for a short time, near beautiful Little Lake Sebago. While we were there, Bobby Darin's latest hit song, *Beyond the Sea*, played often, I still think of her whenever I hear it now. We had a memorable relationship, I just wasn't meant to be monogamous at the time.

One summer I rented a cabin outside Worcester on Lake Quinsigamond, and I kept a small dinghy docked a few yards from the house. The three redneck crackers who lived next door seemed to envy my female companions. They untied my boat a few times and sent it adrift to the middle of the lake, and I had to swim out to get it. My pal Bo Bo sold me a derringer handgun which I kept close to me. The next time one of those psychopaths pushed the boat out, I crept up behind him with my pistol. He quickly became aware of my rage when I demanded that he swim out to bring my boat back or risk getting shot. It wasn't easy to entertain pretty women there, but now I owned a weapon. I even hoped they might try to hassle my friends again, which would give me a good excuse to shoot someone in the crotch.

*****

My tiny black MG sports car tore up the roads between Worcester, Boston and Providence, Rhode Island. Gerry Braccia, was a fairly attractive gutsy young Italian-American lady who tended bar at a popular gay club in Boston. Her lover, Jo Jo, was a hoodlum dyke, and well known for drug problems. The bar closed after her shift, they would fight about money. When Gerry got angry enough with her self-centered partner, she sometimes stayed overnight with me at the little cabin on the lake.

Gerry wasn't very affectionate, and used a lot of drugs; I was attracted to her anyway. Each week I gave her a delightful ceramic Pixie. These imaginary little friends made her very happy, I was glad that something did since she was such a sullen Capricorn. It was my sincere intention to help her to feel better when she needed inspiration. I was eager to put a little sunshine in her life, though it was apparent our relationship could never grow. Her lover Jo Jo died a horrible drug-related death and we stopped dating. She looked absolutely miserable the last time I saw her at that dreary Tremont Street gay bar.

While living at my lake front rental, I barreled down the highways to Providence and had a brief fling with a sexy girl named Marsha. She had two bratty children and a tough sister called Mary who beat me up once when Marsha initiated a quarrel over something which wasn't even my fault. I redecorated her entire apartment with fresh paint and wallpaper from top to bottom, but by the time my work was done, I'd lost all respect for her. She was an extraordinary lover, which was the only thing we had in common. I decided there was no future with her or that crazy family, so I returned to my tiny cabin to appreciate the serenity. Since those hooligan neighbors had agreed to behave, my cozy niche was peaceful again.

Speed kept me going during those days. I worked hard every day at the shoe shop yet continued to cruise gay bars at night. My use of pills escalated, and I was indeed addicted, like many other people then. Phil Mahoney was the ultimate drug connection when Brown's diversified and became a major distribution depot. His assignment was to send pharmaceutical medications to different military bases. Miscellaneous diet pills and vitamins came in regularly, and we checked all the unknown drugs listed in a big red PDR.

Dexedrine and black beauties were already trendy with my friends; hence an illegal business emerged. My entire file cabinet was filled with all kinds of pills, and there was something for everyone. I tested some of the pharmaceuticals personally, just to see what would happen. Within a short time I got hooked on a dangerous male hormone. The pamphlet defined them as potent vitamins, but they were actually steroids. Huge burgundy football shaped capsules which caused my voice to drop a few octaves.

While bathing I began to notice the hair on my body growing longer and thicker. While I enjoyed the strong masculine sexual energy the pills provided, several adverse side effects occurred, and I had to stop using them. I felt nervous, paranoid and moody; nevertheless, it was a chance to feel the physical persona of a young man.

Lorraine Clukey, an exquisite-looking French Canadian belle from Montreal, lived with her mother, but she had a cruel boyfriend, Pete Johnson. My friend Helen knew her well and told me all about the abuse she took from that worm. Helen brought me to the hospital to see Lorraine while she was recovering from the latest beating. I liked her so I gave her a wink, a blink, and my telephone number. Lorraine really turned me on, she was an aggressive Aries, and she called the night I slipped her my number. Without delay we began dating. For romance, I usually took her to my place, but soon after falling in love we rented a nine-room house at number13 King Street. Her mother, Louise, never realized I was a female, my lover simply couldn't tell her. Thank God the old lady didn't live with us or see me enough to figure it out.

In the good old days, my father could down a quart of whiskey before his regular breakfast of oyster stew. He'd take a nap, then dress up and drink at a bar till closing. Someone at Brown's informed me that he had just been rushed to a veterans' hospital. I left work at once and found him strapped to the bed in a crowded dormitory room with several other guys who were screaming and carrying on.

He was ranting and raving about an imaginary bank robbery which he and Duckeye allegedly did together. It never happened, though he claimed: "Thirty thousand people witnessed us robbing my sister Millie's bank, and we got away clean. Wasn't that great?"

After watching him struggle in agony to free himself from the leather restraints, I wondered how he could continue to drink. He soon became the bookie for his alcoholic hospital ward, once he got over the DTs and went through considerable rehab. Dad was always a habitual gambler, but he was proud to take me to numerous gangster bookie joints when I was only four. His friends thought I was darling, even more charming than Shirley Temple, they enjoyed teaching me how to play cards for money. I had a winning personality that gave me an edge.

Fresh out of the hospital after another futile de-tox, my father moved in with Lorraine and me. They wouldn't let him out of the sanitarium until he made arrangements for a place to live with someone reliable to care for him. We fixed up a nice room and everything was going great, but within a short time Dad started taking Lorraine's vicious poodle Shu Shu, on lengthy walks as an excuse to hit the bars. He'd get drunk and angry, and begin to throw things out of the upstairs window. We found empty booze bottles, soiled clothing, besides an expensive pair of brass candlesticks in the yard beneath his room.

My father had to go, and so did my relationship with the dragon lady. I restored that huge dilapidated house completely by replacing old wallpaper, sanding hardwood floors, and ultimately beautifying each room. It was the first time I ever had my own art studio, though I really didn't have much time to practice oil painting since she kept me so busy. Lorraine was also a speed freak.

My father had saved up quite a bit of money during those weeks at the hospital, and while he lived rent free with us. It hurt me to ask my alcoholic father to leave, but he was anxious to have his own quarters to entertain hussies who chased him around with mattresses on their backs. My dad was very handsome; he often wore white Irish cable knit sweaters, which accentuated his dark skin and pearly teeth. Drunk or sober he was neat, and managed to take a hot bath every day. Soon a small basement apartment nearby with a nice backyard became available so we moved him right in, which is where he acquired his first cat.

Lorraine always reached for the sky, and even begged me to help her purchase that nine-room money pit. She would deliberately start petty fights merely to kiss and make up later, which usually fueled wild, passionate, crazy sex. The woman enjoyed lovemaking much more than any of my former lovers.

Although she was an exciting beautiful woman, her extravagant psychotic ways were getting on my nerves. Change was inevitable; I didn't want to buy that enormous old house anyway so I played it safe and decided to leave. We almost came to blows when she insisted on dogging me around town later.

Shortly before I moved out, Lorraine was crossing King Street, when Phil gunned his big finned Chrysler and aimed straight at her, barely missing. My involvement with Phil was another matter to be resolved. He'd become overly possessive, and this recent hostile behavior seemed bizarre compared to his usual passive disposition. I saw the wrath of a Scorpio rear its ugly head, which was indeed disturbing. The guy never acted jealous with anyone else before, so maybe he needed a change as well.

We went to dinner, had a few drinks, and I spoke to him in a heartfelt way. "Phil, you have been an amazing friend, I love you, and appreciate all the wonderful things you've done, only I have chosen to live an openly gay life, and I can't see you anymore. You never really turned me on when we made love, it's clear now; you were simply not the right gender." He drove me home sobbing pathetically.

Everyone was fraternizing the next morning at the shop. A co-worker came over to my bench bawling, "Phil tried to commit suicide last night, he drove his car into an enormous cement retaining wall, he's in bad shape, but still alive."

After a tense day I went directly up to the hospital to visit him. I peeked into the room, and it was no surprise to see at his wife sitting there. She was very pretty, I'd never spoken with her before, and this certainly wasn't the appropriate time. They told me at the nurses' station he was very drunk when he crashed. A broken jaw and a few minor injuries wouldn't keep that ding-toed Scorpion down. I quickly slipped away unnoticed, which was the last time I ever laid eyes Phil Mahoney.

Rumor has it that shortly after his dramatic suicide attempt; Phil divorced his wife and moved to Arizona with a younger man. From the outset we had incredible fun. He always enjoyed going to gay bars with me and loved dancing to a song called *Personality* by Lloyd Price. Occasionally we went out in the country horseback riding, which is how I came to learn a little about horses. At the time you could rent a palomino all afternoon for two dollars. We even drove to Boston to see the latest movies, and attended the world premiere of *Mutiny on the Bounty* in 1962. The Tahitian drum music was awesome, and the details of this whole extravaganza amazed us. Excluding Marlon Brando, an extensive cast appeared with beautiful dancers from the South Pacific while they served us champagne in the huge ceremonial lobby. Phil and I shared some wonderful moments together, but it was time to move on now.

*****

Walshie was busy with her own life while I needed something to do, so I teamed up with a fast-talking guy named Gary who was about to make serious changes in my life. We first met at a local gay bar, but he lived in the suburbs. Gary was a homosexual, Jewish, creative, and anxious to introduce me to his beautiful Greek friend Niki, a contemporary hairdresser. Gary had just stolen a checkbook from a tailor shop and claimed he could cash them without risk. His plan was to use it freely at different bank branches. By sunset he handed me a lot of money, and we immediately became partners in crime.

My mother did the best she could, but our home life certainly wasn't stable. My pal Gary came from a well-to-do family and had every opportunity to recognize right from wrong. Instead, he was a spoiled brat looking for thrills by using his exceptional intelligence to get whatever he wanted. Some kids grow up with too much, others, like my brother and me, had to earn things for ourselves. I really didn't know how poor we were, yet I never resented anyone with privilege, I felt blessed and lucky anyway.

The first time Gary stole checks, he just happened to find his tailor's checkbook lying around the store and helped himself. Then he began stealing checks from everyone everywhere, which consumed much of our day, we scammed banks all over the county. He assumed the male's identity, but if it belonged to a female, he thought of ways for me to cash them. We worked this fraud together for quite a while, and never got caught, but I really had to quit when my Catholic guilt set in. It was amazing to hand over a single little piece of paper and walk out with a stranger's money. This scheme wouldn't last forever, but long enough for Gary to enjoy the finest manicures, while I experienced high-priced haircuts.

The more Gary talked about Niki, the more I had to meet her. He said she was gay and beautiful so I made a date to see her, face-to-face, on November 22nd, 1963. We agreed to hook up at Circe's Coffee Shop, and I wanted to look perfect. It just happened to be the Venus hour at one o'clock on a Friday afternoon, how perfect was that? We simply looked at each other and fell in love instantly.

She waltzed into the restaurant like a prima donna, smiling confidently, and I'd never seen a more stunning woman before. Her teeth were extremely white and perfect, her hair was incandescent gold, and she had a slender body with a gorgeous classic Greek face. I was almost speechless, and I was overwhelmed. The instant we met was beyond expectations, which is when I decided Niki should be all mine forever.

We chatted buoyantly for some time, and I adored listening to her marvelous accent. Then, suddenly, the fastidious waitress began screaming to everyone. "The President of the United States has just been shot." JFK was killed in Dallas, but somehow the extraordinary news drifted right past our enraptured delirium. From that day on we became an inseparable, charismatic young couple in love.

She had to leave after we swapped phone numbers. Niki worked for an exclusive salon, Elegante, where Ronny, a famous gay hairstylist in Worcester, became her personal mentor. He conditioned her to indulge only wealthy female patrons. As her popularity escalated, she stayed booked for months in advance.

I was thrilled when she phoned later. Something dreadful ensued between Niki and her parents on the extraordinary day we met. She called around midnight and begged me to come pick her up. I didn't have a car then, but borrowed a friend's and drove around in the rain to find her house at the end of an obscure, dimly lit, muddy dirt road. When I finally arrived, my beautiful Niki was waiting on the porch clinging to a large overnight leather bag and a heavy flat iron; she was overjoyed to see me.

We went right to my place and stayed awake all night, talking, laughing and cuddling.

It seems there was a terrible fight at home. Apparently her father was a possessive man who cared for her in a very odd way. While the subject of incest never came up, anyone might be suspicious about the way he protected Niki.

My TV was black and white, and every broadcast over the weekend commiserated over the death of JFK. In spite of our sadness, it was a chance to get acquainted and experience some profound lovemaking.

Irving Street held too many sordid memories, the building was full of pushy lesbians whom Niki didn't care to socialize with. Soon we found a quiet apartment, a warm third-floor attic cubbyhole, which we rented from an old naïve Polish couple. Niki introduced herself as a contemporary hairstylist, while I pretended to be her youthful Greek brother who never spoke a word. I just smiled politely and let my big sister deal with the rental agreements. The elderly proprietors chose to see me as a clean-cut bashful adolescent, they had no idea I was a female, most people couldn't tell unless they actually knew me.

Niki and I shared incredible bliss in that dinky apartment, and Ronny kept us well supplied with grass, which was only ten dollars a bag then. After three short weeks the old couple politely asked us to leave, at times we became rather boisterous. My divine Greek Sagittarius turned ordinary lovemaking into a revolutionary free style of expression. Niki was a natural born lesbian without inhibitions to complicate sex, and we constantly experimented with diverse pleasures. As I reflect on our oneness, no other woman could ever satisfy my hidden desires, subsequent lovers were simply not allowed to touch me.

When a friend pointed out a reasonable loft for rent nearby, we paid a visit to our future landlady, Irene, at her lovely home. Everyone had a glass of wine and chatted a bit, and decided to move in right away. She seemed open to gay people, and marijuana, now I could be myself and not my lover's brother. Moving to a friendly place felt good, while Niki persuaded me to alter my appearance. She toned down my masculine image and transformed me into a sharp young lady. Every day she fussed with my hair, makeup, and weighty false eyelashes. I resented that whole girly charade, though I did look terrific.

Ronny used to pull up in his flashy black Corvette and drive us to NYC when we were very stoned. He liked to check out attractive window sets on Madison Avenue. Somehow he hooked up with a trendy gay agent who arranged for Niki to model the first Mink Bikini ever shown in the United States. The prestigious fashion event was held at the Hilton Hotel in New York City. It took my breath away watching her breeze down the runway in that amazing swimsuit. Men and women ogled, applauded, and flirted as she wafted past blinding flashbulbs and spotlights. Niki was irresistible. Spectators were awed by her elegance and long shapely legs. If a person was lucky enough to meet Niki, they wanted to get closer. Important guys handed her calling cards, but celebrity wouldn't change our unwavering love.

Along with her father, mother, and two younger sisters, Niki had escaped from communist Albania by crossing into their native Greece. After years of suffering, and deprivation, they finally arrived in the United States. Luckily a distant relative from Massachusetts sponsored the desperate immigrant family. Niki's birth name was Eleni Nicolidis; her sister Vasiliki was also known as Bessy, and papa's favorite, Anna, was a toddler. These beautiful children were very disappointed and unhappy when they landed in Worcester. They literally expected to see 'Coca-Cola flowing from water spigots and streets covered with gold coins. Sadly they realized that most people here weren't rich or famous movie stars.

Niki survived plenty of hardships in pursuit of the American Dream. Her family began new lives in a dismal cold-water flat, which embarrassed her. Wearing used boys' shoes from a tacky thrift shop wasn't the stylish look she anticipated prior to reaching this land of plenty. Various unskilled foreigners, including her father and mother, gladly accepted menial jobs at the Tabletalk Pie Company.

We lived in a fantasy during our first three years, and up jumped the devil. Her menacing father invited us to move into their current residence to save money, which appealed to my money-conscious lover. I was genuinely opposed, but we relocated to her parents' depressing apartment anyway. Niki and I were only in our early twenties; however, her depraved father didn't allow us much freedom to have fun.

Our tiny room was next to her parents, close enough to hear them making love. We hid warm beer in our closet, if we felt like having one; we kept it near our feet in case someone barged in. Niki smoked Larks, and I liked Marlboros. Whenever we lit up, we had to blow all the smoke out the window. Her cold-hearted family really disliked me; they assumed our love affair was just an immature phase.

One Sunday we were summoned to a family meeting and had to sit on their plastic-covered sofa while her father dictated with great authority, "It's time for Niki to get married now." He offered us a free trip to Greece, but only if we promised to break up after the vacation. We were one, and shared so much. How dare that creep destroy our incredible solidarity? We actually broke up when I refused his proposal. She complied with family protocol, while I became a cynic, relinquishing all faith in monogamy.

Periodically she worked on Sunday mornings doing touch-ups for rich women involved in weddings. Ronny manifested unlimited opportunities, which always fetched her, a considerable amount of revenue. She was a cheerful optimist, with good vibrations and excellent taste. Her lustrous golden blond hair was impressive, hence many prominent ladies referred to Niki as the darling of glamour.

One of Niki's more affluent clients, a complicated woman named Helen Collaro, was married to Jimmy, an alleged mafia member. Niki indulged Helen at Elegante, where they formed an amusing friendship. Her husband was happy to hang out with me while the ladies discussed contemporary beauty techniques. Before I ever met him or Niki, I had a brief affair with Faith, Jimmy's long time mistress. I didn't know the guy then, but Faith admitted she'd always be in love with him. She was free to date others, including gays like me, yet he always treated her with respect. Collaro was a kind man, and took good care of his own family, even if he was a mobster; no one ever clarified his shady profession.

You couldn't blame him for infidelities; his wife was the most neurotic woman we ever met. Helen was a tall attractive blonde, perhaps Slovakian, and experienced a face-lift before anyone else in her circle. The woman was melodramatic, cried a lot, and burst into hysterical tantrums over nothing.

Jimmy senior was a slightly pudgy, good-looking Italian man. Our favorite straight couple cherished their beautiful teenage daughter Janet, and charming younger son Jimmy Junior. Their kids were sharp, smart, and quite humorous; we appreciated being in their presence. Eventually Janet married a wealthy lawyer, though it was no surprise when Junior turned out gay and became the family's decorator.

To get away from the Nicolidis' insults, dirty looks, and cheap innuendos, Niki and I fled to Collaro's elegant home on weekends. The ladies would dabble with contemporary fashions every Sunday, while I learned to prepare tasty spaghetti sauce in the kitchen with Jimmy. He was extravagant, and gave us the best pre-rolled joints we'd ever tried. The lovable guy bought expensive grass, and didn't even smoke. Their large estate was in a community comparable to the Los Feliz area of L.A. It was the ideal retreat from Niki's, but we paid our tab by commiserating with Helen's neurotic dramas. Within those attractive surroundings, we had lots of fun enjoying fine food, awesome weed and constant entertainment.

They had a regulation-size pool table, one of the first big screen color TVs, and several tropical fish tanks, which Helen cared a great deal about. After smoking a bit of Jimmy's dynamite grass, Niki and I would stare at the delicate creatures for hours as they swam around in the breathtaking aquariums.

During an exceptionally cold winter, the electricity suddenly went out at the Collaro's, so they checked into a posh hotel until the power returned. When the family came home about four days later, they were completely shocked to find every precious fish frozen solid. Helen really went berserk since she lost more than ten-thousand-dollars worth. Niki and I were always available to comfort Helen's psychotic ordeals. Besides other perks, we were even given our own room in their house.

After we broke up, fun times at Collaro's house simply became nostalgia when I rented a bachelor pad on the top floor of an old wooden building along popular Highland Avenue. My new address had narrow front hall steps, a huge back porch, and was lodged in a college district bustling with hippies. Neighborhood folks didn't watch TV, yet somehow acknowledged everyday concerns about the war in Viet Nam.

Late one night Niki pounded on my front door unexpectedly. She came to offer me bankbooks and valuable stock holdings I wasn't even aware of. In return for assets, she expected to stay with me forever. Once I loved her with all my heart, but she took it all away by choosing a deceitful existence which would never make her happy. Latent resentments erupted, and I declined her tempting inducements. As she lingered in the doorway begging for reconciliation, I gently hurled her down a flight of stairs.

Niki felt terrible for placing her cold-hearted papa above our amazing partnership, and for a moment I considered starting over with my first true love. Suddenly I realized that Gail Luzzo, an intriguing young lady, was waiting quietly for me in the bedroom naked and drunk. She was quite beautiful, but could never measure up to Niki, the lover I'd banished because of foolish pride. My new flame was spoiled by her wealthy family, who owned a lucrative Italian grocery business. While I was at work, she left huge boxes of groceries on the back porch to make sure there was always plenty of gourmet food.

Trying to fall out of love with Niki hurt, it was the worst pain imaginable. I could have taken her back, but I'd inherited that Irish defiance from my mom. I blamed ancient Greek chauvinism, in view of the fact that a patriarch is always the king. Our relationship was doomed, and her father's reprehensible ruling impacted our lives greatly. Perhaps he was jealous about the way we felt, or how much we really loved each other.

*****

My hippie flat grew busier, and I felt comfortable wearing breezy butch clothes again with a very short haircut. In addition to Gail dropping by, Niki's trend-setting friend Ronny visited regularly. We were stoned when he decided to pierce my ears, and I chose a pair of plain gold loops from his jewelry case. He gave me a tall water glass full of Vodka, told me to relax, then drove a big fat dull sewing needle through each earlobe. While I appreciated current fads, I bled on the pillow all night and cursed Ronny's archaic technique. Whenever I put an earring in, it reminds me of Highland Avenue.

June DePasquale, a kooky acquaintance of Ronny's, became a constant caller at my popular place. She was a gay man's groupie; American-Armenian, fairly short and pudgy. The woman had a weekend heroin addiction, but I didn't know much about drug use then. June wanted more out of me than I could reciprocate, and I quickly informed her we could never be intimate. My free-spirited pal was basically straight, but she would gladly bend the rules for me. I enjoyed her cynical sense of humor; she was funny and made me laugh a lot. If perchance I said something humorous, she'd compare me to a 'One a Day vitamin. She couldn't enjoy casual friendships since it was difficult for her to live without sex.

Before and after Niki, I worked at some dreary factories, but my last job in Worcester was packing pizza mixes for the Appian Way Pizza Company. One Dexedrine daily turned me into the fastest worker they ever had. I earned more than anyone on the line, but the boring work ended abruptly when they announced the entire plant was moving out of town. Our congenial shop manager offered two options. We could accept the same work in Rockford, Illinois for more money, and furthermore the company would fund incidental moving expenses. Otherwise we could take modest severance pay and collect unemployment. It was definitely time for a change, but moving to Illinois wasn't my intention.

When I got laid off in the spring, their modest dividend gave me some leeway to look for another job. Ronny suggested we celebrate on Cape Cod, so we bolted. I'd been there before, yet it seemed different. While admiring the artistic colony, and in its entire splendor, I began to obsess about living in Provincetown.

Tourist towns usually limit females to waitress jobs, sales clerks, or making beds in hotels, but that type of work wasn't for me. I had some experience fixing up and restoring cheap apartments, perhaps I could get a job as a handyperson. Magically, a sign appeared on Commercial Street in front of an adorable place called Angels' Landing. 'Painter Wanted'. I hurried down the alley to a tiny cottage with a ship's bell and a crest which said 'Captain's Quarters'. Angela Calomiris owned the entire charming resort. She was a short Greek woman, darkly complicated, who looked tough and acted more butch than me.

Angela wasn't there the first time I meandered down the narrow sandy path, but I went back until we met. I wanted that job badly and kept ringing the bell until she came to the door. There she stood, holding a cigarette in one hand and a guest list in the other. Locals warned me about her unpleasant attitude, yet she was cordial and offered me a scotch. As an employer she had reservations about my size, she had no idea how hard I could really work. I excused myself briefly, went back to our hotel room, and dropped two black beauties. Soon I returned for the definitive test. My speed and neatness impressed her as I sanded and stained a costly antique desk, consequently I worked at Angels' Landing for the next eight years.

In summer months, the place becomes a Mecca for beautiful gay people, spending an entire season in Provincetown was a dream come true. I couldn't wait to start my new job, which provided room, board, and even a small amount of weekly cash, thanks to Ronny's allusions about changing my life.

Angels' Landing consisted of a few rickety structures next to the beach; except for her cottage, each building housed multiple units. The charming abodes were uniquely eclectic, graced by nautical artifacts. My job was to maintain and decorate the apartments, in addition to some outside duties. Angela kept the place full of tenants throughout each season. Many guests were friends from New York who returned regularly. I worked hard at the Landing and thought of the colorful place as my home. Watering the gardens in the evening was a routine chore. At the end of each day I dropped a tab of LSD to get in touch with the meaning of stillness and beauty. Angela smoked pot with me a few times, but never knew when she was high, and she often entertained the tenants with tacky jokes or absurd costumes.

At a glance she looked like Napoleon and blazed dirt road trails in Provincetown before the illustrious Commercial Street had a sidewalk. When we met in the sixties, she was a part-time photography teacher at NYU; her tiny bug-infested apartment was above a rowdy bar on Horatio Street, in Greenwich Village. Whether she had money or not the woman really lived like a bag lady. She taught a crowded trendy class, which was hard to enroll in; there were many admirers because of her former covert background.

She was a bona fide card-carrying party member working undercover for the FBI, and later wrote a book called *Red Masquerade* detailing her daunting ordeal. Throughout the early fifties, she photographed and documented well-known communist subversives along with their families in New York City.

After the conspiracy trial, Angela developed paranoia, and hid out with old friends on a rural farm in Pennsylvania. During that long seclusion she wrote the book and saved enough money to buy the first parcel of Angels' Landing. When the ruthless commy threats subsided, she moved back to P. Town.

The elegant Chrysler Art Museum sat poised like a dignified clapboard cathedral directly across from Angels' Landing. Angela knew the wealthy owner, Walter P. Chrysler Jr., through community functions. He was a brilliant entrepreneur, philanthropist, and heir to a large family fortune. When young Walter began collecting items of fine art, his dignified father told him those stately pieces should not remain in his hands. "Objects of great beauty must be displayed openly for all society to appreciate." His passion took him around the world procuring from great artists. He actually purchased abstract paintings privately from Picasso. My first season in P. Town was off to a great start, and I felt genuinely happy.

Shortly after the prestigious Chrysler Building in New York City was sold in 1956, Walter bought the colossal Center Methodist Church of Provincetown. Extraordinary renovations were necessary; the 1850s wooden structure was built to embrace the largest congregation on Cape Cod, but he converted the huge citadel into sections. The main gallery was designed for illustrious paintings, next he integrated a grand reference library, and mythical sculptured works occupied other areas. An array of antique glass from Sandwich was featured, while befitting rooms were graced with authentic Victorian furniture.

Walter seemed gay to me, though he claimed to have a wife in Virginia. He scheduled extravagant premier showings for contemporary artists and patronized wealthy audiences. Andy Warhol exhibited his famous *Soup Can* pop art during my first summer. Walter liked me and introduced us personally, which was a daunting moment; Warhol acted cold, looked sickly, and appeared quite narcissistic.

I became addicted to heroin later, and many contemporaries were amused by The Velvet Underground clique. It seemed like everyone in Andy's life used drugs throughout that fearless period.

My paranoid boss took me to every cocktail party around; generally shallow, boring social functions. Lilly Tomlin, Dom Delouse, Joan Rivers, Ruth Buzzy, and The Kaiser Kids attended the same soirees. The upcoming actors did hilarious cabaret shows at the Madeira Club, a place for stealthy talent scouts. Ms. Tomlin looked deep as she sat alone taking notes. Sometimes I'd see her bicycling through town, and one day I noticed her exchanging affections with a mysterious woman who came from nowhere.

Ravi Shankar was the most mesmerizing artist I ever encountered. Thanks to Walter Chrysler, I was able to hear his rousing music in person, a wonderful gift. He performed one show at our tiny crowded town hall while a parade of beautiful Indian ladies threw rose petals all around. There was something very spiritual about this musician, maybe it was the LSD, but I felt ethereal in his presence.

Nina Simone was booked at the A House for the summer. Her temporary quarters were right next-door at the Xanadu Inn. One morning she leaned across our fence to ask where she could buy potatoes. I nearly flew over the hedge and escorted her to the local A&P in Angela's classic yellow convertible. We bonded instantly. After a few visits she asked if I could stay with her three-year-old daughter Lisa Celeste. Nina's gay younger brother Sam, her regular sitter, was anxious to go out and party.

While tourists reveled in the bars, Commercial Street grew quiet, and I'd lie down next to her beautiful child, Lisa, nuzzling my head into her soft, sweet-smelling, nappy hair. Nina usually came home late after her last show at the A House, and when she walked in, I felt honored to be in her company. She drank rum, inhaled bottled oxygen, and read the Sexus, Nexus, Plexus, trilogy. My cultured friend had great success composing songs with dark verses, but what made her think that I was an angry person?

I thought she'd like me better if I related to her gutsy lyrics by acting hostile. She said I was a good person, and my honesty was refreshing, but I should think for myself, it wasn't necessary to emulate. Prior to the Cape, June got me hooked on Nina's music, and we'd ad-lib dramatic tunes like *Pirate Jenny*. Today when I hear *Sinner Man* in the background of a film, I reflect on her great humanity.

Provincetown attracted bohemian characters, intellectuals, and art lovers, bringing rarely a dull moment. From Memorial Day until Labor Day, more than twenty thousand tourists arrive to vacation; only two thousand folks were anchored all year round. I stayed for a couple of menacing cold spells in the sixties when the picturesque hamlet becomes bleak and dismal. On lonely, chilly nights, I raised a glass or two with an array of townie fishermen at The Old Colony Bar. My beloved town now has a local population of thirty-five hundred, while visitors rise to thirty-five thousand. P. Town has always been a homosexual utopia, today gay marriage is legal, and the artistic colony I once cherished is fading slowly.

The legendary Atlantic House was built in 1789, and through

the years it was a favorite watering hole for writers, especially during the twenties. Eugene O'Neill, a frequent patron of the merry A House, caught his first break at Provincetown's Wharf Theater, then went on to Broadway. A life-sized photo hangs above the bar, which flaunts a free-spirited gay playwright, Tennessee Williams, strolling on the beach nude.

When I lived in P. Town, a notorious Portuguese couple, Reggie and Mira Cabral, owned the A House. Rumors spread about their bizarre gay liaisons via our close-knit community. Socialite hotties from Hyannis often occupied the tiny crowded dance floor. One almost needed a secret password to carouse on it through summer. When brisk autumn nights set in, there was a majestic fireplace to enjoy.

A House's cliques seemed smarter, hipper, and groovier than other clubs. Great music, trendy people, and available drugs earned it its popularity. An obscure back bar fared as a cruising bailiwick for gay males hoping to score a one-night stand. Closet-sized rooms upstairs were rented transiently late at night.

The Grand Room where Nina Simone performed was mainly for elite jazz artists. That illustrious stage was simply a crude wooden platform yet accommodated endless celebrated composers. Gazing at her from a table next to the piano was an extraordinary experience. She always ended the show with a long, breathy, exhausting number. Andy Stroud, Nina's famous record-producing husband at the time, cautiously slipped her hits of oxygen from behind the curtain. He rarely came up from New York on weekends to be with Nina and Lisa; their turbulent showbiz marriage was destined to go adrift.

Ronny came to Provincetown regularly, and wore long blond hair while dating a beautiful man called Mark. His Greek Adonis owned Papagalo, the classiest boutique in Hyannis, and always dressed in white. I knew many people with his bloodline, though Niki was the most exquisite Greek female I ever met. They continued working together at Elegante, behaving like best girl friends. Ronny regularly drove his Corvette back and forth from the Cape to Worcester. Just to get a rise out of her, he'd gossip about seeing me out on the town with attractive women having fun, which she later admitted was annoying.

I was pleased she still felt jealous. It motivated her to visit me out of curiosity, or perhaps pure desire. Ronny brought her directly to P. Town from Worcester after work one Saturday. Without a word spoken, Niki and I connected amorously and enjoyed the carefree A House till closing. Then we went back to my little loft while the moon was full on that balmy July night and fell in love all over again.

We made mad passionate love through the night, transcending the usual, and I'm certain the boss heard the lively outbursts. When daybreak came, I introduced Niki to Angela, and they hit it off right away, perhaps because of their roots. Angela seemed surprised by Niki's stunning looks and cheerful attitude. "She's a definite keeper, don't blow it." In any event, my greatest fantasy wasn't meant to be. After an emotional weekend, we never wanted to part, but she proceeded home to accept her responsibility.

Her future husband, Richard LaRevierre, an extremely rich banker, was also from Massachusetts. Niki showed up at my tiny garret to share in bliss a few more times. Eventually she alluded to wedding plans with an unattractive man whom she could never really love. Richard was coping with cancer of the face, which must have seemed horrible to the glamorous young lady who modeled a mink bikini. Niki grew unhappy soon after their wedding and took advantage of his private helicopter and crew to visit me on the Cape. If my girl had nothing else, that darling Greek possessed bold determination.

Niki could marry Richard, or become my lifelong partner; she chose to obey her family's wishes. I broke up with her for good on the subsequent visit. Aware that she'd be sharing a bed with someone else was wrong. Niki was a dynamic force I didn't want to live without; most women couldn't even hold a candle to her. She broke my heart in a million pieces, regardless of how much I disapproved. Our final separation led me to hunt for unsavory characters on the street, who dealt in heavy-duty pain killing drugs. This was the start of a casual, weekend warrior, heroin habit.

At the end of an absorbing season, I went back to Worcester and rented a cheap furnished apartment for the winter. Finding a dealer would have been easy, but I kept a low profile and mused on Cape Cod.

*****

I reappeared in Provincetown the following summer to meet with Angela concerning my employment. 'A Nice Place to Hang Your Halo', was the slogan on the long wooden sign which dangled over the driveway at Angels' Landing. Plenty of halos got lost down there, including my own. The landing had become twenty-two apartments; the latest was a converted fire department building complete with a fireman's pole. What used to be known as the home of 'Pumper Number One' was now a suite called 'Angel Baby'. She bought up every available property near the landing, even though there were many community conflicts.

The Captain (Angela) was accepted by some of the locals but not very well liked. She was arrogant and fought with everyone from the garbage man to the entire power company. Part of my duty at the landing was to walk a few paces behind and apologize for her rude manners, or try to console someone she plainly provoked. Folks wondered why I stayed so long; honestly, it was because I loved the place.

All the units were named after angels: Gabriel, Seraphim, Raphael and so forth. At the hub of this nautical empire was a grand wooden deck, with a heavy iron ship's bell next to my beloved flagpole. At first light, I raised the American flag, and proceeded with other flags to honor the nationalities of our visiting guests. The American flag was always first, then Greece, Israel, Canada, France, Italy etc.

Around five p.m. I raised the cocktail flag and most of our tenants would congregate or mingle all around the huge, pine-soaked, wooden deck. Angela put out some cheap booze, sodas, and paper cups. It was self-service. She loved to entertain her lodgers by putting on unique or funny hats. At one party, she might wear a fez, a cowboy hat, or sombrero, which led up to one of her zany, contrived acts.

When all the flags came down and the gardens were watered, I cleaned myself up, dropped a black beauty and left my drunken employer's crowd. If I didn't get out of there quickly and unnoticed, she would generally try to fix me up with a likeable girl. Some of her guests really surprised me with their open promiscuity, but they were from the city and loved to play kinky games. I wasn't interested and went directly to the A House wearing a simple faded blue work shirt, bell-bottoms and leather sandals.

Another Pisces friend Ronny introduced me to a woman named Freda DeCiccio from Worcester, whose family was fairly comfortable and owned a celebrated wine and dine business. She went to college with Joan Crawford's daughter in Newport Rhode Island and seemed educated, but somehow I never thought of her as being very smart. The A House is where we first met; she came in with Ronny one weekend and though she was slightly taller, we had great fun dancing together on that crowded floor.

Freda had a beautiful face but always seemed ill at ease; whenever anyone made her nervous, she would cough incessantly. We stayed at the landing the night we met, but soon after she rented a room across the street and got a waitress job at a chic restaurant called Plain and Fancy. One of my regular chores around the landing was touching up the paint and wherever I worked, she'd just sit on the fence for hours admiring me. No matter how much I appreciated her devotion, she wasn't my Niki.

The bond we shared was our passion for potent drugs and energetic sex. Freda's tiny rented room on Commercial Street was literally a trip because we dropped acid in there three times a day, usually with a nice hot cup of tea. That creepy flophouse with many rooms was run by a very crazy Canadian woman called Ruby. Frankly, she wanted to have sex with me and didn't mind admitting it, which is why she often became angry with my lover. One evening I arrived at the house extremely drunk and Freda was out, the big, repulsive building manager carried me upstairs to a windowless room hoping to have her way with me, I probably passed out right away, so she locked me in there all night.

I woke up around sunrise with an awful hangover and went into complete shock when I looked around the room; it was the most depraved place I'd ever seen, or even imagined. All four walls were literally covered with disturbing photographs of very young, small boys performing unnatural acts with loathsome adults. I was overwhelmed and sickened, so I continued to scream loudly until Ruby finally opened the door. After that macabre experience, I went exploring through the rest of the house and discovered whips, chains, torture devices, even a stretching rack in the basement. We learned a little later that this diabolical building actually belonged to a pedophile, Walter Chrysler, the famous art tycoon.

Angela was really getting on my case about my vigorous life style, so I quit working for her temporarily and got a job to be near Freda washing dishes at the Plain and Fancy. Before work, I'd drop a black beauty; hence, I earned the nickname 'Super Dish'. Other than the boss, most employees in the kitchen bought speed from me; we all worked so fast and could hardly wait for the diner's to finish eating, just to scrub their plates. One night, a Puerto Rican busboy got angry with the chef and actually urinated into an enormous vat of fresh Portuguese soup, which had just been placed on the walk-in freezer floor.

Pat and Lenore lived in an apartment upstairs over the restaurant. Pat was the energetic, friendly chef and Lenore, the hostess, was a fat, disagreeable drunk who bought me a drink or two at the bar after I finished work, where tried to get me up to her bedroom for a sordid tryst. When I first saw Lenore lying on her bed upstairs, naked and coming on to me, I got sick at the sight of her huge breasts, which could have strangled me. Shortly after rejecting her brazen advances, I quit the dishwashing job and went back to the landing in a hurry.

Earlier, Angela was making a practice out of dining every night at the Plain and Fancy just to hassle me in a brotherly way because she knew that someday I would return to my rightful job at her place. She cared much more than I really deserved at times and said the flowers in her garden missed my cheerful conversations, so I moved back and hung my halo anew.

The structure directly in front of the landing housed the most well-known, prestigious, art gallery in Provincetown, called 'Tirca Karlis'. Tirca and her husband Mr. Cohen were actually tattooed survivors of the Holocaust and had a son named Aaron, who was a very dear friend of mine. Angela got a kick out of it whenever they came into town because Aaron had developed a big crush on me. She jokingly hinted that if I ever married him, I could become rich, which revealed her pathetic way of seeing things.

'Slow' was the only word to describe him, but that isn't to say he wasn't smart. Each day I would simply talk with him for a while about mundane things or current events. Our quality time meant a lot to him. Both his parents were rather sickly, frail and nervous people but highly religious; his mood was serious most of the time, so once in a while I made him giggle about something, his genuine laughter was divine. For the Friday night religious traditions, cultural candles blazed in their modest quarters above the gallery, I admired their decency and knew Aaron would be praying while I was out dancing.

I always wanted to turn Aaron on to grass, simply to help him to feel good and enjoy himself, but he wasn't on stable ground all of the time and getting him high may have proved dangerous. Before every gallery opening, he always gave me first peek at the new show, and I got to see those famous works way ahead of the art critics and rich buyers. Recently, I looked on the Internet to find the Tirca Karlis files. Much to my surprise and joy Aaron was listed as the present owner of the gallery, maybe one day I'll go back to the Cape just to visit him. Would he still remember me? I really think he might.

When I left the Plain and Fancy, I also left Freda because she was starting to act goofy from drugs. She quickly disappeared to Worcester, and my Libra moon compelled me to get another mate right away. The majority of summer tourists visiting Provincetown came from New York City. Numerous doctors, lawyers, and other advantaged men, brought their wives and children for the entire summer season. Some husbands regularly drove back and forth from the city on weekends to relax with their families.

Janet Grigsby showed up for the season once and leased a dingy basement dwelling from the Cohen family just a few feet away from the landing beneath the Tirca Karlis art gallery. Her spouse was a swinging photographer with Vogue Magazine and never once visited Janet, but her two zany sisters frequently camped there. They were well-educated Russian-American women who all laughed hard at their own father's broken English. They seemed to be having so much fun that I decided to get to know them. Janet, the Taurus, was home alone all week, so I approached her first.

"Hi, I'm Carole, blah blah."

After that, I shopped a great deal for us at the corner Spirit shop. We drank plenty of Chablis, celebrating our new friendship. Janet only smoked weed occasionally but laughed a lot anyhow, basically white wine was her turn on and she was an extraordinary cook.

We'd have a glass of wine just before dusk, then walk down the beach to pick buckets of raw mussels from the nearby breakwater. I'd breathe in some clean, salty air, watch the fishing boats come home and linger over spectacular sunsets during my Quixote leisure time. Janet knew her way around that tiny, ill-equipped kitchen and prepared a delicious sauce for the freshly cooked mussels, in addition to other side dishes. Each specialty she created for an average meal was remarkably beautiful and appetizing. After eating the terrific gourmet delights Janet cooked, my favorite tasty hot dogs from the bowling alley could never satisfy me again.

I went with her to a local thrift shop, for the first time ever. It was held in the basement of an old church and I soon discovered many wonderful trappings for very little money. She believed shopping for bargains demonstrated that anyone in America with good taste could look great and be well dressed, regardless of where they traded, or how much they spent. This very down-to-earth lady really proved to me that patronizing an inexpensive store was nothing to feel ashamed of.

Janet wasn't the fine, attractive miss I usually dated, she was older, quite voluptuous, with a slightly muscular body and wasn't at all shy, her charm was even a bit kinky. She wrote a book about her amours while living in Mexico for a short period and it seemed conceivable that she may have devoured several young men down there. Sometimes she was rough, consuming, loud, and aggressive and carried on too long for my erogenous needs.

Angela was jealous of the fun we were having, maybe because she was never included in our constant partying. The late summer night sounds amplified and all the cheerful, happy, voices from the Russian sisters and me wafted right up into the Captain's open bedroom window. We laughed about her too, but if she happened to overhear our nightly, rowdy conversations, her attitude in the morning would surely indicate whether or not she'd be cantankerous that day.

Well, it was too bad if the boss got angry because we broadcasted so much enjoyment; I still fixed her breakfast, hung all my flags and went on with my everyday chores at the landing. When the workday concluded, I dashed straight over to Janet's for a chilled glass of Chablis and a splendid gourmet meal, followed by some all-encompassing lovemaking.

When we made love, it felt somewhat like a struggle or a

difficult thing for me to do at times; I never worked harder at trying to please someone who became so ravenous. This intense relationship went on for a good part of that summer, but I ended it abruptly because I disliked being controlled in any way, and she was much too dominating for me.

*****

There is no place in the world like Cape Cod and I was really privileged to live there for so much time. Let me reflect on a few things I loved about it. Before Memorial Day everyone is busy painting and fixing up hotels, guesthouses and generally preparing for a prosperous season. If you saw the movie *Porgy and Bess*, you may recall the new Todao system used to echo the true sounds of rebuilding that village, after a big hurricane. P. Town sounded like that every spring. Small businesses started to reopen, which meant more people for me to chat with daily. There was always a good sandal maker, some handmade jewelry shops, fine restaurants and numerous art galleries. You could drive all the way to the tip of Provincetown to see the mighty Atlantic Ocean surrounded by mountains of serpentine sand dunes.

Many artists lived in shacks around the sand dunes and some became famous. A woman named Bonny Whittingham was a revered friend of mine and a great artist. She created extraordinary compositions of the Cape, concealing a distinct clown's face somewhere in the painting, which was her individual trademark. If you looked closely, you could find a harlequin hidden within the spectrum of her work. Throughout my travels, I never found or loved any other place more than charming old Cape Cod.

Seasons happily begin and sadly end. After Labor Day the presence of summer tourists dwindled and we began the task of securing our seaside domains before the blustery winter embarked. It was challenging to close down the landing each September for many reasons, invariably it rained a lot throughout that month and every year prior to my birthday on the fifteenth, I came down with an awful cold.

We should have docked the Captain's eighteen-foot boat before I heard the latest news report on the radio, which had just dispatched a dramatic warning to the entire Cape about the arrival of a huge hurricane. Hardly anyone watched television then, so I promptly raised the solid red flag high up on the mast to warn our neighbors about the imminent and hazardous weather conditions. After I hoisted the large danger flag, Angela realized that her own craft wasn't properly anchored in the bay and coaxed me to swim out and bring it back to land. The wind and waves were really picking up, and I wasn't sure if I could get to it safely, but I gallantly opted to carry out her request anyway. I plunged into the cold water, swam halfway out, lost my breath completely and contemplated the end of my young life.

Finally I reached it and collapsed on the saturated floor of her costly Chris-Craft breathless, exhausted and genuinely praying for help. Fortunately, my petitions were answered at once. My friends Bruce, Jeff and Jerry were on their way home and just happened to see me in the water, so they swam right out into the rough, choppy sea. I was lying down dormant in the small boat as they navigated it all the way back to the wet, sandy coast.

When we returned to the landing, Angela declared everyone a hero, I hated her for saying that, but later on, after a brandy or two, we laughed about my paralyzing adventure. The same guys who taught me how to trap lobsters in the summer, were now my saviors and continued to be my favorite drinking buddies at the Rumpus Room through a couple of really bleak winters.

I really loved these men, not just for saving my life or Angela's boat, but they were The Barbarians; Provincetown's own, original garage band/rock group. Moulty was the fourth member, a bohemian-looking drummer who couldn't swim out to help me because he had a silver hook in place of a hand. In earlier years, he blew his left limb off by accident with a Molotov cocktail, but it never stopped him from playing. Their biggest, most recognized hit was titled *Are you a Boy, or are you a Girl?* Each gay person who visited the Cape in the sixties identified and thought it had been written exclusively for them, but I knew those Barbarians were actually describing my long-haired friend Ronny in their famous tune.

The local four-man band never put on Beatle boots, they only wore handmade, Cape Cod, leather sandals. I saw them a few years later in a small Boston club and they weren't doing very well. Their sounds had become passé, but these four young men were still our homegrown, P. Town rockers and we cherished them for being who they really were, great guys with indelible New England accents. Moulty, the drummer, married a good wife and currently performs live music with his three children.

Batten down the hatches, shut off the gas, water and power, board up all the windows and only use galvanized nails, the rough weather and saltwater air can really rot things quickly. We kept the Captain's cottage open all year round with everything running, but those twenty-two apartment rentals needed some final work. To protect objects from the ensuing elements, we removed valuable paintings and delicate artifacts from the exposed, ocean-side apartments, put them away carefully, and locked each place. Now from time to time when closing up for the off-season, we'd find a little spare time to fly kites from a deserted beach. Angela always played to win and would intentionally attach brand-new razor blades, to the tail end of her kite to cut down the other player's rig. She loved to proclaim herself a conqueror.

It starts to get cold in September and dashing from one chilly unit to the next wasn't much pleasure. Between jobs on crisp days, I took a relaxing break to enjoy a nourishing lunch, at the Wharf Diner next to the town pier. I watched people coming and going from the Boston Ferry as I enjoyed a big, tasty bowl, of steamy New England clam chowder with delicious freshly baked bread. I believed if you ate sufficiently, you could stay strong enough to fight off the flu or a cold. Billy, the droll restaurant owner, opened at five a.m. for the fisherman and early breakfast crowd, he closed promptly at four p.m. hence, my pals, the idle townies, left then and headed home to their families, for a fine Portuguese dinner.

At the end of my mission when all the work at the landing was completely finished, I collected a major bonus from the boss, which was certainly earned. I could either stay at the Captain's, or move to a different city to holdup until the arrival of the following spring. Angela, must now return to her little cave on Horatio Street and continue teaching photography. I decided to work in Provincetown at the landing for the entire winter that year to paint and redecorate some neglected units. I really didn't mind my own company when I was alone, it was extremely quiet, but if boredom ever did set in, there was always the legendary A House, or the rowdy Rumpus Room to meet friends and have some fun.

I kept my summer job, throughout each season for eight consecutive years, during which time I acquired many new friends, received employment offers and good advice about places to live, but it was hard to decide which career to take, or where to move. In spite of the many invitations, I needed to be around gay people to feel honest and comfortable with my own essence. Autumn was a scary time because of my real fears and ambivalence about coping with a new location. Cambridge was high on my list of attractive communities, but oddly enough, my next winter residence became Irvington, New Jersey.

*****

Another wonderful summer was over and the best offer for a cozy winter haven came from my drunken Aunt Jenny and sweet Uncle Bill. We always stayed in touch, so I thought it was a good idea when they invited me to stay at their new home for a while, but I told them it would only be until the following spring. Angela approved of this distant family scene because I wouldn't be moving in with a lover; she was still a bit jealous of my worldly activities. Jenny and Bill lived in Irvington, the ticky-tacky, white bread town bordering Newark. Uncle Bill drove a brand-new black Chrysler convertible with huge fins and really enjoyed frequent trips to the racetrack. They never had any children together, which might explain why they favored me so much. I was their pseudo Shirley Temple at five years old when we stayed with them in New York long ago; they absolutely adored me then and I hoped they still would.

Aunt Jenny was a moody Cancer who loved to speculate and gamble. Uncle Bill, a Virgo, came from the hills of Arkansas and never wore shoes in his entire life until he joined the army, but he always kept his charming southern accent, spoke slowly and drank Jack Daniel's mixed with milk because of his ulcers. Their cottage in Jersey was paid for with winnings from the track. They chose that specific city because my cousin Joy had recently purchased a house there with her husband Bob and were planning to adopt children. Joy decided to live in Irvington because it was close to her beloved New York City and far enough away from Aunt Aggie, her outspoken mother. Uncle Bill worked at the post office for many years and retired with a comfortable pension, he also received excellent veterans' benefits.

They were free as birds and crazy as loons, yet this eccentric couple came all the way to the Cape just to drive me back to their home. Angela spotted their big black convertible pulling into her driveway and must have thought: *These people are hillbillies, how is Carole ever going to make this strange kinship work?*

Angela invited them in for a cocktail, they chatted informally for a while and I realized how crude they must have seemed to her. I took a long, climactic look all around my precious summer home, I would definitely return to the landing next spring. We were off to the Garden State, but they insisted I drive so they could drink more and not worry about the car. After that day, I became their personal chauffeur, but I didn't mind, eventually I drove them to some wonderful racetracks all around the East Coast.

When things settled down following my move, I looked through the local paper, promptly found a job and went directly to work for an electronics firm in Irvington. Nearly everyone who worked there was German. They paid well but expected total perfection in our work, or else, repeat, repeat, repeat. This was a strict government job; they designed and produced nose cones for NASA spacecrafts. I learned a lot about precision at that huge, sterile factory. Every day I ate a delicious lunch at a small bar next door which served the best knockwurst sandwiches anywhere, the imported beer was excellent too. Come to think of it, almost the entire population of Irvington came from a German background.

One evening during that fall election, a blond, Aryan-type politician came to the door, introduced himself and defined his platforms. He strongly intimated: "No black people will ever live in this district." I quickly asked Uncle Bill to boot him out on his ass. Noticeably, there really weren't any folks of color living there, or even gays. After that man's annoying visit, I began to see the colorless town for what it really was. Minority figures drove through Irvington in a real hurry because the local police were perceived as genuine bigots then. The Nazi wannabes usually took their young sons out in the woods for target practice on Saturdays, which is how and why some children learned to hate and kill. I was beginning to feel disheartened about living there, but my lovely cousin Joy would be a great consolation.

World peace can never be until all nations who hate other races let go of their ignorant prejudices. There really were Nazis living near us in Irvington. They acted so superior, which inferred that everyone else must be inferior. I began writing this book two weeks before the terrorist attacks on 9/11/ 2001, but stopped for a while because I was sickened by the event.

A Citizen's Peace Corps should now be activated to teach those racist cops in New Jersey, or wherever else that ignorant mindset still exists. Peace and harmony begins with us, look around your own town or area for any signs of prejudice, address the main reasons and figure out how to put an end to it. I had problems in the past with a certain ethnic group; today I try hard to understand their combative manners. Before we hurry off expecting to educate those poor people in Afghanistan about love, life, independence, or even make an effort to teach to them how to grow things without water, we should first acknowledge our own nation's poverty.

Joy didn't have many hang-ups and she was a much lighter Capricorn than most. Long ago, while on a visit to Uncle Leo's summer camp, we slept together for a few nights; I was seventeen and she was about twenty-two. For me, sleeping next to a woman whose company I really enjoyed, generally turned into romance, and those marvelous feelings we shared back in Hopkinton were easy to renew in New Jersey.

While living with her parents in the Bronx, she aspired to become an actress, just like Audrey Hepburn. Joy's delightful father, Uncle Sam, was a talky, cigar-smoking cabby who married a very pushy wife, our Aunt Aggie. Joy was always treated like a true Jewish Princess because she was the only girl out of their five children. The four brothers were: Philly, the cute one; Gary, the sweetheart of a nerd; Glen, the bratty wimp; and my favorite cousin/friend, Kenny. He was a gangly ball of energy and loved tapping with his drumsticks. Whenever I visited them in the Bronx, we had lots of fun hanging out together.

After many hostile years, Mom and Aggie finally made up and agreed to let me visit the Bronx occasionally. My four-eyed aunt, was always trying to shave my eyebrows, or dress me up to make a lady out of me, instead, I grew more boyish by hanging around with my male cousins. Kenny said he was the original drummer with the famous local Bronx group, Dion and the Belmonts (their big claim to fame), and successfully recorded *Teenager in Love*, *Run Around Sue*, *The Wanderer*, etc. Bob Chasey, the most blasé guy on the planet, courted and ultimately married my savvy cousin Joy, during the same period. Chasey's behavior was quietly creepy, and when she accepted his proposal, the family seemed shocked.

I didn't have a car when I lived in New Jersey, so once in a while, Jenny and Bill would lend me their big black convertible, otherwise, Joy offered me regular rides. Her husband Bob, the sullen Gemini, was previously a burnt out stockbroker who changed professions and became an elite house painter. Before I moved there, they'd just adopted a three-year-old little girl and named her Carole, maybe because I was Joy's favorite relative, my little namesake, however, was a difficult youngster and a bit of a brat.

Bob did very well in the painting business, so I tried to pick up a little extra money by working for him one Saturday. Five competent assistants showed up at the job site that day and began to coat their assigned areas. His company emerged around the Newark area and was in constant demand because the expert crew produced flawless work. Bob gave me the tedious job of trimming the fancy windows, which was a huge mistake. I detailed the wood trim all around that big window panes non-stop from eight a.m. to five p.m. thinking that my work was great, by then; the other guys had completed the entire house. Bob graciously paid me but after working with real professionals, I felt guilty for accepting the wages and since his team didn't appreciate my Virgo perfection, I decided to terminate myself.

We were cousins just hanging out, shopping side by side and sharing wonderful conversations as we tooled around the beaches and more attractive sections of New Jersey. Our leisurely time spent together was acceptable to the whole family, at least in the beginning. Bob always stayed home with the toddler Carole and once in a while, Joy and I would go out to a Jazz club in Newark with my new Afro-American friend Allen, who played the Saxophone. Music was always a pivotal part of my life. When Joy and I first became romantic in her car, the hit song that week was *Michelle* by the Beatles.

One night we parked in front of Jenny and Bill's ticky-tacky house for a couple of hours just talking, when suddenly our loud aunt came out drunk and shrieking: "Kiss her goodnight Carole and get right in the house." At that point, we honestly hadn't even smooched yet, but it was a good idea and we wanted to. Before anyone else in the family suspected, that cunning, ugly, inebriated relative sensed our fascination.

It was a crisp, early autumn evening when a huge news bulletin flashed over the television; all the lights had gone out in New York City, we had full electrical power in Irvington but other towns nearby didn't. Joy called me right away and suggested that we drive around the Hudson River to look at the blacked out city, so she picked me up. It was really an eerie sight to behold. We parked on a quiet street to observe this baffling phenomenon and our very first amorous kiss happened; I was breathless. Then I struggled with the idea of going home to face my nasty aunt, Joy had to be back for Bob and Carole. That alluring darkness gave us the autonomy to fall in love and so we did.

Shortly after that night, I had a big fight with Jenny and immediately moved into a small room at Joy's house, with Bob's approval. Our romance had become an all-powerful sexual activity almost daily, but I wondered what would happen when this affair had to end. Bob wasn't stupid and I knew my welcome was wearing out when he began to exhibit some criticisms. Now I was definitely going back to Provincetown before Memorial Day.

Even though it would be a whole month before I started back to work at Angels' Landing, it was impossible to stay at Joy's house any longer. Bob tried to goad me into one of his typical Gemini debates and I refused. This man never raised his voice or lost his temper, but suddenly he seemed to be in a silent rage about something. Maybe he heard rumors about me and Joy from our lecherous Aunt Jenny. In all the years I'd known him; he was completely out of character one particular evening and offended me with an abusive attitude. I really didn't enjoy that town anyway so my basic instinct told me to cast off.

Now I had to confront Joy about the fate of our relationship. "Will you and the baby come to live with me in Provincetown?" (What a nerve; me without any prospects...)

Her answer was typically Joy. "I'd like to, but it's very important that I send my daughter to a good Hebrew school and I think that Bob can provide this. Besides, there aren't any accredited

Jewish schools on the Cape, are there?"

When it was time for my departure, she drove me to Newark Airport and we ultimately embraced for the last time. Our feelings were still strong, but we could never again disclose how we honestly felt. Later I heard she moved to Florida near her mother, Aunt Aggie, who always hated gays and never forgave our liaison.

Remarkably, I did save some money while living in New Jersey; enough to catch a plane headed for Boston and live cushy for a while. Just before leaving Joy's, I called my pal June DePasquale about hooking me up to camp at our friend Bobby's house in Park Square. For an entire month, I could hang around the city, stay loaded and bottom out before returning to a sober-conscious life with Angela in Provincetown.

My Bean Town gay friends met me at Logan Airport and said 'Welcome' by filling both my hands with various pills and a tall, strong drink.

Bobby and Andrew were nice guys who I met through Ronny previously at the Cape. One was a banker, the other a broker and they loved staying high.

We always stayed in touch, which is how I came to nest at their home for a very cheerful hiatus. June hung out wherever there were free drugs and no one ever objected; she was funny, entertaining and made the perfect gofer. Having a huge tolerance for narcotics, she stayed loaded from many assorted brands of painkillers; her infectious laugh gave us all reason to party. When she wasn't putting the moves on me, June was very much enticed by black men, large black men, and subsequently married one of her dates.

*****

After that insane month, I was totally ready to leave the Boston binge and head for my summer Cape Cod job. Enough lamenting and partying, it was time to work and awaken my creativity again. The Greyhound from Boston stopped right at the town pier, a block away from Angels' Landing. Driving into Provincetown is spectacular; you can see the entire tip of Cape Cod at one point and the closer you come to those quaint, narrow little streets the more excited you become; I was going home, to love life once more. From the bus stop, I strolled down the gritty windswept beach to the main deck of the landing while deeply inhaling the fresh salt air. That amazing seascape was like cosmic medication to me. There were twenty-two apartments in dire need of freshening up and I might even be glad to see the Captain again.

Seated at her desk in the small cluttered office, wearing tiny spectacles, Angela looked surprised when I came in a little early. We hugged, she poured me a scotch, and we walked down to The Lobster Pot, one of the few restaurants open all year round. At times, I loved her like a mother, and that night was one of those instances. After a hearty meal, we went back to the landing, had another drink and I unpacked my two old suitcases, thanking all the stars above for my cramped little garret in that cottage. She expected me to work extra hard just before the tourist season began, which left less time for my bad habits to kick in. Tomorrow we'd get started opening up and attentively go through every musty unit.

The boss was cheap about a lot of things, but she gave me an unlimited credit line at the Land's End Hardware Emporium, a place which every resident living there needed. They sold everything from paint to boats. I decorated each unit at the landing with many shades of colors, so I spent a lot of her money in that wonderful store. The proprietors of this handyman's heaven were great to, and for, the town.

Commercial Street was indeed named because of the many small businesses located on it. You could walk the entire length of that narrow street in about thirty minutes and probably say hello to most of the local townies. This friendly image has been likened to some places in Ireland. Never be in a hurry if you are sauntering through an Irish village, inasmuch as you are expected to stop and chat with everyone you approach. Nina Simone depicted this activity in a funny song which she often performed. "I said good morning to the cows, good morning to the hens, good morning to the chickens on the hill, by the time I got through saying good morning, it was time to say good night. Good night to the cows...."

Some folks fell in love with Provincetown last year and might return this spring, determined to start up a chic, faddish enterprise for the season. One such charming boutique, called Mexicana, was conceived and launched by three single women from New York City. This very cool and attractive store was partly a head shop but primarily retailed cheap goods from Mexico. They carried the best rolling papers and conspicuously displayed other popular psychedelic paraphernalia. Within a short time, the four of us became friends, sharing much gaiety at their huge, rented house with an ocean view, which was located on the highest hill of Bradford Street. Earlier arrangements were made with a real estate lady from the city and they leased that marvelous home for the entire summer. Welfare checks began to arrive for all three women, which compensated for their enormous rent. I don't know how that fluke ever transpired.

Three young ladies drove to town in a beat-up Volkswagen bus guarded by a big old German shepherd dog named Sam. Marion was a single Virgo, Debra an Aquarius, and Susan the Cancer were dedicated longtime lovers. These enlightened, savvy, lovely maidens planned their activities well and arranged to receive welfare payments while living on the Cape. Throughout any summer period, Provincetown was commonly flooded with hippies hoping to draw assistance, and many capable people relied on that steady check. If one person accumulated enough for the rent and their partner provided grocery money, someone else in the commune could apply all their welfare benefits toward drugs. Sharing was fundamental.

Patchouli oil and leather were the most prominent essences in their tiny shop, which were only a few doors away from the landing. Each time I passed their spot en route to the hardware store, or when going out for lunch, the Virgo partner would eagerly smile at me. Marion appeared to behave a little more butch than any other girl I had pursued. Her posture was poor; she hunched slightly and exhibited a large white toothy smile, but she was fairly attractive in a nice clean-cut, collegiate way. Her friends believed she vaguely resembled Jean Paul Belmondo; I thought she looked more like Alain Delon. Out of her peer group in Provincetown, she was the brightest. After this season ended, Marion would attend The New School in New York City to complete her thesis on some type of heavy-duty psychology project.

Our new romance was definitely less sensual and more intellectual than any others that I'd known. We saw each other considerably but not with great sexual enthusiasm; actually, she was cold. Marion fared very well through Angela's interrogation and passed the litmus test by agreeing to clean up some of her old paperwork in the future. She overcame my defensive boss partly because her rich dad owned a large chain of department stores in New Jersey. My cordial Jewish companion was in like a burglar.

Angela saw herself shopping in New Jersey for all those tacky items she loved to buy, expecting big discounts from the Ross family, of course. Marion helped me out around the landing and I'd craft a few original leather items sometimes for her at Mexicana. Unlike the New York intellectuals she usually hung out with, I was a very wild and attractive individual whom she adored. She even loved to watch me smoke cigarettes in a tough, seductive, Bogart way. The various drugs we shared were common to me but novel to her; she could well afford them, however, and always obeyed those naughty cravings.

The only bad acid trip I ever experienced started at the house on Bradford Street one peaceful, lovely, Cape Cod summer's night. Shortly after dropping a powerful tab of acid, all things became purple and beautiful. I stepped out into the yard, where a strange black jeep was parked and climbed into this open car to sit quietly and absorb the awesome panoramic ocean view, while breathing in the balmy, jasmine-filled air. Suddenly, my body became petrified; I noticed a deranged, crazy, Lhasa apso sitting right next to me on the passenger side. Every tooth was exposed, and he growled ferociously while charging at my face with very long, sharp toenails. His eyes became red and glowing, like when they show the devil's glare through special effects in movies. That hairy little beast dogged me around town all night, chewing and tugging on my Levi's; I was too high to elude him. I hoped to get rid of him or make friends so we struggled all the way to the bowling alley for a juicy hot dog; when we got there, he simply vanished.

We were both productive Virgos, who worked as hard as we played, but our happy summer season was quickly coming to an end. I finished closing down the landing, while Marion helped them to pack up Mexicana.

Meanwhile, Debra and Susan wanted to make a pilgrimage through the United States and Mexico, if only they could use Marion's banged-up Volkswagen bus and bring along their old dog Sam. After reading a Jack Kerouac book, these wannabe freedom-loving hippies dreamed of such a journey, so they agreed to sublet their apartment to us and began charting a courageous road trip, which would continue until mid-spring. We happily traded Marion's van, for their sixth-floor walk up on West 13th Street, located between 6th and 7th. Fortunately, their chilly flat was within walking distance of The New School, just around the corner from Cookies gay bar on 14th and close to Washington Square, where I spent many enjoyable hours with my cat Heather, who casually stayed perched on my shoulders. That particular block of West 13th Street had several chic restaurants and even a few dependable drug dealers.

*****

On the first night in our Greenwich Village sublet, we had to turn five dead bolts and arrange the fox lock before cracking open a good bottle of champagne, to celebrate our crude new digs. We woke up early the next day with headaches and anxious for a hot cup of coffee, but the bright morning background manifested a whole different image from what we pictured the night before. Discovering objects covered with roaches is simply a fact of life in New York City, but a frustration I couldn't get used to. The empty wine bottle on the living room floor looked like an animated chocolate decanter, and the sticky glasses were likewise surrounded with millions of busy little creatures. Maybe it was the weather or atmosphere, but I never once saw a cockroach on Cape Cod. "Now, I'm really in a New York state of mind." (Panic!)

We cleaned up most of the bugs in that apartment, but before we moved in the ladies coped with filth from their dog Sam, who had no control over his bowels and serious hip problems. That nasty smell and old leather aromas never really disappeared. Regardless, this place was worth some adjustments because the rent was only ninety-two dollars a month; we needed to stay through winter and part of next spring. Marion promptly trotted over to The New School to arrange her schedule and sign up for several classes.

She chose evening classes at school to be available for daytime employment. After verifying her courses and things settled down at the apartment, we agreed to look for jobs which might pay some real money. Her thesis focused on psychology; therefore, I'll never understand how we both ended up taking a very long, difficult examination to become ordinary letter carriers for the United States Post Office. She was fairly well-off and highly intelligent, so what made Marion decide to go for this type of mundane job?

On a chilly, late-September afternoon, we had to keep an appointment for the postal test at some old school or office building way downtown. We sat in an ugly cold classroom with thirty other applicants for the numbers challenge. A large, chunky, serious, black woman was the examiner and handed out number two pencils along with a thick questionnaire booklet. After several good hits of smoke from a bong before we left home, I was in no condition to deal with this strict lady, or any type of math calculations, which were always difficult for me anyway. The test involved zip code listings and I was absolutely lost. After a meditative minute or two, I put the pencil down, winked at Marion and excused myself. My clever companion aced the quiz and genuinely became a mail delivery person for the U.S.P.O. The downside to that job was carrying at least forty pounds of letters at one time. Oh Poor Marion.

Everything for Everybody was a tiny storefront on 8th Street and caught my attention, so I went in to browse. A two-dollar fee let you search through their files all day; a full membership was good for a whole year. 'Help Wanted' was my only interest since we had a place to live. All their files were alphabetically sorted by categories and I got lucky. A very hip, thirty-something couple needed an energetic person to pack special effect screens for television sets. The work environment at their vogue apartment seemed casual; pot smoking was openly permitted and it was only a block away from our own place.

Marion put on the ugly postman's uniform for the job and I began packing those psychedelic TV screens, which gave a black and white television set bizarre, warped, colorful effects. People in New York frequently started up homegrown businesses and failed, yet these cheaply made optical devices did well at the time. I was permitted to smoke pot at work because they smoked too, and the female boss made regular passes at me. Both employers invited me to participate in a threesome with them. Doris was certainly worth a tumble, but I absolutely rejected her wimpy husband John's role. This sexy, delightful Piscean woman liked me a lot and suggested one night that I go with her way up town to see a friend's extraordinary apartment on Park Avenue, so I said all right and we left after work. She had a key to the place and fortunately no one else was there; I tend to get very nervous and cautious around new flames.

It was overwhelming as I looked around this sophisticated but erotic residence, openly flaunting sadomasochistic apparatus, which I chose not to get acquainted with. Whips, chains, leather outfits, cuffs, mirrors and every perverted toy commonly used for kinky liaisons were all out in plain view. New Yorkers have a lot going on behind their Fox-locked doors. Doris supplied all the drugs and just before having sex, we turned ourselves on with a little cocaine, plus a pipe full of hash. I made wild, passionate love to my appreciative female supervisor without ever using any of those eccentric toys and excited her much more than she anticipated. My dull job would soon come to an end now because I couldn't stand to see either one of them after the Park Avenue odyssey. I never told Marion about my affair, just in case I had another escapade while she was still attending night school for her valuable, higher-minded dissertation.

During the previous summer at the Cape, we were weekend warriors, chipping away at heroin, a very bad habit which I couldn't stop reverting to. Marion also loved feeling mindless and totally anesthetized.

Gradually we began the same pathetic, part-time routine. Dealers were everywhere in New York, and once in a while we'd share a ten-dollar bag just to get comfortably numb. Marion was one of the most blasé people on the planet; I constantly stayed high on heroin, it was a gratifying alternative inasmuch as I felt devoid of sexual excitement and fun. White-hot sex is rarely ever achieved between two Virgo lovers.

The only way to beat the dealers' price was to become my own distributor, so I saved enough money to accumulate a hefty cache of smack. Washington Square was my primary location for dealing to the desperate narcotic consumers who anticipated my valuable goods; I was always on time and dependable. Success came easily because I was a fair and honest merchant with a cheerful attitude and a beautiful cat named Heather, usually draped across my shoulders. By December, three young fellows were trafficking for me, and we all made enough money to support our own diabolical habits, when the drugs ran out, we divided up our daily profits. My assistants encountered a few maverick clients, but the most treacherous part of that dirty business was getting ripped off. Regular customers would rarely ever think about menacing their own dealer, but one corrupt cop could shanghai your dope and money instantly, it happened a lot.

Marion and I had become quite distanced by now; she had no concept of the enormous amounts of narcotics I was using and really didn't want to know. Her wealthy father would have died instantly from a heart attack if he ever learned that his only daughter was involved with drugs, and would certainly never appreciate knowing she was having a gay relationship with a precarious lesbian character like me.

Late in April, my most productive and ambitious helper got arrested for possession of heroin, a clear warning that the law might be catching up to me soon. If I were to be compromised, my big city opiate bondage must stop right away; I also needed to get back into good shape for my wonderful summer job at the Cape.

Marion was planning her own sanitized agenda as well; she hoped to become a professor in the near future and began to abstain from all substance abuse. Through a former customer, I was able to score enough methadone to painlessly withdraw from my full heroin addiction in a comfortable, gradual manner.

Meanwhile, my suspicious, evil-minded mother came to visit us unexpectedly but didn't stay long when she sensed what was going on. The six flights of stairs to our hippie-styled pad nearly killed her and there was nothing in New York to hold her interest. Each time we suggested something to do or somewhere to go, she declined. I was glad when it was time to take a taxi up to the Port Authority to buy her a ticket for a fast ride home. Mom always seemed to be around when there was a crisis in my life, but I couldn't really converse with her. She felt angry and negative about my sexual preferences, hence, Catholic guilt.

That frigid winter passed slowly and all I could think about was my buoyant life in Provincetown. Our relationship barely stayed cordial until May when Debra and Susan came back; I honestly couldn't wait to get out of there. We had officially broken up but stayed friends for a long time. It was shocking to see poor Marion's van when they finally returned it. The vehicle reeked terribly from their sick dog's messy bowel movements, I doubt if any type of deodorizing process could have restored it decently.

My well-trained cat would stay there to be taken care of and loved by the girls on West 13th, but if I ever could get Heather back to the landing, they said it would be fine. Once more, I was taking a Greyhound home for the dawning of a fresh summer in P. Town, which promised new hope, bold adventures and plenty of beautiful people. During the long bus ride, I reflected on my recent life in the Village and concluded that it was too easy for me get into mischief when I wasn't living at the Cape.

*****

I returned to Angels' Landing feeling fresh, ready for a new season and there was a great deal to do, preceding the anticipated guests. Each unit was aired out, hot water tanks were tested, heaters had to be checked thoroughly and most quarters needed some minor paint touch-ups. I was indeed a frustrated decorator at heart, reaping great personal satisfaction as each apartment took on its own distinctive personality. I dressed up one suite, called Gabriel, with all different shades of purple; in addition, there was a fabulous, handcrafted hobbyhorse in that unit, designed by Angela's friend Gabby, a famous artist from New York. Placing costly pieces of art, in focal sites to enhance their auras was my real talent.

After much preparation, we were ready to indulge a few unscheduled tourists who might wander down the path for cheaper, off-season rentals and the boss was eager to earn some extra money. This would be a good time to find out if things were working properly before any regular tenants showed up. Sometimes we had to change a mattress or fix a leak at the last minute and up to Memorial Day we were making needed repairs so everything in these tiny, celestial units looked respectable.

Our busiest day was Saturday, people were checking in and out, then came the clean-up chores. I felt awkward about accepting tips, but Angela said I earned them, making sure her lodgers were quite generous. Thank God for speed.

When the big push to get the landing open was finally over, I was free to carouse around town, which is what I liked best about summertime. Nancy, was our very first pre-season guest and came to P. Town for a mini vacation, she'd just broken up with her boyfriend and needed a quiet haven away from Boston. She stayed at the landing for about a week and decided to extend her visit, but she couldn't afford Angela's rates. I directed her to a cheap rooming house nearby so she could stay longer and ponder her future. We became lovers right away; it was easy, this girl was the essence of American pie, beautiful and smart.

Nancy looked very much like Katy Couric, star of the Today show on NBC. She was an attractive, foxy wasp, with blond hair, blue eyes, milky-colored skin, medium height, twenty-eight years old and flaunted a carefree, Leo desire for passion. Right up to my collective boredom attack, we were a delightful couple. Angela adored her; everyone did, but somehow, she was persuaded to go back to her abusive boyfriend in Boston. We met up again a few months later in Cambridge, which was a very peculiar experience.

I yearned for a playmate once more and thought about hooking up with Freda, who liked me a lot and was easy to be around, I took a chance and phoned her family's home in Worcester. She was bored too and didn't hesitate to join me at the Cape right away. I rented a room for her at a place called The Captain's House; she then set sail for another waitress job. Freda would just shadow me all around, which I didn't mind so much, but she never stopped staring. Later on in time and space, I came to believe my overly affectionate feline, Habib, was a true incarnation of Freda. That little cat constantly followed me for blocks, meowing loudly all the way. Now, I can appreciate the children's song *Mary had a little lamb*.

Both Freda and I worked hard, shared plenty of drugs and made love regularly. My enormous sexual energy was an enigma to some people, but I didn't get any complaints from ex-lovers.

The summer season flew by really fast and so did our limited money. Acid was indeed a thrilling drug; the most draining phase of anyone's trip, however, was the struggle to come down. Numerous people in P. Town began using small amounts of heroin because they couldn't handle the aftermath of LSD. Without exception, dope helped to appease discomfort but could turn into a daily habit, kindling an inescapable addiction. I was lucky the boss never knew that her tiny, cluttered kitchen was being used for providing drugs to a handful of my intimate friends. I felt ashamed and anxious whenever I did shoot up in her cottage.

I got wasted a lot, but I was rather a controlled doper and didn't show it as much as Freda, who was really obvious after getting off on heroin. She would nod constantly, scratch her face a great deal and usually quarrel with customers at work. It didn't take long before she became a very unpopular waitress. This meant smaller tips and less money for drugs, she was eventually dismissed by her ethical employer.

When it was time for me to close up the landing in late September, Freda left ahead of me for Boston to find us an apartment, and I would join her later. She decided that we should live in Cambridge and quickly found a modest place right next door to a huge Catholic church. While packing up those two old suitcases, I felt depressed about leaving the mystic, beautiful and gracious Cape Cod, yet I looked forward to new interests within the elite Harvard Square area.

*****

Head shops loomed on every corner, seductive drugs were cosmic and you could get openly stoned at some old movie theaters while watching groovy films. Many folks spaced out at these funky cinemas; it was the hip thing to do. Coffee houses were great sources for intellectual conversations, or you could just browse through unique economy shops for odds and ends. Hippies put thrift shops on the map; those worthy stores dressed us and basically decorated our homes.

Freda accepted a job at an exclusive lady's shoe store near Copley Square in Boston. She was cosmopolitan, accomplished in the arts and had exquisite taste in women's apparel. I conveniently found work at a nearby chocolate factory in Cambridge as I wasn't very educated. After a while, the powerful smell of chocolate boiling and swirling in gigantic vats all day made me quite nauseous.

We lived on York Street and did our best to beautify that hollow-sounding, unfurnished apartment. I bought a neat couch at the Salvation Army and a brand-new mattress, which went on the floor. The rest of our pad was sparsely furnished with orange crates and a small wooden kitchen table we found at a yard sale.

Freda dropped an unexpected bombshell on me when she alluded to befriending my ex-lover Nancy. They met in town accidentally at Freda's expensive Italian shoe boutique and soon discovered Nancy knew me earlier from the Cape. She wanted to see me again and insisted on visiting us. Her egotistical boyfriend, Richard, drove her to our humble abode on a Sunday afternoon. This cruel-looking Libra fellow turned out to be a notorious drug peddler, conducting business throughout the entire Boston area. Richard immediately placed a generous pile of pure heroin on the kitchen counter. Freda and I didn't want to appear desperate or anxious but took out some clean works in a hurry. Blood spilled on our little wooden table, but none of it was Nancy's, she was too smart and beautiful to ever use a needle. We enjoyed their fruitful visit, and I felt cavalier when she quietly indicated that our brief romantic tryst was all good.

We really hit it off that day, and on their way out Richard left his private phone number in case I decided to embark on dealing narcotics for personal profits. Several motivations or incentives to start a new venture came to mind at once; I could leave that awful-smelling chocolate factory and liberate Freda from the agony of hawking those gaudy, five-hundred-dollar pairs of spaghetti-strap shoes for small commissions.

Weed was generally our daily drug of choice, whether we used heroin or not, since we weren't altogether hooked yet. I called Richard to set up a meeting about dealing, and he made an offer I couldn't refuse. His initial proposition urged me to take advantage of a great closeout sale on some mediocre Mexican grass. Each kilo would cost exactly fifteen dollars, but the kicker was that I had to buy a large quantity, one hundred kilos to start with. We never could save money; therefore, Freda made an express trip to Worcester, pretending it was just for a nice little family visit. The next day, she reappeared with plenty of cash, likely taken from their downtown restaurant safe, and more than we needed to clear Richard's introductory offer. Now all I had to do was sell off some marijuana and use that cash for my next heroin buy.

I continued working at the icky chocolate factory for a bit longer and made friends with a young man named Danny Farmer.

He seemed like a good kid, he was very polite and had plenty of nerve. After I turned him on with a healthy stash of my personal weed, he facetiously suggested we should have at least one car between us, but it seemed hopeless to ever buy a car, pay for insurance and get it registered without any money.

Danny knocked on our door late one night, quite excited and asked me and Freda to go outside with him to behold our new car. There it was, my first Volkswagen bug, just stolen within the past hour. Our adorable little hijacked coupe was a soft mint green color, in superior condition but had no keys. We hot-wired it for a few days, and paid someone at a regular gas station to install a brand-new ignition. The ideal enterprise had simply and magically manifested, I felt blessed to have my own transportation again.

All around the Harvard University vicinity, there were at least ten Volkswagens for every regular car and the vulnerable, nerdy types were at great risk inasmuch as they rarely locked their autos. Danny had no qualms about stealing and even got a few of his good friends to help. Whenever we met, I warily instructed this motley crew to heist only the clean and flawless ones. Each time his pals brought me a classic bug, they were paid off at once with a whole kilo of grass, ergo, and the grateful stoners routed numerous VWs to my designated locations. In less than a month, I had one guy changing ignitions for new keys and another man quickly shuffled number plates around; some from out of state but the majority were local. The next undertaking was to place a current inspection sticker on the windshields. I did the fine art work myself very carefully with pen and ink; that year the emblems were crimson on little pieces of red paper, I counterfeited, 'The State of Massachusetts; blah blah'. In fine print it read, "F... you."

Danny was a pint-sized twenty-one-year-old with a bad case of acne and dressed like his friends; plaid shirts, tacky jeans, old sneakers, they were all sloppy, but I knew our association in the illicit auto business wouldn't be permanent. I preferred to be around neat people and couldn't respect anyone who looked shabby or dirty. Basically, I dressed in the definitive uniform of the sixties; spic-and-span faded blue work shirts, ageing Levi's, Birkenstocks in the summer and Chukka boots for winter. My hair was coifed in a blunt Beatles cut; the natural color was blue-black, but I usually dyed it windswept blond for summers on the Cape.

Freda was a thrift shop fashion plate. She wore those big old black ladies' shoes with the fat heels because they felt good on her feet and kept her posture more uplifted. Adorned in brightly colored Hoover dresses, she usually draped a finely woven shawl over her shoulders as a chic accessory.

Freda quit her stressful job at the shoe store and went to work part-time for our priest/landlord next door cleaning the rectory. He asked her for temporary assistance because the regular domestic person was ill and wouldn't be coming back.

Old Father Flynn was a tough Irish guy who didn't mince words. Without any warning, he came over to visit us for the first time ever and the distinct smell of pot throughout the house was pretty overwhelming. He never actually said that we had to leave, but I got incredibly anxious when he bellowed, "Clean up your filthy house, it's on God's property." (My Catholic guilt kicked in.) Without delay, we moved to Revere Street on Beacon Hill in Boston, fairly close to the awesome Charles River.

Beacon Hill was the hippest place to be and we had arrived. We left our worthless furniture behind on York Street, to the great disapproval of Father Flynn. A friend referred us to a sweet attic apartment on Revere Street because he thought I could sell more drugs in that area. This delightful studio unit was in a very elegant old building and nicely furnished; nevertheless, it was a long, winding, four-flight walk up.

Freda got a waitress job right away at the Holiday Inn on Cambridge Street, just around the corner from our attic loft. This exclusive hotel indulged many affluent patrons and having had previous experience, she soon became head hostess in the main dining room. Whenever well-known celebrities or big name stars from the music industry performed live in Boston, they usually stayed at this distinguished inn.

Welcoming customers and seating them properly in the deluxe dining room was her basic function. She began to notice that some people chose not to look at menus or eat any food; perhaps they were drug users. Word quickly got around the hotel from co-workers that Freda could readily obtain grass, coke, or heroin and would even deliver it to the artists. She wasn't shy about making money or stealing it from her parents.

I can honestly tell you, several of the lackeys who acquired drugs from us carried them directly to Liza M's penthouse, or to The Rolling Stone's suite. Taj Mahal, Tracy Nelson, Ritchie Havens and Janet Joplin's group, Big Brother and The Holding Company, also shopped with us. I actually met a few notable celebrities face to face while cautiously circulating my illegal substances by way of Freda. The visible cash was amazing; now we could really afford those wholesale narcotics. Richard and Nancy had simply vanished, so I put the word out on the street that we wanted to buy large quantities at once.

I explored the entire Holiday Inn for secret places to exchange drugs and money with Freda, also to learn about escape routes in case we needed to leave the building abruptly. Soon, I came upon the spacious but nearly empty parking structure in the basement. My next challenge would be to make friends with Oscar, the Puerto Rican garage manager. After I turned him on with some great smoke, we drank a little rum, while I began to discuss the possibility of leaving my hot VWs for a brief time in his relatively empty garage. Until Oscar and I reached an amicable agreement, the recently abducted cars were parked on dark, narrow streets, all over Beacon Hill, now I could store ten or fifteen autos at a time down below. He did very well by us financially and could never challenge the potentially risky consequences because he had five kids to support, along with two wives. Coke was his drug of choice, so we were always generous with him, and Danny's refer boys kept busy obtaining more coupes from the well-off Harvard community.

After much bribery through the streets and alleys of Boston, I finally connected with a man known only as Maurice who sold heroin in very large quantities. This young black gentleman was a handsome, dapper Leo, serious about taking care of business and we got along just fine. It took a while for him to learn to trust me; nevertheless, I encouraged Maurice to expand his drug trade. He could lease my cars daily, and dispatch experienced crews to small towns, circulating more narcotics to boost his profits considerably.

Guests usually arrived at this Holiday Inn by means of taxis or limos; there were seldom any visitors in the subterranean lot. After we made a fair deal concerning the garage, I then coordinated the pickup times to coincide with Oscar's work schedule. Maurice's dealers showed up early in the morning to claim their cars on specific days (just like Avis), who then sped off to dispense their goods around Amherst, Lowell, Lynn and even Worcester. Occasionally, the drivers returned the vehicles in messy condition; therefore, they had to reimburse me with dope or cash. The zippy little beetles paid off, through that timeless winter.

Freda and I were the only freelance female dealers on the hill at the time, which was rather dangerous. We had a lot of moxie but constantly needed to be aware of rip-off artists; slowly, paranoia began to set in; it was hard to get comfortably high, take care of business and keep your eyes in the back of your head.

We had to stay sharp, wear a confident look and act calmly at all times; the presence of danger constantly lurked all around those ageing hilly, cobblestone streets. In the narcotics business, it's only natural to want everyone nearby to pay for your quality cache, but you must determine first who the real customers are. "Can these shady people actually pay for a bag, or is this the petty rip off we've always dreaded? Is he, or she, an undercover cop? Could this be the day that we ultimately get killed for our stash?"

You may judge or criticize my habitual opiate use or colorful lifestyle; nonetheless, I have always tried to live as an honorable person. I did the best I could with what I had and dealing dope was the most lucrative resource for me to work with because it was really hard in those days to function as an obvious, butch lesbian unless you were an affable gay with enough money to dress properly and live in suburbia.

We were doing well by December, so I decided to start my own Christmas tradition; passing out free bags of smack to all the hookers I knew. That particular holiday was usually a very slow day for the working girls on the street, the majority of their tricks were husbands obligated to stay at home for family celebrations.

Most heroin users are instilled with deep inferiority complexes and subconsciously work their way down to low self-esteem. I stayed loaded much of the time, choosing not to acknowledge how imperfect my life actually was, but the prostitutes really liked me and thought that I was a genuinely happy person all the time. My diverse lady friends just assumed this because I never dumped any of my problems on them; they had too many burdens of their own. Picture me driving a freshly stolen VW through the snow-covered streets of Boston on a cold Christmas morning handing out bags of goodies to some very grateful women who might have otherwise been dope-sick that day; no one should feel bad on Christmas.

The length of a drug dealer's career depends on how carefully they operate; one could get busted or killed in a New York minute. People are literally being watched all the time unless they are safely tucked away at home, behind locked doors and closed curtains. For example, if an individual walking down the street thinks that no one else can see, they might make an awful face or scratch their body parts enthusiastically. Meanwhile, a stranger could be observing from a remote window, or a rooftop just around the corner, believe me, someone is always watching; now, hidden cameras are everywhere, even on public streets.

A person's daily habits make them fairly predictable; if I see the same figure at the same time every day, doing the very same thing that is a routine. For months Freda lived by a certain timetable and by now someone was covertly stalking her. She always walked fast when commuting to the inn and never noticed anyone behind her, yet the skulking presence of obscure agents was all around. Those smart, Ivy League, FBI suits blended very well in Boston (the hub of universities) due to its large collegiate society.

The cash that passed through our hands was amazing, we only saw Maurice every so often when he planned to pick up extra large sums of money. He never did drugs or booze, kept a low profile and was driven around regularly in a big black Cadillac by a sinister bodyguard. A huge, flamboyant Caddie happened to be the only obnoxious thing about him. No one in the area had any idea about where he lived, or the nerve to ask; we were simply given telephone numbers to call. This almighty drug tyrant appeared and disappeared like Osamu Bin Laden, making it a challenge for lawmen to locate or catch up with him. We heard rumors about two murders they say he committed; a disturbing fact later verified by a fellow doper, fortunately, we never witnessed any of these bold crimes. Two bunglers perished because they tried to cheat him, the younger guy was actually an informer; the highest priority on any scorned dealer's hit list.

During our first business meeting with Maurice, he explained the company rules in a very cryptic way, we understood completely. I braved Beacon Hill daily, selling only to users who could afford these drugs and made a fairly good living. However, my profits were considerably smaller than Freda's gross from the Inn; she moved the really big money. Cell phones were nonexistent then, so we planned all deliveries and cash exchanges by way of certain payphones. We were lucky to have survived that dangerous game for almost a year but had in fact, changed physically and almost turned into lowlife, strung-out junkies ourselves.

Out of the last six years, this was the first summer that I wouldn't be going back to work at the landing; I can scarcely remember anything about that demoralizing heroin stage, except for attending a few loud summer band concerts on the Promenade.

The greatest place in Boston for contemporary rock groups to perform was called The Boston Tea Party and I went there quite a bit to see some very famous bands while dispensing a few forbidden treasures. Before I realized that almost a whole year had vanished, Angela got a replacement for me at the Cape; actually she hired several workers, I was irreplaceable.

By spring, we were getting sloppy at home, likewise with dealing. One bright sunny day, I took a long hard look at my eighty-pound, track-filled body and suddenly felt unnerved. Methadone options were scarce then, so maybe it was time for me to check into a de-tox hospital. I began to inquire right away because my intuition was screaming, "It's time to get out of here and this business." Sure enough, one clear March afternoon, the FBI picked Freda up on her way to work. She had been under surveillance for months; they also had a warrant with my name on it. A woman who knew Freda promptly called me from the street to let me know. Within minutes, I fixed, got dressed, packed a few things in those two old suitcases, to slither into a waiting taxi. Just as my cab was pulling away, the cops arrived to pick me up.

The federal agents simply asked Freda to locate and help prosecute Maurice. She could have gotten out of the whole predicament but was too frightened and absolutely refused to give up any information about him. When the trial began, I didn't think she'd be strong enough to withstand any part of that nightmare, consequently, she got a seven-year sentence at the Club Fed in Lexington Kentucky, where she grew very fond of black women. I was legally untouchable, sheltered at a local hospital withdrawing from heroin.

Freda's wealthy family was truly brokenhearted about her misfortune and admonished us to not see each other again. It was easy to obey their orders because I didn't plan to visit her in Lexington any time soon. We really didn't see each other for many years after her dubious incarceration. Meanwhile, before the trial started, I had already checked into an old veterans' hospital in Dorchester Massachusetts. Sections of this huge place were used for tuberculosis patients, other wards were for studying the addictions of acute drug abusers. Lucky me, I entered a rehab program which only required a two-month stay, and at the end of that period I would literally collect one thousand, tax-free dollars for participating in experimental tests. The law couldn't touch me now, but I always wondered what I might have done in Freda's place.

*****

When I made that quick departure from Revere Street, I had some money and a modest stash of dope, which had to go before I arrived at the sinister institution. My favorite customer, a hooker called Sandy became the recipient of my limited valuables and was one of the few visitors I ever received out there. Other than a small dumb nursing staff, this enormous hospital had very little supervision. It was apparent how many different drugs were brought into and freely used on my ward; even the mop-swinging janitor was a dealer. Many addicts attending this clean-up therapy were just as hooked inside as they were on the street. If you did get loaded, you could take a nature walk around the charming grounds, or just quietly go to bed.

They expected us to be in bed a lot at the hospital because we were supposed to be convalescing and reflecting on how much pain our addictions had brought about. The one thing I didn't foresee concerning the healing process, was gaining weight. If I became bored or frustrated, I'd munch on comfort food, even the starchy institutional kind like mashed potatoes or bread, seemed tempting. Judy, my roommate at the asylum, was moderately into drugs but her primary health issue was alcohol. On the few occasions when I did receive a visitor, she begged them to bring back a cheap bottle of Jean Nate cologne on their next trip. It turns out she was drinking the stuff and had been busted for doing it before. After the callers left, two nurses always looked inside Judy's mouth and throat to see if there was any inflammation. When the sparse staff thought everyone was fast asleep, I'd sneak down to the big empty bathroom to fix in private.

The research program was all about electric shock treatments, and a psychologist named John O'Brien became my new best friend. I went upstairs to his office three times a week, sat in a comfortable leather chair; he would then place wires around my body in different spots to record electronic responses, whenever I got excited from hearing certain key words. First, he needed to learn street language where he could tap into my inner thoughts. Until this assignment, John had no prior knowledge of anyone who had ever used drugs. He was a smart Gemini, cashing in on his recent diploma and being further educated by our generous government.

During the initial sessions, I fed him many scenarios about the actual life of a junkie and he recorded every word. "I need to get off. Where are my works?" These rhetorical doper expressions triggered some painful jolts. For instance, if John got the idea that something seemed to excite me, he would zap me with small amounts of electricity until those familiar words were no longer arousing. "I am going to cop some drugs." Zap, Zap, Zap. Following the debilitating shock treatments, they practically had to carry me back to my room.

After each draining treatment, it was hard to move around, but I could usually catch up with Juan the janitor to score a couple of bags. The impact of those shocks to my body caused adverse side effects and I wasn't exactly cured of my ongoing heroin desire. John kept increasing the jolts of electricity as he filmed our sessions; the video later became an educational documentary. I wondered if the physicians who watched my face grimacing with pain and anxiety ever anticipated using this brand of therapy on their own patients.

Volunteers lured into this rehab program gravitated there for different reasons. Several youngsters who were being sought by the law and other users decided to honestly clean up their intolerable dope habits. This prototype of experimental therapy seemed like a fluke, nevertheless, I'd still be paid a thousand dollars.

Late in the spring, I appreciated that I wasn't as psychologically, or physically addicted as I was prior to this weird psychotherapy game. It took every ounce of courage within me to call Angela; I definitely wanted to get my summer job back, but first my lofty aspiration had to be deliberated by John O'Brien and the entire hospital staff. They wouldn't allow me to leave without a chaperon and a place to stay; John talked to the Captain at great lengths about taking me home to the landing. Angela listened to the whole story concerning Freda and me, she also learned of our heroin business and seemed a tad reluctant to commit, who could blame her? As the season neared, she agreed to let me return, assuring John I would see a good shrink regularly.

We drove to Provincetown in silence, settled into the cottage, and soon discussed, the forthcoming work. I focused on the urgent jobs until the landing was totally prepared for our guests. Without delay, I began to enjoy periodic visits to a sandy beach with a lady psychiatrist, sipping chilled cocktails as she analyzed me. This lovely, feminine and benevolent doctor was a good friend of Angela's; she didn't charge me a penny for the intimate service. My boss was simply told I had problems because I was overly sensitive and too aware.

For the first time ever, I opened a passbook savings account at the Seaman's Savings Bank with my one thousand-dollar government check, the compensation for those daunting shock treatments. Angela was on her best behavior at this time but watched me very closely. She walked all around Provincetown just to find a couple of part-time helpers for our busy Saturday schedules; I appreciated the extra hands because the landing had grown enough to triple my work. The boss did everything possible to assist my recovery process, but the truth is, I wasn't at all tempted to use heroin throughout that crucial summer and graciously thanked John O'Brien for his help and support in alleviating my former addiction; I loved being free from that dreadful habit. Throughout this very chaste period, I enjoyed peaceful inner contentment, then I began to notice a few of my old pals who never used smack doing it routinely now and I felt sorry for them.

Fortunately, I decided to stay clean for that season; since it was an election year, the local police began to crack down hard on hippies, or anyone else using drugs; essentially, they hoped to get rid of all the dopers in town forever. These crude cops started using new devices to bust people; they had small, state of the art vacuum cleaners to check a suspect's pockets for marijuana shake. Inexperienced lawmen were getting educated and smarter by the day, although they were still yokels. For the entire season, I firmly resolved to stay clean and behave more cautiously in public, but I absolutely refused to ever give up smoking pot.

    Weed seemed to be my religious right, if I ever got busted and the issue came up constitutionally, I would challenge the legality, which must exonerate anyone who is part American Indian. While abstaining from acid that summer, the wonder of fabulous sunrises and sunsets in their true colors felt instinctively therapeutic. I used to think that one could only reach God through the sundowns and colorful twilights by tripping on LSD; it was a divine revelation to behold those identical visions just from smoking a little grass.

Carole,
A Lucky Little Rabbit

Part Two

*"Change is good, even healthy.
My Dad said 'familiarity breeds contempt.'
He also believed that one should use the back of the chair more
to relax.
At least he was right about a few things."*

That was the last year I worked for Angela Calomiris as a personal assistant. After staying there for eight tedious summers and two frigid winters, I could no longer tolerate her arrogance, but I held my temper long enough to collect my big bonus when we finally closed the place down for winter. Many good things did ensue during that season, yet I felt quite unhappy through most of the summer. I wasn't doing any heroin, my head was exceptionally clear, and I could really see right through her Leo, imperial, spoiled, selfishness. It seemed like much of the time, all I did was take care of her daily needs; she was the ill bred, self-proclaimed king of Commercial Street.

I've always been an early riser, consequently, I served her breakfast in bed and went off to do my chores; the next scheduled drudge was to fix her a creative lunch. At times I felt like a Chinese bride, walking three steps behind, offering amends to anyone she antagonized. The Captain saved me in the spring with a shrink, yet killed me with hard work all summer for my payback.

My boss was one of the most frugal people on the Cape. Whether shopping for food, linens, or paint, she would only buy the cheapest brands. If her feline, Mackerel, didn't eat all of her canned food, Angela would keep putting the tin can back in the refrigerator, adding water until the cat finished; sometimes it took days. She broke my heart with her penny-pinching ways, especially feeding her pet with that old stuff. It has always gone against my grain to be cheap, which is probably why I'll never have much money. Angela made lots of money, and banked it to play the real game of Monopoly, diversifying her property holdings. As I said earlier, she was popular but not at all well liked by most people. In a strange way, we were like a mother and daughter, having the usual discussions about where and how I spent my wages; she constantly tried to control me.

There is an old Greek expression that says: "When you do your work by the moonlight, the sun comes out to laugh at it." Light equals truth, clarity, expansion and positivity; darkness suggests contraction, distortion, negativity and depression. Heroin represented oblivion or death. I truly love the sun; it makes me feel warm because I dislike feeling cold; the rays seem to rejuvenate me. Throughout any given year; I attempted to catch a little sunshine, inasmuch as everyone looks better with color; my father was dark, so getting an ideal tan was easy for me. My mother hated to be in the sun; she was quite fair skinned and got sunstroke while fishing on the beach in Bridgeport.

The landing occupied most of the early sunrise hours but I seldom missed a spectacular sunset and practiced countless meditations from that friendly beach. "I am free, at peace, alone and in a state of grace, thanks to all of my guardian spirits; I am having a heavenly moment." Things seemed great when every flag was taken down and the garden watered perfectly, then soft ocean breezes blew fragrances from the flowers. I was privileged to have so much and so little to care about. When I think of nothing, I am at peace and harmony with the universe; all is right with the world: Selah.

When my chores were done at the end of the day, there was one delightful soul to actually care about at the landing. Amanda Bedlington Calomiris was Angela's dog, a rat hunting, Bedlington Terrier who always brought me half-dead trophies, but in spite of her awful breath and need for grooming, she was more comforting than her cold-hearted owner. Mandy brought a rat home every single day and slept on my bed when I didn't have company, she even boarded with me once when I lived in Providence Rhode

Island, and I certainly enjoyed her. Currently at twilight, my esoteric moments are less frequent and shorter now because of real responsibilities; nevertheless, I still meditate at sunrise.

Perhaps it was because of the strong police presence in Provincetown that year, but the whole place seemed extra quiet, even the usual celebrities were sparse. I didn't mix with many strangers and as the weeks hurried by; my big dilemma was where to live after this job. Angela suggested I return to New York with her, but that was never going to happen. If she exasperated me in the summer, how could we share a rather confined winter environment? I hadn't met anyone interesting enough to coerce me toward another area, so I thought long and hard about moving back to Worcester. It was 'Niki Land' and there were plenty of my former lovers to hook up with. This largely industrial city, had always embraced a huge gay community, I felt downright comfortable going back to my roots.

Angels' Landing was now officially closed for winter and once again I was on a Greyhound bus with my trusty old suitcases. I saved a lot of money at the Seaman's Savings Bank that summer, starting with those thousand dollars from the drug research project. Now I had to choose between buying a reasonably priced used car, and renting a cozy bachelor apartment. Before I made that big decision, I needed to visit my favorite gay bar on Main Street in Worcester, The New Yorker, just to say hello to old friends, catch up on current gossip and drink like a vagabond for a while.

The first person I noticed sitting there, was my good friend Louise Welch, a Gemini who lived with her crazy mother. In between my wandering, we had a lot of fun together, she was easy to get along with and always ready to follow me through any kind of shenanigans. A couple of years ago, we elected to do something different so we hitchhiked out of town, got a fast ride, in a small truck and landed at a dingy, redneck bar in Oxford, about twenty miles from home. We ordered a glass of wine, only the yokels began absurd dialogues to hit on us, even though we looked gay.

To make them equally apprehensive, Louise whispered that we were actually working in their town to research UFOs, she exposed this dramatic conversation deliberately and made it sound like an episode from *The X Files*; the bumpkins really fell for it. After a little more wine, we forewarned everyone there: "Do not watch us leave or you might see something you will regret and never be able to explain." One chump, an auto mechanic, begged us for a glimpse at our imaginary, scientific car, but he was afraid to follow, so we walked out of the place, softly bidding all a good night, then ran like demons, laughing all the way to the main highway. We hitchhiked back to Worcester; this time we got to ride home in a huge trailer truck. If Louise and I were any place where people really didn't know us, we'd always act out crazy scenes, fabricating and improvising different characters.

Louise stood about five feet eight inches tall, medium weight, short brown curly hair, dressed neatly, and was certainly cute. She always had a mischievous twinkle in her eye and expounded with jovial, happy laughter. I was about five feet, one inch tall; some folks referred to us as Mutt and Jeff. It was indeed a stroke of good luck when I came in from the Cape on that chilly autumn night and hooked up with Louise. We reveled in the New Yorker until two a.m. She encouraged me to stay at her house, while I thought about my next move, which made me feel relieved and elated.

Her place was rather far so we took a cab; I sobered up quickly when Louise's mother met us at the front door. She seemed drunker than we were but genuinely glad to see me. Flossie had been to gay bars with us many times and always expected me to dance with her; she was taller than Louise, asserting that I was the only woman she'd ever consider turning gay for. I appreciated this futile tribute and let her to call me 'Pi Wi', even though I began using my adult name 'Carole' again.

My best friend Walshie originally started calling me 'Pi Wi' when we were kids, and it stuck for many years.

They lived in a nice apartment; Louise turned their only bedroom, into a well-locked, private space. Flossy created a lavish, ultra-feminine boudoir in the enormous living room, hoping to receive callers. The dining room was a communal area for meals, chats, or heavy drinking. I slept well in Louise's secure room that first night, then made my way to the kitchen to fetch some coffee; I took the easy way out and made the instant kind, now all I needed was a couple of aspirins. When they woke up, we all sat around the table with dreadful hangovers trying to hold a cordial conversation.

Louise had a day job in a dirty mill, but her mom worked nights at a restaurant. Flossy donned a paper Tierra with a very short, black and white uniform; they both hated their jobs. Louise was seriously involved with a flaky woman named Betty, who had an abusive husband and a young son. Her marriage situation seemed hopeless, so Louise finally admitted, even though she loved Betty, it was fruitless to continue their dishonest, part-time relationship. Rather than buy a practical car or rent another dump, I suggested that we try going somewhere else for excitement, like Miami perhaps.

It didn't take much of my fast talking malarkey to convince Louise that this would be the perfect time to adjust her life. We both yearned to find a fresh new adventure; Worcester had nothing but factories, gay bars, homely women and freezing cold winters, so why not Florida? After more friction between her and Betty, they decided it was best not to see each other again. Quitting her job was easy; she simply told the boss to send her final paycheck to Flossie's house. We hardly knew anyone then who flew on a plane, so we stuck to the conventional means and we took a bus. Louise's inquiries confirmed that Trailways was cheaper than the 'Greyhound and actually took less time to get there. The distant jaunt seemed exciting at first, but forty-eight uncomfortable hours later, it reeked.

I gladly bought our bus tickets and still had plenty of money left over to pay for a place to stay once we got there. Louise's mother gave her a few hundred dollars, which made her feel a little more secure about leaving her familiar surroundings in Worcester. There were many short rest stops on the way to Miami, our stomachs stayed full, but we did get constipated from eating too many cheese sandwiches. My only regret was not taking some booze along to keep us numb for the lengthy ride. Maybe then we wouldn't have noticed the terrible smell from the toilet at the back of the bus.

The further south we traveled, the hotter it got, so piece by piece we changed out our heavy fall clothing into lighter jeans and short-sleeved shirts. Louise wore feminine-looking blouses, even though she was quite butch, I always sported a T-shirt underneath my size fourteen, boys' plaids. My friend was about four years younger but very sharp and smart; we usually had a lot of fun.

When the bus finally stopped at the terminal in a shabby area of Miami, we needed to give our stiff legs a good walk, so we parked our suitcases and gear in two separate lockers at the crowded station.

I approached the first person I saw and politely asked how far it was to the ocean, but they didn't speak English. It dawned on me later that this town is almost all Cuban and neither of us could speak a word Spanish. A good-looking American guy came to the rescue and gave us simple directions to the closest beach, which was my fervent reason for being there; I really love the sun. The bus got in before noon and it was already ninety degrees, yet we felt terrific being in this new and exciting place. My face was exposed to sun all afternoon; I had no idea how strong it was. My head and arms were as red as a lobster and there was a ridiculous white line, from my neck down. We walked until the sunset on the countless boats; next, we needed to find a room for the night close to the water.

When it began to get dark, we walked east on Biscayne Boulevard, then spotted a neon cocktail sign nearly a block away. The place was called 'Hotel Senate', a three-story building, with a small bar at the front entrance on Fourth Street. We needed to rent a temporary room, they had a few vacancies and the rates were cheap, now we only had to get our belongings from the bus terminal. Cabs were easy to hail, so after retrieving the luggage, we checked into the Senate. The desk clerk gave us a large room with twin beds, overlooking the street. After securing our things, we went back downstairs to the bar; the owner came over, bought us a drink and seductively said: "I am Omara Sanchez."

Omara, a petite, thirty-eight-year-old Cuban woman, wore big blond hair, was rather cute but had the early stages of a washed-out look from heavy drinking. She was particularly friendly and helpful to us; it was our first time there and we didn't know anything about the city.

Now that we had a room, it was time to think about jobs, so we picked up a Miami Herald, which seemed huge but featured many help wanted ads. A male bartender served coffee at the bar downstairs in the morning, which is where we planned our days, located directly across the street was a tiny White Castle hamburger joint.

The owner of the entire Senate building was a nice man called Ernesto, a former general in the Cuban Army, who migrated to

Florida when the majority of affluent people abandoned that country. He was a sweet person, and we shared many interesting conversations while enjoying Cuban sandwiches and coffee. Ernesto taught me one very profound lesson, which really stuck: "Carole, if you ever discover a rat in your house, you must sweep that creature out immediately. Never even think of moving, just get rid of the rat. Fidel Castro was a dangerous beast in Cuba, but if all the people picked up a broom and swept him away, we wouldn't be living in Miami, we'd still be happy on our own beloved soil."

Not knowing one person in Miami reminded me of an alien trip that Freda and I took long before our final episode in Boston involving Maurice and her arrest. While living in Worcester, I did a foolish thing and the cops just wanted to question me. We were steady lovers then, so Freda panicked and suggested we go to Canada, a hasty decision considering how cold it gets in the winter. Before we headed up to beautiful Montreal, she magically scored a lot of cash from her family.

We soon located a local street map and an English newspaper; the very first apartment we looked at sat in a dark basement, but the rent was only thirteen dollars a week so we took it. Our new cave was just around the corner from St. Catherine Street, where there seemed to be a flurry of hippy activity. The first thing we bought was a small black and white television set, and discovered most of the programming was in French. Once again, it was difficult to find employment and prospects were bleak, basically, one had to speak French or exhibit a certified green card. After nearly six weeks I gave up, so we took a bus home. At the border crossing, an inspector opened the bus cargo area, noticed our TV and said we couldn't take it back to Massachusetts without a permit so it got trashed.

I analyzed and dissected the Miami classified ads; there was plenty of hotel work, but I'd be damned if I would wear a dress for any reason, my buddy agreed. It seemed like even factory jobs required employees to understand some Spanish. We went down to the bar at sunup to have our usual coffee and read the daily paper, when suddenly, Louise screamed out something about a revelation that just popped into her Gemini head. "I can become an assistant veterinarian because I really love animals and here is the enticing ad for a person with my many-sided abilities." The job was in

Hallandale, pretty far from here and since we were never lovers, she was certainly free to go her own way.

Louise promptly called that clinic for an interview and made an appointment to see someone the same day. Her only pet experience was limited to feeding Flossie's horny cat Igor, but I had no doubt she would get this job. She memorized the bus route and spruced up nicely, hoping to impress her potential employer. People around the hotel lobby wished her luck and said the long ride up the picturesque coast would be well worth it. It took over an hour to travel one way, but she always carried a book.

After she reached the designated bus stop, there were four more blocks to walk just to reach the place. This pristine area was totally residential, not at all commercial like Fourth Street. The pet hospital was very large, clean and sterile, with a young black woman seated at the reception desk.

"Can I be of any help to you, Miss?"

Louise gulped, blushed, and whispered, "I'm here about the job advertised in the Herald."

Just then, a handsome young man came out of the office. "Hello, I am Dr. Bodine, please fill out this simple application and by the way, when can you start?" How lucky was that?

He hired her at once; perhaps her résumé said all the right things; or it could have been her congenial manner; she had a way with words. Louise was Caucasian, as was the doctor, and the majority of residents in that neighborhood were blonde. These ingredients may have aided or facilitated her newly acquired forte, but I believed she earned this position because she was alert, strong and very tall.

Her tasks included a little of everything; she cleaned cages, washed dogs, assisted in some surgeries and handled paperwork very efficiently. She loved the place and fitted right in; it was the first time I ever saw her look happy about going to work. Losing nearly three hours a day going out there was rough, but it didn't take her long to find out that the gentle veterinarian was gay, which soon proved helpful.

At first, Louise was on a tight schedule because of her new job in Hallandale; meanwhile, I continued to check newspapers and told everyone around that I needed a job. When my roommate finally got home after a long hard day, we'd have some dinner at a nearby restaurant; go back up to our hotel room, then she'd take a hot bath and fall asleep instantly. Through our wide-open second-floor French windows, noisy fiesta sounds and exotic aromas wafted into the room; these rhythmic activities rose up from Fourth Street and if you didn't know better, you might actually think you were in flamboyant Havana. When I couldn't relax or sleep, I'd go downstairs to the dreary, smoky bar, drink a couple of Cuba Libres (Meaning free Cuba) and listen to some overplayed tunes from the antique jukebox.

The late customers seemed like a sad bunch, they wept whenever they heard the Johnny Rivers song *Baby, I need your Loving*. Omara's patrons were politely curious about me; I was gracious, yet rather boyish, wore short hair, madras shirts, sandals, Levi's and sported a light-hearted, perky attitude. The crowds at Omara's were mostly unmarried, folksy, Latin men who incessantly played an emotional song called *Guantanamera*; it seemed to be their very own Cuban national anthem.

There was a full moon one Friday night around midnight, I'd had quite enough to drink, so I decided to go upstairs and sleep. As I was walking through the lobby, I heard some loud shouting; it was Omara and her night bartender. She was very drunk at the time; I didn't have a clue about what was going on, but Omara was screaming hysterically at him to leave. He acted creepy, so it wasn't hard to believe that the guy could be stealing from her, which was the reason she fired him. As soon as he left, she got right behind the bar to serve the shaken customers. I went back inside, sat at a table and began to feel sorry for her life. She laughed courageously, and asked if I knew how to open up a bottle of beer.

The full moon over Miami is notably a great object of beauty, unleashing boundless energy. Omara's fiasco turned into my first bartender job. She really liked me and thought I had a great personality, especially with the quiet customers; even macho guys appreciated my frankness and enjoyed the innocent conversations we shared together. After locking up the bar at two o'clock, she asked me to join her for one last drink across the street at a huge dance bar called The Flamingo, which it stayed open until four. We really didn't need another cocktail, but she had to come down from that ugly scene.

Her saloon opened at six a.m. and closed at two a.m. The morning man, John, started at six, worked until noon. Another person took over around seven p.m., which is when it started to get busy. Omara switched the day guy to nights and gave me the afternoon shift, which was really in my favor; that was a quiet time to experience and practice mixing drinks. I could get a suntan on the roof, have a meal, take a shower and easily be at work by twelve. Louise and I were in Florida for less than a week and already had jobs. I really was a lucky little rabbit because my funds were dwindling.

Omara lived in a large, private suite on the third floor of the hotel, but I never went inside, I got a tiny glimpse of her place, once while carrying packages to her door. Through the crack, I could smell gaudy perfume and the foyer seemed extremely colorful. Rumors circulated around the hotel about her mysterious, bad boy husband in Cuba; perhaps that's why I never saw her act intimate with anyone.

Most of her daytime customers were tourists from different places; some were way off the beaten path. Characters would walk in, order a drink and ask for all kinds of information. "How far is it to South Beach? Are there any good drugs around? Where can I find a hooker?" I was of little help to them.

There was a bar on every corner of Fourth Street; women generally worked the day shifts because it was safer than after dark. at times I'd just glance inside different places to see what other barmaids looked like; some of these gals resembled old hags dressed to kill. I heard that they enticed their male clientele, hustled and even stole from many lonely, dumb hayseeds. I never wanted to be thought of as a contrived servant exploiting people, I was simply a natural friend to my customers.

Prior to leaving Worcester, I bought an ounce of grass, but once we got to Miami, we hardly smoked. Once in a while, I'd take a couple of tokes from a joint, which turned me into a ball of energy to begin work at noon. I stayed on my best behavior all day at the job, when my shift was over, I could cut loose to do anything I wanted. Fortunately, heroin never entered my mind, I was too busy living in this amazing new world, besides, and there was plenty of booze around to keep me buzzed. Drugs were easy to buy anywhere down there; cocaine was considerably cheap and nearly as accessible as Jack Daniel's, however, I didn't care to use it then; coke was a rich man's sport and I wasn't rich.

The Senate Bar was starting to get really busy now, even though I wasn't the usual ladylike, bourgeois barmaid; I still attracted an array of gallant patrons.

One quiet afternoon, four good-looking chaps walked into the place; they appeared to be dressed like sailors but not in the American style. I knew they were English after they ordered four warm beers. They were part of a twenty-four-man crew from a huge yacht docked in Biscayne Bay which belonged to a very wealthy French architect. We became friends instantly as I casually joked with them about drinking hot alcohol. The following afternoon they showed up with a few more sailors, eventually this place became a hangout for the entire traveling crew. Omara was ecstatic; every day she had to order more and more beer and ale.

I can't remember what their yacht was christened, or the French owner's name, that rarely used the vessel but kept a full time staff on board all year round. He would tell the guys how long to stay in each port, then send instructions, as to where to drop the anchor next. Every so often the architect would have elaborate parties on board, but the crew never knew when or where. During this voyage to Miami, he didn't show up at all, ordering them to stay there for thirty days, next stop, Jamaica.

The charming crew had two weeks left on Biscayne Bay, so they came to the bar more frequently. One evening as I was just finishing work when a bunch of my sailor friends showed up with their captain, he rarely ever left the launch. His name was John, very handsome, suntanned and his snowy white, starched to perfection uniform was outstanding. The commander was an educated gentleman who had the time of his life along with me and his staff. He had so much fun that night that he offered me a reward for genuinely making him laugh. That blessing was an unexpected tour of their huge yacht.

Early the next morning, a sailor met me at the bar and hailed a cab to the dock. From there, we took a motorboat out to the glistening ship. I never saw anything more beautiful and polished; the rooms were endless with so many things to see, but I had to cut my wonderful visit short to be at work by noon. I thanked John with all my heart and he said I was welcome to come back again before they left port.

I got a lot of invitations to go out somewhere after work from people I liked and trusted, but usually I preferred a quiet nightly walk around the boats in the bay. One evening, a guy named Pete, who was a regular, asked me to go to the Flagler Dog Track with him. I'd never been, so he drove us out to the crowded track and paid for everything. When we got up close to the dogs, I wanted to cry for them. I could hardly stand the presence of abuse and cruelty, so I begged Pete to get me out of there fast.

It was high time for Louise to get some good news. Dr. Bodine, her gay boss, was truly sympathetic about her daily plight and by chance he happened to have a small, vacant, two-bedroom bungalow. This was his first house after successfully opening the pet clinic but soon moved into a larger place when he got a steady boyfriend. It was a typical Florida home, with a large yard, just two blocks away from her job. The good vet only charged her a small rent and paid for the gardener because he believed she was trustworthy and responsible. If ever my friend had a dream house in mind that was it.

Louise could move into the place right away, he didn't expect the first, last, or a security deposit all at once. I was glad for her, yet sad for me; now I would be living alone at the Senate, but at least she wouldn't have that long bus ride anymore. Lou made a map of how to get there and asked me to please visit her when I got some time off. Right after she moved out of our space, I had a cup of Cuban coffee with Ernesto; he brilliantly suggested that I take a smaller room on the third floor, so I wouldn't hear too much street noise. Besides, it would actually be much cheaper and I could save some money.

We saw little gay activity around Miami other than when we got dirty looks at an unsociable, Latin dyke bar once. Now that she'd nested in the new digs, it was time to check out gay scenes in the area. Next to quiet Hallandale was the City of Hollywood, which had plenty of gay sections to peruse. Louise found her way around quickly and felt comfortable, frequenting a bar called Happy's, where the daytime female bartender sported a fairly thick, natural, and well-groomed mustache. Mostly the regular crowd was young, white and wild. I went there a couple of times with Louise, who seemed unhappy and frustrated with these new-age gay ones.

Now that she had a good job and a house, she thought maybe it was time to find out what her ex-lover Betty was doing; Christmas was approaching.

Ever since my sailor pals shoved off to the islands, the bar was practically lifeless in the afternoon, but once again, my mojo was working because a new group of big tippers started hanging out at the Senate. They were all associated with thoroughbred horse racing, one guy was a well-known jockey, another man was a top trainer, and the two quiet ones simply handled horses. Out of the numerous racetracks around Florida, Hialeah seemed to be their main axis and not very far from there.

As usual, I made friends with them right away and unlike those adorable English boys who loved their beer and ale; these guys only drank heavy-duty booze. They joked about me becoming a jockey because of my size and weight, but I really did love to ride. Our heartiest laughs came when they tried to picture me in the male locker room, or having a physical exam each time before riding. The trainer's name was Dave; he gave me his phone number and said if I ever wanted a job at the track, to just call.

Christmas in Miami was surreal; some trees were spray-painted in pastel colors of pinks and yellows; there were even gold ones. It was time to do my seasonal shopping but the list was very small this year. I wandered over to Flagler Street a couple of blocks away, which was bursting with 'Joyerias' or jewelry shops. Each store blasted Latin music out to the street, every salesperson was a hustler, nevertheless, I adjusted my patience long enough to choose a sweet necklace for Omara, a thin, handsome, gold chain for Ernesto, and I would buy Louise something nice for her new home.

Louise and Betty were deeply in love again by way of endless, romantic telephone chats. Things were horrible between Betty and her husband; she suspected he was molesting their child, which gave her the ultimate reason to leave. She flew directly to Miami with her son on the day before Christmas.

You can only imagine how happy Louise felt waiting to be united with her significant other again. She asked a friend from work for a ride to the Miami International Airport to pick up Betty and her son Eli. After they arrived at the immaculate bungalow, Betty acted openly disappointed with the place, perhaps Lou embellished when she first described their honeymoon cottage, regardless, and Betty was a shrew. I'd only met her once before we left Worcester and easily pegged her as a bitchy little snit. She was about five-six, wore cat's-eye-shaped glasses, the black ones with the silver specs; her clothes were mod, she was rather thin and barely cute, but Louise cherished her every criticism.

Each lovely piece of furniture which came along with the house would be replaced by some very tacky furnishings. Once Eli entered the nearby preschool, she went directly to sign up for welfare payments. Her husband disappeared after the sexual allegations, so she didn't receive child support, but now she could collect a hefty, monthly relief check. Life with Louise seemed easy, providing the house was clean with plenty of food left on the stove. I think Betty was Sag, but I never really asked; she was quite outspoken and said exactly whatever flashed through her simple, narrow mind.

*****

Men always tried to score with Omara; she may have teased them a tiny bit but never got involved unless it was to merely join them for a dinner, which had to be in close proximity of the bar. She said that she could never be bought; yet she took a lot of expensive baubles from many willing givers. During the day, she'd show up for a while to do the ordering etc., have a few drinks, then go back to her suite for a nap and a shower. Omara was usually there when the bartenders changed shifts, hoping to find a benevolent guy who might pay for her evening meal. I believe that she felt some kind of inner sorrow or secret pain, which could be why she drank much more than she should have.

She admonished a hateful drunk once so he turned around and told every person there that we were lesbian lovers and claimed this was the real reason for her brush-off, but I'm sure people knew better. I assumed Omara was an optimistic Leo, with a great deal of pride and never wanted to be thought of as anybody's concubine.

One night I was tense and couldn't fall asleep, so I went downstairs to the bar for a nightcap, also to drown out those echoing conga drum sounds from the block. My boss was totally ripped when I walked in, and noticed a debonair, sober looking man asking her to go out with him after work. It wasn't like he made a physical pass or said anything abusive, but she absolutely went ballistic on him. The guy really bailed out fast, as she yelled, screamed and called him a dirty swine.

Omara's abrupt breakdown might have been caused by PMS; she really needed to relax and get some rest. After closing, she asked if she could go to my room for a while. I always thought of her as sexy and desirable, but this wasn't the right time to experiment with lovemaking. My tiny room was only two doors away from hers, with a small single bed. However, she climbed right on it, took off her clothes and stretched out as I perched on a hard chair pretending to write a letter at my desk.

She coaxed me over to the bed, and we began to kiss in a very sensual way. I quickly pulled back because of my basic shyness. Omara was deeply offended and asked, "Carole, you have always treated me like such a lady, so just for tonight, why can't you imagine me as your private femme fatale. Am I not pleasing or pretty enough?"

We kissed and fondled passionately for a while, but I don't think either of us were comfortable with this fleeting fantasy. I truly understood that she was lonely and love-starved; however, I didn't want a broken heart. Maybe the right man would walk into her life, or perhaps her enigmatic husband could safely reach the shores of Key West from Cuba, what then?

Omara slithered out of my place at sunrise; I didn't know if I could ever face her again. She'd never thought about being with a woman, therefore, she must have felt a certain sense of guilt; I was always openly gay. When I saw her the next day, we tried to act cordial, but underneath the artificial smiles we felt incredibly awkward, whether or not anything sexual did happen. We couldn't look at each other after the quasi-amorous encounter, so now I had to really think about some other type of job, knowing that I might never see those huge tips from my drunken acquaintances at the Senate again.

I made an instant decision to quit my job and move from the hotel as soon as possible. Ms. Sanchez would understand. The apprentice barmaid career wasn't exactly what I had in mind when I first came to Florida anyway. Omara graciously accepted my notice, and it probably wouldn't take her long to find another employee, but I doubt if anyone else could assert my personality, or attract so many new and cheerful customers. It was fun for a while; the money was terrific and my diet was perfectly healthy. Every day, I had a few Woof Cookies (cheeseburgers) from the White Castle and in between, lots of Cuban sandwiches. Generally, I ate dinner around the corner at an oriental restaurant; there was a large population of Chinese people living in Cuba at one time who also migrated to Miami.

Before Louise moved out of the Senate to the suburbs of Hallandale, she told me if ever I needed a place, I would always be welcome to stay at her house, but this was long before Betty and her son moved in. I wasn't sure if her warm offer was still open, so I just called. She told me to come right out there. Lou always liked me and would really feel good having her most congenial buddy around again. Betty, on the other hand, might not be so inclined. Eli would have to sleep in their room if I moved in, anyway, it was a done deal; my last day at the bar, would be my first day in the boondocks.

A nice guy named Jose, who lived in the hotel, offered to drive me way out to Louise's house with all my stuff at no charge because he liked me. I said goodbye to Omara just as I was leaving, which was the last time we ever saw each other. I felt sad and welled up when she explained, "It is best for you to go now, I am starting to like you too much and I'm not worthy of your faithful devotion."

Ever since my breakup with Niki, I became a classic untouchable, which didn't mean that I couldn't have an orgasm with the right woman, it simply meant I would never permit anyone touch me in the carnal way. If someone really turned me on, the charged feelings in my body fused directly into the core their sensations; hence, we climaxed simultaneously. I could levitate my erogenous zones, even wearing clothing, yet I expected my lovers to be naked and cherish the ultimate physical ecstasy. One of my regrets was not achieving this magic with Omara, who sensed I was different from other gays.

*****

Now that I'd moved into Louise's, I didn't have a clue about what to do next. I assured the ladies that I probably wouldn't be staying very long but promised to pay them a fitting amount for room and board, besides helping out around the house. Lou worked five and a half days a week, Betty, the happy homemaker, cooked well and kept the place clean and tidy. I saved a decent amount of money from working at the bar, so I didn't have to run right out to score a job. In a short time though, I began to despise Betty's depressing country music, got tired of chitchats and doing my nails, I needed to bolt.

Within days of living there, I got a great suntan, felt strong, healthy and terrific, so I decided to explore this white bread community. Every house within a square mile looked exactly like the last one. It was the dullest place I'd ever seen, getting somewhere else required taking a bus, even to the grocery store.

Guantanamera continued to play in my head, I might have been hankering for the excitement of downtown or perhaps being with Omara again, but I resisted the whole concept of going backwards. There was a bus stop a couple of blocks away from the house on Biscayne Boulevard, so instead of taking the long ride south to Fourth Street, I chose going north to the closest gay bar. Lou told me how to get to Happy's, her favorite joint, so I rode to Hollywood, expecting to relieve some boredom.

It was early when I got there and a few tough-looking gals seated at the bar kept staring at me in a very hostile way. Maybe if I bought them a drink, it would help us to become sociable; they said thanks but never reciprocated with a simple smile. I had a few single malt scotches, and found my way back to the bus stop. It showered off and on while I was being ignored at that unfriendly, cheeky saloon.

My main complaint about Florida was the creatures that came out after the rain. I also hated that my clothes constantly felt damp. There were no sidewalks on Lou's street; I heard squishing noises and felt things crackling under my feet as I walked. The critters I disliked so much were known as land crabs, other pests included mosquitoes, frogs, palmetto bugs and cockroaches. Several canals in the area even had small alligators running around. Their house had tiny steeping stones up to the door, If I got home drunk; the rascals always seemed to attack me on the path.

With time on my hands, I reflected back on riding horses with Phil Mahoney and I thought about the hours I spent at the Suffolk

Downs racetrack with Jenny and Bill; I learned a lot about the ponies whenever I hung around the stable grounds waiting for them to stop gambling. Dave's friends said he was a great trainer; his phone number was still tucked in my wallet so I just decided to call him.

It took a lot of moxie to call him, several weeks had passed since he'd given me the number, but I chanced it anyway. I didn't need to identify myself when he answered the phone, and Dave was indeed happy to hear from me. I wanted to know if he meant what he said about finding work for me at the track. Without hesitation he replied, "Absolutely." We set a date and time, and he came to pick me up.

Dave drove an old pick-up truck and knew his way around the area; he had no trouble finding Louise's. First we went to his messy apartment, which was in the city of Hialeah and I met his disagreeable wife, Mary Lee. The woman was inebriated when we arrived and got drunker by the minute. I couldn't wait to leave but the main reason for going there was to borrow a pair of old riding boots which his wife could no longer wear. A big mystery to me was how such a sweet man could be so faithful to a witch like her; apparently, she was the reason he enjoyed those frequent visits to the Senate Bar.

Dave came up with a very nice pair of leather boots for me, only Mary Lee didn't know it. We passed through a heavily guarded gate a few blocks from his place. All vehicles had to have the proper stickers etc. to enter the huge and sacred grounds of the Hialeah racetrack. He escorted me around the entire awesome venue to show its colorful beauty. I was impressed. Then we parked behind the stables where he worked. Trainers are celebrities of sorts when they are winning, and my friend was a winner.

The start of a new racing season was in less than a month, so he tried to form a hardworking crew, which was difficult, most of the common racetrack workers appeared to be heavy drinkers and not very dependable. Dave was commissioned to train six thoroughbreds; it was hard dirty work, stables had to be cleaned and the high-priced equestrians needed to be exercised, fed and groomed constantly.

The job as a stable boy (person) was mine. All I had to do was figure out how to get from Louise's to the track by six a.m. This jaunt would require taking two buses and a long walk. If I missed one, there wouldn't be another for an hour. After about a week of calculating the best way out there, my Virgo record for punctuality became perfect again. Dave generally showed up around nine a.m.

When I lived in Miami, I usually dressed in white linen shirts, white pants and never shorts because of my complexes, but now my work clothes would be strictly Levi's, T-shirts and rubber boots. I didn't get many chances to jump on horses wearing Mary Lee's jodhpurs; I had to wear rubber ones for the dirty stable work, shoveling and more shoveling. The real reason for taking that filthy job was so I could ride extremely fast and often, although most of the time I was stuck in the smelly barn.

Dave understood that it was hard for me to get there on time, he suggested I stay overnight at his house to see if it would help, so I slept there for one night only. His wife prowled around their disheveled apartment, clutching a big water glass full of bourbon, never cooked, hardly ever ate and ranted about whatever popped into her crazy head, in particular, how she felt about gay people.

"I truly like you, Carole honey, but the Bible says it's wrong what you're doing. You can be saved if you want to be." I finally fell asleep on their couch but decided it was much less painful to take the bus.

It really made my day when I got a chance to freely ride a horse; otherwise, I had some great moments just walking around the grounds. Pink flamingos were a big part of the Hialeah image, and there were plenty of them, which meant they also needed care. I visited their area occasionally and made friends with the guy in charge of them; I learned many things about those aristocratic, noisy birds.

This was my fourth seven-day workweek at the track and I usually got home between five and six. Louise and Betty started to bicker a lot then, which made me feel pretty uncomfortable; I think the honeymoon was basically over. Poor little Eli must have really been confused, but I could never interfere with their personal arguments. It seems Betty was bored playing the adorable housewife role, and Lou didn't have much energy to do anything after work. Things might have been better if they had a car since their place was in such a secluded area, but they could never see their way clear to buying one.

Dave had my absolute devotion and assistance until the grand opening of Hialeah in mid-March, but I told him after the great event that I needed to move on; he was very understanding as usual. I went to his house for the last time to collect my final wages and slyly return Mary Lee's boots. We wished each other luck, shook hands, hugged, then I alleged to Dave's god-fearing wife that I'd deal with getting saved once I got back up north. Excavating all that horse manure paid off, I left with a hefty paycheck.

I had a morsel of regret about not being more familiar with Omara because she seemed so very sad. Some women decide to turn gay when they are troubled and in need of a woman's shoulder to cry on. Appreciating this gentle comfort oftentimes results in physical love, but it never happened with us.

All things considered, I did have some fun in Florida, but now that it was spring again I very much wanted to get home to my beloved New England roots. The first person I called was my best friend Mary Walsh; she was glad I was coming home and said I could stay with her for a while. Betty and Lou wished me well and even got us a ride to the airport from the same chubby gal who picked Betty up. This was my first trip on an airplane ever; I was a bit nervous but thrilled to be taking off, and going home.

An American Airlines jet would fly me from Miami International Airport, to Logan in Boston, where I could take a bus to Worcester. When the plane started to climb straight up, I felt somewhat tense but shortly afterward the stewardesses came around in their neatly tailored uniforms and asked everyone what they'd like to drink. Vodka and tonic was my preference, you could even smoke cigarettes on board then, and I became more relaxed quite quickly. Massive clouds were all I could see from my window seat, and I vanished into a dreamlike state, reflecting on my past. This climactic trip to Miami with Louise wasn't really my first time being in Florida, I drove there long ago all by myself.

*****

When I was about eighteen and fed up with slaving at the shoe shop, I quit my job for the hundredth time, got my 1949 Ford in good shape and hit the road for Florida. I stored some stuff at my mother's and had enough of a nest egg to feel secure for a while. Just trying to get out of Worcester was a hassle. The first thing I had to do was shovel my car out of the deep snow banks in freezing temperatures, which is one reason I chose to go south, I've always hated the cold and loved the sun. I left during the week before Christmas and my Nana was staying at Mom's for the holiday, as well as my kid brother Earl. They all said this journey was crazy, but I was really determined to travel.

My first stop for gas was in New Jersey, from there, I raced down the highways even faster. I took some Dexedrine in case, but eventually became extremely exhausted and stopped at a southern truck stop for breakfast. They had a men's room with showers; you simply had to pay for soap and a towel. I generally braved going into a gentleman's restroom because I was a young dyke in full drag. Just as I was about to undress and shower, an enormous burly truck driver approached my cubicle space and said: "Boy, you sure enough got pretty black hair, can I touch it?" I got scared and ran like a rabbit.

The creepy scene at the truck stop left me wondering about how many unreported rapes or assaults actually happened in that type of place. The next time I felt drowsy I checked into a well-lit motel in Georgia, tested the locks and windows, and went next door to buy a sandwich with a bottle of beer to go. I slept very well that night and decided to make Miami, my ultimate destination, but first I had to have a good breakfast before driving; hopefully I could make it all the way down in one day.

Women usually put on makeup before they go anywhere, I did the same, but it wasn't the pancake or powder kind, my sole implement was a basic black eyebrow pencil to darken my faint mustache and lengthen my side burns. I slipped into the large, hollow café without being noticed, the locals just assumed I was a typical young chap having breakfast, and so did Hattie, the angelic blond waitress.

While masquerading as the perfect boy, I lowered my voice a few octaves, spoke from the abdomen and conversed softly. Hattie took my breakfast order without looking too closely and we bonded the minute she asked if I wanted grits with my meal. I felt pretty ignorant and must have blushed when I told her that I didn't even know what grits were, we began to laugh uncontrollably. Feeling confident that she didn't know I was a girl, I conjured up the nerve to ask her to join me after work, perhaps we could see a local movie or go to a very fine place for dinner, and she answered yes with an open smile.

I left her my room number and she agreed to join me after work at three. Hattie never showed up; perhaps she actually knew I was a female and was putting me on, or someone at the restaurant tipped her off. I honestly thought we had something going for a brief moment, and if we really did have an affair, she might have five big, ignorant brothers pointing shotguns at me, so maybe I was lucky.

My heart wasn't broken; I've had some experience with disappointment, this southern whim only cost me a little travel time. I gassed up the car; put the pedal to the metal and the next big interstate sign read: 'Welcome to Florida, the Sunshine State'. Various advertisements on billboards emerged about every fifty yards after that. 'Take your next right to visit Alligator Land', or 'The greatest freak show on earth is only five miles away'. I couldn't believe how many tacky ads popped up on one highway.

From the border of Georgia, through the City of Jacksonville, the pungent smell of rotten cabbage lingered in my head, though it could have been decaying cotton. I drove right by that city, hoping to elude the awful stench. As I got closer to the ocean, the air became much sweeter and when I arrived in the City of Saint Augustine, it was like a religious experience, the place was absolutely pristine. It is known as the oldest city in America and has many breathtaking residences. Neon road signs touted it as the legendary site of the 'Fountain of Youth and birthplace of the Oldest Jail House in the U.S.A.'

Ponce De Leon couldn't offer me youth from his magic fountain; I was only eighteen and didn't really want to be any younger at the time. I drove all around the magnetic locale, dipped my feet in the ocean and wished I could move into the fabled lighthouse. There seemed to be much grandeur to savor, and I promptly realized that I should have taken a camera, it simply never occurred to me to buy one.

What I concluded from this lonely trip was the understanding that all beauty is even more splendid while sharing it. The wonders that I'd seen and appreciated could only be affirmed by me, and writing about exquisite things could not replace a real photo. From then on, I would never travel without a camera or a companion to partake in the pleasure of visiting a special place like Saint Augustine.

I spent one very fulfilling day in the oldest city, and when dusk approached I checked into a friendly motel near the oldest jail. At times it was risky making simple conversation with strangers for fear of being exposed as a male impostor, so I didn't speak much.

The inn was charming, clean and had a small pool, but there were a few straight folks swimming around with their kids. I got something to eat down the road, enjoyed a good night's sleep and at sunrise, when no one else was around, I dove into the pool, wearing only jeans and a T-shirt. Bathing suits or shorts were never included in my wardrobe.

The chlorinated water must have awakened my senses during that swim because I decided to pack up immediately, hit the road and make it home by Christmas day. My old Ford held up very well for the ride south, but now I had to get it back in good shape for the long drive to Massachusetts. An elderly man changed the oil and checked my tires at a nearby gas station and the gypsy was ready to travel.

I didn't make it to Miami, but as for the trek home, I carefully analyzed the fastest routes on the map and planned to get one night of sleep at a motel; the rest of the stretch I would drive like the wind. One of the few places I wanted to visit was a well-known establishment called 'Stuckey's'; their signs were endless. 'Relax – Refresh – Refuel - Only five more miles to Stuckey's, four more miles.... etc.'"

With so much advertising being flaunted, I had to browse through one of their stores to see what they carried. There were many choices about Christmas presents for the people on my list, but I got hung up in the eye-catching Mexican section and bought a lot of junk. For Mom, a colorful wall zarape, my brother Earl, the clown, deserved a giant sombrero, and Nana would embrace a full collection of turquoise jewelry. I also bought some stocking stuffers like castanets, small bongo drums and plenty of pecans.

My final motel stay was in Baltimore. I drove nonstop to the slushy streets of Worcester, arriving at my mother's house early on December 24th. The family was shocked to see me saunter up the steps, especially Mom; she had prayed hard to the Blessed Mother that I might come home before Christmas. I handed out gifts which made them happy; it was an outstanding holiday and a rare time for all us.

After the merriment ended, Nana went back to Pakachoag Street, Mom continued to work as a waitress, Earl just wasn't doing well in school so he decided to join the Navy in two years and once more, I showed up at the H. & H. Brown shoe company to ask for my inspector's job back. Charley Kaplan, the boss, was really glad to see me; subsequently, I became good friends with Phil Mahoney.

*****

The plane from Miami was now taxiing at Logan Airport and my heart was in my mouth, not because of fear, I was simply anxious to be back in familiar territory. After hoofing down all the ramps, Walshie surprised me by parking right outside to pick me up in her new Datsun Z. She brought along a cold six-pack of beer and we chatted briefly about my trip to Florida with Louise. During the next forty miles home, we drank and laughed a lot, as we clearly recalled my very first visit to California.

Before Niki or Provincetown penetrated my life, I decided to see 'The Golden State of California'. Joyce Huey, an aimless gay Gemini, who hung out at the New Yorker, heard about my whim and wanted to join me on this distant tour. Joyce was the only available person I knew who was willing and able to leave on three days' notice, first she had to say goodbye to her sweetheart Rosemary. This pretty eighteen-year-old lived way out in the country, but couldn't leave home except to go to work; the reality was that her father had been molesting her for years and Joyce couldn't do anything about it.

Joyce met sweet Rosemary while working at a factory; somehow they fell madly in love sharing thirty-minute lunch periods. Joyce had a single room, not far from work, but her girlfriend lived in Auburn and took a very long bus ride each way five days a week. They began to carry on during coffee breaks and baby Huey would walk her to the bus stop every day right after work. Rosemary had to be home by a certain time for dinner, leaving them little time to make out or make love. Joyce didn't have a car, so she'd take a bus out to the farm on weekends. Just before our trip to California, she learned about the domestic incest affair and begged her young darling to leave with us. The crestfallen maiden said it was impossible to flee from her father. I thanked God because my tiny car only had two seats.

I was still working at the shoe shop and Phil helped me to save several hundred dollars for an anticipated vacation, then I navigated Joyce all the way cross country to California in my 1957 MG.

We left on a Saturday morning in the early spring, yet the weather was still quite cold. I packed my small car with one big suitcase behind each bucket seat, the trunk barely held anything, so that space was for Huey, who owned or carried very little in a small duffle bag and had absolutely no money.

Joyce bundled up the belongings from her place and left several boxed items in a friend's basement. We literally dreamed of living in California forever. I gave up a ten-dollar weekly apartment for this change in geography; fortunately, all my stuff would be stored safely at Walshie's. There was one final stop to make, we had to say goodbye to Rosemary, possibly for the last time. After Joyce told me about the incest problem, I could barely look at the forlorn girl and just as we were saying farewell, her disgusting father came out of the house. The mere sight of him made me sick and I actually wanted to kidnap her. I peeled rubber pulling away from their depraved farm and we finally hit the road.

My little MG convertible was not hermetically sealed and leaked like a sieve. On the first leg of our trip, we ran into a terrible snowstorm in the mountains of Virginia, then more rain with huge floods throughout West Virginia. Many bridges had washed out, so we were forced to stay at the first hillbilly motel available. It was my intention to drive all the way out west on Dexedrine and only stop if it was absolutely necessary. When it cleared in the morning, we filled all the leaky gaps between the windows and the roof of the car with lots of newspaper, and soon we'd be cruising on the legendary route 66.

Because of tire trouble, we checked into a motel in Oklahoma, and I realized that Joyce never took a shower. When the car heater was on and she put her feet in front of it, I gagged from the smell.

So I began to build a list of complaints in case I ever decided to get rid of her. Out-of-date plaid pants which rose way above the ankles were her style and she looked sloppy no matter what she put on. Joyce was a bit taller, pudgy, with two front teeth missing, which caused her to talk funny. When we reached Oklahoma City, I offered to buy her a plane ticket home, but she whined, I felt guilty, so we advanced.

Joyce was quite butch; she looked like a female Brian Dennehy wearing ugly shirts, with high water pants. I was sharp, crisp and in a boyish way resembled Sal Mineo. These shallow contrasts didn't really change our friendship, but from now on she would have to make a conscious effort to dress better.

Finally, we were driving down the Hollywood freeway and I was thrilled. At the first motel sign we exited and checked into a clean place on Sunset. I insisted she take a shower before we did anything. Basically, all I remember about Los Angeles then was the awful smog, and I couldn't really see the sky because the air was brown. After a diet pill and a blasé take-out meal, we got directions to the ocean. By fluke, we landed at Venice Beach and strolled along that very diverse boardwalk.

What would a trip to California be like without delving into a gay bar? So we asked someone on the boardwalk and got directions at once. The Barn was a huge, cold, open hangout and reeked of everything, including pot. I hardly felt secure in this weird roost of bizarre people, but I noticed one group at a table, having a lot of fun, so I approached them. A heavyset, cheerful woman was at the center of this rowdy bash and turned out to be the famous gay singer Bonnie Guitar. Her biggest hit song, *Dark Moon*, was vague in my memory, but it seemed like now she was down and out in Venice. The older, washed-out-looking star was accompanied by a large butch woman, and they both accessorized with tacky guitar jewelry. Bonny sang a few notes after we bought them a beer, but the whole experience depressed me. I'm sure L.A. had many excellent gay bars; we were simply disenchanted by that one.

The few gay women that I noticed working in Los Angeles were slaving at car washes; I could always get that kind of job in Worcester. We only stayed for about a week and I don't mean to judge or be hard on L.A., but how could I ever become brave enough to start off fresh as a stranger? I couldn't. My hometown embodied all my good friends and family. Moving out west then might have left me virtually nowhere. At least I felt comfortably hitched to my earthy, Pi Wi Johnson image at the New Yorker Bar and Grill. "Joyce, put your face in the sun and tan quickly, we're going home right now."

*****

After sharing old stories all the way from Logan, we eventually reached Walshie's house half loaded. I went right to bed in the guestroom and further reflected upon my life. At sixteen, I left home with the carnival, at eighteen, took a lonely trip to Florida, at twenty-one, Joyce and I went west, though I lived on Cape Cod through most of my twenties. Now, I was more than thirty and didn't have a clue what to do next. Would I always be a gypsy or a happy wanderer? It was time to find a nesting kind of woman.

Walshie had been my best friend since I was ten years old, always eminent in my life. At this time, her lover was a sweet but talky Sagittarius girl named Cassie Stewart who was a newly arrived southerner. She came up north with her nice, quiet friend named Pat. It seems some redneck yokels in Georgia were very abusive to conspicuously gay people in certain areas; those two gals had been victimized enough, so they migrated to Worcester because someone told them it was a Mecca for gay people.

Friday night was best for meeting trendy people at the New Yorker; it was always packed with horny women. Walshie, Cassie, Pat and I joined the raucous crowd to drink, dance and cruise. I danced with Pat, who wasn't my type but a nice kid; she helped me to scope out other girls. Suddenly, a young woman attracted my roving eye. That pretty face belonged to Kathie O'Malley, a very cute Irish girl who was tough, streetwise, yet showed the greatest dimples whenever she smiled. I liked her instantly, though she was more spirited than the passive, ladylike femmes I was used to. Ultimately, we kissed, dirty-danced together and ended up staying at Walshie's place for the night. I didn't know where this affair would go, but we were white hot. We dated for a while, then decided to become monogamous and began to shop for our own apartment. Now I'd be getting involved with the entire crazy

O'Malley clan.

Betty O'Malley Rose was Kathie's mother, a matriarch to five kids from two different bad marriages. She was even tougher than her daughter and worked indirectly for the city as an organizer for some local grassroots program throughout the seventies, when our government was being excessively generous with grants. Perhaps because she was a powerful Leo, Betty didn't do very much other than to criticize everyone and delegate different people to do her personal work. Kathie held a good position in her mom's office, and before long I would have a job there too, thanks to those federal funds.

The oldest brother, a Scorpio named Timmy, was really a dangerous guy. He'd been in and out of jail for heavy crimes like armed robbery. Tim was fearless because he was a long-time, hardened heroin user. He was notorious for pistol-whipping people on the street just to get a twenty-dollar bag. Then there was a younger brother named Mike who was also an addict. He was a nice guy, not just because he was a Virgo but this sibling really helped me out later in time. The bright-eyed, handsome brother Kevin was a bit different from the other O'Malleys. He wanted to become some kind of minister because of his need to experience religion, but basically he was a Taurus bull who always had the heifers chasing him. Betty spent most evenings analyzing court dates for her troubled and rebellious kids. A litigation, which concerned Kevin, was an ultimatum from the court: marry her, or pay for the child.

From her previous Rose marriage, Betty produced a monster son named Buzz, and at six years old he was declared an absolute incorrigible. This family was beyond dysfunctional, even Kathie had been to reform school because she was wild, hard to handle and unmanageable, yet you could never tell from her angelic Libra smile. She learned a few necessary office skills at the Framingham farm for bad girls, but I had to wonder why I even associated with these coarse people. Kathie was desirable and possessive; I stayed with her for nearly seven insane years, after which I moved to California to get away, far away.

We led a somewhat commonplace existence at first, but then up jumped the devil. Eventually, I turned Kathie on to heroin and her brothers were thrilled that we could share this trashy lifestyle with them, confirming who the best dealers were, or finding the strongest dope. It doesn't take long to get a mean jones when drugs are so easily available. Worcester was loaded with dealers, stuff is always cheaper when you first start using; the peddler knows it takes but a short time before you're maintaining a big habit.

Prior to becoming addicted, our lives were pretty ordinary. Kathie worked at the office every day with Betty, and I took a job in a factory. As a couple of thirty-something lesbians, we were smart, sharp and joined in regular poker-playing party nights with other gay companions. Kathie and I were indeed sexually compatible; I never wanted to be touched and she didn't want to do it anyway. Other petty tensions did result from my chronic Virgo impatience, which probably began with Mom's hasty potty training; nevertheless, I disliked my body being fondled. Considering all the females I chased, you may ask why I became a physical untouchable after Niki; I was modest and simply chose to adopt this tenet.

Phil and I had sex a few times at a motel out of town; it was over quickly since I was the top. He was very good to me, so it was a dutiful act of tolerance, not a fun thing. I was only there for him on special occasions but that was long ago. Fortunately, Kathie never knew about Phil or she would never stop badgering me. She was insanely jealous, but an extremely sensual woman prone to being quite noisy while making love. When the sound of her passion reached a certain pitch, it meant that with all her Libra lust she was getting ready to climax, and simultaneously I would release my own poised orgasm. Any woman can peak at will through sexual levitation, by positioning certain body muscles just right.

We were admired by our peers and were role models for younger girls who were afraid to attempt gay life. In public, we dressed well and behaved properly, but when we got home, if she thought someone else looked at me, she'd charge into me like a demon. Kathie had a vicious temper, so mainly I kept the peace by making love to her whenever she got upset. After the intimacy, she would flash her Irish smile, though we might survive through another day or night. Our bickering was evolving and I couldn't escape her filthy mouth; maybe some dope could help us now. 'When sex just isn't enough, try drugs.'

Her brother Mike copped a bag of heroin for us, but Kathie was hesitant to try it. Wow! After the initial phase of being sick and throwing up, she became a different person and I liked her much better. That was the start of the worst period of my life. At first, it was a dime bag once in a while, which we shared; then it was a dime bag for each of us; soon it would be a dime bag every day. There are just so many things you can do to adjust your daily funds; luckily, Kathie had access to the petty cash at work.

We lived in a really nice flat close to everything, and for the first few years we regularly entertained friends and family. On Sunday mornings, Kathie would read every word of the weekly newspaper in bed and always expected me to join her. I don't read much now, and I surely didn't read much then. Staying still when not sleeping was a very hard thing for me to do and relaxing around her was futile. The Libra mind is dedicated to finding a balance; the Sunday paper could begin an aggressive debate between us which might last until Tuesday. If I chose to go out for any reason, she accused me of having an affair. How could I ever find the time to run around when we were together about sixteen hours a day?

All good things must end; the interim at our first apartment ended abruptly. A notice came from the landlord stating that the building had recently been sold and we had to move out within a very short time. Kathie was livid. It was all I could do to stop her from showing up at his private residence with a butcher's knife. Let me remind you that she could be vicious and graduated from a tough correctional school. Losing our niche set the scene for a major fight, as though it were my entire fault. This argument somehow became her mother's issue. Betty was happy to interfere because she really didn't like me anyway. I couldn't take any more attitudes then, so I retreated to my mother's place, a large, one-room studio on nearby Lagrange Street. Mom was always there for me and felt useful when I needed her.

The three-story brick structure had exquisite woodwork throughout the interior and classic old New England architecture. Theresa lived on the first floor and the psychotic managers of the place, Marge and Eddy, lived on the second floor. It only took about three days of being around Mom to make me crazy. Conveniently at this time, someone was moving out of a small unit on the third floor and the place could be mine for thirteen dollars weekly rent, so I took it. The custodians liked me a lot and really wanted me to live there, at least in the beginning. Most of the tenants in that dark chateau were elderly, eccentric or behaved strangely, but I'm sure they all thought the same of me in other ways.

People in Worcester only knew me by the nickname, which was selected by way of Walshie's father, Patty; a good friend of my dad's who was in love with my mom through their teens. I was a very short ten-year-old when I first met Patty and he inquired: "Do folks call you Pee Wee?"

I quickly answered, "Yea, but I spell my name with the letter 'I', instead of an 'E', like Ki Wi, the shoe polish."

Ergo, Pi Wi Johnson was conceived. With a name like that I had to shape an image for myself by aspiring to look cool, I just wasn't quite sure how to go about it. Regardless, my individuality would develop later on.

Kathie and I saw each other often at the New Yorker and played asinine games to make each other jealous. During our break up this time, I discreetly began to date a charming girl named Cheryl Plitnik. She was what you might call moderately chubby but very pretty and remarkably sexy in a way. Her body was soft like tofu, and she always enjoyed huge, wet, and emotional climaxes. This affair went on for a while, but in case I forgot to mention it, I was deathly afraid of Kathie. We had a couple of violent, physical brawls, which I despised, she really fought to the bitter end, or whenever I fell to the floor from complete exhaustion. Periodically, Betty would ask for Kathie's help to control her barbaric sons.

Mark Twain knew what he was talking about: "Clothes maketh the man." One wouldn't expect visits from debutantes in our low-class gay bar, but I managed to have fleeting rapports with other attractive ladies. One foxy cruising gesture was simply not to speak. Never chatter; keep your lips pursed as you strike an artistic pose, you could be confronted with an amiable conversation, even if you weren't in the mood. My dapper Scorpio father traded at an elite men's store called 'Shacks', and when I had the money, I'd also shop there. Downstairs had a great youth section with an array of fine boys wear, where items fit me well. Walshie used to copy my wardrobe; if I bought a gold sailcloth jacket, she got one too. If I spotted a new style of shoes, she'd buy them, even those ugly Ginny boots. My slacks were creased and long enough, shoes well shined and my boyish body was always buffed.

Gay people live to celebrate, regardless of the reason, but on this particular New Year's Eve there was a big party scheduled at the New Yorker. I stayed over Walshie and Cassie's the night before to get dressed up, and rode with them to make a grand entry. On that much anticipated party day, the temperature in Worcester literally fell to fifteen below zero. All the pipes were frozen solid and you could barely get any water out of the spigot to wash up with. Taking a perfect shower would be out of the question but we did the best we could to get bathed and polished for this huge gala.

Walshie's car battery was dead and cabs were unattainable, so we coasted all the way on a sheet of ice in our party apparel, marching two whole frigid miles in very thin shoes meant only for dancing. Our chic clothing couldn't keep us warm enough, as the merciless wind chill took our breath away. After we paid an entrance fee at the door, everybody downed a stiff shot of something; I favored a double brandy. All of the so-called 'In Crowd' was there, including Ms. O'Malley, dressed in scarlet red.

The pub was really crowded and a few good-looking girls that I used to date were there as well. Every once in a while if I felt lightheaded, I'd step out into the freezing shadows for a breath of cold air. I quickly scored a joint from a stranger as the bewitching hour approached, and the moment I lit up, Kathie was standing next to me. "Can I have a hit?" She smiled like an innocent maiden and I couldn't resist her Irish charm. We kissed in the center of the ballroom at precisely midnight, and left together.

Kathie came home with me and we made love on my tiny bed all night long. Following that interlude, she moved in until our next fight occurred. Out of all the places I'd ever lived, this third-floor berth was the most poorly decorated, yet I had no interest in enriching anything there. We began doing heroin without delay, which meant additional traffic at the house. Marge and Eddy soon placed a mirror in the hallway, to watch the weirdoes coming and going. Our cryptic lifestyle became a daily soap to them.

Kathie's two junky brothers were regular visitors at our dump. Tim slept all day at Betty's house after everyone left for work or school, there just wasn't enough room for him to live there, and consequently he prowled around all night. Tim stalked defenseless people on dark streets to rip them off, or burglarized quiet shops. Mike had a good day job at a funeral parlor, though he never acted the part, he was gay. Bob, the undertaker, truly idolized him and this Aquarian lover gave Mike everything possible.

Other guests at Lagrange Street included a very tall, explosive, Aries guy named Legs who walked with a prominent limp, drove a Harley hog and was, in fact, a genuine psychopath. His crazy, wild-woman girlfriend, Rachael Capputo, a treacherous Pisces, usually rode shotgun on the back of the bike. If someone made her angry, she'd threaten to send Legs after them, and he was our drug connection.

We both worked but the money was never enough to support our budding habits. This was a bountiful time; free merchandise offers began to arrive in the mail every day. 'Just fill this coupon out, mail it in and receive your brand-new electronic... with no money down.' These complimentary deals kept coming; the companies were constantly sending us goods, which we promptly sold. Certain firms risked small color TVs, portable short-wave radios and other diverse products on consignment to people like us who didn't have any credit; this was the dawning of junk mail. Buy now, and pay for it later. Our mailman never knew that he was delivering the potential capital for our daily fix. I was in my lucky Jupiter period and able to sell every item to dealers, or anyone else on the street that could pay for the stuff.

The frenzy of peddling objects, which weren't really ours to sell, got to my conscience. I worried about who would pay for this electronic paraphernalia in the end. Sooner or later, bad karma catches up, so I thought about how to justify selling drugs again for a profit. I was actually wealthy once but didn't know it, now I was broke and hated it. Though we existed as addicts, Kathie and I were admired for being fair, honest and aboveboard, so I hoped to find a dealer who wouldn't mind fronting us a few bags.

Slick was a big black guy with a heart of gold, I approached him about dealing, and he offered to front us a hefty stash. We met him daily at a bar to do an inventory, he was a very fair person unless you came up short with his money and I prayed that would never happen. Kathie continued working as an accountant in the office and finally I could quit that dreary, grimy, factory job. It wasn't so much the work I hated; it was the greasy, lecherous little boss, who used to follow me around the place asking if he could take Polaroid pictures of my breasts for fifty dollars. I would rather deal drugs on the street than ever give in to a disgusting pig like him. Now I'd be working for myself, and that really felt good.

Most of the heroin action took place within a four-block radius of my apartment. A popular restaurant owned by a nice black couple was at the hub of all this and they didn't make much profit, because many of their customers were addicts who ate very little food. I got friendly with several hookers who hung around there; Sweets Café became my new space for retailing. Cars pulled up to me on the street, but I walked carefully and just couldn't trust every new shopper. They had to have bought something from me previously or knew someone close to me; otherwise, I was dubious about serving newcomers.

I'm certain it was a full moon on that indelible, hellish, Friday night and there seemed to be more street activity than usual. I ran out of drugs to sell and only had a couple of bags left for our wake-up, so we hurried home to Lagrange Street. Just before entering the house, we noticed a car with three guys in it, and they wanted to score. Somehow they knew we were dealers and became really persistent. "Please, please, sell us one bag?" We ignored this appeal but two of them followed us all the way up to the third floor while sweet-talking us. These guys were obviously not from our hood, and we never thought about getting hurt, nevertheless, they did some harm. Once my key went into the lock, we were abruptly knocked to the floor, seriously beaten, robbed of Stick's money and our morning wake-up bags.

Kathie was being punched hard in the face by a hooligan wearing a bulky graduation class ring. I think it was from Grafton High School. The creep did a lot of damage with those sporadic jabs, while the other guy who restrained me, acted more civilized. For some odd reason, Kathie did attract a certain amount of violence in her life, which was the flipside of what I hoped for. Her face was a mess; these savages took every penny they could find in our pockets and even things from around the house. We were bleeding conspicuously, battered and exhausted, but we had to go right back out again to tell Stick.

We showed up looking wretched, just as he was walking into his hang out, which was a disco bar on Main Street. In the past, we were always on the level, so he had no reason to be suspicious of what had just gone down, but now he may have some reservations. The bottom line was, we owed him a couple of hundred bucks and definitely needed two bags for our morning wake-up. After he exploded, swore a lot and told us how stupid we were, he gave us two bags on credit, then we made an arrangement to bring most of the money to him by the following afternoon and he would set aside additional dope to get us back in business again. We were seriously cautioned; if we fouled up again, just leave town immediately. Kathie had access to some petty cash at work which made us feel better, but we still needed to fix.

It was after two a.m. when we got out the works, shared half a bag and saved the rest for morning. I let Kathie get off first, and took my shot. "Oh my God, he gave us coke instead of smack." Stick dealt both cocaine and heroin, so it had to have been a mistake. If you've never done drugs, you're smart, but if you have, you might understand what a terrible thing it was to get the wrong kind of narcotic. Coke wires you, it's an upper, we really needed to sleep and I couldn't bear to think about morning without a heroin wake-up, so I trotted right back to Stick and exchanged the coke for what we needed.

Most tenants living in that gothic house on Lagrange Street were seniors or people receiving disability checks. My mother was able to work at a job most of the time, but every once in a while she would go on a major binge. She'd lock herself in the apartment and drink alone until she got sick enough, then go back to sweat at the dirty brush factory where she seemed to be happy. I really didn't see Mom too much through any of my stay in that quiet building because of my drug use, but when she staggered up to Marge and Eddy's with her rent money, she got a full report about my comings and goings.

The front hall stairs in that old house made creaking noises whenever anyone walked up or down, and Timmy O'Malley used them regularly. Like Dracula, he only appeared at night, generally after making a score. Once in a while, he'd buy or borrow a bag from us, but a few times he actually hustled some good dope somewhere and turned us on for free. If he couldn't make any money, he'd just rob Betty again. Marge and Eddy finally detected our drug-induced lifestyle but were really afraid of Kathie and me, so they hesitated to ask us to move. After the obvious beating and rip-off episode at our place upstairs, they became distant, in a polite kind of way, and we continued living there for a while longer.

Because of my continual narcotic use, I was beginning to feel paranoid, depressed and even a bit suicidal. I was sick of everybody and woke up each morning feeling great despair about my damaged spirit. Kathie's mom kindly put me in touch with a psychiatrist named Conrad Nadeau. He ran a storefront office once a week where numerous clients lined up just to speak with him. In time I became comfortable enough, to entertain him with my astrological magic. He liked me a lot and arranged for me to collect SSI right away. This would take a good deal of pressure off of my dope dealing misery, and I was especially grateful for those extra few hundred dollars a month. Likewise, other benefits would come now because I was a documented sick person; on certain days, folks like me carrying an ID card would line up like cattle for free welfare food. It was humiliating, but those packaged mashed potatoes and blocks of cheddar cheese really came in handy when we were broke.

I referred affectionately to my handsome shrink as 'Conny', but he didn't mind. Conny was Canadian by birth, and he said after he became rich and famous he planned to return home someday. He was a Taurus, the same as Freud, and evaluated individuals in a similar way; he could be a little freaky too.

Following our long painful sessions, he would try to make me feel good by telling me how smart I was, or that I was born with more natural class than anyone out there. (Out where?) He gave me his personal telephone number in case there was a serious crisis, but I never used it. I'm not vain enough to think that he ever wanted me physically, yet he focused a great deal on my sex life. I revealed many intimate, embarrassing details about myself to him because of his enthusiastic and genuine concern.

Ever since her psychotic boyfriend, Legs, went to jail for forty-five days, and Rachael's wealthy family threw her out of the house indefinitely, Capputo then surfaced as a hooker. With a big habit to support, she worked the streets and profiled tricks rather well, but she couldn't always handle their requests alone. She received special instructions from a regular client one day to hire a couple of lesbians for lovemaking scenes. He wanted to watch two women graphically demonstrate wild passionate love. That specialty could make good money if a person had enough nerve to cope with the personal degradation.

Kathie and I were hiking down East Main Street when Rachael approached us. "I have this john and he's willing to pay you a hundred dollars each just to watch you make love the same way you do at home. Okay?"

It was winter, and we were cold and broke, so we said, "What the hell."

She called the guy and he came right over to her trick room in a crummy building not far from Sweet's. The burly simpleton arrived with a fifth of bourbon to help us relax for this kinky, voyeur soiree. Now that I was a bit drunk, Kathie looked attractive enough to turn me on, but how could I ignore the obvious and keen presence of the others? The repulsive trick sat in an old stuffed chair holding a towel and facing the bed with his legs spread and zipper wide open. After another drink and a cigarette, I kissed my lover erotically, removed her clothes delicately and with the first bodily touch, she moaned with real desire.

By now, he was enthralled in frenzied masturbation, and even though he wanted her to participate, Rachael could only watch because I absolutely refused to let her near us in a sexual way. She had long, greasy, stringy black hair and a big furry mole on her face. Maybe she turned Legs on, but I could never get myself to kiss a woman who looked liked that, let alone listen to her loud, abrasive voice.

Kathie and I hurried through this fabricated act and I never took my clothes off. The guy was really happy and imagined that we both had fabulous orgasms, he said it would be great, if we could do this again, Rachael would call us at the earliest opportunity. Our relationship could hardly be considered amicable; I agonized while pretending to make love to Kathie. Afterward, we had enough money to buy a lot of dope; therefore, our junky peers presumed we were actually hookers now. As prostitute partners, our contrived lovemaking was the only carnal exploit that we ever capitalized on. Rachael called and we arranged to playact a few more 'female-to-female' exhibitions, then we chose to break up again.

When I was a baby, Mom used to really soak my gums with paregoric for teething pain, and I can almost believe the original roots of my drug dependence derived from some of that stuff. Paregoric, anisette, licorice, pot and Sen Sens, are still my favorite flavors, they all taste similar to opium. Could my addictions have evolved from family genes, or did I simply choose my own self-destructive behavior?

My brother came from the same alcoholic, heavy-smoking parents and never drank or smoked. He was a good kid, joined the Navy at seventeen and married the first girl he ever dated. I could never even get him to try the smallest amount of marijuana, which I thought was admirable. He had four kids by his first wife Pat when they married in Connecticut; today he lives in Georgia with his second wife, also called Pat.

My mother had been dating a Pisces guy named Bob for about two years; in the beginning he seemed like a terrific person. They drank a lot together, and at times he would become very abusive to the dragon lady. One day he threw some boiling hot water at her, which went in the right ear and she lost all hearing on that side permanently. Bob was a changeable person and I didn't know quite how to read him, but most of the time he was good to my mother. It turned out he had a large brain tumor and no one knew that his intense boozing made this pain even more overwhelming to live with.

I arrived home late one night after bumming around town and noticed an ambulance right in front of our building. They were removing Bob's blanketed body from Mom's room; he'd just passed away and I think she felt relieved; Saint Theresa never really wanted to be obligated, controlled or dominated by any man.

My mother had a few little secrets, like when she hid her income tax refund check in the oven so I wouldn't find it, a fact which didn't stay guarded very long. She told my father, who lived around the corner, and he told me. Mom was smart in a way since no one ever used the oven at the time. She knew I wouldn't be baking a pie, but I might ask for money if I thought she had any. To a hardened user, getting a fix comes before anything; I was a very unhappy addict and honestly wanted to quit.

After the shock of Bob's sudden passing, Mom began to attend AA meetings and quit drinking completely. She was saving money and talking about moving to California; one day, she just packed all her belongings, gave me the good stuff and left the rest for neighbors. She would be taking a Greyhound bus one more time to a place she'd never been without even knowing anyone out there. It would be hard for me to live in Marge and Eddy's building without my mother's presence. The two lushes aired their contempt while monitoring my guests and bitched about everyone who passed by.

Things were changing quickly, but my very soothing doctor Conny was always there for me. This compassionate psychiatrist recognized that underneath all my grumbling, I would experience the infinite loss of my mother's presence when she finally moved out to California, he was right. His body was a bit pudgy; he had rather long, dark blonde hair, smoked a pipe and sported a well-groomed beard.

Kathie and I were really finished now and my keen Virgo instinct, told me to quit using heroin at once. She moved back in with her mother Betty, and I promptly got in touch with Dr. Nadeau. He was happy to make the arrangements for my de-tox at Worcester State Hospital, originally known as the 'Bloomingdale Insane Asylum', near Bell Pond.

*****

The colossal stone asylum was a one-mile walk up from the boulevard, positioned on a majestic hill, surrounded by lush green grounds. Nevertheless, this huge place could also be characterized as gothic, dark, morbid, sinister and macabre. Many diabolical filmmakers have profited by framing this eerie locale for spine tingling, sinister backdrops.

My acclaimed doctor was the director of this institution and occupied a lovely home with his family on the same compound. They put me on a ward with some very crazy people, and I thought it was just a big mistake. The regular daytime nurses were all right with me, but through endless, sleepless nights, the evening crew didn't want me to get out of bed and walk around the place at all. A young jock who worked there nights constantly tried to entice a female nurse into fooling around and really despised me because I was hip to his tasteless act. One time we all argued and I gave them some bristly flack, so they forced me to wear a straight jacket for the rest of their shift. Later, I heard them making love. Conny got a full report from me and they were reprimanded, I was clearly his favorite patient but not very well liked by the staff, apparently I seemed more dangerous to them than the real lunatics.

Conny placed me on that specific ward so I could have a certain amount of freedom, otherwise, if he put me in with the regular addicts, I'd have to be locked up for the entire de-tox period. The staff was right to believe he really indulged me. After the morning routine of braving a disgusting breakfast, taking the medications and participating in psycho babble dialogues, I was free to leave my sector and go anywhere on the grounds of the immense hospital property. Soon, I discovered small, empty, padded cells in the basement, strange chamber areas, where eerie sounds echoed and water seeped from the old stone walls. The endlessly long, cold, spooky corridors way down there could channel you from one building to another, but I got lost several times. My first impulse was to peruse for secret places to shoot dope, and after that I'd find a safe niche for making out with the girls who might come to visit me.

When I felt better, they allowed me to have visitors, I worked hard at looking good and my mind was still coherent. The physical craving for heroin had subsided, now they wanted me to take drugs like Stelazine and Thorazine. Those two in particular could actually make a person feel lifeless and like a zombie. The hospital coerced their patients into behaving complaisantly; these pills made people cooperate more readily. While observing some of the sick ones moseying down those long hallways, I noticed they were all doing a dance step called 'The Stelazine Shuffle', or 'The Mellaril Mambo'.

Not me, babe! At first, I honestly took their pills because I wanted to do the right thing, but that strong medicine made me feel totally awful. My body literally stiffened, and I couldn't speak right because my jaws got all locked up. These drugs inhibited my thinking process, but I can only imagine the hindrance to one's sex life, although, that place did seem to have a lot of feeble pregnant women around. I soon began to hide the tablets in my mouth until I could spit them out without a nurse catching me.

The withdrawal process took about thirty days and I needed some company. Thanks to Kathie's outbursts of neurotic jealousy, the names of desirable young females had dwindled in my little black book. There was one person that I could count on to visit me out there, Cheryl Plitnik, with the big hair.

It was a perfect Sunday afternoon when she appeared and I was happy to see a friend. Cheryl was very accommodating to all my whims because she lived for lust, and I could always satisfy her insatiable needs. This wonderfully blasé woman was short, buxom and immature, with a tofu-like body. She wasn't my dream lover, but I adored her shallowness. The Beach Boys were the greatest, coolest and grooviest according to her. We were never on the same page, but she was a very loyal Leo.

My ward was on the third floor of the hospital building, the second story was completely empty because of a major renovation going on and no one ever worked there on Sunday. The layout was about the same as upstairs; only it had some compact private chambers with tiny beds, so you can guess where Cheryl was taken first. I chose a bright, cheery room far from the beaten path; it even had an inside lock on the door. What a lucky little rabbit, I am. We did the deed in unison and did it again with rapture. This rather sex-crazed woman never took a bus; she always arrived and left in a taxi.

I politely escorted my matinee date to the main entrance where cabs made their pickups. Cheryl was all smiles, beaming about our amazing corporeal visit inside a madhouse. That's when I decided it was time to ask her to bring me back some dope on the following Sunday. In her mind, using heroin was pure malarkey, so it wasn't easy to persuade her to go out and cop for me. I gave her enough money for two dime bags and the cab fare. She'd have to call Rachael to get the drugs and some new works to shoot up with. In a curious way, Cheryl enjoyed getting acquainted with these underworld characters.

Back at the New Yorker bar and grill, Cheryl bumped into Kathie after her Sunday visit with me. Metaphorically, Ms. Plitnik didn't hesitate to mash the toes of her stiletto shoes into Ms. O'Malley's face. They never really liked each other so Cheryl made it public knowledge that I was doing well and looked great. Kathie walked out of the place fast when Cheryl commented that I had never performed better sexually. The two blazing barfly femmes did have a few things in common; they were short, cute, and rounded, with soft bodies, their mannerisms seemed a bit tough, but they both loved me.

Throughout my brief stay at the stone castle, I didn't participate in basket weaving or making potholders. During physical therapy sessions, I simply found a comfortable bright spot to focus on my astrology work. The more I studied planets, the more insight I gained to amaze people with. Conny was impressed when I made a chart for him featuring the seven yearly changes that we all go through. He followed my astrological systems with great comprehension and enjoyed this newfound knowledge. The staff continued to express further petty resentments relating to my influence on him.

I kept my place on Lagrange Street while collecting those monthly SSI checks; Marge and Eddy were ecstatic about my recent recovery. Theresa even called them from L.A. to see how I was doing and was delighted to hear the good news they related. A couple of times, Cheryl went to my quarters to get clothes or some personal items for me. The drunken managers made sure they got a complete report from anyone who came near my door. When a person stops using, it is possible for one to become productive, busy and useful. You may even seem happy, sappy, wappy and grateful to the whole world, however, if you continue to use drugs, you will indeed feel ashamed, dirty, insincere and not worthwhile or vital. A junkie is habitually deceptive, shrewd, and cunning, never relaxed and feels guilty constantly.

Cheryl called Rachael to hook up for the small amount that I asked her to bring me. Our amorous Sunday affair on the hill would be a bit different this week. All I really wanted from her were those two bags of heroin she scored from Capputo, and since Cheryl didn't use, the smack would be all mine.

It always seemed to take a long time for this blonde bimbo to get ready for anything, but eventually she showed up that day riding in a spotless taxi, looking fresh and lovely. I watched her cab drive up the hill rather slowly, when it went all around the lengthy circular road to the huge front entrance of the citadel. As I waited anxiously in a cold sweat, my compulsive craving for dope was still apparent.

Cheryl and a few other women I knew weren't the least bit shy or ashamed of their gayness. She insisted that I kiss her right there in the hospital lobby with all those weekend visitors mulling around. I put off her advances and we headed directly toward our secure room. Even though I was a brazen dyke who could usually pass for a boy, I had deep reservations about improper displays. I hated to see anyone, especially homosexuals, tongue kissing or vulgarly arousing each other in public areas.

We proceeded to the same airy niche on the second floor and I began to stimulate her erogenous zone with a long, passionate, penetrating kiss, then I could reward myself with a strong opiate. She chatted nonchalantly as I got the new gimmicks ready for this highly anticipated fix, and I quivered with excitement. It had been nearly a month since I had used any heroin and vomited the minute I put the bloody needle down. Cheryl was cool about it; I warned her beforehand, even so, watching a lover heave isn't attractive under any circumstances, let alone, at The Worcester State Hospital. Intense heat came over my body as I started to feel comfortably numb. Making love would be futile for me, but I got through it anyway to gratify her. When I am not being genuinely honest, Catholic guilt sets in.

I was near the end of my stay at the hospital, and thank God they never discovered me using; Conny, who was so devout and generous to me, would have been heartbroken. The fact of the matter is, I was still a conniving drug abuser who might be addicted forever, or so I thought at the time. The future didn't concern me very much while I was in there, so I'd probably just go right back to Lagrange Street when I finally got released from the asylum, then continue to see my beautiful shrink once a week. Drugs were probably on my mind more often than guys who constantly obsess on lower body parts.

As I walked down the one-mile hill to a bus stop, I took long quick strides and plenty of deep breaths. Perhaps the institutional food, which put quite a bit weight on me, did some good for my previously emaciated body. Superman could have been a Virgo inasmuch as I felt dynamically strong when I was detoxified and not using any dope; I could almost levitate my body at will, or fly to any place at all. "Why would a person initiate an atrocious heroin habit, after feeling the wonders of being clean, healthier and smarter?" Sadly I admit that question would not be answered for quite a while.

For the first time ever, I enjoyed a bus ride home. It passed restaurants and familiar places, which made me, feel happy to be free. As the coach reached the illustrious Main Street, my nerves became jangled. Should I stop at the New Yorker, maybe a few of my friends would be there.

It was sundown on a Friday afternoon when the driver finally let me off at the front door of the bar, and the very first person I noticed was Kathie O'Malley. She was sitting by herself and conspicuously looked at me all over, smiling with that Irish grin and exposing her cute dimples. I parked my neat leather suitcase brazenly sat down next to her, had a drink and we chatted until the evening people began to show up in their fashionable cruising duds. Lagrange Street was only two blocks away, so we left side by side.

Ever since I can remember, Friday has been a day of jubilation to me. I was born on a Friday and the day belongs to Venus, perhaps that's why I enjoy it. Kathie and I buoyantly hoofed up the street from the bar, not saying a word and felt happy, at least until we walked past Marge and Eddy's place, then suddenly the loud mouth Marge bellowed through the open door, "Welcome back from the funny farm, Carole, but don't ever think of doing any more drugs in this house."

I quickly said, "Hi," and we flew up the stairs to my pad. Those people were beyond contemptible; I really had to move out of there soon.

There was a payphone downstairs in the hall and after our anger with Marge settled down a bit, Kathie tiptoed down and called Rachael to locate a Friday night dope special. Since I had been on 'holiday' at the hospital for a month, there was plenty of money left over from my government check so we could get really loaded. Caputo told Kathie she was totally broke, but if we could lend her enough for a fix that night, she would leave Legs' favorite pistol with us for collateral. The abrasive-voiced, foul-mouthed loony came right over and not very quietly. We gave her plenty of money for a few bags and she left the revolver, which belonged to the wildest man God ever created. I tucked his weapon in the hamper under some dirty clothes, and remarkably, Rachael came right back with the correct amount of smack. That extremely large .45 caliber loaded gun would remain safe with us for a little longer, but not too much.

It was clear to me now that Cheryl and I could never really make it as a couple; we simply enjoyed each other in bed. She wore Charley perfume and loved the Beach Boys' Good Vibrations. I was a definitive Beatles fan and hated all colognes. Kathie resented me having any friends, so without her ever knowing, I wrote a gracious goodbye note to the pleasantly plump Ms. Plitnik after realizing O'Malley would never permit this friendship, and she might be my jealous partner for a while longer.

*****

Kathie and I were sitting around the kitchen table about a week later on Saturday trying to figure out how to get some money for our next fix when all hell broke loose. Legs had just been released from jail and managed to track Rachael down instantly. He pulled up in front of our house with her on the back of his Harley and dragged her all the way up the three-story hallway stairs by the hair. Did you know, more murders occur on Saturday, than any other days of the week and many firearms called Saturday Night Specials are especially used on that day? It's true because Saturn is quick to anger.

She was all bloody and screaming as he dragged her up the steps. "Please give him back his gun." We could hear her every cry from the minute they entered the building and all the other tenants did too. When they finally reached my apartment, he went berserk with Kathie and me, though I tried to explain that Rachael had only borrowed some money to secure a temporary loan and left his gun for collateral. Legs didn't want to hear anything. We gave him back the weapon immediately, but just to make sure we understood that no one should ever mess with him, he punched us all over again. Having his gun was a cardinal sin and afterward he really punished Rachael since she was the one who stole it.

There is no doubt about it; I really have to move now. Marge and Eddy called the cops that day, but fortunately they arrived too late to witness the brawling scenes. Legs disappeared and there were no drugs in our house for the police to find. My whole life seemed hopeless. Consequently, Kathie and I had a serious discussion about entering a free methadone program. We had to find an apartment close by and move out of there as soon as possible.

Legs dumped Rachel permanently, and she seemed helplessly abandoned, nonetheless, she continued to work the streets. But soon Rachael chose to commit suicide with a lethal dose of heroin and died all alone at her parents' affluent country home.

After the ugly encounter with Legs and his evil behavior, we found a furnished apartment the next day. The house was about one block away from our favorite watering hole, The New Yorker, and owned by an old Albanian widowed woman. It was a small but cozy one-bedroom unit decorated with a great deal of heavy floral material; the furniture had all been upholstered with fine European fabrics. Our new landlady, Alma, worked a forty-hour week at the same place as Niki's mother, peeling apples for Tabletalk pies. This homey little nest was to be the start of a fresh, clean, drug-free life for us.

It seems hard to believe now because all my friends here in L.A. are so pure and beautiful, but back then almost everyone we knew was a user except for Walshie, who wisely never tried narcotics. Some of our peers didn't have jobs, own cars, or even have enough to eat. Betty was ecstatic when Kathie and I announced at the office that we were entering a methadone program in Lowell, Massachusetts right away. In the beginning we had to scrounge a few rides to get out there from other addicts who also appreciated this beneficial treatment. Once we completely stopped using dope, our most basic needs would be good transportation and a telephone. Now was really the perfect time for us to evolve.

I can never recall which years certain things happened, somehow I have a mental block for dates, but for sure Kathie and I entered the SHARE inc. methadone program in the spring of 1975. Through the years I managed to keep a few important documents intact which were dated during that year when I got an actual job working with Kathie in her mother's office. Betty created and developed a well-paid position for me. My office title was 'Survey and Assessment Analyst', I'd be counseling people who were already involved with, or trying to get assigned to, a drug-free program. It felt wonderful to be absorbed in a nonphysical, legitimate duty. I could dress nicely, yet look as butch as I pleased.

Our office was called, the Main South Neighborhood Association, and it was on Main Street in Worcester. Twice a month, we cleared a healthy paycheck, and soon we were able to buy a used 1967 Dodge auto, which was a rugged little tank. We went to the SHARE program three times weekly, and my Dart was adequate for the eighty-mile roundtrip to Lowell. We gathered a few regular paying passengers who didn't drive but still needed to go way out there for methadone doses.

We took an older black guy named Wallace with his white girlfriend Debbie, also a woman named Crazy Carol. The salt and pepper pair lived a few blocks away from us, but Carol lived out in the country with her parents.

For a few Valiums, or some extra money, I would drive out to Auburn and pick Carol up, but only when she couldn't get a ride to town on her own. She was the most drugged-out character I ever knew and I don't know how that Pisces beauty got through life in her constantly stupefied condition. Most of the time I couldn't even understand what she was saying; regardless, she was a very pretty female. My disabled passengers all collected SSI and had access to benevolent doctors who didn't mind handing out a lot of free prescriptions of various sleepers and strong tranquilizers for doper tensions.

Junkies are forever scheming. During some of our trips to Lowell my riders came up with a lot of brainless plans to make money. For example, one of them may have had a slight injury from a previous incident, like the time Wallace gave Debbie a black eye. They went right to a supermarket, dropped some cans from the top shelf, and would pretend the cans caused the damage to her face. At the same time, she could fake a back problem or even twist an ankle. That kind of hustle might work with a dumb store manager, but not every time. They even calculated a phony car accident involving me, but I would never invite their type of bad karma if I wanted to continue as a lucky little rabbit.

Kathie and I got Betty's approval to leave the office early on Monday, Wednesday and Fridays, so we could get to Lowell for our miracle medicine. Each time we arrived at the clinic, we were required to give a urine sample. This very small wooden house was originally a single family home and the bathrooms barely had enough room for you to sit down to pee in a cup. Since there wasn't enough space for a nurse to accompany you in that area, most of the urine tests came up clean. If any of the staff became suspicious, they would simply ask you to keep the door open, but they rarely ever did.

Throughout our trips back and forth to SHARE, we discussed various educational issues. One useful topic was learning how a junkie could come up with clear urine analysis, even if they used heroin the day before. A fresh specimen from someone who didn't use could easily be put into your sample bottle while you were locked in the tiny, three-by-three bathroom. Another popular maneuver to distort that test was to carry some vinegar in a small vile, then discreetly pour a few drops into the pee cup.

At the time, methadone came in the form of a large, orange, square-shaped pill and these precious drugs were called biscuits. They started us off with huge doses, but after a while they began to slowly decrease the amount until we were at zero milligrams. The objective of this program was to help clients become totally drug-free, painlessly. Kathie and I initially were very sincere about not using ever again.

Jackie Lloyd was a cute little married gal and the supervising director; she lived in the fabulous town of Rockport, Massachusetts with her husband. Somehow, I was lucky enough to have her as my personal counselor. She was very easy to talk to and I had a big crush on her, but never made a pass. For the limited amount of time we spent together, I literally poured my heart out and she always understood.

We earned our wages squarely, owned a car, paid the rent on time and finally got a telephone, which began a fresh dialogue between my mother and me, since she moved to California and become sober. It was a pleasure to speak with Mom and likewise for her because I was free of the heroin addiction. My job was exactly what the title implied: 'Survey Assessment Analyst'. Experiences from my past dependence and having the awareness to profile addicts were my only credentials. I wasn't academically minded, and never had a certificate or diploma regarding a formal education, though I genuinely understood people.

The survey aspect of my job meant going out into the streets and interviewing addicts who needed information concerning government assistance; they all had dilemmas. One place to canvass such unfortunates was right outside the Chandler Street drug and mental treatment building. Cliques of desperate-looking characters hung around there, a few of them knew me from junkie haunts and were familiar with me by sight. After cultivating comfortable rapports, I'd ask if they were presently receiving any benefits. Many of these ill-fated folks were really paranoid about going to large agencies like welfare or Social Security offices, and to survive they stole or hustled, much more than someone receiving monthly checks and food stamps. The lucky ones who passed my litmus tests for honesty were happy to arrive at our ticky-tacky office to fill out the proper forms for countless advantages.

Assessing my new acquaintances was the complicated part; they all lied a lot, so intuition was my only guide to determine who deserved free federal money or any other commodities. My unwritten contract demanded an earnest pledge from my clients to go directly into a program and quit drugs. Most were sick to death of their lives and sincerely longed for hope, but a few cretins assumed they could get one over on me; they were very wrong. If they scratched an itch, or let their eyes drop, I noticed.

I smiled with gratitude because of my new and ethical occupation. The average client was analyzed on paper first to find immediate solutions for their needs, and later addressed at center meetings among the entire staff. We put people in touch with the right agencies and met with them as much as possible so they would stay occupied with things to think about. If they were with me, they weren't high. Medical care and food stamps were necessities, but they also had other problems. Perhaps someone missed an appointment to see a probation officer, neglected a court date, or had pending warrants on them; my function was to clear up some of these matters. I strived to rehabilitate a handful of troubled folks with kindness, which was fulfilling, as long as they stayed clean and were above reproach with me.

My client list was growing fast and people were coming in right off the street to see me, apparently, they were told that I was fair, and that any issues we discussed would be kept strictly confidential. I was only trying to be a professional counselor, but some newcomers thought of me as a priest, except a few rogues registered at the office resented my current authority and hated that I was really clean.

Typing wasn't my forte; I did a lot of corresponding with judges, lawyers, probation officers, courts, doctors and welfare agencies. Ms. O'Malley learned to speed type while attending reform school and fortunately, after a hand-drafted letter of importance, she would type it out neatly and expertly. One of my younger clients, named Beth Mann, was in deep trouble with the courts because of one excuse after another. It's too bad I liked her so much; I frequently went to bat for Beth then finally had to drop her. I felt awful about this termination, yet I couldn't let her petty, little criminal mind jeopardize my primary career with deceptions. There is a fervent need in me to be honest whenever I felt badly about something, I would inevitably call Walshie, and we'd go to church just to sit and quietly pray.

Church has always been a place of comfort and strength for me. When I was a little kid living in Bridgeport, I attended Sunday services with every denomination within walking distance of our crestfallen house. The Berean Church held a bible study at ten a.m., after the lessons, they served up a nice lunch, but before that I had to go to Mass at nine a.m. If they claimed you when you were young and vulnerable, the Catholic religion would be a hard habit to break. A person has to withstand many rhetorical prayers and say the whole rosary when in despair. Walshie and I shared everything, we felt the same about going to church; she was just as hooked as me. After growing up, we continued to honor the Catholic Church; no one there ever recognized me wearing shades and a babushka on my head.

Not having much to do and being a curious kid, I would walk around a lot to get familiar with our neighborhood wherever we happened to be located at the time. This was the phase when Pete kept Mom in bed all day with a huge bottle of cheap wine next to her. One beautiful Sunday afternoon, I approached a very boisterous and obscure storefront, on a crummy street in Bridgeport; it was a Holy Roller Church. The windows were painted black but the door was slightly ajar, so I was able to sneak a peek inside. There were about forty African-Americans sitting around attentively on folding chairs.

A wide passage through the middle of a small room exposed a

young animated minister. Lively music was being played on the piano and someone shook a mean tambourine. I was beguiled with this bizarre ambience, when amidst all the singing and frenzy a heavyset woman suddenly came rolling down the aisle on her knees crying and everybody exclaimed, "Hallelujah, praise God." This was her confession; the hysterical woman was admitting she slept with her own brother the night before. Maybe divulging things to a priest in a dark confession box through a screened window should become obsolete.

The despair I was beginning to feel couldn't be healed by saying the rosary. We had become too busy and too serious behind all this Main South Neighborhood outreach work, Kathie and I began grumbling at each other and there wasn't enough time left to carouse at the bar. Between regular trips to the SHARE clinic and a growing client list, we were wearing down. I was required to attend many community meetings with cops inasmuch as I was now an esteemed member of every drug advisory board within the City Council assembly district, but ironically I still relied on methadone.

A notable satire concerning my job began at local meetings with a cop named Joseph Tracimowicz, more commonly known as 'Joe Track'. This big, heavy, pockmarked, red-faced Polish dick admired every word that I conveyed at those meetings and genuinely liked me, but I couldn't say the same about him. Joe was now a police captain; previously, he was my father's consummate nemesis. Dad was always attracted to sleazy bars, looking for women of any sexual preference; he'd even been chummy with a few lesbians. Joe was a beat cop then and occasionally checked the place my father frequented called Coney Island. Half of this huge hangout was a restaurant, famous for their tasty chilidogs; the other section where dad parked me was a smelly barroom with shabby booths and a sawdust floor.

My father (Earl Johnson) was a scrapper; it didn't matter if his fight was with a man or woman. He got into an argument once with a big butch gal named Ruth Pointer, so she cracked him over the head with a thick beer bottle, and he had a scar for life. At that exact moment, Joe Track walked in off the street and stopped their fight. From then on, he would be relentless in his pursuit to arrest my dad for any reason at all and would find plenty of grounds later. Sitting next to this tough cop at City Hall made me grin, he appreciated me as Carole Markarian, yet he had no idea I was Earl Johnson's little daughter.

Judge Morris N. Gould was a man I had great respect for because he was honest and really listened. A few of my law-breaking clients went before him with me being present to back up their tales of speedy recoveries. A shady character named Beth was trying her best to get over on his honor, but he looked at me for a heads up, and I was candid with him; she was still hooked. To this day, whenever I have to go into a government building, I get nervous; I developed a phobia about going to courthouses, which cause panic attacks, perhaps because I spent a lot of depressing hours in those cruel chambers.

Frank G. Rourke was the probation officer for almost everyone registered with our office. I thought he was too lenient, but I never questioned his kindly decisions because it was possible that I myself might need a benevolent friend of the court one day.

One important person who didn't attend many meetings was John J. Hanlon, the chief of police. Whenever he missed these conferences, he would attain regular reports on my recent good deeds through Joe Track. He would send memos to our office proclaiming his gratitude for my work toward a cleaner city, and that was what my job was all about. It amazes me that I actually saved much of that correspondence. I discovered several letters from the SHARE center and notes from distinguished people that I worked with during the seventies.

They say morality can cheat you out of life; Kathie was gradually coming to that conclusion. She threw a few subtle hints about getting off once in a while over the weekend but got no response from me. My whole life flashed before my eyes as I reflected on how far we'd come in such a short time. After all the lectures given and promises made, I didn't want to become an absolute hypocrite. It was a white-knuckle hold out, but I ignored all her rational arguments at the time and abstained from using. I came home from work early one day and there she was with her brother Mike putting a needle in her arm. My mind became confused and I felt fragile. I ran from our apartment, jumped into my car and headed straight for the bar to call Walshie.

My dependable buddy drove over at once in her yellow Nissan. She learned to drive much later than I did, but she didn't steal cars to teach herself, instead, she went to a legal driving school for lessons. Mary always did things by the book unless you count the times we got drunk when we were way too young and her father caught us. Walshie was my dearest friend and stood about one inch taller than I, with huge round, expressive flashing brown eyes and extra long thick lashes. Her mother, Margaret, was Assyrian and her dad, Patty, came from Irish ancestry. She was great fun to be with and expressed childlike feelings through those laughing eyes, I positively loved her.

"Kathie is using smack again with her brother Mike and I fear this is the beginning of the end for us."

Walshie had a beer, listened to more of my self-doom theories and as usual said: "Let's go to church."

That simply wouldn't work for this huge defeat. "I'm scared about everything now. I'm scared to use again, I'm scared of losing the finest job I ever had, and I'm scared to be alone." It was common knowledge in this town that Kathie could probably beat the hell out of anybody, so if I said I was leaving her after nearly seven years, there would be an awesome fight and she could be vindictive.

We didn't go to church, but we did get smashed. That night, I stayed over Walshie and Cassie's place, it was beautiful, they seemed so balanced and really cared about each other. Now I had to plan a future course. "Will Kathie continue to use drugs or will I get foolish and become tempted again? What about us working together, and how do I face Betty Rose? Think of how unpleasant it will be driving out to Lowell with her for our methadone. What should I do, my friends?"

They responded: "You must do the right thing, Pi Wi, leave her right away, move in with us temporarily and never use heroin again."

I went back to my place the next day to pick up a few clothes and lucky for me, Kathie wasn't there. Through my clear eyes, I flashed on the kitchen table and there were still a few drops of blood along the Formica, probably from her last fix. Just seeing it made me feel both angry and excited. I hurried to leave before she returned, after glancing at that odious scene, I gladly returned to Walshie's.

Crying in any chapel was a weakness of mine which I can't

explain, maybe it was because I usually went to worship with a guilty conscience and that's why I broke down. Walshie insisted we go to confession that day so we could receive communion on Sunday. I'm not good at admitting my sins but quite skilled at atonement, so we went. The Sacred Heart Church reminded us of my cousin Patsy.

Mamie was a Virgo, Mom's youngest sister and my favorite aunt. She had three children with her second husband, big Uncle Pete Kilmonis. He was a dedicated Navy guy, very tall, towering over Mamie and seemed deeply in love with her. Patsy was the oldest child, went to college for a while. Soon she joined the convent. Peter enlisted in the Navy, married a sweet girl named Louise and they are currently retired in the small town of Auburn. Mary Anne, the youngest, became a charming nurse, married a rich doctor and that's all I know about her. She was kind of an uppity kid, totally spoiled by Uncle Pete. Mamie was tough on her kids and firm with my brother and me whenever we visited.

During my freshman year in high school, I lived on Pakachoag Street and shared a bed with Nana. Patsy walked across the street almost every night to study and do homework in our quiet bedroom. I would play classical music and even coach with her lessons. We got along fine, but studying came quite hard to her. In the second semester, she broke out with a bad case of shingles and became extremely sick.

It is a glorified honor for a Catholic family to have a priest for a son, or a daughter who is a nun. When Patsy was ultimately accepted by a convent, all the relatives felt proud and blessed. She tried to get into many different orders but some had strict rules about divorce. Mamie had been married once before Uncle Pete and certain hierarchies rejected Patsy for that very reason. The Maryknoll alliance of nuns agreed to accept her, so she packed up immediately and moved into a local seminary for sisters.

Walshie and I used to visit her when we could, but I always got depressed afterwards. She revealed to us how hard novices worked. The white habits they wore were laundered by hand with strong soap until they sparkled, then carefully dipped in starch many times. After gently drying, the habits had to be ironed in a certain way. What a total drag. Patsy lived at the convent for nearly five years; however, just before taking her final vows, she had an epiphany about bearing children. To the disappointment of the whole family, she left the cloister and married the boy next door, Chuck Jackman. They found out very early in their marriage that Patsy couldn't ever give birth so they promptly adopted two toddlers.

This was a Monday I shuddered to face. I was generally at the office by nine, but went in a little late that day; Kathie wasn't there yet. Anxiety was setting in, my nerves were shot and I had no idea, what to say to Betty, if and when she arrived. I sat at my desk in the back of the room and made detailed lists of things do before moving out of our place. The car was definitely mine, Kathie didn't drive anyway and the furniture belonged to Alma, so all I needed to pack were my clothes. I could stay at Walshie's for a while, but I really needed to have a personal space. Betty took that day off and Kathie strolled in buoyantly about noon, looking as cocky as ever. She boldly sat at her desk in front, wafting those cute Irish smiles my way and finally came over to ask me if I would join her next door for a coffee.

We went to the coffee shop and ordered something light. Kathie's eyes were obviously pinned, indicating that she had already fixed. The meal ended before we ever commented on our issues, I felt so angry inside because she had used heroin with her crazy brother Mike. After all our courageous struggles to get clean, we would have disappointed countless people, starting with Jackie Lloyd, the SHARE program, agency workers and all my own clients who really believed in us. The Main South office employed about thirty people who were starting new lives and they all had different motives. Some were victims of crimes and others were formerly criminals. Betty Rose had a big heart.

When we finally got around to discussing her indiscretion, she said it was all Mike's fault. He came into a cash bonanza by some kind of fluke and was moving to New York City in a hurry. For her help with past favors, he gifted Kathie with a large pile of dope before leaving; he wouldn't be coming back any time soon. No one knew what he did, or how this newly acquired fortune was gained, but a stable Virgo guy like him doesn't just pack it up without good reason. Mike's business didn't interest me; I only cared to know whether Kathie planned to continue using, or if that was only a weekend slip. She paid for our lunch. She begged me to drive her home, so off we went and there we stayed.

My conscience stopped bothering me from the moment we entered the house. Kathie kissed me at once with such passion I became totally intoxicated. Next, she took out some works and a plastic bag loaded with smack, I forgot about the job and my clients, I just had to get off without delay. She gave me the first shot; I was nervous, but after the crude vomiting stopped, I became very high and we made delirious, erotic love all day long. How lucky we were, Betty had the flu and we didn't see her all week. The potent smack which brother dearest left might only last a short while so what would we do?

We stayed blissed, or high, for about a week and it doesn't take much using to get hooked all over again. What a shame, after all the breakthroughs we made. I couldn't look anyone straight in the eye and felt constant guilt since we relapsed into our miserable habits. Kathie and I were back to the same ugly arguments from the past, and she became really unattractive to me. I called my mother in California a couple of times a week, which accelerated my interest to join her. It was all good timing; the SHARE program took me back, but O'Malley wouldn't swallow her pride to go out there ever again.

That was the frigid winter of 1975 and we were finally ending our reckless seven-year relationship. I barely endured work at the office but stayed on methadone and never used heroin with Kathie again. As tensions built, Mom was genuinely influencing my decision to move out to sunny L.A.

One cold day after a big snowstorm, Kathie and I were fighting violently in the apartment and dragged this battle outside to the street. I can't remember the dialogue, but she just kept screaming at me, so I jumped in my old Dodge to leave, but she continued yelling vulgar insults. Jockeying my car out of the snow was hard because she stood there arrogantly, causing a scandalous scene. I shoved the gear into reverse, when she still refused to move out of the way, I gunned it and bulldozed her into a deep snow bank.

This cold invincible woman sobbed for my help, so I pulled her out of the frozen drift. She was bleeding from her head and hands. Devoid of words, I forced her into the car and drove up to the back door of the city hospital emergency room. Apologies weren't necessary, we knew this was the end and said goodbye forever.

My well-kept car would be easy to sell; now all I had to do was call Mom to say when I would be arriving at LAX. My councilor arranged for me to enter an interim L.A. methadone program and I would be eligible to collect unemployment for a while. "California here I come."

Carole,
A Lucky Little Rabbit

Part Three

"Don't try keeping up with the Jones family. You are the Joneses. Simply maintain a clear mind, and generous heart. When greed vanishes from real estate, and there is goodness in everyone's soul, world peace is a possibility."

When it was finally over with Kathie, I appreciated the end of our destructive behavior. I sold my car without delay, then I bought a ticket to Los Angeles, the sun went into the Aries sign as I was paying for my airfare, ending a cold, unpleasant winter period, bringing in a fresh spring season, which would be filled with big adjustments and inevitable challenges. I felt some anxieties about going to an unfamiliar methadone clinic, making new friends, finding a good job and was greatly concerned about the type of neighborhood I would first be living in.

My jangled nerves would be fine since smoking was permitted on planes then. The flight to L.A. on American Airlines went smoothly; I relaxed through the long trip thanks to several Vodka tonics and a few Marlboro cigarettes. No one on this jet seemed very sociable so I drifted into the reflections of my childhood when life seemed simple to Walshie and me, we trusted our families, walked with our Guardian Angels and depended on all the saints. Mary always said, "Pi Wi, if you stuck your hand in a bucket of shit, you would come up with a handful of diamonds." Luck is timing and opportunity, nonetheless, I think my spiritual awareness also kept me protected and blessed.

Mom gave Eddy Martinez, the building manager, some money for gas to pick me up at LAX, they were both standing there when

I stumbled down the ramp. My condition was grounds for a fight, whereas she was now a sober member AA. I arrived conspicuously drunk but snapped out of it fast when I saw the disappointment in her face. Perhaps this meant that I could never drink booze in her presence again.

As we headed toward downtown, there wasn't much to see, but the closer we got to her house, the essence of Mexican food wafted through my head. There were many taco stands which reeked of refried beans, chilies and cilantro, the aromas seemed alien to me.

I really wanted to ask Eddy, who was a nice guy, if he wouldn't mind stopping at a liquor store so I could pick up a night cap, but when I realized how angry that might make my mother, I dismissed the thought right away. This place was a different world to me and Mom was a different person now.

Her apartment was located close to downtown in a rundown Latino area which had an enormous Mexican population. Los Angeles seemed like a foreign country and I was not at all familiar with the language. I couldn't communicate very well with these uptight locals because to this day I still don't know enough Spanish to connect one basic sentence. Later on, I found out that many of these really poor people were illegal aliens from somewhere and lived in fear of the INS every single day.

Mom's apartment house was on Union Avenue, close to 6th Street, just a couple of blocks south of MacArthur Park. It was a well-kept, narrow, two-story stucco building, with twenty small, one-bedroom units. She assumed I would be sleeping in the bed with her, but I really preferred the couch in case I ever came home with liquor on my breath, which she always noticed. This was indeed my second trip to L.A. and once again, the weather stayed overcast for quite a while, frustrating the sun lover in me.

I went right out to survey my new surroundings. To say this location was a colorful place would be an understatement. Brightly painted carnicerías, zapaterías and botánicas were businesses I don't remember seeing in Worcester, although Miami had its own fascinating similarities.

RTD, the bus system, sold little city guidebooks to help visitors find their way around this sprawling town, so I studied one. My first bus ride was way out to East L.A., past the County Hospital. The busy methadone clinic was on Macy Street and most of the clients were Latinos.

Not one person on the whole staff was the least bit friendly, they seemed hostile when handing out the doses of methadone, but I didn't feel bad about their superior California attitudes. After going out there a few times, I befriended a wonderful Chicano guy named Victor who welcomed me; I was beginning to think that everyone in this town was a total snob. Our common denominator was heroin, which is how we became instant friends and basically the only topic we ever discussed.

Victor lived down the road from the clinic in the town of El Monte. He was medium height, very thin, with long, straight, blue-black hair and could have played the lead role in Viva Zapata. His tattooed macho image was just a façade, besides heroin, his other passion was growing incredibly strong marijuana and he amazed me with his skill for grafting unusual plants. After we became friends at the clinic, he invited me to his place to see this amazing work, so I took a bus to El Monte. It was a courtyard apartment complex and behind his tiny place there were grass plants thicker and richer than I have ever seen. We sat on a bench, drank some cheap red wine and admired these creations.

My next long RTD ride was the excursion to the unemployment office; fortunately, I could collect checks for next six months. The agency was in Hollywood, a community very different from the eclectic Westlake district, or East L.A. There seemed to be far more Anglo people in that area with a smattering of gay ones who inspired me to look at the whole metropolis, especially the beaches. Perhaps now it was time to shop for a good car and Mom could help me to finance one. To soften her up for buying a car, I reminisced about the good old days. "Remember all the Saturday nights when Nana played the radio? From seven to eight, a priest recited the rosary, then for the next hour they played authentic Irish music, she drank a glass of beer, danced the jig and was very happy."

Mom had a regular routine of attending daytime AA meetings throughout the city. Whenever she smelled booze on my breath, she would hint that I should go with her to one of these gatherings, so I joined Mom a couple of times but couldn't wait to go out for a drink afterwards. It was unthinkable; there was no way I would ever get up in front of a group of strangers to say: "Hi, my name is

Carole, blah, blah, blah." Most of these meetings were held in the sleaziest places, filled with unattractive, dreary characters. We went to visit a friend of Mom's once at a crummy looking halfway house, and the environment depressed me for days. Mom believed strongly in the Reverend Billy Graham and all his propaganda but never really strayed from the Catholic Church and seldom missed a Sunday mass.

Victor and I had a couple of things in common; we both received checks in the mail and always wanted to stay high. The methadone clinic didn't take one urine sample from me for the first month, which I thought was careless but fine with me. On his payday, my faithful amigo scored two balloons of heroin, a.k.a. Mexican mud, so we went to his place in El Monte and shot up immediately. It was the first time I ever saw dope packaged in a balloon, but since I hadn't used for a while, I was a little apprehensive. The stuff was terrible; I didn't even throw up, I assumed this is what he was used to and thought it was okay. When he sensed my letdown, he admitted it wasn't close to China white.

While riding on a bus down Sunset, I had to chuckle about my first trip to California with Joyce Huey. The television show called *77 Sunset Strip* was popular at the time, so Joyce and I decided to find that famous place. We drove the entire length of the boulevard, until we reached number 77. It turned out to be an old abandoned taco stand which was falling to the ground. Nowadays, I'm hip to Hollywood illusions but back then, we were disappointed because we didn't get to see Kooky, or his comb.

My mother enjoyed a few good friends; Dorothy was an older dyke and lived with her longtime lover Bertha, a tiny Mexican woman. They had occupied an apartment in the same building for many years. Mom also had some gay men for chums; one guy named Bob was a Virgo accountant, his black Libra soul mate, Joe, was a former monk and worked as a great chef. This group frequently played cards together, but I could hardly stand their pastime. Bob would become very angry if he lost at poker, but so did my mother, the dragon lady. Another player connected to this clique was Richard Coyne, a gay schoolteacher and ex-priest. The Catholic Church is presently involved investigating many sexual abuse cases and homosexual activities within the clergy. After listening to these grown men, I concluded that they all liked being with young boys, which has always bothered me, but how dare I judge them. Who would choose to be a man of the cloth today, cognizant of those degrading stigmas?

Years ago, when I told the family that I was gay, Mom went into a rage. She ripped a necklace from my throat because she thought it was some kind of lesbian symbol, but it wasn't. For a person who hated gays earlier, she'd collected plenty of homosexual pals at this time. I honestly didn't have any feelings for this bunch, yet they were very kind to my mother and I will always be grateful for their constant friendship to her. She was difficult at times, but Mom was basically a good person, quite religious and worked hard at the busy Woolworth's lunch counter on Wilshire Boulevard.

I found my way around L.A. on the RTD rather well, but learned that one does not hitchhike because this town was full of weirdoes. We often bummed free rides in Boston, it was different here, people drive Mercedes instead of Volkswagens and motorists aren't meek college professors, they are movie producers or television big shots; everyone seems to say: "Have a nice day."

Neither Victor nor I had a girlfriend, so we spent a lot of time together. He was the only person who I could actually communicate with, since my mother's friends bored me with their mindless small talk and useless information. I was open and honest about my preferences but this never bothered him. My Pisces pal was a man of few words and mumbled when he spoke. He kept a lush, gracious garden, which was perfectly groomed, healthy and extraordinary. My companion was passionately into nature, which indicated to me that he was very close to God, right in his own backyard.

Usually when I went to visit him, I would always take the bus home before dark, but one afternoon he asked me to stick around until sunset to see something fantastic. I agreed to hang out for a while and just before twilight, we went outside to the courtyard; I could not believe my eyes. Victor pointed toward the towering palm trees, and there sat countless numbers of huge white owls perched on every limb. I had never seen a white owl; it was an absolutely awesome and supernatural sight.

We did a couple more balloons of that Mexican garbage, but I decided it frustrated me too much; the stuff never got me high enough like the East Coast China white dope, so I quit using. Perhaps my focus should have been on getting a car, then an apartment, Victor and I would remain friends for a long time.

Mom figured out that I was getting really bored with my routine and suggested we shop around for an affordable auto, which was nearly as exciting as when she took me to Sears for my first bicycle. I saved some money from unemployment checks and she offered to kick in a couple of hundred more, so I found my way to some used car lots on Western Avenue, then purchased a compact blue, Ford Fairlane. It looked very clean and was in good mechanical condition, now I could drive out to Malibu every day. It was a huge mistake taking my mother to the beach because she hated the sun.

Mom used to be much more fun when she drank, but now I practically had to stand on my head to please her. She hated the beach; it was too sunny, and she didn't like the movies because the sound was too loud. My mother was a dragon lady and I am a peaceful little rabbit, how could we ever get along? I must admit that she was really needed throughout my nomadic life, but now I had to have my own place, though it might be hard to find something suitable being an obvious gay.

When the right time came to look for my own niche, I drove around town quite a bit to get a feel for each area. The nicer places I wanted to live in were too expensive, or the almighty building manager had some kind of prejudice; straight landlords preferred renting to straights. Somehow, I ended up renting a decent place in the Mar Vista district; my new apartment was on the ground floor and resembled a motel. The price was right and it had a large swimming pool, which I used every day. Each night, I noticed young people gathered at the pool playing sweet guitar music. Most of this structure was occupied by Filipinos who were always welcoming and gifting me with exotic foods.

Many folks there were related and all seemed to be happy; one of the guys played the song *Feelings* so many times each evening I actually got to hate that tune; perhaps it was the only music he knew. A pretty nurse named Mary was becoming overly affectionate with me; I wasn't sure how to read her intentions. We became friends and shared a lot Rosé wine together, then sat around the pool, eating dainty treats.

One balmy night, Mary was feeding me by hand, when she began to breathe hard into my ear, instinctively, I decided to kiss her, then she screamed loudly: **"I am not gay."**

All I could say was: "Oh my God." This was the first time I'd made a pass at a straight woman and got totally rejected; yet she sent out the very same signals as all the other heterosexual women I'd turned on.

Mary was a delightful girl, around twenty-five and I was in my mid thirties, I never felt guilt about ages, since I really wasn't a leche, I only liked her. She was constantly touching me, even if it was just a shoulder massage, she fluffed my hair, adjusted my collars and let me assume she was coming on, yet alleged that she wasn't. She toyed with me in a perfect lesbian genre, but evidently a strain of inner denial must have inhibited her before our first kiss. I will never hit on a straight woman again.

When I moved from Union Avenue, I was required to change methadone clinics and receive my doses from the West L.A. branch. This meant I wouldn't be with Victor very much, but now I could actually drive to El Monte to see those beautiful white owls again. I promptly became friends with a straight couple named Cathy and John when I started at this new clinic. Many drug deals went down right in the front window of the dispensary; there seemed to be no such person as a real ex-addict. The Midwestern twosome became a huge source of street narcotics; pills, pot, coke, smack, you name it and they sold it. My first buy was very large stash of assorted downers, besides a small bag of weed.

The moment Mary screamed on that awful night, I bolted into my apartment to swig down some more wine. I was so ashamed and embarrassed, how could I ever live this scandal down? Every person in the place knew everyone else, or they were related, and most of them worked in hospitals. If ever I needed medical attention, or had to go to an ER, God forbid, I'd probably bump into someone from her family. I genuinely believed she wanted to have a romantic episode with me; nevertheless, there was only one escape from my shameful personal error. I dressed completely in white, drove to the liquor store before closing, bought a pint of top-shelf brandy, went home, swallowed sixty Seconal, in addition to Ninbutal and sipped cognac while relaxing at the edge of the pool until I fell in.

The pool was in the rear of the building, I don't know how long I'd been submerged there, but sometime during the night, a kindly old neighborhood gentleman observed me floating and pulled me out. He woke the manager who had my mother's number. After phoning the paramedics, she called Mom at once. They would be taking me over to the UCLA Hospital emergency room.

She took a taxi way out there, arrived at the crisis center and looked on the blackboard relating to incoming patients, a thick line had been drawn through my name, so she asked the nurse what happened and was told that I had been pronounced clinically dead, but they were still trying everything possible to revive me. Saint Theresa sat on a hard bench for many hours repeating the entire Rosary. Finally, they told her I had awakened and she believed this miracle came from the Blessed Mother; nevertheless, I'm sorry I didn't appreciate her prayers but I did go to heaven for a while.

Every inch of me ached all over when I finally woke up, they had to pump my stomach for a long time, which made me think that I was punched by Muhammad Ali, and the awful chest pains came from those electric paddles. The worst part was not getting my regular dose of methadone on time. I never felt sicker; I failed to escape from my miserable life, which is, a mortal sin and a coward's way out.

The room was really sunny when a big strapping, female doctor with a thick German accent came in and sat down on my bed. She said: "I'm the person who saved your life."

My voice was very weak, but I managed to whisper to her, "What for? How soon can I get my methadone, Doc?" I was sure that this suicide attempt was absolutely fail proof and would have ended all my despair, only Mom believed her numerous prayers to the Virgin Mary forbad me to give up on life just then.

I didn't really have much stuff at the Mar Vista apartment, so Mom asked Bob and Joe to move all my things back to her place. I'd only been living in L.A. for about six months but my unemployment checks were running out. When I went back to my mother's, I knew I couldn't bear to live with her again, or even think about finding a job here. The experience with Mary left me so humiliated, I decided to sell my car and go back east, just in time for winter. One of the great things about this country is that if some crazy or distraught person attempts suicide, they routinely become recipients of SSI because foolish actions like that confirm they are genuinely psychotic; God bless America.

A hoodlum type guy named Leo was also a client at the West L.A. clinic and was permanently confined to a wheelchair. He had been shot by the cops during a botched robbery, became crippled for life and received lots of money from the city; he always carried plenty of cash and heroin. One morning at the infirmary, I announced that I was selling my car to pay for my plane fare home. Leo offered to buy my well-kept Ford right away but couldn't drive, so he hired a junkie bodyguard right on the spot to chauffeur him around town. He insisted on paying me more money than it was really worth.

*****

On the first day of November, all my official paperwork was in order for the trip back east. An American Airlines flight would jet me from L.A. to Boston. I would then catch a local bus into Worcester to brave the coldest winter ever. At the bus station, I got a cab and asked the driver to cruise around the main streets; I was hoping to see a familiar face. Sure enough, my old pal Shorty George was standing in front of a dark bar and seemed happy to see me. I told him I needed a place to stay temporarily, so he jumped in the taxi and took me to his rooming house around the corner. The tiny place had a single bed, bath, good heat, a community kitchen and the rent was very cheap.

I would be receiving my methadone doses at the Chandler Street clinic, which, luckily, was very close to where I roomed. The people there were familiar with me since I'd worked at the Main South office and I knew the junkies from the staff. I believed it was a permanent arrangement because no one ever mentioned discontinuing this marvelous, legal, and free addiction. The procedure there was easy, all I had to do was pick up my prescriptions three times a week and see a counselor twice a month. When I did use heroin in between, I could always fake the urine test thanks to my former Lowell passengers, Wallace and Debbie, who were also picking up their methadone at Chandler.

Shorty George did some pimping and sold small amounts of smack. He was a very short black man with an extremely loud, high-pitched voice which intimidated most people. A regular character that appeared on the Miami Vice Show during the eighties was called 'Nougy', or the 'Noug man'; he could easily have been Shorty's twin brother. Their facial expressions consisted of squinting as though in pain and both showed their teeth like growling dogs when they were aggravated. Mr. George went berserk if someone owed him any money. His narcotics were very low quality, but once in a while he would front me a bag; it wasn't the greatest high but getting drugs on credit was still a luxury.

It was Christmas time in 1976. I took long brisk walks in the snow to escape the confinement of the rooming house, and it snowed a lot that year. I felt especially lonely whenever I passed by a warm-looking, well-decorated residence. Would I ever have a home of my own instead of a twelve-by-twelve rented chamber? The fresh polar air seemed to clear my head because I realized only then that I was controlled by and totally married to dope; it was absolutely time for a change. My life had become a huge waste; I sincerely wanted a stable address, a good partner and my own Christmas tree to decorate.

I thought of myself as rather a smart user, but I didn't know what a stupid human being I was. Ask any junkie why they use and you will learn that dopers plainly enjoy the high because of its likeness to death. There is no balance; the bad things inevitably outweigh the good. The pain of an addict is endless and personal sacrifices are beyond measure. Twice I became infected with hepatitis, everyone shared their needles then, fortunately, AIDS hadn't arrived yet. Emergency rooms were accessible 24/7 to lance my abscessed arms and ankles. In addition to this damning lifestyle, there were the sins of lying, cheating, stealing, prostituting and even petty shoplifting. If a junky is determined enough to get off, they will shoot up in urinated hallways, rooftops, or maybe even an empty elevator. Besides regular vomiting, another persistent malady is constipation, which means that your finger must be applied at times to remove rocks of feces down through the rectum. Shall I continue the list of pathos?

My councilor's name was Kathleen, a pretty woman whom I felt very comfortable speaking with; I could tell the truth about anything and she really understood. Whenever discussing her favorite brother, who lived in California, she beamed and depicted artistic images of how green it was all year round, unlike the constant gray complexion of Worcester in wintertime. The more she glorified The Golden State, the more I hoped to return. It was a huge mistake for me to go back east that year.

I decided to return to L.A. for a third time; this might be the charm. My plan was to fly from Logan on April 1st, then move in with Mom briefly. Kathleen agreed to get my paperwork in order so I could register at another program out there, but she ran into an unexpected snag. The State of California was getting strict with longtime recipients of free methadone and every clinic that she contacted said the same thing, the only way I could get any more was if I went to an expensive, private clinic.

The costly, but discreet, infirmaries catered to movie and television people, or anyone else who could pay two thousand dollars a month. If I had that kind of money, I would simply buy the best heroin. I was still receiving a hundred and sixty milligrams daily, which was the maximum dosage, the same amount given to enormous people. If I really wanted to go back to L.A. badly enough, I would have to reduce my dosage to practically zero. There were two months left to lower my intake, which seemed impossible to accomplish by April 1st. Kathleen worked very hard with the organizations out west, so they agreed to keep me at a small dose, but only for the first two weeks after my arrival.

If I had to recall the worst period of my entire life, it would have been those last six months in Worcester. Not having a car kept me staring a lot at a black and white television, and I very seldom left my closet-sized room. Once in a while, I'd bundle up in my pea coat from the army and navy store, and hoof down a few icy, slippery blocks to the New Yorker just to be with a few gay friends. Kathie O'Malley always seemed to be there, but nowadays she had a new lover called Star. The tough little young butch reminded me of myself in earlier days, I was a legend of sorts, and this probably intimidated her. As usual, Kathie was stirring up trouble by trying to make me angry. She'd yell ugly, negative, belittling remarks from way across the room. "Why did you leave California? Did you miss the common people?" I never wanted to see her again, and never did once the spring came.

It was almost April 1st. Forty milligrams of methadone a day is what I got down to, but that's still a lot to completely withdraw from. My craving for heroin became more intense as the dosage was lowered, but I didn't even consider buying a dime bag from Shorty because I needed every penny for my definitive trip to Los Angeles. This time I would be starting over, with more reason and logic.

Without ever having been involved in a twelve-step program, I knew I had genuinely bottomed out. It was clear now that drugs could no longer do anything for me except cause pain and keep me broke. I promised my councilor I would hook up with a psychiatrist as soon as I got settled. The issue regarding my faux pas with Mary would be discussed first, as well as my endless cravings for narcotics. Medical would pay for a doctor anywhere, and I was sure I could find a good one out there.

I picked up a moderated supply of travel doses at Chandler and spoke with Kathleen for the last time. I thanked her for the generous help she gave so freely, and honestly promised I would never use heroin again; indeed, I haven't used any since then. Maybe I had some kind of epiphany or revelation, but this time around I imagined myself doing all the right things in that sprawling City of Angels.

*****

When I arrived in Los Angeles for the third time, it was a warm, sunny afternoon; my mother was waiting for me at the airport terminal with Bob and his partner Joe Lewis. They were all glad to see me, but I was still a little finicky about them. Bob was a well-paid accountant for a big oil company and Joe was a master chef at a hospital in the valley. They owned a small house on Lemon Grove Street and frequently held poker games. Joe would cook all the time and drank a lot while preparing things. He wasn't into cards, so the drunker he got, the more he would play religious songs on the organ; which he probably learned when he was a Catholic monk. To say these nice people bored me would be a vast understatement, but they always cared about Mom, who loved her card games.

Mom had moved away from her place on Union Avenue into a nicer, one-bedroom apartment at the corner of Third Street and New Hampshire, the brick building was called the El Prado

Apartments.

The statuesque five-story building had fifty similar units which housed some pretty strange people; perhaps that's why my mother felt so comfortable being there. Once I moved in, it was easy for me to become friends with several of the tenants, like a very nice Korean guy named Joe Chi. He was a Cancer and the wheeler-dealer type, always hustling cheap merchandise; once, he gifted me with a handsome grandfather clock, which I kept for ages. We went out drinking a few times and had fun.

Mom would host a card game often; she always invited Bob, Joe, Dorothy, Bertha, Richard and a woman named Tina, who seemed to have light fingers. Dorothy, the fifty-year-old Capricorn, wore thick glasses, had clacking dentures, and thinning hair, which was always cut badly by Bertha, and hobbled with a cane. Bertha was a dreamy Pisces who giggled a lot, ate huge amounts of sugary candy, and worked in a sweatshop but saved every penny she earned to visit her family in Guadalajara once a year. My mother must have spoken well of me because Dorothy developed a silly crush on me; I never actually knew why, I was barely polite to her. She followed me around and called me 'little brother' incessantly while smiling through her food-filled uppers. Bertha simply laughed at everything I said, even when I was being serious. How could I ever relate to these unattractive people?

I sincerely kept my promise to Kathleen; I didn't use heroin again, but I still needed to get free from those last forty milligrams of methadone. The new clinic was way out in West Hollywood, which meant another long bus ride. They told me on the first visit that I could only receive it for fourteen days, and the state demanded that I become free by then unless I chose a private place. Luckily, I was able to reach my gallant Dr. Nadeau, who quickly recommended a great shrink named Muriel Streightz. Conny always had the correct solution to my problems, but I don't know how he knew about her.

Conny spoke frankly with Dr. Streightz using his influence to coerce a direct appointment for me. Her office was on Wilshire, near Lafayette Park, a short bus jaunt from our place. She shared a lovely suite with other psychiatrists, who each seemed successful. The doctor's secretary called my mother's apartment to set up a hasty appointment, so I went over the next day. Muriel was an average-looking Jewish woman, she appeared very smart and ladylike and her soft manner promptly comforted my anxieties.

We discussed a great many things during that first fifty minutes, but time was running out on my fourteen-day completion agenda. Dr. Streightz delighted me when she suggested, I could virtually sleep through the entire, unpleasant withdrawal period to become totally drug free in just seven days. We had one more meeting at her office to make plans for this particular hospitalization. I agreed to enter the Glendale Adventist Hospital for one week right after my final dose of methadone and the bureaucracy would never again have to pay for any more of my futile, narcotic recoveries.

For the last time, I was going to a lowlife clinic and would finally be liberated from that humiliating pageant. After an early ride to and from West Hollywood, I went back to Mom's, where we charted the trip to Glendale. They told me to pack lightly, and simply bring pajamas, underwear and a toothbrush. Three different buses took us out there, I assumed the place was about fifty miles away, but it wasn't. It was a long walk to the admitting office after the commute; however, the grounds were attractive, peaceful, lush green and pastoral. The director gave me several forms to fill out for this curious week of benign slumber, and escorted me to a small room which had two beds. A tall nurse told me to put on my sleepwear, and soon a charming doctor came in to give me the first shot. All I can remember after the injection was going into a shadowy bathroom to change clothes a couple of times.

The image of Saint Theresa sitting next to my bed was vague but she came out to visit faithfully for seven days just to watch me sleep. I didn't see Muriel Streightz until I was finished with the procedure and find it hard to believe that doctors nowadays don't advocate more sleep therapy to help their patients withdraw from any number of addictions, like food, smoking, drinking, or drugs of course. Why would anyone choose the cold turkey method over a gentle hibernation remedy?

When the sleepy time sedatives wore off, I awakened to a glorious sunny morning feeling absolutely free, more alive than ever and anxious to seize the day. The gangly nurse came into my room and congratulated me for a great accomplishment, then asked if I was hungry. I quickly opened the window blinds and noticed a swimming pool outside; I said forget about food but asked her to find a pair of shorts so I could go swimming. No one was around, my jeans and a T-shirt were handy, and so before she got back, I jumped in to baptize myself with holy water from Glendale. Once again, I was a lucky little rabbit, oozing with gratitude; California would now be my indelible home.

After leaving the pool, I called Mom and told her I didn't mind riding home by myself so she wouldn't have to make the trip, I really felt great. Everything looked green and pretty on the way back home, and for the first time in years, I saw things through clear eyes, even the bus drivers were beautiful. My body felt stronger, animated and I gradually began to walk with some pride in my step, someone who thinks guilt free is a blessed individual.

The RTD dropped me off at the corner of Third and Vermont, suddenly a bar called the Monte Carlo appeared which I'd never noticed before. From the moment I paddled through the mob getting off the crowded bus with my suitcase full of dirty pajamas, I was magnetically lured to this place; I should at least go inside to check it out.

The large, red-leather-padded, circular bar was nearly empty; it was only one o'clock in the afternoon. Who could drink that early anyway? I sat on a stool in a dimly lit corner away from the few folks who were already enjoying themselves. Then it dawned on me, this place was totally straight, the type of saloon my father always took me to when he roved for women and I was very young.

My taste in booze was limited, dopers never considered drinking to be very fashionable and I never drank much until I drifted into that cave. The owner of the place was a Chinese woman named Pola, who married Dave, a redneck guy from Montana, just to acquire her green card. She was a pleasant Cancer and quite hospitable considering she probably hadn't served too many butch characters like me at her heterosexual bar. Since I really didn't know anything about mixed drinks, I ordered a vodka tonic, which became my standard cocktail for a while. One drink led to another and the lovely Pola basically heard the story of my life. It was easy for me to bond with her on that special day; however, a little later on, her really hot-looking sister Susan Lee waltzed in and I fell in love instantly.

This was my first drug-free day, so I didn't see any harm in stopping at the Monte Carlo to celebrate. My mother was raving when I staggered in after seven p.m. and wanted to know why I didn't call to stop her from worrying. I regret that I forgot, she was still going to AA and no matter what, she didn't appreciate me getting drunk. When she caught her breath after the boring lecture, I gave her some good news. "Mom, I fell in love with a beautiful Chinese woman today, which is why I was too preoccupied to phone. I'm sorry." Why is it, she didn't mind if I went out to get drunk with Joe Chi, but the idea of me courting a female lover really upset her? Perhaps she was jealous, but from then on, I'd be going to the bar a great deal to see Susan and I needed to find my own quarters close by.

It was becoming difficult to live with my mother in that small place, she always heard me creeping in and I didn't sleep well on the sofa. The Monte Carlo opened at six a.m., sometimes I went there for breakfast, which was generally a plain croissant with a cold bottle of beer, depending on how bad my hangover was. Susan worked nights from six p.m. until the two a.m. closing time, that's when I got to see her in action. She was an extremely cheerful and talkative Taurus, and we became friends by sharing conversations from across the bar. Our first chat was about the song *Hotel California*, which played incessantly; she was curious about everything and asked what that song really meant. Her smile was infectious and everyone loved her; she remembered the favorite drink of every customer.

When I was young and living in Bridgeport, someone started a cruel rumor; white kids should never go near Chinamen because they will grind you up, that's where rice comes from and you could be someone's dinner if you weren't careful. I never even met any Asian people until I moved to California, so I quickly became addicted to these ethnic women. Susan was sharp, very sexy and lived with a Thai boyfriend who couldn't stop her from playing the field. I became her first gay lover.

I made my way to the Monte Carlo almost every night to see her; she knew I didn't have much money, so I was gifted with free drinks regularly.

After a short period, Mom expected me to find a job and stop running to the saloon. Working would be great, providing I could hang out at Susan's bar nightly and party until two o'clock. The

SSI check was my sole income and finding a cheap apartment in this straight area would be a challenge. The majority people who lived around Third and Vermont were foreign; there seemed to be huge numbers of Latinos, Koreans, Chinese, Thai and a smattering of Japanese. I simply needed my own place and could care less about accents or diverse cultures.

Kathie O'Malley was the last woman I'd been sexual with, which was roughly a year before. I never had a problem finding a lady, but in this neighborhood, I was like a duck out of water and what seems strange right now is the fact that I never bothered checking out any gay bars, maybe because I fell in love with Susan Lee so fast. I didn't mind hitting on this straight woman; she was more than willing to experience romance with me. I learned from Mary the attitude of Filipinos is just to be happy, Susan taught me that Chinese people are business-minded, lack a sense of humor, but are seldom ever bashful.

After she closed and locked up the bar, we'd go across the street to a Korean coffee shop and feast on a huge breakfast. One thing led to another, and Susan invited me over to show off her new townhouse. I was ecstatic about the invitation but recalled that she lived with a boyfriend. She assured me he would be at work all day, so she picked me up at the El Prado on a Saturday morning. Going to her place made me a bit uneasy and apprehensive, but once we got through the door, she told me to relax and fix a drink, so I poured a large glass of Absinthe from their bar. Many pillows were scattered around the marble fireplace, I propped them up carefully on the floor, while she nonchalantly did a load of laundry. Although I wouldn't dream of using their bed, our lovemaking was inevitable.

More than once it overwhelmed us as we made extraordinary love that day. Susan had never been with a woman before and having sex with an Asian female was even more arousing to me. The only lover I could ever compare Ms. Lee with might be Janet Grigsby from Provincetown, who was highly erotic and also a Taurus; they both had great stamina and could overpower anyone with passion. Susan kept a clean house, garnered large tips from the bar and took a few classes at Cal State in business management. She worshiped money, knew how to save and allowed everyone else to pay.

Her mother, Ming, a Leo, taught all her children the genuine value of money and likewise its power. A family member told me that she originally had ten children but swapped four of them for safe passage to Thailand to flee from the hostile situation in communist China. The proud matriarch traded the kids who didn't have much of a future and kept the ones like Susan with money in their stars. Ming always referred to a thick red book, which turned out to be classic, Chinese astrology; her life was ruled by these explanations or theories. My attractive new lover was born to be fortunate.

Pola was among the lucky six who ultimately came to America from Thailand, along with a younger sister Joanne. They all wanted to own a saloon or bar business because these establishments were able to bring about huge daily cash flows. Their Mom managed through some kind of bureaucratic lottery to acquire a couple of bars for her children. This family seemed above board and honest, yet all the females appeared to be constantly hustling men, simply to buy them trinkets of gold; they all loved jewelry. I met quite a few Thai women through the Lee family and they were all friendly.

In between quarrels with Susan, I dated one of her friends named Pal; sometimes we made love in her rented room, right above the Monte Carlo. All I seem to remember about our inebriated affair was that she had the blackest nipples I ever saw; every so often, she'd even ask me for money afterward. I seldom left her any cash, but she enjoyed seeing me anyway. Whenever Susan went out with some strange guy, I simply got drunk and went upstairs to see my Pal. Ms. Lee dated a lot of guys, but for all kinds of absurd reasons. Perhaps she thought they were sexy and smart, or merely assumed they had money. One night she went out with an Armenian man to see if he made love differently than others. She was never my formal lover, therefore, we had no strings; it was all about her convenience.

The majority of male customers often enjoy buying the barmaid a drink, and Susan's drink of choice was Kahlua and milk. This was a cheap drink for the house; she fixed it with a lot of milk and didn't have to worry about getting too drunk while on duty. A few gentlemen even brought her take-out food regularly; she wasn't the least bit shy about accepting a meal, or anything else, from a stranger.

If you ever need anything, tell everyone you meet that they might just have it, or possess germane information. A buddy from the bar told me he saw a place for rent on Catalina Street, so once again, I got lucky at acquiring my own apartment. It was a single, two blocks from the Monte Carlo and one block from Mom's. The landlord, Mr. Sheridan, seemed like an all right guy, and the rent was cheap. There were a few kickers to this convenient abode, it didn't have a heater and the large French windows which went from ceiling to floor would be a problem later on when Susan stayed over.

She didn't know the real source of my meager funds, or how much I received; she merely assumed I inherited a small monthly income. Since it was her car, she always chose the places and most events we attended. We toured Disneyland, but I hated the crowds and all that waiting. She wanted to see *Hello Dolly* at the Pantages Theater; she bought the tickets, but we were seated so far from the stage that Carol Channing looked like a blond ant. Sometimes we'd go to Venice Beach, which I enjoyed because of the ocean; I jumped in once with all my clothes on; Susan was quite embarrassed.

Her Thai boyfriend, Michael, whom she had known since childhood, started to wonder why she wasn't coming home to him at night; hence they began to fight a lot. He was a crazy man, insanely in love with her, jealous and possessive; although she denied it, Susan was absolutely terrified him.

I began to seek employment for extra cash and one such job was working in a boiler room called The Preview House at Hollywood and Vine. I had no experience, but I'm a quick study. This office was crowded with unemployed actors and people like me who simply needed the work. It was a bit intimidating at first; being confined to the simultaneous uproar of screaming telephone dialogues from fifty diverse workers. Between five and ten p.m., we hustled at getting folks to attend free screenings of contemporary films in the main Preview House just to critique or rate what they saw. We coaxed them with various gift offers, like free gasoline or Shakey's Pizzas if they pledged to go. A list of numbers was given out nightly, and the staff attempted to book everyone on their roster.

Today you can use DONTCALL.GOV, but telemarketing was

out of control then, at any given dinner hour, these tacky phone calls were likely to disturb you. My desk was right next to a fervent Christian convert, Carol Marcus, who was in fact born Jewish. This woman spoke softly, but quite often told the pigeons on her list, "Jesus loves you." In spite of the innocent malarkey, she booked more than almost anyone else there. At the end of our shift, the office manager rewarded the person who hoodwinked the most prospects that night, and the competition for cash was routinely between Carol and me.

A couple of cocktails might help to relieve the aggravation of all that screaming and pitching, so I found a bar to get energized before work. It was a dive on Vine called The Firefly, after which I felt like I could win it all. Hardly anyone at the office acknowledged I had downed a few drinks, no one especially cared, and I usually obtained the highest number of bookings, except for a few times when Marcus did a little better. What I disliked about the office, besides throwing the bull, was Carol sitting right across from me rolling her big eyes and quietly advising me to get saved.

Most days I took the bus to work, but once in a while Susan would drive me if she wasn't too busy with own duties. We hardly ever discussed my obscure, part-time job. She stayed at my apartment quite a bit then and even did some cooking; only I couldn't identify many of those exotic dishes.

I had only seen her boyfriend, Michael, from a distance once or twice and quickly determined we could never be cordial because of his sinister, intimidating, angry personality. Neither of them were legal citizens, somehow they got to L.A. unnoticed by immigration and lived in constant fear of deportation. Both hoped to get lucky and capitalize on an American spouse, at least they couldn't marry each other.

Susan and I fared through a very public love affair; she wasn't bashful about broadcasting to everyone at the bar that we were lovers. With folks talking behind our backs, I felt awkward regarding her flamboyant, homosexual declarations. She was still going out with other guys under the pretense of husband hunting for a green card, or some good jewelry. The attractive Asian ladies whom I came to know could smile and fascinate anyone, and they had no sense of guilt about accepting gifts. Perhaps they were brought up to take advantage of people; they used men, but never really robbed them.

We made love every day, regardless of what happened with her straight escorts, yet Michael would repeatedly claim she belonged to him. Susan had awesome sexual needs, which never bothered me because I had plenty of energy and stayed drunk a lot. One night after the bar closed, we were about to get into her Datsun, which was parked right in front on Third Street; the moment we approached the car, Michael showed up out of nowhere in a brutish rage. I stood dumbfounded as he snatched the keys from her hand, threw her in the passenger's side, and sped away. She glanced at me when he drove off as if to say; "Don't worry; it's okay; I've been through this kind of drama before."

By that hour, I was usually pretty drunk but after he kidnapped Susan, I sobered up fast. A few locals were outside watching this unbelievable spectacle and called the cops, they came right away. I wrote down their names, addresses and identified her car, only the men in blue didn't seem very interested because they figured it was just a normal girlfriend/boyfriend quarrel, so they left. That was a very long and daunting night for me; I worried for the safety of her life and didn't really want to lose her.

Michael drove to a desolated beach, raped her with all his might, and dragged her back to their townhouse. She showed up at my door early the next morning unscathed and flawlessly beautiful.

Mom couldn't stand Susan but I had one good friend named Jim who knew and liked her. He was a sensitive Cancer man, somewhere in his sixties; I could easily discuss personal matters with him. We first met at the Monte Carlo and became friends right away; perhaps I sensed he was a closet case. My tiny buddy could have been a jockey in earlier years but chose to become an accountant; he was now a retired bank auditor. Jim didn't look gay, but once we struck up a conversation it was obvious. His suits were dressy; however, his actual signature was a black fedora with a wide curvy brim. Like a true crab person, he grumbled a lot, discussing which brands of toilet tissue tore off more easily, or he would rant about his displeasures with the MacDonald's quarter pounder.

Sometimes I hung out at his adorable little apartment around the corner from the bar. Jim liked to talk about his unofficial, much younger boyfriend John, who seemed to be using him. The guy came over a few times while I was there; he walked with a cane, collected disability and always bummed poor Jim for money. In my estimation, he was just a cheap hustler, but Jim believed they really loved each other; who could say otherwise? I found an old photo and they didn't even look compatible.

Before I got on the Hollywood bus headed for the Preview House, I would pick up a few things for Jim at the market, the primary staple being a quart of vodka. We'd have a drink before I left and Jim would tell me everything that happened at the bar on the previous night, which usually entailed a hefty brawl. Pola worked days and Susan was the night manager, but regardless of what time it was, some jerk would always try hitting on these ladies. Dave was Pola's jealous husband and a mysterious type of guy; he had a wicked temper and was probably capable of homicide. Once I saw him catapult two guys out the door simultaneously, just for looking at his wife in an affectionate way.

Michael abducted Susan on a Friday night, so she moved out of their place the following Monday morning when he left for work. Without any warning, she was ringing my doorbell carrying a king-size sheet, which was tied up into a giant ball filled with some of her clothing. Grinning like a Cheshire cat, she told me that she was moving in with me right away. I was thrilled about her presence, but how could we both live in my tiny studio? Suddenly the place was bulging with plants, groceries and her cheerful charisma, yet I had to wonder if this could really be a gay relationship.

We began to develop a comfortable routine, I'd make the morning coffee or tea, and she'd jump out of bed, shower and start doing her personal chores, Susan's needs came first. She washed her car every week at a fifty-cent do-it-yourself carwash; in some ways she was penny-wise but dollar foolish. Her parents were pure Chinese ancestry, so the vanity plates on her car, read 'YEN HIN', which was her true birth name, it had something to do with three sisters, but I don't recall the whole story. About once a month, we drove out to North Hollywood and took the Buddhist monks some food and offerings. This gives person insurance for the afterlife; the more you give, the more you are blessed.

All the monks wore orange togas and looked forward to cash gifts, which were pinned to a money tree inside the temple; they likewise enjoyed refreshments from dedicated subjects such as home-cooked purified meals. Susan prepared some special dishes for them on certain Chinese religious holidays. One Sunday morning she was cooking chicken, I started to take a tiny piece and she slapped my hand instantly; I didn't even know why. The edibles bestowed upon these bald, pious men, must never be touched by anyone except the cook. After the clerics devoured a huge banquet, they would burp loudly, smoke a heavy-duty cigarette, cough hard, and began to chant or pray. This was not the image of holy men that I chose to perceive; they seemed too sloppy and lacked basic social etiquette.

Things were going well for us; I still worked nights and hurried back to Third Street to sit around the bar with Susan until closing. Sometimes we'd go out to eat, but most of the time we just went home and made love until dawn.

She generally parked right in front of my house, however, one night we were laughing hard while getting out of the car and didn't notice anyone else around. We barely entered the apartment, when her crazy boyfriend, Michael, crashed his whole body through a French window; he was like a wild bear and really frightened us. There was a lot of loud screaming and somehow we all ended up outside on the front lawn. I tried to get between the two of them because they were struggling to kill each other, but he clobbered me to the ground, boldly broke my nose, and carried her off for the second time in a month. She had to get rid of this savage, once and for all.

When they left, I called the Rampart station; fortunately, the officer who showed up was familiar with Susan and her deranged sweetheart. The cops took my emotional statement and drove me to a hospital emergency room to treat my badly broken nose; I looked terrible and felt much worse.

Just like on television, the cops put out an 'all points' bulletin on Susan's car, it wasn't hard to find because he always dragged her back to their place, and that's where he was arrested. No one would volunteer to bail him out, but still it took months to ultimately bring this thug to trial.

Susan and I were seated in court along with two strapping detectives, who may have noticed the smell of last night's Vodka on my breath, but seemed to be in our corner regardless. The case was never a gay issue; it was all about Michael breaking my nose and carting Susan off whenever the urge struck him. We didn't have to say much, the evidence was conclusive, this wasn't his first run in with the law, therefore, the INS deported him to Thailand and he could never to return to the U.S.A.

The Lee family arrived from the Far East at different intervals, Pola brought their youngest sister, Joanne, here first, then Susan entered with her former boyfriend, Michael; the matriarch was the last to arrive. Her mother rented a huge apartment half a block away from my place on Catalina Street, and two brothers lived there as well. I think the male siblings must have watched lots of gangster flicks because they tried to look and act tough. Thin leather vests were worn instead of shirts; they brandished tight black Levi jeans and blasted loud, heavy metal stereo music, defying all complaints from neighbors. I hated to visit them; her hostile mother couldn't stand me and sneered constantly.

Now Susan was completely rid of Michael and didn't have to account to anyone regarding her bohemian behavior. She could sleep around and do whatever she pleased; her recent independence was made very clear to me whenever she stayed at my place. "I am not married to you." After a while, I simply came to accept her as a cheap hustler and tramp, which never stopped us from being amorous. I managed to stay drunk enough, so I actually didn't care what, or whom, she did.

Susan informed me on September 14th that she would be leaving for Hawaii by herself in the morning, which happened to be my birthday; how could she be so cold? While packing, she said: "Oh, I'm sorry to miss your birthday. Should I take a leather jacket, or will it be too warm?" She gifted me with a tacky greeting card and a gallon of vodka just before her five-day trip to Oahu.

One of her affluent bar admirers furnished the ticket for this vacation as a reward for being free from Michael. She confessed it was a lonely experience without me and was sorry I didn't go. Susan couldn't remain alone for long, so she approached an older, wealthy gay woman while checking into an elegant Waikiki hotel. The dyke drank excessively and was ineffectual to her erotic demands.

Things changed when she got back from Hawaii, I began to realize what Susan was all about. She was selfish, aggressive, ambitious, and not always honest and more than anything wanted to have her own bar, if her mother could draw another one from a state lottery. The clients with any measure of cash became potential investors or live wires, she wasn't afraid to ask for anything. The subject of money was her preferred topic and my least favorite. I never liked to think much about finances.

I was still seeing Dr. Streightz, I needed to complain about my only partner who could never be a faithful lover or monogamous. Muriel advised me not to expect anything. "Susan is what she is. If you were a beggar in the square asking for alms, some may give and others may not. Whenever you ask for something, always be prepared for rejection, if you beseech Susan to change, do not be disheartened if she can't." From then on, I learned to listen to my inner voice and rarely wished for anything unattainable. Independence is my strength now, and I will rely on myself for sensibility.

We shopped in Chinatown for certain groceries, but I really didn't like going down there, everything smelled terrible. Dead ducks hung upside down in every store window, fresh fish was openly sold outdoors and nothing looked hygienic to me except for one bakeshop, which made beautiful pastries. After shopping, we went back to my place and she began to cook, at first I thought rubber was burning outside. I realized the awful smell was coming from the stove. She put stuff in a big pot, which looked like strange roots and barks all boiling in muddy water, so I told her I could never eat that garbage. She turned off the gas, gave me a dirty look and marched right to her mother's place.

If ever I committed a cardinal sin - that was it. By implying the food she cooked was garbage, I had insulted all Chinese sustenance, therefore ridiculing the entire culture. Susan stormed out of my apartment and it was divorce Asian style. Later she returned with a handyman to help her move from my place back to her mother's. I watched with amazement as she stuffed a closet full of clothes into one big sheet, and hauled it over her shoulder. It was a quick maneuver, almost professional; she was certainly used to moving. The next day she called to ask if I would go to the movies with her.

I continued to work for the Preview House, visit my friend Jim, meet with my shrink and stop at the Monte Carlo every night to gaze at the stunning Ms. Lee. Sometimes she came home with me, but if I happened to notice a cute young guy waiting around, I simply left. It was easy to identify those hopelessly horny guys who lined up nightly expecting to score with Sexy Susan. How could she possibly know who might end up abusing her or even force her to do bizarre things? I didn't want to think about the dangers of those blind dates, yet I shared the same desire for her as the guys who loitered outside at two a.m. She was exotic, beautiful, funny, intoxicating and addictive.

Susan was living at her mother's but sleeping with me almost every night. One Friday before she left for work, I promised to cook something special for a late night supper after the bar closed, we needed to take part in some old-fashioned romance. She thought it was a sweet idea and promised to be at my place shortly after two a.m. something had changed during the evening; she didn't show up or even call.

I spent a lot of time and money to prepare a fabulous dinner, yet she chose to go out with a little creep to bask in unsafe sex. By three a.m. I was beyond angry; I could only imagine what she was doing. I drank several vodkas, got drunk and became pretty crazy. Thrifty's drugstore was open twenty-four hours a day, so I went over and bought four cans of bright red spray paint. I knew she felt ashamed and wouldn't show up at my place. Even though a great dinner was waiting, she would go to her mom's. I sat on the cold steps in the next building until her 280 Z pulled into the driveway. She seemed happy when dashing into the house; I waited about fifteen minutes, and painted her entire car. The original color was burnt copper, however, that night, it became crimson red.

It was very foggy that night and I wasn't sure if the damp car would hold the paint. The spray cans were kind of noisy when I shook them, the clack, clack, clack sounds, echoed loudly at four in the morning, but by luck, no one actually saw me do it. I know that was a childish, asinine thing to do, but I just couldn't stand her breaking my heart anymore without some type of payback. This paint job would be the absolute end of our insane relationship; she would never disappoint me again. Susan didn't really cheat on me because we weren't actually monogamous and since no one could ever hold her, I was ready for a serious companion change. How could she be considered reliable when she couldn't even show up for one fine meal? I am now clinging to the adolescence of maturity.

Her younger sister Joanne was leaving for school that morning and noticed the fresh paint on the car. She ran back in the house to tell Susan. When my phone rang, I knew who it was, so I took it off the hook while I went back to sleep to cure last night's hangover. Later, I put the receiver back on and the first caller said, "This is Susan Lee, I know it was you who decimated my car last night, you will have to pay four hundred dollars to get the red paint removed."

Then I argued, "Susan, you can't prove a thing and even if you had any real evidence, trying to get money from me would be futile." There wasn't much chance of her becoming vindictive; nevertheless, she still had my keys.

I waited a couple of days before making my grand appearance at the Monte Carlo. It was a Friday, around midnight, the place was packed and I knew everyone there. Susan declined to serve me a drink when I sat down, I deliberately went there when it was crowded to make a public scene and get my house keys. She literally refused to return them, so I told everyone Ms. Lee was a thief as she still wouldn't give them back. The bar had a big old-fashioned, wooden telephone booth, I slithered in unnoticed and called the police at Rampart. In a fearful, quiet, sultry voice, I told them there was a guy here waving a gun, and hung up. Several cops arrived within minutes wearing bulletproof vests. When the dust settled, I demanded my keys and she readily handed them over.

*****

I didn't really know how karma worked at the time, but I was about to find out that my ugly prank on Susan's car, would boomerang, sending bad luck my way. A bar called the Catalina on Third Street became my new hangout since I could never set foot in the Monte Carlo again. On the first day of every month I got my SSI check, put my rent money aside and went out celebrating. Perhaps the moon was full on that crazy day. Everyone seemed excessively jovial and bursting with fun.

Like a cat with my back to the wall, I took my usual seat at the end of the bar so I could see the whole place. A couple of guys I'd never seen before sent over a drink, I had to reciprocate and buy them one, which was how we all came to be friendly and smashed by nightfall. Somehow the three of us ended up at my place, no one thought about getting any food, but I did have plenty of vodka to guzzle, eventually I passed out and didn't hear them leave; they must have been expert sneaks.

I was fully clothed when I woke up the next day and still had a few small bills in my Levi's pockets, however, the rent money, which was carefully and secretly stashed in the closet, had disappeared. They stole three hundred dollars, which was all the money I had in the world and Mr. Sheridan's monthly cash payment of two hundred and ninety-five dollars was due. I couldn't have been more shocked since it was the first time I'd ever been bamboozled like that; it was my own bad karma for getting drunk with complete strangers.

One of the thieves let it slip that he worked for Phil's Moving Company and the depot was around the corner on Vermont. I took two aspirin and a stiff drink to clear my head. I hoofed right over there, but the creep who ripped me off quit his job. There was no way I could come up with that amount of money unless I asked my mother, and she definitely didn't have it then. I met face to face with Sheridan to tell him I was moving in with Mom, which I did very soon after. His building wasn't the luckiest place I ever lived in, so once again I landed back at the El Prado, where I was safe on Mom's couch contemplating another residence of my own. It seems like I was always just one monthly SSI check away from personal difficulty and starting to feel hopeless. Fortunately, my job at the Preview House filled some gaps, but even that place was getting me down. I drank just to function through those scripted deceptions. (Bull crap!)

Hustling nice people out to see a tacky movie, or even a series of commercials, wasn't always easy to do, sometimes we promised them gifts which they might never receive for attending any kind of screening. Luckily these poor suckers didn't know where we were calling from or else they could have confronted us at the office on Vine Street for an argument regarding our phony promises.

The only person on the staff who would never lie to a prospective client was Carol Marcus. One night I went to work feeling depressed and maybe it showed because my fellow employee, the Jesus freak, suddenly began to preach to me about being saved, but she picked the wrong night to convert me with that nonsense. "Your whole life will change for the better if you get on your knees right now and ask Jesus to come into your life as your personal savior." I took a deep breath, and politely asked her what I needed to be saved from. She plainly replied, "From your blatant, sinful lifestyles."

The Firefly Bar around the corner absolved me; otherwise, if I didn't take a break to have a couple of drinks, I might have really offended Carol. I didn't know if she was referring to gay life or my drinking, nevertheless, our shift went by very slowly. Carol really was blessed, not only with her Jesus power, but because I chose not to flatten her that night. I decided I couldn't take anymore, so I told my boss, Louise, to send my final paycheck to my mother's because of the insanity throughout the entire boiler room. She was sorry to lose me but understood.

Now that I only had a monthly check for income, Mom started to worry and my luck wasn't getting any better. I simply trotted across New Hampshire Avenue and got busted for jay walking. The cops ran a check on me and it seems I had about thirty unpaid parking tickets, so they arrested me.

Leo was the guy in a wheelchair who bought my Ford when I was leaving L.A. the last time. His bodyguard, or driver, racked up all those parking tickets because the car registration was never put in his name legally, I didn't know about transferring the pink slip so it was still registered to me and I was responsible for those tickets. The policemen carted me off at once to the Sybil Brand Institute like a common criminal, I felt frightened, angry and nervous about going to jail. I was completely innocent of any parking violations; Leo's friend had even demolished the car while I was back east.

Karma translates into cause and effect. I didn't know about California car registrations, so that was the cause; the effect was ending up in jail for my ignorance. They booked me, took terrible mug shots, fingerprinted me, and tossed me in a crowded holding tank until they decided which dormitory to house me in. The majority of inmates were black or Latino and they were there for all kinds of serious crimes and laughed aloud when they learned that I was in jail simply for not paying parking tickets.

It seemed like time stood still in that big cell with all those tough women, but I got an education when I spoke to a few real convicts. A jovial fat lady showed everyone how to boost huge amounts of expensive seafood and meats from supermarkets. She wore long baggy dresses, chose the products she required, then balanced the goods between her chubby legs and casually walked out. Another woman, who was a professional shoplifter, described in detail how she took off alarm wires placed in leather coats, which made a lot of money for her. All of this information was useless to me, but listening to stories about how some people barely got by gave me new incentive to work harder and stay out of jail. Their comments were amusing to a point and made the time pass quickly, but many of these people were totally insensitive about the way they existed and saw no future hope.

 I barely spent any jail time in the east, and when I did get busted, I was bailed out immediately, but now I couldn't leave Sybil Brand until I appeared in court to face each of the thirty indictments. To adjudicate these charges, a big black prison bus transported me to distant courthouses every day. The creep must have spent a lot of time in Santa Monica; he got ten parking tickets there, which brought down the number of my appearances. I felt humiliated when one of the hearings was in Beverly Hills, my jeans were tattered and my shirt was old, but who cared? Ultimately, my last obligation was in Pasadena, where a pleasant judge who really understood dismissed everything for time served.

 About time served, I hope none of my friends will ever go to jail for any reason, it's awful. I was only there for a week, but I lost more than ten pounds. The food tasted like it was all cooked in the same chili pan. An inmate who worked in the kitchen said some of the canned foods were dated before the Korean War. As a Virgo, using public restrooms has always bothered me, but coping in a dormitory with two hundred messy women and having only twelve toilet stalls was beyond disgusting.

 The reason I couldn't get bailed out during this incarceration was because Mom didn't have any money, she did come to visit me when Joe Chi was able to drive her out to East L.A. After the final court appearance in Pasadena, Joe picked me up and I was happy to get back home to the El Prado. He turned out to be a really good friend. Subsequently, I kept a low profile and only went out drinking with my Korean buddy once in a while.

I wasn't looking too hard to find a job other than through the daily newspapers, which didn't seem to have anything that I might care to do. It was easy to become passive when I came home from jail, I watched a lot of television and walked over to Shatto Park to observe tennis matches whenever I needed to get away from my nagging mother.

I was feeling rather blue when Mom handed me a letter from the Social Services Department requesting me to go to their office for a conference, I immediately got nervous. All I could imagine was they might be canceling my SSI checks for some odd reason, and I couldn't bear to think about that. For many years those government checks followed me no matter where I lived and always made me feel secure. The office was within walking distance from our house, so I called to set up a speedy appointment.

This interview was with a good-looking young black man named Ted who sensed my apprehension. He was very nice and calmed my jangled nerves by explaining that the government was willing to pay for training me in the occupation of my choice. Now my luck was about to change for the good. Selections of vocations were limited; however, learning how to key punch didn't tempt me. Ted finally asked how I felt about animals and I said bingo, I really love pets, so he gave me the opportunity to enroll in a dog grooming school, which was the greatest gift I could ever hope for. The only kicker was that I had to stay clean and sober throughout the entire six-month training program.

The first thing I had to do was call Alcoholics Anonymous to find out when and where their meetings took place. I mentioned that I was gay and preferred to be around my own kind. As it happened, there was a strictly gay meeting hall called Alcoholics Together or the AT Center. It was a smoky room on the second floor of a building conveniently located at the corner of 1st and Beverly Boulevard, about six blocks from my house. Since my mother was an old hand at this, she accompanied me to my very first AA meeting. As we climbed up the long staircase, I really felt like turning around, but Mom saw it coming and pushed me all the way into a room filled with drab-looking strangers, and there was no going back. If I was really sincere about starting a new life, it had to begin right here.

Everyone was more than friendly, but I felt sick when they

asked my name. It took about ten meetings for me to stand up and say: "Hi, my name is Carole, and I'm an alcoholic and drug abuser."

Then they would all shout: "Hi Carole." My whole life had bordered on discretion and secrets, why should I bear my soul to this bunch of misfits, whom I didn't know from Adam? These sober individuals were a little too happy, joyous and free, their whole concept seemed hokey to me and I hated these meetings. Were they really as blissed out as they all looked? The group contended that if they did not drink or use, they could do whatever they wanted. In other words, it was okay for an alcoholic to kill a spouse, burn the church house down, or even drown a cat, as long as you did it sober. I was confused.

The regular members always seemed to have a cup of coffee in their hand, perhaps to replace that glass of booze they were used to; I began to dislike coffee after that. At certain meetings, I noticed little cliques gathered regularly, they seemed to do a lot of backstabbing with other members and I wanted to totally be free of the small minded 'In crowd'. All I had to do was show up, sit around for a while, have a card signed by an AA secretary and show it to my councilor later.

Anyone could have signed that card to prove I went to AA meetings, but I was honest about it. Now it was time for me to embark on my training as a pet groomer at The Bark N' Purr School on Beverly Boulevard.

*****

Three women ran Bark N' Purr; Mickey, a Capricorn, was the owner and had a tiny Japanese Aquarian partner named Aki, Katie, the Taurus, was Mickey's daughter-in-law and took care of the bookkeeping. The first day at school, I wore a good pair of jeans with a nice shirt, then I asked Mickey what we should be wearing for classes and she said, "Wear anything you hate because you will constantly be covered with hair and all sorts of dirt while you're learning this occupation."

Bark N' Purr was a certified grooming school, but they were also a boarding facility for dogs and cats. This huge property had many large enclosed dog runs in the rear, which were always noisy.

In a large room on the second floor they boarded many cats. There were several closet-sized rooms upstairs which they made very affordable to the immigrant workers from Mexico who took care of all the outside jobs and construction projects. There was a foyer as you walked in which had a lot of old pictures of Mickey in earlier years; she must have been popular in the pet world. Aki was very serious about everything and did more work than anybody. Katie was just happy taking care of the money.

When I started going there in May of 1979, there were only about eight students attending. One girl, called Brandy, was there on the same type of government grant that I was. She was on a methadone program but confided to me later that she was still using heroin every day, so I stayed away from her as much as possible. Another student was a Mexican woman called Maria, who was really disabled. She only had the use of the left side of her body and could barely hold a broom; I don't know how they thought they could make a groomer out of her. These three partners enrolled anyone who could pay for the tuition through bureaucracy funds or their own money, like a few Japanese students.

A peculiar person named Ruth, also an apprentice there, worshiped the British television show *Doctor Who*. This Libra character used to follow me around the place all the time wearing a nine-foot scarf just like the one the alien doctor wore; as a matter of fact, she collected numerous scarves. We were supposed to start school at nine a.m. and be there until four, but not everyone did. I went to school early, stayed late and worked hard, hoping to accomplish something useful and learn a genuine profession. Treating and tending to the sick animals was what I did most of the time.

Mickey asked me once to take special care of a huge Irish wolfhound named Rory. His owners had to leave the country on a business trip, so they boarded this one-hundred-and-twenty-five-pound dog with us. He started to drop weight immediately because he pined for his masters. It was my automatic reaction as a Virgo to become his friend, servant and nurse. Each day I would boil a pot of rice and add a little meat to it, he refused to eat anything unless I fed him by hand, and I was glad to do it.

That building had many rooms and there were five bathtubs. If someone was washing a dog in one place, I could go to another tub.

Cats were my specialty from the first day, I learned the art of bathing felines without any problems; it was just a matter of being faster and anticipating their swift moves. There was an area set up for drying big dogs like Rory which used an enormous fan as a dryer and there were always dirty wet towels on the floor. My favorite place was the lunchroom where novices socialized and learned some textbook lessons. Two Japanese girls were pupils at this weird school and they simply went there to keep their student visas current. One girl was called Suzie, we didn't communicate very well, her English was terrible and I couldn't speak a word of Japanese.

Suzie's best friend, Yasue, was in Hawaii when I first started at this school, and I found out later that they were having long-distance conversations about me. She told her pal that she couldn't tell if I was a boy or a girl, but I seemed much more interesting than the other students. When Yasue returned from Oahu, we bonded and became fast friends. Sometimes we went around the corner to a taco stand for a meal, or other times I would just bring some hard-boiled eggs and bananas to the lunch room. Everyone smoked cigarettes, so I was generous to them with mine. Several Japanese students were registered there, but the three of us stayed together constantly and ignored the other apprentices.

My mother's light-fingered friend, Tina, recently moved out of the El Prado, into a lovely, baroque old building around the corner, called The Parkview on Fourth, which was originally purchased by William Hurst and given to Miriam Davis as a gift. I ran into Tina at the market one day, and she told me that she got a great apartment under the section eight ordinance; meaning she would only have to pay one third of the actual rent payment and the government would pay the balance. I ran right home to tell my mother about this deal and suggested that she venture to do the same thing. Mom wasted no time and acquired an apartment in that elegant structure for herself, just across the hall from Tina.

Fortunately, I inherited her old fifth-floor place at the west end of the building, now I had my own quarters again. All my neighbors on that floor were rather old; there was Ms. Gibson, a Leo who would never discuss her age, Mr. Nelson Welch, a Libra actor who always played the butler role on television, and a sweet gay Scorpio man named Charlie. Having my own space and being surrounded by friendly people made life seem good then and I wouldn't be ashamed to bring home any of my new Japanese friends. As soon as Mom left, I started to decorate, and bit-by-bit, I made a cozy patio area up on the roof. It was sunny there all day, so I began to grow my own marijuana plants. I would invite the old folks to come up for ice tea just to get them out of their stuffy dungeons for a spell.

Yasue, Suzie and I saw each other every day at school, from Tuesday through Saturday and became inseparable. Suzie drove a little Dodge Colt clunker and lived in Hollywood with a photographer friend called Miharu. Yasue didn't drive; she lived with her roommate Eriko at The Executive House a couple of blocks from my place on New Hampshire. At this point, I had become very fond of Asian women; they seemed more refined than the American girls I usually dated.

Whenever these fine ladies came to my place for dinner, they would have the dishes washed, dried and put away before I digested the meal. They worked quietly and never had resentment about the clean -up jobs; it was like they were glad to be serving someone. Maybe it was a Japanese thing.

With two new friends, I expected to make one of them my lover. This caused a slight dilemma; I liked them both. Yasue and Suzie were Sagittarius sun signs; they dressed well and were very cute in different ways. Suzie had a blank expression, and I'm sure she was born with Mercury in retrograde. I just assumed she was taller than Yasue because she always wore high wedgies shoes; nevertheless, her legs were longer. Yasue was sharp, smart, and much more cheerful and even though her legs were short, I decided she would become my special love, so I began to court her with enthusiasm.

I started school at Bark N' Purr in May and fell head over heels in love with Yasue Nakamoto by the middle of June. This must have been the year of intimate relationships because my mother was starting to talk to my father. She was having regular phone conversations with him in Worcester and wanted to rekindle their marriage after being divorced for thirty-five years. At one time Mom was quite beautiful and Dad was extremely handsome in his day, so she made all the arrangements to bring him out here from the east and Joe Chi would pick him up at LAX.

When Dad hobbled down the runway, Mom almost fainted; she didn't expect him to look that old. He had aged since I last saw him; evidently the boozing had caught up with him. When he was thirty, his liver was badly diseased, and I'm sure it didn't improve. Dad's hair had thinned, his shoulders were hunched over, his eyeglasses were as thick as coke bottles and he looked much older than sixty-seven.

Mom began to criticize my father the minute he arrived and had instant regrets about sending for him. They never got along before, so why should things be different now? She was always too persnickety and difficult with her men, yet she believed this time would be better because they had some wonderful chats over the phone before he arrived about remarrying for the sake of the church.

Within two weeks she was really sick of him and wanted to throw him out. If he stayed with her any longer, the nagging would have driven the poor old man crazy, so he ended up moving in with me. There was a Murphy bed which pulled out of the wall for Dad and I would be sleeping on the sofa for a while. The rent was only ninety-five dollars a month and I still received the SSI checks, so things were good. When he moved in, he had one suitcase with a few clothes, a couple of pieces of silverware and a mallet, which seemed curious because he'd never swung a hammer in his life.

I wanted him to be happy here, but it turned out to be a big mistake when I left him to his own devices. The first place he headed for was the Catalina Bar, my old hangout. He would get very drunk and pick fights with anyone for no good reason. Remember he was a Scorpio ex-boxer who imagined he couldn't lose. The guys he challenged were younger, stronger, and meaner, and he regularly took a beating. After a while, I couldn't stand to see him come home with any more bruises, so I told him it was fine to drink in the house, but he could not go to any of the neighborhood bars.

Dad quickly settled into the little old man's routine; he enjoyed shopping at Ralph's market and going to the bank to see the young ladies. If his balance was ten dollars, he'd draw out five just to get some cute female clerk to pay attention to his flattery, he complimented every woman he ever met.

It had been less than a month since he moved in with me and

the woman who lived across the hall passed away suddenly; we didn't know her but she was very old. This meant that Dad could move into her apartment, I was good friends with the building managers, so they readily gave him the place. He was delighted to have his own quarters and I was happy to have my private bachelor pad back.

I looked forward to going to school just to see Yasue. She would stroll in about eleven a.m. and leave about two. We became very close and now that Dad was out of the way, I could entertain more. It was impossible to obtain a thirty-day chip from the AA program, as soon as I got to the twenty-ninth day, I'd go out to get drunk. Forget about that, I was anchored at school, in love with Ms. Nakamoto and had no guilt about sharing a couple of canned vodka gimlets with her during our leisure time.

We didn't communicate perfectly but one day I got up the nerve to ask her for a date, and she said yes right away, she just thought I was a colorful person with many different types of friends. It was all arranged for me to pick her up in a taxi at The Executive House on a balmy Saturday night. When Yasue got in the cab, I told the driver to take us to the Palms, on Sunset. This was the only women's gay bar I knew of then, and when we got inside the place; she promptly wanted to know where all the men were. I told her it was still early, so maybe we could dance a little before they arrived.

The bar was lined up with the usual butch ones, but I took her focus off that image as we began to dirty dance. This scene had to be confusing to a straight foreigner who assumed everyone there was merely acting out a Hollywood fantasy. We became quite amorous while dancing, so we took a cab back to my house and cuddled on the sofa all night. That was the dawning of our relationship.

*****

There was a room upstairs where they boarded cats and much of my time in school was spent up there taking care of them. I learned how to carefully bathe them, clean their ears and give them certain medications. My hypnotic rapport with cats has always been stronger than any of my feelings for dogs, although I loved canines too. Katie called me downstairs one very rainy day, knowing how I felt about felines. She was holding a small, dark, calico kitten and said a woman just brought it there to get the poor baby out of the rain. It had been living behind a restaurant and was being abused by some sick teenagers. As soon as I entered the foyer, this hungry, drenched and bedraggled little cat flew into my arms. Somehow, the name 'Habib' came to mind right away, which means 'Little Darling' in the Arabic language. She was mine instantly and the first of many more pets to come.

Yasue also enjoyed spending her time in the cat room when they didn't have a yappy little poodle for her to groom. Maybe it was because I was very strong then, but they gave me all the big dogs to work on, like Rory the Irish wolfhound or the Old English Sheepdogs. The hardest part of that dirty work, was brushing the animals. Cutting hair was the easy phase of grooming and when Yasue finished her one poodle a day, she could leave; I stayed much longer to finish up the hard jobs and big dogs.

Once in a while, I would stop over to see my good friend Jim and since I was so devoted to pets now, he decided to get a dog for himself. He ended up with a tiny Chihuahua and did his own bathing; I cut the puppy's toenails as we continued to sit around drinking and bitching about mundane things. Jim was old and wise, he said, "Carole, animals are your forte, stick with this profession, you will do well if you start your own business." Little did we know that later on Yasue and I would become admired as the owners of the best and most popular pet grooming shop in all of Silverlake.

When Yasue entered my broken life, it was definitely a miracle. Following the fiasco with Susan and shortly before I attended the Sybil Brand Institute, I was feeling depressed one day so I drank some booze and swallowed a bunch of Valium. I wasn't really trying to commit suicide; I just wanted to sleep for a long time, only that was impossible. My mother had a spare key to the place and when I didn't come right to the door, she let herself in. I was passed out on the Murphy bed and she couldn't wake me up. She called 911 right away and an ambulance took me way out to the Brotman Hospital. They kept me there for several days for observation until I convinced them I wasn't suicidal.

A very eccentric woman wrapped from head to toe in a white

sheet was sitting on the hall floor between two different wards. Evidently she was in a more confined area and asked if I could take her beyond an imaginary line into my sector. The nurses told her not to leave her own area, but she longed for conversation so I crossed over to her side. She called herself 'Tsitra' or 'Sidra', which was the word artist spelled backwards. Her true birth name was Kathie Moriarty and readily informed me that she was gay, even if she was nuts or damaged, it was comforting to be with a sister. The government gave her SSI benefits permanently because she could never endure the real world as we know it.

It turned out that she dropped some acid and was driving her truck erratically on the freeway so they busted her. This woman was totally crazy, yet fascinating in a way. She carried a small address book, which was penned in tiny letters, she asserted that everyone's name was alphabetized, categorized and wrote comments about her lovers. Sidra seemed to be the smartest person I ever met, and I got past the insanity by exploring her inner soulful feelings. We remained friends long after our Brotman Hospital association. She was a captivating artist who made me think hard about things.

Sidra was a large woman of Scandinavian descent, raised as a Mormon and her father was a blind minister. She was a May Gemini, with an Aries moon and thought that everything was all about her. We were never lovers, but I stayed at her house a few times when I first started school. Once in a while she would drive me to Bark N' Purr in her classic Karmann Ghia. Her aristocratic attitude was about getting the maximum out of any situation. For instance, "Why are you going to dog grooming school when you could easily become a veterinarian?" Sidra never thought about the amount of money it would take to get into UC Davis or the procedures to become an animal doctor, fortunately, I didn't take her very seriously. My mother couldn't stand her for that kind of distorted logic.

The school took in all types of students as long as someone doled out twenty-five hundred dollars for tuition. Our government paid for drug addicts and the mentally challenged, but foreigners from Japan and Korea were expected to pay the full amount in cash unless other arrangements were made. This place was like a zoo, Mickey was constantly screaming at someone and the dogs were always barking, which is why I looked for peace up in the cat room. There were couple of beautiful Persian felines who had been left there to board, and we were told their owners had called from Mexico to say they had been busted for something and wouldn't be coming back to pick up their nameless kittens.

Yasue fell madly in love with those two and came upstairs to visit a lot. She very much wanted to take them right home, but the school was obliged to keep them for a certain amount of time before they could be adopted out. Yasue christened them in advance, the silver gray male was named Sebastian and his shy black and white sister was called Tama. Sometimes we let them out of their cages, but the room had lots of places for spooky Tama to hide and she hid from everything.

Things were good now, Dad enjoyed his own place, school was fun and I had my sweet little cat Habib, who was very affectionate and talked to me a lot. My life would really be complete if Yasue became my permanent partner. After our date at the Palms, we acted somewhat more demonstrative toward each other, but I wanted more than hugs. Maybe if she moved in with me, we could bond and stay together forever. I needed a dedicated relationship, I wasn't getting any younger and my sexual energy might decline someday, so I better get busy with my future lover.

Yasue paid four hundred and ninety-five dollars a month for rent, plus the utilities, at the very fancy Executive House. My place was only ninety-five bucks a month, with everything included. I asked her to move right in with me and assured her she would not have to pay any rent, I also promised to make her coffee every morning. She would be leaving a secure building with a swimming pool and all the amenities, for a fifth-floor bachelor apartment and an animated view of Third Street.

It didn't take her much time to think about my proposal; she was a smart Sagittarius and the idea of not having to pay rent attracted her. She moved right in with me and never looked back. Unlike Susan Lee, who threw all her belongings in a sheet, Yasue had some attractive luggage and many small cases to carry makeup etc. Prior to coming to California, she lived with her married sister, Toshie, in Hawaii for a while and did some very hard restaurant work for her tough old aunt. L.A. was a huge frustration to her, it stayed overcast for a long time and the sunshine was minimal when she first arrived here, this place could never compare to Waikiki in any way. The Japanese read a lot of cartoon-type magazines and she was always swapping them with friends. I don't know how she came to know so many people here, but she was very popular and I enjoyed all her companions.

When Yasue first moved in with me, I knew my luck and my life would change for the better. I only had a black and white TV and a couple of lamps, lit with red light bulbs. It wasn't a cheerful place because I didn't feel bright or lively. We redesigned what we could; she insisted we turn those dreary surroundings into a comfortable, lovely home. Once in a while Sidra would lend me her Ghia because she was trying to sell it, and the more I drove around, the more people would see it. I planned my errands around the days I'd be using her car. It was a small coupe, but I managed to get two-by-fours in it to build some bookcases for my studious, book-collecting partner. There used to be a large department store on Sunset called Zody's which carried all the household articles needed. In a short time, we put up fresh curtains and made our tiny fifth-floor home quite charming.

Someone called one night to ask if I was interested in purchasing a brand-new, twenty-one-inch TV, so I jumped at the offer. Within a few short days, this colored television was delivered to my door and all I had to do was make outrageous payments for a while. The interest was ridiculous, but there was no other way that I could buy such a wonderful appliance, so I considered it a miracle. Another telemarketer called me after school from the Broadway, which happened to be my favorite department store. They asked if I would like to have an account with them and I answered with a positive yes. Now we had a color TV, and Broadway gold card to buy everyone a Christmas present.

In the beginning of most courtships, sweethearts are at their best, and I couldn't have been more pleased to enjoy Yasue as my lover, she was great. I won't discuss the details of our lovemaking, but I can tell you that we weren't afraid to explore erogenous zones. She wasn't at all shy or inhibited; we were very compatible, deeply in love, and still feel the same after all these years.

We were finally able to take Sebastian and Tama out of Bark N' Purr legally, which made Yasue really happy, only now that we owned three cats, Katie from school begged us to take yet another one. Her name was Lady Bug; she was about a year and a half older than the others and nurtured Habib as her own, which was good because Tama and Sebastian had bonded from the moment of their birth. My father adored Tama, but couldn't stand her sibling, which was how he acted with my brother and me. Our cats were free to roam around the back section of the long hallway, providing the doors were closed and Dad was at home. The landlord would never permit us to have any; he disliked felines and would soon be making a surprise visit, meaning that we had to hide those four little critters.

The country was in a recession, a reality which never entered my mind, and Christmas was coming. I went shopping down at the Broadway, to buy my family some presents and a few for our neighbors. After purchasing gifts, I threw a big party up on the roof for all the tenants in the building. We served apple juice, some beer, wine and assorted snacks. I played a portable radio and the old folks danced together. Those moments were precious; I vowed to have parties for the elderly whenever possible.

Ginny, the manager called to let us know that our landlord, Mr. Horowitz, would be arriving in the afternoon. She confirmed that he was allergic to cats and we really needed to hide them somewhere before he came over. This abrupt apartment inspection was the day after our Christmas bash on December 23rd. The only place we thought we could conceal them was up on the roof, where supposedly he wouldn't visit. We took all four cats upstairs, left a huge blanket, an umbrella for shade and lots of food and water. Lady Bug and Habib adjusted well, but Tama and Sebastian found a small opening in a vent, climbed in and disappeared through the crawl space of the fifth floor.

As soon as the landlord left the building, we ran straight up to the roof to fetch our four cats. Habib and Lady Bug were very happy to see us, but there was no sign of Tama or Sebastian. We realized where they had disappeared and began to panic, there seemed to be only one way into the tiny place. I called the Department of Animal Regulations and two uniformed officers came over very quickly. The small vent cover was bolted to a metal wrapper and they didn't want to rip the whole thing. After taking off part of it so we could look down there, they asked us to get some talcum powder to pour onto the crawl space floor, this way, if they walked around, we could track their paw prints, then later, we gingerly lowered a bowl of fresh water and some dry food as we continued to call them.

Before the officers left, they assured us that cats are able to survive for weeks, even without food or water. They told us to get someone to rip off the entire vent cover the next day. There was only about three feet of space between the roof and the ceiling beams of the fifth floor. Darkness came fast and we were feeling sad and frustrated, so we went back and forth to the roof all night long, whispering their names. It was nearly dawn when Yasue decided to just rip that metal apart, and she did. I didn't want her to climb down there because creatures like bats or other things might be there as well.

Once she lifted the metal off, I slithered through the small opening and gently set my right foot on a solid beam. Then I lowered the other one, but I had to hunch way over since the access was only about a yard deep. I wore old Birkenstocks so I wouldn't make any noise, but somehow I lost my balance, causing one foot to bulldoze right through June and Joe's ceiling, just above their beautifully decorated Christmas tree. The old couple scrambled out of bed in shock and thought we were having an earthquake, instead, they plainly saw one brown sandal bursting through the high ceiling.

As I was trying to get my foot from the hole in the ceiling, my worn out Birkenstock fell off my foot and landed on their living room floor, I apologized to them face-to-face once I got free. All I could say when I got to their door was 'I'm sorry', but I was wearing a guilty smirk because, in a way, it was funny. June was about seventy and Joe was much older. They were basically nice people, but I knew they were slightly homophobic and this incident wouldn't help my social standing with the naïve, retired couple from Idaho. Yasue got down into the crawl space and ultimately rescued the cats on Christmas Eve; I probably wouldn't be inviting these old people to any more rooftop parties.

Dad had a serious crush on a flaming red-headed woman named Rita who worked at Ralph's market as a cashier; he made several daily trips over there just to see her. One day she noticed that he was buying a lot of Kal Kan cat food, so she asked if he owned one. He said not really, but sometimes he took care of ours. My fickle father coveted this woman and might have done anything she asked. Rita mentioned to him one day that her daughter's cat recently had kittens, and he could have one of them for his own if he cared to. Naturally Dad said, "Sure I'll take one, how do we arrange this?" The very next day, she brought a small white kitten to the house and now our family owned five cats.

We weren't really sure if this kitten could hear or not, some people said that all white cats were born deaf, but even if he did have a hearing problem, Dad was still happy. He was a very peaceful little pet who actually could hear; soon we named him 'Mello Boy'. My father fantasized that someday he might get a visit from Rita to check up on Mello, but she only came to his place that one time. It seemed like Dad's health might have even improved since he became surrounded with cats, so we spruced up his dingy apartment and bought him a colored television to watch his favorite sporting events.

Yasue and I went to cinemas quite a bit and sometimes we'd even take my father. We also attended live outdoor concerts to see Alice Cooper, Pink Floyd and others. We were madly in love and tried to enjoy everything that life offered us. It was impossible to get Mom to go anywhere, especially to the movies because one time we took her to see *Jesus Christ Superstar* and she blamed the loud music for her deaf ear. She'd lost her hearing a long time ago from being scalded with hot water, which her old boyfriend Bob threw. Playing poker was her only real source of fun and entertainment.

It was a Friday night and I was committed to a red-hot card game with Mom, Bob, Joe and Tina. We started playing early, but I cautioned everyone I would be going out promptly at eight fifteen and had to stop playing by then, they all said it was fine. At exactly five minutes to eight, I won the biggest cash pot the group had ever played for, which meant we could pay for the movie and dinner; I was ecstatic. Mom's serious poker group showed their exasperation immediately, but I felt no guilt.

*****

No one ever really graduated from Bark N' Purr, when a student's time was up, Katie handed them a chintzy-looking certificate which simply stated they had completed a course. Now that we were both finished with school, it was time to find a job.

In the beginning, Mickey explained that a groomer made the big money, but if you worked as an assistant veterinarian, you would only get minimum wages. I wasn't planning on becoming a professional any time soon; I didn't have enough experience or speed. It would take me one whole day just to beautify a tiny poodle because I tried to do a perfect job. Yasue dove right in, cut the dog's hair nicely and went home in a couple of hours. She was very good and had lots of patience. I figured if this strange cast of characters at school could make a living in this business, we could too; it became an obsession to have a shop of our own someday.

Yasue knew a lot of Japanese women, basically her age, who were all here on student visas. A few of them, including herself, worked at the home of the Japanese consulate. Their duties varied at the huge mansion off Third Street. The Council General graced many diplomatic dinner parties and retained a full-time, highly acclaimed Japanese chef. Our friends did all the preparing and serving for these elaborate feasts, and my honey frequently brought some amazing food home. She only worked out there on certain evenings and the master chef would always drive her home; he really liked her.

She also labored as a part-time groomer at a shop called The Clip Joint on Melrose. The owner of the place taught her many tricks of the trade which you never learn in school, but paid her a very small amount for the work she did. In those days, a groomer was supposed to earn a certain percentage of the charges, but he only gave her two dollars for each finished dog. I heard from someone later that an old groomer named Loren Hawk needed an assistant, so I borrowed Sidra's Ghia and drove Yasue out to his place, which was called The Silverlake Pet Shop. It was on Hyperion Avenue, and she remarked about how rural the area seemed, she said she expected to see a cow or two ambling down that quiet street.

The whole area was different then, a gas station sat on each corner of Hyperion and Griffith Park, and the original Zen Restaurant was just a tiny place. Next door, Camille's Pet Food store did very well; they sold a lot of fresh horsemeat for animals. Yasue gladly accepted the job from Loren, but ended up doing much more than grooming. Before she could use his filthy toilet, she took one whole day just to cleanse and disinfect it. Suzie helped her out once in a while, but Loren made it clear that they were only apprentices and would have to perform hard work for little or no pay. This man cheated at everything; once we saw him spray a German shepherd with Lysol in the tub and he called it a bath.

Throughout our first year together, we became totally monogamous, with five cats and my dad across the hall. In my eyes we were married, Yasue accepted me as a husband figure in her life and she was my sweet little sexy wife. Even though we took a vow under a light bulb in our dressing room and she placed her mother's wedding ring on the third finger of my right hand, which will never come off, her denial was fascinating. When it was time for the annual Gay Pride Parade, she refused to go with me because she actually said she wasn't gay. To this day, we have never uttered a word about our relationship around her Japanese friends, though our existence together was and still is, quite gay.

She was comfortable financially with two part-time jobs, so it was definitely time for me to find some full-time work. Katie called from school one morning to say that a famous L.A. veterinarian was looking for an employee at his office on La Brea. Occasionally, some professional people in the pet business would call Bark N' Purr seeking employees, and I was very lucky to be offered the chance to even work with someone such as this celebrated doctor. It took two long bus rides to get out there, but my initial interview with him went well, and I gratefully accepted this badly needed position.

Assistant Veterinarian was my official job title, but it turned out to be much more work than that. Each morning, before eight, I would open up the place and basically straighten out the front desk of the reception area to get caught up on the filing. Next, I had to clean out all the messy cages because he did a lot of boarding. He designated certain kennels in separate rooms for the sick animals, and there were many outside dog runs. I began in the cat room by feeding and taking each animal out of its cage. I then put them into another cage until I finished disinfecting and cleaning. Sometimes we boarded up to twenty felines at a time and even more dogs, which was a lot of pooh to clean every day.

His clients couldn't see the doctor before eleven a.m. but they would line up with their sick pets much earlier to sit around and chitchat with others. He saw each one separately, made a diagnosis, to schedule all surgeries following his daily Big Mac sandwich for lunch. Goodman was a Taurus, around sixty years old, kept a steady girlfriend and had two ex-wives. Eleven hundred dollars monthly was what he had to pay his last wife for alimony. The skilled doctor drove a fairly new Cadillac, dressed sharp and loved Las Vegas showgirls; he generally favored very tall ladies.

At the outset of working for Dr. Albert Goodman, I felt confident that I had the aptitude to get through any doubtful circumstances. The first morning went very well, so he scheduled a cat to be spayed at two p.m. When he came back from MacDonald's reeking of onions, he meticulously set up the surgery room. This tiny female calico kitten only weighed about seven pounds. First he gave her a strong sedative, then tied all four paws to the table and while she was lying flat on her back, he told me to hold the container of ether, directly over her nose until he said to take it away.

He proceeded to make an incision straight down the abdomen and even though it was a very neat cut, I could see her innards swimming in blood. I was in a total state of shock when he told me to take the ether away, and I froze and became paralyzed. The poor little kitten stopped breathing and died. Goodman screamed at me, untied her and skillfully began to massage the open heart. Fortunately, he revived her at once, but I got nauseated and shaky anyway. The doctor told me to go outside to take a few deep breaths or have a cigarette, so I did. My first day in surgery was daunting after that unnerving scare; I would pay much more attention to the instructions and try to make my job easier. Since then, I've seen many veterinarians at work, but never anyone with his competence or technique.

At one time during his career, he indulged many famous Hollywood celebrities but vowed never to make house calls for these people again. He explained that several well-paid actors didn't pay their bills. They told him to deal with their business managers or accountants, however, the bigger the star, the longer it took him to get reimbursed. The doctor went to their mansions to treat all the sick pets but was never compensated to his satisfaction.

When I began to work for him, I wondered why he shook his clients' pockets so hard. I was always chagrined by his insensitive way of dealing with cash, especially when he rousted the really poor people who couldn't readily pay him for treatments. This troubled guy had to earn major money for alimony payments and hustled to the bank daily.

Dr. Goodman was famous through part of the sixties when he and another veterinarian invented some new type of plastic limb for animals. They were acclaimed for coming up with the first pet prosthetics, and they wrote about and lectured other vets about this procedure. He was a smart and caring person, even though he was terribly rude about collecting fees. There were times when an animal was in very critical condition so Doc would sleep at the clinic all night until the crisis hopefully passed. The building had a small room with a bed for a caretaker but was only used if he stayed over to monitor a pet. He never retained a twenty-four-hour staff; I completed all the work during the day.

It was early in March of 1980 and Yasue's sister was about to have her first baby. Asian ladies are very good at being helpful throughout an event like this, so Yasue decided to leave for Hawaii to comfort her until the baby arrived. I was surprised and overwhelmed because this meant that we might be separated for a couple of months. How could I deal with being alone after we had been dedicated lovers for nearly a year? Now it would be just Dad, the five cats and me.

Yasue left for Oahu with my blessings and I promised to behave while she was gone. I worked very hard, six days a week at the animal clinic, cleaned our apartment frequently and over-watered all her plants. One night I had to work late in surgery with Dr. Goodman, so he was kind enough to drive me home in his chic Cadillac. He came upstairs to meet my dad and remarked about his cataracts. Our cat, Lady Bug, was quickly diagnosed as a dry-food junkie, he told me to change her diet right away. Doc believed that felines should only be fed with canned foods. My opinionated boss really did appreciate our place; he said the ambience was just like New York City.

It would soon be time for Yasue to come home now, so I replaced the dead plants with new ones, but I knew she would notice.

Regarding my earnings as an assistant vet, Mickey was right, I was only paid twenty-five cents per hour over the minimum wage, but this experience was priceless. He taught me a great deal about healing my own pets, so the need to visit any pet clinic would be minimal. I survived on that tiny paycheck, and I continued to draw SSI checks since I concluded that this job might not be permanent.

There were plenty of heartaches in that business, especially while watching an animal being put to sleep, I sympathized with the owners when they chose to be with their cherished pets as they passed away. Later, we stored all the dead bodies outside in a large freezer until Animal Control could pick them up. A huge German shepherd that weighed more than one hundred pounds had to be put down one day and this dog became a problem after he expired, we just couldn't seem to get him in the refrigerator. There were several small cadavers in there already and the city wasn't coming to collect the bodies for a week. After much grappling, we finally got that enormous canine into the freezer and my back began to ache. Women are more sympathetic to pets but men are physically stronger.

Yasue was finally coming home; her sister had a baby boy called Chad on April 1st. Our house was immaculate and I was in good shape when she arrived, however, my father seemed to be feeling some genuine distress. He only had one lung and continued to puff heavily on Camel cigarettes. Smoking was very taxing on his heart and maybe he shouldn't have been running over to Ralph's to see Rita, the red-headed cashier, every day. It was obvious whenever he walked that he could barely breathe, so I made a deal with him. If he stayed home while we were at work, I'd bring him a half pint of whiskey in the evening to help him sleep. Meals on Wheels delivered nourishing food to him five days a week and we took him to the doctor regularly, but at times he flatly refused to take his medications.

*****

You may be wondering why I introduce people by announcing their Zodiac signs. My fervent interest in astrology began in Provincetown during my early twenties when a pretty girl named Candice, who was the town oracle, did my natal chart by hand for five dollars. She assured me that I would be a late starter in life, but I wasn't convinced of her prediction until I met and fell in love with Yasue at the age of thirty-nine. Since the Candice period, I spent many years trying to disprove the influence of planets and studied enough to know there was really something to it, so I continued to investigate.

Astrology became my second language, so I asked everyone about their sign before anything else. With an uncanny memory for birth dates, I began to see how the influence of stars could determine what we are like and how these planets affect us. Before I went to work for Dr. Goodman, I took a college-level course at The First Temple of Astrology downtown. I was blessed to have lived so openly in Provincetown but frittered away my youth on drugs and booze, which was usually the fastest way for me to find bliss, but now I am a real adult with a family, and I was indeed a late starter.

The urge for some kind of spirituality or magic would frequently accelerate within me; I recall a fleeting friend named Belinda who was also interested in mysticism. I met her during my bachelor days when I hung around the Catalina Bar. She was a very tall waspy blond with blue eyes, working as a part-time exotic dancer. We were both analytical Virgos, and in between the bumps and grinds of her performances we discussed astrology with keenness. Belinda was smart; she understood the Tarot cards and was extremely accurate with readings. I wanted to learn more about this absorbing subject, so she told me that all the necessary books, materials and tools could be found at a mysterious occult shop called The House of Hermetic on Hollywood Boulevard at the corner of Serrano.

It was a long walk to this spooky cabalistic store, but the place hypnotized me at once and became my focal spot for shopping. The large smoky room reeking of incense displayed countless books on astrology and other fascinating occult topics, including how to conjure up personal magic. The owner was a good White Witch named Reio, pronounced 'Re ya'. Her Gemini daughter, Lola, ran the business and a smug Leo guy named Matthew worked for them as the manager. They stocked all the fundamental materials for one to manifest riches and good fortune by way of white witchcraft.

Reio was a tiny older woman who appeared to be the main

figure in the Pagan coven that I stumbled upon, she was the wisest person I ever met. Lola was friendly, sweet and tended to the financial part of their business. The cynical Matthew spooked me with the dark and chilling glances which he gave to people he didn't like. We became friends because I never wanted him to dress my candles with evil. He told me that he got angry with a client once and dispensed his own smelly arm pit sweat all over the person's candle, presumably while he was anointing it for luck in the back room.

Years ago when I lived in Cambridge with Freda, I bought a pair of little boys' cowboy boots at a thrift shop. The moment I put them on, my feet seemed to carry me to magical places, including an occult shop near Harvard. This tiny store was quite cluttered but one item which stood out was a small booklet written by the Rosicrucians, a timeless organization that distributed many cabalistic publications. I chose to buy a pamphlet which included a round plastic gold coin with letters and times. Their intriguing system explained the merits of each weekday, also the seven daily periods of change. After dissecting the text, I learned we also go through these seven changes every seven years.

The small imprinted plastic coin was a reference indicator and the booklet was an abbreviated digest from the big book *Self Mastery and Fate with the Cycles of Life*, written by H. Spencer Lewis. It detailed how you could achieve harmony by means of timing your seven life cycles. Health, happiness and prosperity are available to those who know what period they are living in; one could enhance the success of countless activities. Eliminate chance or luck, cast aside fate and try to replace those entities with Self-Mastery. Once you understand the cycles, you can control your own destiny.

I appreciate analyzing systems, if this technique lived up to the author's promise, I could abide by his method and come to depend on it. The main book covered personal and business phases, health and disease periods, fortunate times, inner soul characteristics, opportunity seasons and success interims. If you follow these seven major changes, you will always know the right time for the coming events in your life. For instance, which period would be the right one to start a new romance or take a vacation? It is especially helpful to know when you are going into your fortunate period. I have studied this approach for a long time, simplified it and live by the seven cycles of life to this day.

Eventually I figured out that the Rosicrucian system of seven simply characterized the seven main astrological planets. If the day of the week was Sunday, the planetary ruler was the sun, the moon ruled Monday and so forth. The plastic coin indicated seven daily changes, but I concluded that each and every hour, one major planet was dominant, which happened three times a day. This system seemed complicated, but I'll give you one example of how I applied it to Mom's advantage.

My mother was taking a two-day trip to Las Vegas, with her hard of hearing friend Marge. I stayed up late the night before they left to make them a very basic chart. I marked the twenty-four hours for each day in red or green. If the hour was colored with red ink, they must not gamble, if the hour was marked with green ink, they should really go for it. Mom genuinely followed my stop/go chart and won a lot of money. The doubting Thomas Marge gambled to the contrary and lost every penny.

*****

Yasue and I didn't have a car; once in a while I would walk all the way from Third and Vermont up to Hollywood Boulevard. We were usually broke then, if I needed a two-dollar candle, I'd cash soda bottles at Ralph's then hike to The House of Hermetic. You can buy white glass candles anywhere, but I needed to have mine anointed for luck. My first altar was out on our fifth floor fire escape where I sat at a tiny white plastic table, set an ashtray there for a joint, next to my astrology lesson and The Book of Psalms to say particular daily prayers. Later on, I set up an altar at my small desk. I would neatly place a few sheets of art paper over the whole surface, the center a multicolored candle arrangement, leaving space on the paper to write astral messages. Clouds of incense were sent to the universe as offerings to bring about our wishes. Whether a person's religion is Pagan or Catholic, the ideology of repetitious prayer and sacrificial fragrances manifest the same miracles.

I don't think the average person realizes what astrology has to do with certain events. For instance, Easter always comes when the moon is full in Libra and the sun is in Aries. Jews attend synagogues on serious Saturdays and Muslims worship on Fridays under the lovely influence of Venus. Christians glorify Sunday as the family church day, as the sun is a life giver. Doctors' play golf on Wednesdays, and that day is ruled by restless Mercury and performing surgery when one is inclined to feel nervous isn't a good thing. The lessons I learned through studying astrological timetables became vital to my life. If I ever intended to bring about a miracle, it could only manifest through astrological timing and pragmatic work. Soon, we would attract some unbelievable magic.

It was almost the spring equinox of 1980 and I was getting tired of taking those long bus rides to Dr. Goodman's place. He began to get on my nerves, along with the heaps of animal excrements which I constantly resented cleaning up. What I hated the most was apologizing for my employer's bad manners. Dad was getting sicker and I wanted to be closer to him in case he became critical. I phoned Bark N' Purr to see if they had any job leads closer to home, Katie said they didn't have anything then, but would call me right away if she found something I was qualified to do.

Yasue was still out in the boondocks slaving as an apprentice groomer for Loren Hawk. At one point she was ready to leave his shop, so he promised to sell her the business as soon as he came into his Texas oil inheritance. She continued her part-time job at the consulate's house while the chef, Toyo, grew more in love with my darling Sag. She kept in touch with many former English school chums who came to visit us a lot; it seemed like I was in the middle of a Japanese soap, but her friends had too much class to ever ask about our relationship. They were all polite young ladies.

When I was a kid living on Pakachoag Street, my Aunt Emily kept a large statue of The Infant of Prague on her bureau and believed that this little baby Jesus saved the entire harassed country of Czechoslovakia from financial collapse. She explained its deep symbolism and always kept a dime scotch-taped to the bottom. Her shrine became a lending place for me whenever I needed ten cents for Coke money, sometimes I would borrow that dime but replace it with another coin as soon as I could. This dignified plaster infant was really my first fountain of miracles. At times, the handy ten-cent piece provided soda money so I could camp in Ponya's Spa for hours with my friends.

Many years later, I attended a mass with Mom at a huge

Catholic church on Sunset and decided to rummage around the religious article store adjacent to the main structure. To my surprise and delight, they carried lots of printed material regarding The Infant of Prague. This store sold statues of him and one looked just like Aunt Emily's. I couldn't afford much, but I purchased a few pamphlets relating to requests and desires. After reading some facts, I accepted the idea of making a nine-day novena and would dedicate all my prayers to the infant, who was good to me long ago.

I could never ask for a favor without giving something in return. The germane thing to do was to abandon one pleasure which I really enjoyed but could live without for nine consecutive days. Booze gratified me, so I gave it up as a sacrifice through the novena period. My altar was energized with a white candle as the focal point, flanked by many jumbo, colored candles. The charcoal to kindle resin-type incense was ignited, when each candle was lit. One should pray or meditate at the altar just before sunrise and breathe in a yoga mode. Inhale deeply, hold it, exhale and relax. My meditation practices were never taught by Catholics, however, I did burn Frankincense and Myrrh at the shrine regularly.

My greatest tool for information is an astrological calendar. If one knew what was occurring every day with the planets, they could figure out activities for approaching phenomena. For instance, police personnel and hospitals could plan for the many hassles which arise during a full moon. I use a planetary guide to layout agendas as far as one year ahead. The easiest way to learn this system begins with the days of the week. If today is Wednesday, we will feel the need to care of details.

Almost everything on my altar came from The House of Hermetic, but the most informative book for practicing magic, is called *Perfume Oils, Candles, Seals and Incense*, written by Aima, a dynamic white witch and good friend of Reio. This manual described candle color significance, depicted the use of compelling oils, precious stones and gave great insight regarding their legendary powers. Through earlier times, Egyptian priests appreciated the numerous magical mysteries of religious ceremony, which always included incense, perfumes and oils, as part of their sacred rituals.

The idea of making a religious novena is to bring about

miracles of sorts. One might consider anticipating a new car or a nice home, but my heartfelt desire was to own a simple pet grooming shop. After Loren alluded to selling us the business for two thousand dollars, we imagined there was hope. I began to conduct a personal novena once a month, beginning on the sixteenth and ending on the twenty-fourth. Abstaining from booze was my only sacrifice, which wasn't a problem, but I usually got a little anxious by the twenty-third. I continued to make these novenas through all the years that followed and still do. Miracles only come to idealistic people with trusting hearts and childlike minds. Faith is the key for dreams to come true, and I will forever place my trust within the spirit world. In all this time, I could never keep track of the countless wonders, for which I am truly grateful.

Katie called with a desirable job offer in the early spring of 1980. The magic was working because this position would pay much more than I earned from Dr. Goodman. I was to become a receptionist at The Ambassador Dog and Cat Hospital and wouldn't have to clean up any more animal feces, other than from my own pets. I gave him a two-week notice and was amazed when the grumpy old Taurus said he didn't want me to leave; he even offered me a healthy raise. The new office was within walking distance of our house, which meant no more long bus rides, amen.

The Ambassador was right next door to Bark N' Purr and I knew everyone there because when we were in school Mickey always sent me over with the sick animals. A charming Scorpio doctor named Lyle Price was the main man and had a business partner called Rosalinda Fernandez, a Filipino Sagittarius who was all about prosperity. Joanie, my associate receptionist, was a Pisces woman who married all the wrong guys. It seemed like she always needed extra money and sometimes helped herself to the available cash. This animal hospital was extremely busy and made tons of revenue from caring people with ailing pets, though many folks in that area were poor and couldn't always pay.

A strange lady named Ruth had been working there for a long time and did most of the pet bathing. This character always walked around the clinic holding a newspaper in front of her face. No one really knew why she did it; we just assumed it was because she had some heavy-duty complexes. There were some very odd people involved with pet occupations and I came to believe that Yasue and

I were more normal than most. A very sweet Virgo guy named Marty worked there and also attended Bark N' Purr. One afternoon while he was assisting Dr. Price, a sizable Golden Retriever bit him right through the cheek, causing a huge hole and much depression, which continued for a while.

When Yasue and I were first getting to know one another at grooming school, I asked her what she cooked; she smiled and said that she could only make packaged ramen and salads. Those edibles wouldn't be enough for me to survive on, so I promptly learned to prepare the meals. She ate some chicken, but seafood was more enticing. One time we made a deal, I would try eating raw fish if she agreed to eat some steak. To this day, she has never tried red meat, yet I continue to enjoy sashimi. Before we met, I never had to fix a healthy meal. In the old days, there used to be one butch and one femme, the feminine partner usually acted as the chef and former lovers like Janet Grigsby were so great with food, I never had any desire or reason to become accomplished in the kitchen.

Fortunately, my new Japanese pals knew how to cook many different kinds of food. They would come over to our apartment regularly and share meals. Each time this circle of young ladies visited, they would bring assorted ingredients for our eclectic banquets. Once in a while they'd make some tempura and the next time they might show me how to cook sukiyaki, the meal I liked the best though was chicken curry. Eventually I learned how to prepare all their dishes and still make a lot of spicy curry with rice. My father felt ecstatic whenever he was surrounded by those pretty girls.

It was good that Yasue stayed in touch with her Japanese roots. Her friends constantly exchanged diverse cartoon-type storybooks; they read a lot and took many naps. I think they were all virgins except for my little princess, she had been sexual with men, but we never really discussed it. The ladies would fantasize about meeting French movie stars like Alain Delon but never did. We really became good friends and since they shared those outstanding cooking lessons with me, I was glad to help them learn English. They were charming women to be around and I learned a great deal.

On Sunday, May 18th 1980, Mount Saint Helens volcano

erupted. The following morning, that catastrophe became a sensational topic at the Ambassador and everywhere else. Ruth actually took the newspaper away from her face and began to talk our heads off. The natural disaster turned her on in a weird way; everyone was delighted over the fact that she was actually communicating about something. After she initiated a friendly dialogue, I didn't mind sharing my lunches with her.

We still didn't have a car, but occasionally I'd borrow Sidra's. Usually on Sunday we tried to go out to Venice Beach, even if we had to take a bus from Third and Vermont. The RTD trip was a long and noisy ride, and the rear of the coach was always packed with teenagers carrying ghetto blasters, but we ignored their uproar to focus on a lovely brunch at the Sidewalk Café. It was spiritual whenever my feet touched the cold ocean water, and sometimes I'd cast some flowers in for the dearly departed.

The Pacific was about sixteen miles from our house, but it might as well have been a hundred. Most of my free-spirited pleasures emerged when I lived close to the ocean, I believe whenever I am too far inland, my creative efforts become stifled. Even when I lived in New York City I had to go out to Coney Island periodically just to breathe the pure salt air and savor a famous Nathan's hot dog.

I couldn't swim at Venice Beach as the water was too cold; it seemed more frigid than Provincetown. I stood lofty on the shore, blessed myself and sent good thoughts to my faraway buddy Walshie. Yasue walked buoyantly along the coast in her own lovely realm of dreams while I made new friends on the beach. Plenty of characters were attracted to this colorful locality and sometimes I'd share a joint or a drink of cheap red wine with total strangers, simply to absorb their bohemian essence.

Life was good for us that summer, Yasue and I were deeply in love, Mom continued to have the usual companions at her poker games, and Dad was still able to sweet talk Rita at the market. I had a few more rooftop parties, but things were changing fast at the El Prado with our neighbors. A few of the old folks had passed away quietly and the new tenants all seemed to have language difficulties. When Joe Chi moved away, I felt a loss, he had been very kind to us, but we were proud of him because he bought his own house. Ginny, the manager was having problems with her man

Jack, so they split up. Sometimes things unfold for the better and other times for the worse, but change is inevitable.

Cats love to look out windows and our five, had a wonderful time glancing from the fifth floor at the street activities below. Once in a while, a bird might land on the windowsill and they would try hard to catch it, but they couldn't because of the screens. One day I came home from work and noticed that Tama, the spooky one, was missing. Dad didn't even realize that she was gone and felt terrible about it. We hunted through the whole building calling her name, but it was futile, she'd disappeared. The only explanation I could think of was perhaps Dad's paperboy had taken her, she was the most alluring one and that kid was the only stranger who came into the back hallway where our felines hung out.

A couple of days went by and we'd almost given up hope of finding her, then Ginny's daughter called with good news. Smitty, the manager of the apartment house next door, told her that a freaked out, black and white cat was lying motionless in his laundry room. I ran over to his place quickly and there was Tama, dazed and all scrunched up on a towel. I cried with joy when I saw her and carried this beauty right home. Early the next morning we brought her to see Dr. Price, he said she had a broken pelvis but would recover if we kept her quiet in a large cardboard container for a week or so.

I went right to Ralph's market and retrieved a huge toilet paper box from the back. I then placed Tama in some soft bedding, which would be her new crib for a while.

It was nearly three days since she came home and she refused to eat or drink anything. She just laid there in shock, staring up with her big frightened eyes. We tried hand feeding her real tuna sashimi, but she wasn't even tempted. Finally I decided to blow a few small puffs of marijuana into her cardboard sanctuary, and believe it or not, within fifteen minutes, she began to drink some milk and swallow food, what a relief that was.

The doctor said she would never be able to have babies because he had to spay her, but we always fixed our cats regardless. Eventually we figured out that she must have been chasing a bird and shot right through the window screen, plummeting down five stories from Dad's place. Apparently she landed on the concrete, pulled herself over a wooden fence and dragged her tiny broken body into Smitty's basement. Soon after that, Lady Bug also fell out of a window, but we were watching when it happened. She landed in some bushes, picked herself right up and started yelling, which was natural for her. I raced down, carried her back up five flights, then she went directly to the food like nothing had happened. All the window screens were solidly nailed down after those alarming ordeals.

*****

Yasue had been working for Loren nearly one year without pay, and while she assumed that his shop would be hers for two thousand dollars, he secretly advertised it for much more. Meanwhile, we had another serious problem to solve. Yasue went to the Bark N' Purr school on a student visa, but soon that permit would expire and she began to feel paranoid about being illegal. She would either have to go back to Japan permanently, or deal with immigration regarding a permanent residence status. Amnesty programs weren't in place yet and sooner or later she would have to hire a lawyer.

Loren Hawk recommended a young gay lawyer whom he said was bright; we called him right away. The man's name was John Monte and his office was close by in Glendale. He seemed to be a novice but a smooth talker, good-looking and swore that he could easily obtain a green card for Yasue; all we had to do was pay two thousand dollars for this document. We had just enough money to compensate him without hesitation, she signed some papers and that was the end of it for a while.

John told us his strategy for acquiring her green card would be based on the fact that Yasue spoke fluent Japanese and Loren couldn't replace her with just any ordinary American worker. He alleged that forty percent of his business involved Japanese clients. Imagine almost half of Silverlake speaking Japanese? This guy could never tell the truth, but I was glad that he lied in our favor; we could only hope the immigration people would accept this absurd fabrication. John's application stated that she was the best pet groomer in the city to account for the numerous Asian customers, but in actual fact, she was fresh out of school and Loren had merely engaged her as an inexperienced apprentice.

When she finally heard from immigration, they requested more proof regarding her routine duties at work. They especially scrutinized how or why a Japanese person like Yasue could do this kind of work more competently than an American operator. We called John Monte as soon as we received the notice, but he was nowhere to be found. His phone had been disconnected, so we checked out his office in Glendale, it seems the charming lawyer who took our money had apparently left town. Loren swore he had no idea what happened to John, but we couldn't believe anything he said. We came to the conclusion that the guy earned two thousand dollars for one hour of work. Nowadays we are very suspicious of all lawyers, unless we get to know one for a while and build trust in them.

*****

I hadn't seen my kid brother Earl since his first wife threw me out many years ago, but Mom always stayed in touch. Things weren't going too well with his livelihood in Connecticut at the time, so my mother suggested that they all move out here to sunny California. My brother, his second wife Pat, and her two young sons, C. J. and Kenny, from a previous marriage packed up their belongings, stuffed everything into a U-Haul and drove cross-country in an old station wagon. They went directly to Mom's when they arrived, and we all seemed very glad to see each other, for the moment.

Earl's first wife, also called Pat, despised my gay lifestyle and made offensive, hurtful judgments, which generally made me feel bad. Today, I don't allow anyone's opinion or displeasure with me to disturb my happiness. For the first week or so, Earl and Pat slept at Mom's. We put one boy on Dad's couch and the other lad on our sofa. They left their things in storage until they figured out where to live.

My brother decided that he could easily get a good job out here because of his wide knowledge and experience. He was an alumnus of the Navy, so he got hired right away at Hughes Aircraft in Burbank. I thought the wages they offered were really excellent, but that amount didn't quite satisfy him. He always expected to start off a new career as a vice president but never quite gained the title.

The job was a long ride from Mom's by freeway, and soon after the first paycheck they rented a small house in Burbank, directly behind a place called Del Taco, diagonally across from a busy gas station. The two-bedroom cottage on Burbank Boulevard had no trees, scrubs, or even a blade of grass around it, yet to my brother and family, it was Beverly Hills. The boys began school in September; Earl worked long hours and Pat stayed home, watched cartoons, sipped vodka and enjoyed take-out food.

*****

The Tuesday after Labor Day, Yasue showed up for work at Loren's Silverlake Pet Shop as usual. Hawk promptly told her that he had finally come into his inheritance and found a likely buyer for the business. My wonderful Sag partner, who slaved for this creep for over a year without pay, was never consulted about the sale. We couldn't believe his cold, underhanded and heartless decision was made without giving her any prior notice or options to buy it. She cried hard for the entire week.

A man named Bob D'Amato acquired the shop for five thousand dollars and Yasue no longer had a nonpaying job. Soon after he occupied the store, I borrowed Sidra's Ghia and drove out there with a fresh bouquet of flowers to bid him good luck; he turned out to be a nice Cancer guy. Without the details, I explained that before he came along we planned to buy this shop but Loren screwed us, so if for any reason he ever decided to sell it, to please call us first. I boldly left our phone number on the back of a note pad, wished him well and sadly slithered away from the place we nearly owned.

*****

I was still working at the Ambassador and collecting a monthly check, while Yasue calmly served exotic foods at the Japanese Consulate. We were trying to save money in case another grooming shop became available. There were a few places being advertised, most of them were in the valley, and we didn't have a car so we continued to visualize our own place, praying that someday it might happen.

One morning we went to look at a shop for sale way down on South La Brea. The weird woman was asking thirty thousand for a hole in the wall and seemed very reluctant to offer us any financial details about her business. It was a small dingy spot in a strip mall with many homeless people camped all around the complex, and parking was impossible. From then on, we would just wait for a miracle, hope for a blessing and go on making petitions for our own shop through my regular novenas.

Sometime during 1980, I fell madly in love with my vinyl copy of *Double Fantasy*, by John Lennon and Yoko Ono. Yasue didn't always share my taste in music but really enjoyed this album. We associated with certain songs which seemed pertinent to our lives then, and I'd like to think that John wrote the lyrics to *Clean Up Time* just for us. We are still affectionate about his ideologies.

> *Moonlight on the water, sunlight in my face.*
> *You and me together, we are in our place.*
> *The gods are in the heavens, the angels treat us well.*
> *The oracle has spoken, we cast the perfect spell.*
> *Now it begins, let it begin...*
> *Clean up time.*

The words to that tune applied to us in one way or another. I am a Virgo, who has always had a bad habit or two to clean up, and Yasue simply cleans everything, she is Japanese. When I first listened to the ballad *Woman*, it became a manifesto which expressed everything I felt then and still feel about Yasue. She has taught me the meaning of success, and I will forever be in her debt for encouraging me with optimism and faith. '*It is written in the stars; I love you now and forever.*'

Close to Thanksgiving on a warm autumn day, my bossy brother told everyone that we all had to take part in a huge holiday feast at his house, and he would come to pick us. People assumed that I was an only child; I never mentioned having a sibling because I was ashamed of his bumpkin personality. My father denied that Earl was his real son and claimed when he was in the army, Mom fooled around, ergo, he couldn't be his child. Earl's body was huskier than Dad's, but there was still a strong likeness, I now believe he really is my blood brother, yet I often have a difficult time relating to him.

My father was barely cordial to his son little Earl and never cared to bond with him, perhaps because they didn't have much in common. Dad was kind of a wild reckless guy, and my brother was the ultimate husband and family man, forever at the helm. I used to think about what would happen between them if they ever got really drunk together, Earl never drank very much.

Finally it was Thanksgiving Day and we all got ready to join the Beverly Hillbillies in ticky-tacky Burbank, except for Dad. He apologized and said he didn't feel well that day, but I knew he just wanted to stay home to watch a football game on television as opposed to children's cartoons; the old man was smart.

Whenever I had to spend more than thirty minutes with the 'Clampetts', I took a lot of deep breaths while sitting in quiet desperation. It was hard for me to look cheerful when I listened to their boring small talk; I would have preferred no dialogue at all. Yasue, however, was completely patient with those rowdy children. She kept them entertained with nothingness and they adored her for it. Neither Pat nor Earl were very good cooks, but they put a traditional meal together. My brother loved new toys, so he bought an electric carving knife just for this banquet. When the half-cooked turkey came out of the oven, he cut huge, thick slices from the breast, and tore the rest apart by hand.

I never had much experience around children, so I really didn't know how to deal with them, but what was my mother's excuse? She showed Pat's kids absolutely no patience or tolerance, her face actually took on an ugly, mean look whenever she scolded them. Maybe she resented the fact that these youngsters weren't her kindred grandchildren. We took a complete dinner back to Dad, but he didn't seem too thrilled. The turkey was partly raw, the mashed potatoes were runny, the peas were hard, they forgot to make gravy, and the mincemeat pie was mush. Earl and I were very different.

The only rewards I ever accumulated from the Ambassador were some happy moments I shared with clients while their pets were getting well. My friend Jim said animals were my forte and I really liked working there, but other than regular paychecks, I never compensated myself with a penny from that business. On several occasions at the end of the day, money from our cash box was missing, usually a small amount like ten or twenty dollars. Dr. Fernandez approached me one morning and asked why we were always coming up short. Joanie and I shared one large metal container at the time which held the currency and checks, I was certain my skinny co-worker was helping herself.

Joanie was a forty-five-year-old woman with a gritty cigarette cough, she recently married a short Latino guy who spoke very little English and sported a fairly old Nissan. Her husband picked her up every day at lunchtime, drove around the block and they returned within five minutes. A common drug deal took longer; I just assumed she was giving him some of the missing cash from work. This hard-luck lady always needed money, whether it was for new tires or a tune up, she was supporting a loser for a spouse, and in my mind there was no doubt about her guilt, even with that poker face.

The first few times money went missing, I thought perhaps I added wrong, so I began to keep a little sheet of paper to record all daily transactions and my math was quite accurate. I absolutely went berserk when Rosalinda alleged that our daily receipts were short again. We went upstairs to talk in the doctor's lounge and I asked, "Do you honestly think that I am stealing money from this office? If you do, I will quit right now." Fernandez said she didn't believe I would ever cheat, but she suggested Joanie and I keep separate cash boxes from then on. We each got a locked receptacle, but after one week, money from my box was gone again, I soon determined that the same key fit both containers.

We took our lunches at separate times, which was convenient for Joanie to do whatever it was she did. Dr. Fernandez went upstairs every day to eat and watch portions of her favorite daytime soaps. One morning she took a fresh blood sample from a dog, and went up to the lounge. Instead of putting the vile right in the refrigerator, she sat down to watch television and fell sound asleep on the sofa. I had to go up there later to give her a message from Dr. Price, so I awakened her softly. She was still holding the container, but the blood had coagulated during her carefree nap.

On coffee breaks, I had numerous short conversations with Fernandez and assured her that I was an ethical, ring-around-the-collar Catholic, a huge believer in karma and presently focused on Saxon witchcraft from a book called *The Tree*, by Raymond Buckland. The fundamental prayer for the celebration of Esbat written in this manual introduced a splendid philosophy for me to abide by.

> *Man learned as he was taught, with patience and love.*
> *Naught did he receive for naught, but well rewarded for his pains.*
> *As ye give, so shall it return and this he learned well.*
> *Give of yourself, your love and your life and so you will gain immeasurably.*
> *Take that which is not yours to take and you may find it is not what it seemed.*
> *The Gods are just and all they do with reason.*
> *Work well with them and you will be rewarded, more than you might dream.*
> *As we need them, they need us.*
> *Let us live and love together, all in their sight.*
> *Love is the law and love is the bond. So be it.*

Quite a while back, Sidra had given me a few hits of Orange Sunshine, but by now it was probably old and not very strong. At sundown, on Monday, December 8th, 1980, I took an acid trip for the last time. My energy level would always surge after dropping LSD, and I needed to do something productive. As a conventional Virgo from New England, I have a great penchant for neatness. On that particular evening, I decided to press some clothing. I was tripping frivolously, watching the flat iron levitate all around my blue button-down shirt, just like it was gliding over a mystical Ouija board, and each song playing on the radio seemed as though it was written just for Yasue and me.

Everything was perfect until a shocking news bulletin flashed over the radio. John Lennon has just been killed. The sobering message overwhelmed us and I was no longer high, I was sick. Through all the years of cherishing music, The Beatles were always my favorites, and I regarded John as the smartest, having more imagination than the others. Maybe the LSD amplified my grief behind this tragedy, but I really felt psychologically debilitated, extremely sad, and just numb. Yasue and I imagined that our lives were comparable to John and Yoko's, whenever we heard the song *Starting Over*.

*****

Christmas season was here again, fortunately, I had a Broadway charge card. My gift list was rather large that year, but at least I could still buy everyone a simple present. My brother drove us downtown and we headed straight to the chic men's department. Mom always dressed him in black pants with a white shirt when we were kids and he wore the same kind of modest apparel all his life. I decided he needed to look more fashionable, so I told him to get anything he wanted. Sure enough, he chose a pair of dark trousers and a light shirt. I yelled at him and quickly exchanged those boring duds for some crisp chino pants and a couple of stylishly colorful sport shirts, and he looked great.

Mom gave a big Christmas dinner party that year and invited Bob, Joe, Dorothy, Bertha, Tina, with her new boyfriend Sam, as well as my brother and his family. Yasue, Dad and I sauntered over to her house, which was only a block away, but I noticed that my father was coughing a lot. He walked slower than usual, constantly trying to catch his breath. My mother fixed a really good meal, so everyone gathered around talking while enjoying the food; I sat in silent madness because Mom's dismal friends bored me. Dad said he didn't feel well and looked quite pale, so we took him home at once.

We whispered a sigh of relief after leaving Mom's and felt free of all the useless information those quaint people were so anxious to provide us with. Nowadays, I manage to make a lot of small talk but back then I wanted everyone to think I was cool, so I didn't say very much. On our way home to the El Prado, we walked over New Hampshire Avenue slowly, then rode the tiny elevator up to our safe, cheerful, fifth-floor haven. It was early on a Thursday evening, so we decided to watch a little television together. Yasue and I sat on the sofa while Dad rested in a comfortable armchair.

That whole week was warmer than usual; even our Christmas tree was drying up fast, and when the windows were open, the traffic noise was terrible. The five cats were sitting around us when

Dad started to really cough hard; he was sweating profusely and turning colors. Somehow I got an ambulance right away, even though the 911 systems weren't in place yet.

The paramedics gave him oxygen and told us he was having a major heart attack. As they wheeled him out on a stretcher, Dad smiled sweetly at gaping neighbors. They took him directly to Hollywood Presbyterian Hospital, I rode with them to the emergency room and honestly thought he was going to die that night, I clutched his cold hand with all my love. He never meant so much to me, and I felt genuinely scared.

My first experience with death was attending Stanley Kowalski's wake. He was already dead so I didn't see him go through any torment. The next time I faced this anxiety was when my Nana called for me to be at her bedside, then passed away five minutes after I left. Following that heartache, my favorite uncle, Leo, was dying of lung cancer because he smoked all his life and worked in a dirty rag shop for years. Before he died, I went to visit him one Sunday on Pakachoag Street; the whole family was there. When I leaned over to kiss his forehead, his eyes lit up and he smiled. His hand was cold and frail, but I held it for a long time, reminding him of our regular weekend trips to his summer camp in Hopkinton. The next day, they told me that he passed away at midnight, practically grinning. I've always been squeamish whenever people I know pass away; it makes me feel abandoned.

While riding with Dad in the ambulance, I felt more frightened than ever. I loved all the other people who had departed, but my father meant much more, I cherished him deeply. He was my hero and pal, but maybe he really had used up his nine lives. What could I do? Was this heart condition our fault? I froze with guilt at the mere thought of him dying and leaving us now that we were a family again. They stabilized him at the hospital that night but how much time would he actually have left?

It was about one in the morning when I left the hospital. Before this trauma I'd been a nonsmoker for two months. As I made my way home, I noticed that a dimly lit, Latino bar was still open, so I marched in and bought a pack of cigarettes from a machine. The terrible habit came back immediately and I choked on Marlboros all the way home. Yasue was waiting up for the news and was relieved to hear he would be fine; her caring ways are characteristic of a true princess. My father adored her and unusually, my mother appreciated Yasue more than anyone I'd ever been with or loved.

Dad remained in the hospital for about five days, which is when I found out how much Yasue really hated visiting places with sick people. We took him home in a cab and he was thrilled to be leaving. While he was away, we cleaned his apartment thoroughly, added a few homespun touches and filled the pantry with lots of goodies. He now had to go on a strict, salt-free diet and couldn't smoke or drink, which was hard. Meals on Wheels began to provide him with nourishing food five days a week.

My father, 'The Phoenix', looked much older after this ordeal and we needed to keep closer tabs on his health. He was a Scorpio with a flair for insult. By insult, I mean some vulgar expressions he used or things he said spontaneously. Dad always referred to my Indian friend Lucky as 'Son of Cochise', if he glanced at a woman wearing a white dress, he might remark jokingly: "She looks like she's about to make her first holy communion." He mocked my skinny legs and said they looked like hockey sticks. Because of constant ridicule, I avoided wearing swimsuits or shorts for many years.

My mother became much more patient and considerate with Dad, and while we were at work she would run to the store and help out with chores around the house. My brother was still living in Burbank and I didn't expect that he would ever bond with our father. Earl paid him a few short visits, but their moments together were uneventful and not bubbling with dialogue. It seemed like Dad agonized just to make a little friendly conversation with his only son, who would never commit as to how he actually felt about his estranged father. Dad would be leaving us soon, I wanted everyone in the family to ultimately maintain good karma by honoring his current weariness, and not reflect on any prior flaws. Earl wasn't at all like him and didn't have a mean bone in his body. Dad could easily offend a person devoid of feeling any remorse; he was never aware of his hurtful scorpion sting.

Dad was our main worry, then there was Yasue's immigration status, which was a central issue, and we were still upset because of just being screwed by Loren, our hearts had been set on buying his shop. I made regular novenas and began to think about how we could conjure up some financial magic. The House of Hermetic is where I went, whenever I needed metaphysical advice. Lola listened well while I told her what was going on, she recommended another manual by Aima called *Ritual Book of Herbal Spells* and advised me to try a special ceremony from the book using prince's pine herb during any full moon. The alleged spell is said to evoke the gnomes who guard the treasures of the earth. If you follow this detailed procedure, you will be summoning the 'Little People' for assistance. When one seeks gold, silver, or gems hidden beneath the earth, the same rite is performed.

My work was competent at the Ambassador, the clients enjoyed me and their pets thought I was the Pied Piper of goodies. Sometime in January of 1981, Dr. Fernandez bitched once more about missing money, that's all I could take. I dropped everything and insisted she hustle upstairs to accept my notice. People could probably hear me yelling from a block away; this time I was very angry. "Joanie is the guilty one, how could you not see it? I've been telling you since I started here. My partner and I were saving money to buy our own pet grooming shop; do you believe ten dollars more will do it for us? How dare you think I could ever take something which didn't belong to me?"

On the way out, I picked up my personal stuff and gave Joanie the thief a killer, dirty look. That was the end of it, and I became jobless again. The monthly SSI check would always be there; as long as I could convince the government I was still crazy. Every once in a while, I had to keep an appointment with Dr. Streightz to give her progress reports, but quitting my post didn't indicate evolution.

I decided to try a prince's pine ritual, and the ceremony would take place when the moon was full in Leo. Yasue and I went by the book and got stark naked as we shared a few sips of wine from a golden chalice. This magical blend was made up of prince's pine, eucalyptus, acacia, bayberry, juniper berries, Job's tears and red cinchona bark. All the herbs had to be blended in a mortar and worked with a pestle until finely ground. Next, we had to select an outdoor clearing for this ceremonial rite, so we chose the fire escape for igniting the herbs in a brass container. When it was burning well, we faced west and sprinkled handfuls of this concoction into the flames. We then said: "Hearken to us, guardians of the earth! Yield unto us, thy goods of worth!" More spices were cast into the inferno as we repeated those words three times. The fire blazed fiercely, so I finally put it out.

It wasn't easy for either of us to get naked and go out on the cold fire escape, but after a little wine, we got more comfortable adapting to the ritual. When the ceremony is finished, one must sit quietly for thirty minutes to meditate on a sincere desire. Yasue still had the old key to Loren's shop, so she placed it at the base of the cauldron and focused on having that business. We ignited too much prince's pine mix and the flames got so high that night, we could have burned the El Prado down. I wonder if anyone saw us nude as we experimented with invoking blessings from the universe.

You may find this hard to believe, but the very next day after our cosmic ritual; Bob D'Amato called to let us know he was ready to sell the shop now and wondered if we were still interested in buying it. I was taking a hot shower when Yasue charged in screaming, "Bob wants to sell us the business." I called him back at once and confirmed that we were whole-heartedly interested in having the place. We simply asked him to give us ten days to come up with the money, and he agreed to wait.

Now we had to come up with four thousand dollars in ten days. We were both unemployed and didn't have much money saved. Bob was in fact letting the business go for one thousand less than he paid. He claimed he made his initial investment back, but he was in a hurry to sell the shop so he could move to Palm Springs and be with a guy whom he recently fell in love with. In the short time that he had the business; Bob had fixed up the place very nicely. He paneled the walls, did some painting, carpentry and provided the store with a respectable image, though the floors were still covered with seven different kinds of tiles. Bob's shop smelled a great deal cleaner than when Loren owned it.

My mother usually managed to save a little but seldom accumulated more than a few hundred dollars, whenever she had enough, she would jump on a bus headed for Las Vegas. Gambling was her greatest enjoyment, we never asked her for any money, but she gave us some anyway. Yasue called her mother in Okinawa and discussed this rare opportunity to buy her very own pet grooming shop. Her Mom's sugarcane field had done well that year, so she sent us four thousand dollars via special delivery without hesitation. To this day, I have never met the sweet and generous woman, my mother-in-law!

A couple of Yasue's close friends helped us out with additional funds. Kako, a Japanese woman who lived close to our house, lent us three thousand and the lonely chef named Ouda from the consulate doled out another three thousand. We had enough cash to buy the business now and even some left over for a good car. I called Bob to set up a meeting regarding our financial exchange and he was delighted that things were working out favorably for us. We met at the shop and drove over to Bank of America, where a public notary witnessed the sale of 'K-9 Tubbs'. I couldn't wait to take the bus home and present Yasue with this special document. We were finally business owners.

We purchased the business on Thursday, February 5th, 1981; the Year of the Rooster, a favorable time, representing the sign of Virgo in western astrology, therefore, our shop had to be immaculate, with a system for everything. Just before Bob and I signed the bill of sale, he walked me down a few doors to introduce me to Bob Cameron and Al Beal, the owners of the building. They ran an elegant company called The World of Wallpaper and were deeply rooted in the area. Their major clients seemed to be designers, I felt comfortable in this conspicuously gay setting; I loved to decorate.

I guess Bob chose to name the shop K-9 Tubbs for a play on words, but by mistake the painted window sign was only spelled with one b, so I changed the D.B.A. to K-9 Tubs with one B. After completing a verbal deal, I signed a very simple two-paragraph rental agreement with Bob C. and Al. The foundation of our new business began with a basic handshake and we always remained friends, they even said if we were ever short on rent money, we could pay them weekly. The monthly cost was only three hundred and twenty-five dollars, which included all the water and power bills.

Even though Yasue believed that cows might come moseying down Hyperion, there were other stores around. An alteration shop right next to us called Buttons and Bows belonged to an older Pisces woman, Helen May, who behaved like the local sheriff. Del Matheny, a sweet Cancer, occupied a hairstyling salon next to her. For lack of money, I was cutting my own hair, but Del noticed.

One day he said, "I don't do poodles, you shouldn't trim your own locks." After that remark, he became my regular hair cutter. Body Builders' Gym was next to the wallpaper store; Jim Mielke and his lover Bobby were the proprietors. Although Yasue was a bit shy about not speaking perfect English, the gay community fell in love with her anyway, and we were affectionately welcomed by all the locals.

The entire inventory at Bob's shop consisted of one bath tub, six, rusted wire cages, two old tables, two dryers, a huge spider plant and a stuffed pheasant, which had to be dusted daily for dog hair. When Yasue and I finished grooming school, we only had two combs, two brushes, two pairs of scissors, and we each owned a pair of clippers with a number ten blade. Originally we borrowed ten thousand dollars, four thousand would pay for the business and in addition to buying a car, and we needed other things. Brooms, mops, pails and cleaning products were our priorities. Next, we required grooming tools, supplies, stationary and maybe some cheap advertising. We had to get a business license, a permit from the State Board of Equalization, and place the new D.B.A. notice in a local newspaper.

We bought the shop on a Thursday when the sun and moon were in Aquarius, an excellent time to usher in a fresh enterprise. The planet Mercury, however, would start to go retrograde on Sunday. When this phenomenon occurs, our logic goes completely into the dark, causing a void within one's mind, so we began to consider all the important matters which might soon be imminent.

Yasue reviewed a Japanese daily called Rafu Shimpo and as she fanned the newspaper out, she became a lovely art form. Only forty-eight hours were left to locate a decent car before the retro period kicked in, so we needed to find one quickly. I checked the L.A. Times, there were many listings, but we could only afford to spend about a thousand. She suggested that I look over the Rafu classified section; the ideal auto might just be advertised in there. A simple ad in the tiny paper literally jumped out at me, it said, 'Student going back to Japan, and must sell a 1968 Toyota Corona, excellent condition, $800 firm.' I called the phone number and a young gentleman came right over. When he drove the small white sedan into our yard, I noticed the license plate read, 'WCH108'.

When I first saw it, I decided to name this neat little car, 'The

White Witch'. It was all white and the number plate said WCH, how perfect was that? Yasue worked out the details with the Japanese guy, whose name was Hiro. He was willing to sell us his well-kept Toyota, but he needed the car for his last ten days of school at UCLA. It would be well worth the wait, since all the planets seemed to be in our favor. The small square-shaped sedan was flawless, so we checked his identification carefully, and gave him a two hundred dollars deposit. He absolutely promised to bring it back to us in ten days.

It was only a matter of hours before Mercury stole our logic, so we shook hands and it was a done deal. This delay just meant we'd be taking a bus for a while longer. I continued to make novenas from the sixteenth, to the twenty-fourth of each month, no matter how early I had to sit down at the altar. I made coffee, fed the cats, cleaned their litter, packed a brown paper lunch bag, said goodbye to Dad and off we went to Silverlake. For the long and noisy bus commute, I usually carried an interesting witchcraft book to study. People tend to get nervous when they see things concerning the occult, so I disguised these manuals with plain, wrapping paper; no one ever knew what I was reading.

We were now the proud owners of a business, still riding the RTD and couldn't believe our dreams had actually manifested. It was literally the power of rituals and novenas which brought about the magic and blessed us with this little shop that held so much potential for our future. Crocker Bank on Wilshire was near our apartment, so we promptly opened a checking account there and felt like little big shots, embracing our big brown leather checkbook. In the beginning, I tried to do the bookkeeping but failed miserably, Yasue took over the bills and money transactions, doing most of the math with an abacus. After all these years, we are still using the same leather checkbook.

*****

It was the first day we were actually going to work at K-9 Tubs as the new owners, and we were very excited. The bus had already gone a long distance when Yasue suddenly realized she'd forgotten her wallet, but it was too late to turn back. Mercury was retrograde and things would be governed by Murphy's Law for the next three weeks. Bob accumulated a few local clients, one of them was a lovely woman named Emily Smythe, who became our first customer. She owned a brown cocker spaniel called Mensch, which meant 'gentleman' in Hebrew, but he didn't act very gentlemanly.

We wrote down her name, address, phone number and all the information about her dog. Emily was sharp, smart and pleasant, but as she was leaving she said, "By the way, Mensch was just castrated yesterday and may not be in a good mood."

He really did have a bad temper, and when we tried to work on him, he bit us both. Since he was our only appointment, we patiently worked around his nasty attitude for six whole hours. After feeding him many treats and bribing him with all the tricks we knew, his disagreeable behavior continued. If this was any indication of what the future might be like, we should quit right now. Mensch would always be a problem pet, yet for the next ten years, we groomed him anyway. Emily soon opened a children's bookstore around the corner.

Mensch wouldn't cooperate that day, so we only charged her ten dollars; we did a terrible grooming job.

Yasue didn't have her wallet, and I was exactly eleven cents short of our bus fare home. We had hoped to earn some cash, but received a check instead. As I was sweeping up his hair, I found a single dime and one penny; once again, I was a lucky little rabbit. It was a great relief to finally get home to Dad and our five mystical cats. I really do love dogs, but they are definitely different from those tranquil little felines, they can drain you of energy and require your undivided attention.

A nice guy named Joey Curran owned a tiny sandwich shop called Joey's Sub Station a little further south on Hyperion. His food was made to order, remarkably fresh and tasty. He also carried unique candies and little teddy-bear-shaped cookies. Del was a good neighbor who appreciated having us on the block; he always brought us back something sweet whenever he went to Joey's. At the outset of our friendship, we shared many conversations. The topic we dealt with most often involved my lover's illegal immigration status. Perhaps if we offered him two or three thousand dollars, Del would say 'I do' to Yasue, simply to help her get a green card through a contrived marriage.

We discussed the marital options thoroughly, but Del didn't

have a birth certificate. He claimed he was born in a barn somewhere in West Virginia and the midwife who delivered him, died shortly after, also his schoolhouse floated downstream during a huge flood. I asked him if he had a baptism certificate from his Baptist religion, he said, "No, I don't, because all the church records burned up in a terrible fire." So far, he could only provide a California driver's license to authenticate who he was and after all that bull, we never knew whether or not to believe anything he said. He probably lied because he really didn't want to marry Yasue, or maybe he was a Russian spy incognito.

Del was a Cancer, lived in a tiny courtyard apartment then and rode a big Harley Davidson; he searched for young boys whenever he rode around on his hog. I never judged him for his choices, but I didn't want to hear about them. Every day he would have a bad joke or two to tell, except I wasn't interested in dirty stories. It seems he went to a lot of bingo games and that's where he got this corny humor. Rather than risk our friendship by daunting him further with the idea of marrying Yasue, we decided to totally drop the immigration issue, I was delighted that she wasn't getting married.

The ten-day wait for our compact car was over. As promised, Hiro called to say he would deliver it to us and have someone waiting to drive him directly to the airport once we paid the balance. Ironically, he was going home to Japan because his student permit had expired. Once again I was lucky; Yasue had no plans for returning to Okinawa any too soon, regardless of her present visa status. We sat inside the little sedan for about an hour just admiring our finest possession. To avoid future screw-ups, I drove out to DMV the next day and got the White Witch registered properly.

The darling UCLA student actually brought the car all polished with a full tank of gas. The gods were kind and I would take good care of this cosmic gift. Hiro advised me to warm it up for ten minutes in the morning and asked me to drive the thirteen-year-old auto carefully; he was very fond of this classic Corona.

We took my father for a quick daytrip, so he could ride in the car and see our store. Dad lost a lot of weight after the heart attack and kept tugging on his baggy pants while strolling up the driveway. We guided him along the steep path until we got inside the shop, his eyes opened wider as he looked around in amazement;

"Is this place all yours?"

"Yes, Dad, it is really ours."

At the time, the parking lot behind our shop was plain dirt, and not paved at all. The contractors were rushing to add a huge extension onto the structure which would make the place seem quite different. The new annex went from our store to the Body Builders' Gym; they were creating two more shops and building a much larger gym area.

It was a cold rainy winter when we first opened, but we got settled in before they finished the annex. Every stray dog in Silverlake lifted their legs on a huge wooden partition next to our place. One of the new sites became a lovely gift shop called A Piece of Class and the other turned into The Boy Next Door, a fine boutique which featured chic men's wear.

We felt lofty in our little car even though it wasn't brand-new. The upholstery was plain, gray cloth material with red piping throughout, which complimented the flawless exterior white body. There was only one thing wrong with our dandy little sedan; it didn't have a decent radio. Yasue said to just go and buy one, so I did. A Korean guy around the corner, who retailed all kinds of car stereos, installed a mediocre system on the same day, but aligned the two speakers along the rear window. I didn't like flaunting those speakers; they were rather conspicuous to someone who might want to steal our stereo. My favorite music sounded awesome now as we eagerly traveled back and forth to work.

K-9 needed odds and ends, so we frequently shopped at Fedco while I was collecting SSI, which gave us the right to patronize government stores. I accepted checks for three more months after buying the business, but ultimately my conscience told me to stop collecting assistance as I no longer felt crazy. 'Take that which is not yours to take and you will find it is not what it seemed.' Those Pagan words haunted me until I got up the nerve to visit the Social Security office on our next day off.

The agency was on Wilshire and it took all day to see a claims adjuster. I was lucky to encounter a very smart black woman who evaluated my case and didn't seem to hate her job like others I noticed in that office. I told her I wanted to stop collecting benefits right away and genuinely explained my situation. "Mrs. Smith, I am happier now than I've ever been, my domestic partner and I recently bought a small pet grooming business and I really want to make it on my own without any aid from this administration. An undeserved monthly check can sometimes take away a person's self-esteem; I want to be proud of myself for actually working hard." She completely understood and appreciated my sincerity, then she gave me a number to call anytime if I ever needed her help again.

It felt wonderful to be free of my old heroin addiction and now I would be independent from all government assistance. I was ashamed of how much money the state had probably paid me during the time when I was a strung-out junkie or a crazy person. It must have been a huge amount because those SSI checks maintained me all around the country for years. When I left Mrs. Smith at the Social Security office, I wanted to dance in the street; it was like being absolved and pardoned by a priest. Since I wouldn't be receiving any more Medical benefits, it is imperative to stay in good health.

Things can change quickly. We enjoyed having the stereo for about a month, then one gray, wintry morning, it was gone. As we approached the car to leave for work, we noticed that our new system had vanished. Sometime during the night a thief had broken in through the back window, ripped out the radio and removed the speakers from the rear. I was really angry, but Yasue remained the cheerful optimist. It was hard to tell one desperado from another in our building; they all looked alike.

The parking lot was usually full of Latin macho men screwing around with their junk cars. Even if they knew how, they never had the courtesy to speak English; I sensed they actually hated my adorable Asian partner and me because we were obviously gay. I couldn't do anything about our stolen stereo, but I continued to give those greasy creeps contemptible looks whenever we came face to face.

I have since learned that anything you leave outside becomes public domain, whether it is here, or in the middle of Mexico. Yasue, my protector, decided we should just buy another one right away. Kenwood recently came out with a handy portable car radio, which could be taken out at night and easily put back in the morning, so we ordered another stereo setup for the White Witch.

On my first visit to the rehab office, the caseworker mentioned training programs other than pet grooming. Certified career electives included keypunch operating, auto repair and mechanic courses at L.A. Trade Tech. A huge roofing school was also subsidized by the government, but in spite of big earnings, that course seemed like the hardest work of all. It was a filthy occupation with tremendous heat, terrible stenches and sometimes-wicked heights; hence, my decision to groom pets was easy. I didn't know how right he was, but old man Jim predicted the animal world would be my forte.

Jim was supportive when I first entered school and celebrated with us the day we bought the shop, only now his health was failing and he needed our loyalty. This frail heavy smoker was diagnosed with lung cancer. His friend John called us one rainy day to say Jim was in the hospital and didn't have much longer to live. I practically had to force Yasue to visit him; she hated medical centers but came along anyway. Our elderly friend had lost a lot of weight and really looked like he was dying, but he still grumbled with sarcasm. He criticized the entire hospital staff and directed a great deal of animosity toward the ones who were trying to save him. My ailing drinking buddy never got a chance to see our shop, yet I knew he was very proud of us. We saw him two more times, but on a very cold winter night, he just passed away. No one ever held a requiem; yet, he remains in my prayers.

*****

Our business began in the Year of the Rooster and became a Virgo entity. We cleaned the place constantly, washed floors and walls several times a week, and I even got a pink feather duster for whisking over that hairy pheasant. Local people began to notice us when the pee-stained wall finally came down; hence, we got very busy with new clients. In the beginning, we took countless photos, even snapshots of ourselves sitting on the Murphy bed covered with cash and smiling.

Weekly payments to our debtors were serious priorities, but soon we wouldn't owe anything for the shop. Suzie came to work for us in the beginning and always wore platform shoes to make her legs look longer. She was a fairly good groomer and helped

Yasue with much of the hard work, while I raced around town gathering supplies for the business. When certain elderly customers were unable to bring their dogs to us, I went to pick them up. Some of these little old disabled folks really took advantage of my home delivery service. "On your way in, Carole, would you please bring me the mail and when you come back with the dog, could you take out the trash?" Sometimes I had to climb fifty stairs to get to their homes, but I didn't complain, they were my clients and I was their servant.

The bathtub at K-9 was built very high, and without using steps we could barely lift a dog into it. One of our customers owned a huge, overgrown, Old English sheepdog; the hairy animal weighed more than a hundred pounds. Yasue and I hiked this pony into the tub while we each stood on a small stepladder. It took more than an hour just to get him down during his first appointment, then another two hours to bathe him. We worked from mid-morning until nine p.m. After all our fussing to make him look gorgeous, the owner doled out a measly eighteen dollars and didn't even leave a tip.

After Jim passed away, I decided to make an effort to take better care of my father, who was becoming weak and sicklier. Whenever he shaved, he'd miss big patches of hair, his vision was terrible and his eyeglasses were as thick as coke bottles. One doctor said there was nothing we could do about his cataract-covered eyes unless we could afford to have some expensive surgery done, which was out of the question then. Nevertheless, he managed to hold the newspaper to his face and read every line. Dad refused to wear his dentures at meals because they bothered him.

Dad only had one functional lung, the right one had collapsed long ago, making it very difficult for him to breathe. This condition taxed heart muscles, so he stayed home a lot wearing pajamas. He might have been more comfortable using prescription inhalers, but I don't know if such devices were available then. People with respiratory problems today can cope very well through modern inhalation drugs.

I owned a good cassette recorder which was used for copying different eclectic songs from the radio; I've always loved music. One day we came home from work early and Dad was in our apartment watching television. For a change he was all dressed up,

I asked him where he was going, and in a deep raspy voice he grumbled, "I'm going to a disco, where the hell do you think I'm going?" My recorder was taping spontaneously as he spoke that memorable line and long after he passed away, we played it by accident. It felt eerie listening to my father's cantankerous echo again, yet he was amusing.

He was a snappy dresser, a meticulous guy, if I had to compare him to a movie star, Walter Matthau would be the obvious choice. My father was much shorter and wore glasses; otherwise, there was a charming resemblance between them. Whenever someone approached Dad too quickly, he'd jog back several feet, he was overly defensive. I thought these nervous reactions were throwbacks from former boxing days, now I know that paranoia is a common trait for the average high-strung Scorpio man.

At that point, my best clothing consisted of frayed Levi's, blue work shirts, white tees and a couple of chic, thrift-shop jackets, but I was a fresh business owner, and it was time to spruce up my wardrobe. My little brother still wore dark pants and white shirts, so I took him downtown occasionally to share fashion ideas. I didn't like his wife and even encouraged Earl to get a divorce, but it never happened.

While my brother was living in California, he tried to change the way we did everything. He even suggested we run weekly specials on certain breeds of dogs. For example, we could discount Poodles one week, then Cocker Spaniels the following week. His thoughts on reducing rates cheapened my goals. I expected the integrity and reputation of K-9 Tubs to advance simply by doing an outstanding job and giving each and every pet our personalized, meticulous care. Trite gimmicks were never my intention since our prices were already too low. If we put a sign in the window advertising specials, it would surely attract bargain hunters, seniors, penny-pinchers and the miserly. Basically I thought we should pursue and cater to the well-off clients, this way we might never receive a bad check.

In spite of minor disagreements, my brother was a handy guy to have around. He ran an electrical outlet from our dirt basement, and up through the wall to where the future air conditioner would be connected. He also replaced the ballast for two eight-foot light fixtures and did a few other small jobs around the shop. Our next priority was to buy a large air conditioner to keep the entire place cool. There was a tiny unit in back, but its chill couldn't reach the front during those hot sunset hours.

Silverlake was our little town now, and we believed this Utopia was edification from our spirit friends. The first time Yasue walked up to the Mayfair market, she came back smiling and had plenty to say about those poised customers. She mentioned that the shoppers spoke in a whisper rather than a shout, unlike many characters at Ralph's; she also noticed that no one disbursed food stamps, coupons, or cashed welfare checks. Most people in this area seemed to be well-mannered, gainfully employed, middle-class Caucasians. Years before that Hyperion property became the Mayfair Market; it was a celebrated Walt Disney studio; perhaps that's why it was such a happy store to patronize.

When we first opened K-9 Tubs, the people in the neighborhood accepted us right away, which we appreciated. A nice-looking man named Russ worked at the wallpaper store, he and his long time lover, Ray, owned a beautiful home around the corner on Tracy Street. We made friends quickly with the whole block, especially the guys at the gym. Bobby, the owner, was a very good oil painter, yet all of his work depicted the grimace in Jesus Christ's face, and those unnerving images seemed rather morose to me. Bobby came from a strict Italian Catholic family; perhaps because he felt guilty about being gay, he needed to assure his pious parents that the beloved Messiah would be dear to him regardless. His best friend was Mark Barker, who worked at the gym as a Yoga instructor.

Jim and Bobby lived a few blocks from the gym and invited us to their gorgeous home on Panorama Terrace for a wine and cheese gathering one Sunday afternoon. My facial expressions probably showed great surprise as I stepped into their dazzling living room, which was filled with pieces of crystal. I couldn't take my eyes off the rainbow prisms drifting through the house. They were the only people we knew with a swimming pool. Yasue couldn't make it to that particular party, but later I gave her a full report about all the attractive gay men who attended, as usual, I was the only woman there.

A brand-new store called A Piece of Class had just opened up next to the gym and a couple of gay guys named Ed Steckley and

Jay Byrnes were the proprietors. They arranged to launch this business even before they signed the lease, and it didn't take them very long to establish a five-star gift shop. The showcases and furnishings were elegant, most gifts were produced from expensive glass and every article displayed in the place sparkled. It was a beautiful store and their prices were reasonable. Since it was so convenient to our shop, we bought many great gifts for the occasional birthday etc.

During that same period, another new business called The Boy Next Door opened right next to our shop. Bill Mortenson and Richard Alonzo, the owners, had been domestic partners for twenty years at the time and knew a great deal about decorating, as well as their boutique specialties. They retailed some awesome men's attire and always flaunted a huge supply of 501 Levi's, which was the basic garment of most local gay men. Broad pieces of grand mahogany furniture embraced and displayed their fine apparel, it was quite a chic emporium, however, the only items which seemed to fit me were the size small Silverlake T-shirts, size twenty-eight Levi's and assorted socks. Yasue bought several tie-dyed tank tops in every color, but I was too pudgy then, to wear clingy clothes.

Zen Restaurant was diagonally across the street from us, but it was less than half the size it is now. We ate there occasionally and became friends with the owners. Tomi's Coffee Shop was the best spot for a hearty breakfast or cheap lunch, and Janet Joe was the ultimate cheerful waitress there; her Chinese/Japanese family owned it forever. We still see Janet after twenty-three years, she brings her dog, Lucky, to us for grooming, but her dad sold the coffee shop, and now it's a Sushi Bar. Bogies' Liquor Store was another landmark in the neighborhood. It was managed by the Bogasian clan, who were said to have been there since prohibition; they lost a lot of liquor sales when the AIDS epidemic struck.

To the right of our store, an alteration shop called Buttons n' Bows was owned by an older woman named Helen May, periodically she would hem a pair of Levi's for me. She seemed like a very grumpy person, tall, with straight gray hair, donned thick glasses and generally looked kind of ashen or gaunt. After we got closer to her, she confessed something profound to Yasue. Helen came home from work one night to find her daughter's body on the bathroom floor; she was dead from an apparent suicide.

Except for my wicked stepfather, I never really hated a guy, I simply felt more amorous and attracted to pretty women. Yasue and I were enveloped by many attractive young gay gents in Silverlake; most wore penny loafers, appeared well groomed and were above average intellectually. However, we soon realized there weren't very many gay women in our lives, so I asked Sidra candidly to hook us up with her foremost female friends, basically to balance the Yin and the Yang in our social lives.

Sidra knew a lot of women, yet seemed rather connected to a lesbian couple named Sharon and Shelley who lived in the Hollywood Hills. Soon we were invited to their weekly Saturday night gala; however, I had to ask myself a few cliché questions. What should we wear to this bourgeois party? Were we hip enough to impress these lipstick lesbians? Would we fit in, or did we even care to?

Shelley came from an affluent family; she was the ultimate schizophrenic Libra, who likewise met Sidra in a mental institution where they became long time friends. Shelley received money from her wealthy mother in Long Beach and had never had a real job in her life. Sharon her partner, received almost a million dollars from MacDonald's, she claims that she slipped on a freshly mopped floor and broke a tiny bone someplace. Easy money enabled these two women live very elegantly for a while.

The rustic party house was deep in the hills, and was equipped with a wooden hot tub, which is why we were asked to bring bathing suits. I could never undress in front of a strange group of women, so we just sat around drinking and boring everyone with droll stories about our newly acquired pet business. Most of their guests preferred to talk about the people they knew in the film or television industry. Those immature status-seeking egomaniacs drained us, so we asked Sidra for a quick ride home.

*****

Yasue and I got really busy with the shop and new acquaintances; nevertheless, we tried not to neglect family or friends. Since the days are shorter through the winter, we didn't have much time to spare after a ten-hour grind, but we did pay considerable attention to my father when we realized his poor health was worsening all the time. On a good day, Dad would stroll over to Ralph's Market to say hello to Rita. After one of his little shopping trips, he came home with a tall blue candle in glass, which seemed strange because he never admitted to being a pious man. I asked him why he bought a religious candle, he said abruptly, "Just for the hell of it." I think he was really praying.

Most girls love their fathers and I loved mine, regardless of his wild shenanigans. During the forties, he came home from the army on furlough and played an incredible prank on the folks at Pakachoag Street. Even though cigarettes were rather hard to get, Dad managed to buy a carton of Chesterfields via the black market. I was very young then, but can still remember how handsome he looked in that crisp green uniform with the shiny brass buttons, I told my all my friends he was a general.

One Sunday, Dad informed everyone at Uncle Leo and Aunt Emily's house that he had hidden that whole carton of cigarettes somewhere in the cottage, which brought about a wonderful fiasco. Then he said he was going to the local bar for a while and wished everyone good luck in their pursuit. The hunt for butts began around midday and several heavy-smoking relatives from the area heard about the grand prize, so they came right over to help us search. They explored the attic, the basement and browsed through every nook and cranny in that small home, but they never found any smokes. By evening it turned very cold, and just as Uncle Leo lit the furnace, I noticed Dad staggering down the bumpy dirt road very drunk and now he had to face those angry desperate people, who were waiting for an explanation.

Little Emily's outspoken husband, Jimmy, was the first one to yell at Dad. "Goddamn it, Johnson, we searched for those bloody cigarettes all day, we even rummaged through Aunt Emily's sachet-filled underwear drawer, so where the hell are they?"

Dad grinned and answered in his typical cocky, sarcastic way, "You dumb son of a bitch, I hid them in the furnace, and your father-in-law just burnt them all up." To avoid being killed by desperate relatives who were panting for a smoke, Dad whipped out a fresh pack of Camels and passed them around, the clan lit up right away, exhaled and laughed.

My charismatic father was full of life then, but he was elderly now and many things seemed to be physically wrong, the thought of losing him forever scared me a lot. We'd owned our shop for about two months when he suffered another heart attack. An ambulance took him to the Queen of Angels Hospital and we were able to follow since we had a car.

The doctor said, "Wait and see what happens, it is possible for your father to recover fully once again."

Dad identified with the Phoenix because he had died and come back to life several other times, and we prayed he could do it again.

This occurred early in April while my brother and his family were still living in Burbank, so we took turns calling on him every night after work. Dad would be fine one minute and in the next, he babbled utter nonsense, his brain was damaged from an overworked heart. Yasue and I went to visit on Monday night and Earl saw him Tuesday. By Wednesday evening we were exhausted from working and really didn't feel like going, but I took a quick shower, got ready and dragged poor Yasue along; she never complained about the imposition. We got to his room later than usual and he looked quite healthy, remarkably alert, and even happy to see us. At first our conversation seemed normal and buoyant but as the minutes passed, we noticed how confused and unstable his mind had become.

He was experiencing a kind of dementia that evening and said odd things. "I have plenty of cat food over there in the pantry, just take whatever you want." The cats were always on his mind; they provided unconditional love, something he'd never known before. Even though he was curled up in a small hospital bed connected with tubes and wires, he thought he was at home, which made us believe he was feeling good that night, in spite of the brain damage. We went along with his feeble-minded gibberish until it was time to go, he kissed us goodbye and continued smiling as we left.

We drove right home and a very uneasy feeling came over me, perhaps because of his extra-cheerful demeanor. All the cats were fed before we climbed into our cozy Murphy bed and soon we fell fast asleep.

Mom was staying in his apartment across the hall to keep the place tidy; she did care about him in her own way. The phone rang around two in the morning and a soft-spoken foreign doctor from the hospital told me that my father had passed away peacefully in his sleep; he expressed deep sympathy. I thanked him for calling, let out a huge scream, waking everyone in the building. His death was inevitable, but was I prepared to accept the loss of my dynamic father's being?

Mom called my brother, and it only took him about fifteen minutes to get to our place. He left Pat home with the kids, insuring less stress. I became totally numb and couldn't function at all, no one knew what to do next, but for sure I had to drive Yasue to K-9 Tubs at first light to put a sign on the door announcing the death in our family, she also notified clients who booked appointments for that day. We had very little money, so we agreed to contact the affordable Neptune Society, who would take care of the entire cremation and scatter his ashes in the Pacific Ocean. They were courteous people, trained to comfort distraught characters like me; I couldn't speak a word, and I sobbed endlessly.

My father was sixty-nine years old when he passed away on April 11th, 1981 and never saved a penny in his life. There were tedious things to arrange, but my brother helped a lot by making the necessary phone calls to Social Security, the Veterans Administration, etc. Mom found Dad's bankbook, which had a balance of two hundred and twenty dollars. It would have been much less if he hadn't gotten ill. He'd dash to the bank almost daily to make small withdrawals and chitchat with the pretty clerks. In the boxing arena he was a killer, but anywhere else women could easily subdue him.

The Neptune Society was down in San Pedro, so Earl drove Mom, Yasue and me there in his old station wagon. I couldn't drive or do much of anything, I just cried. This was the greatest loss I had ever experienced, and I wondered if this awful pain would ever end. It didn't take us long to find their office nestled upstairs in the marina, but we were a little early for our appointment, so Earl decided we should go to an adjoining restaurant for a snack. When we sat down, my brother actually ordered a cocktail for me and Mom didn't raise an eyebrow. My appetite for food, or booze, was nonexistent.

It was time for Earl and me to go upstairs and give those nice people a check for Dad's service. The arrangements were completed without a religious ceremony. My personal observance would take place later at Venice Beach by casting flowers into the ocean and offering up a few simple prayers. I floated bouquets to him from the bay of Provincetown and the shores of Hawaii whenever possible.

Our neighbors were very kind and sympathetic, but it was time to dispose of Dad's belongings. Mom did most of the packing, Earl took what he liked, and I removed all the John Lennon posters which I placed on his walls originally. 'Give Peace a Chance' signs were visible to Dad every day.

My father was a great guy to me and there would be a big void in my life now. We won't be able to watch a football game together, or even get tipsy just for fun. Did I ever say that I appreciated him; did I compliment him enough when he deserved? This dapper man was my hero and I miss him. The cats would miss Dad too, especially his favorite, pretty Tama. He used to hand-feed her gourmet cold cuts because she was shy. Each spiritual trip I took to the ocean released some frustration and anger; the acceptance process began when I realized how badly I was treating my kid brother.

Social Security sent a check for two hundred and fifty dollars and the Veterans Administration issued the same amount, which barely covered the Neptune Society expense. A short time later, the army shipped me a giant American flag since he had served in the military. My brother became heir to Dad's wardrobe, such as it was, along with a color television and the fancy electric shaver we gave him last Christmas. I was appointed his sole beneficiary and received the two hundred and twenty dollars from his bank account. He always promised to leave me his entire fortune when he died.

Ginny, the manager, began to screen potential tenants for Dad's place, she had a soft spot for senior citizens and promptly chose a tiny Filipino lady named Anna, a retiree living on Social Security who soon became our newest crackpot neighbor. The apartment was at the end of the hallway, which led to my favorite retreat, the fire escape, I got high out there, gazed at the universe and meditated at my first altar, a small white plastic table. Anna's kitchen window had a full view of this iron porch, subsequently we found out how paranoid she was.

Our door was always open when we were home, so the five cats could run and play in the hall. No one ever complained, but this crazy old woman could raise some issues; regardless, we would never compromise the cats' therapeutic routine.

*****

My brother was dissatisfied earning a measly twenty-three dollars per hour at Hughes, and Pat was upset about her own father's waning health, so they decided to pack it up and join her family in Buffalo, New York before autumn and the coming school term. Part of their decision may have been due to the fact that after Dad died, I acted like a bitch for a while. Everything these silly people said or did aggravated me; maybe it was time for them to move on before we became enemies.

Once again they tossed all their effects into a U-Haul and drove cross-country in their Chevy wagon. When they got out there, Earl couldn't find a decent paying job, so he accepted some menial work for eight dollars an hour, fifteen less than he bellyached about. Buffalo is the snow capital of the U.S.A. and they were in for a rough winter. My brother never had much luck with careers, but he knew how to persevere. His family went through a terrible phase that year. Was their bad karma my fault?

Shortly after moving in, Anna waited by the elevator to speak with me about a problem. "Carole, do you know that your cats have been coming into my kitchen from the fire escape when I am asleep to steal my coffee and sugar." I told her I wasn't aware of such magical happenings and asked if she ever saw them doing this. "No, I didn't see them; nevertheless, your naughty cats are thieves."

She made me laugh and that was the first time I even smiled since Dad died. Perhaps the crazy old woman imagined our felines could, in fact, accomplish such a trick, or was this her neurotic way of telling me to stay off the fire escape. The cat dialogue with Anna was amusing, but I got very angry later on when she closed and nailed down the hall window. That iron balcony was my personal sanctuary, how could I live without an altar, the ever-changing colorful sky, or the cool night air?

I tried to open the window but there were more than a hundred nails anchoring it, so I went down to tell Ginny, who laughed hard when I told what Anna had done. "She said our cats were burglarizing her unit and carting away her coffee and sugar."

Ginny phoned Anna at once to explain that what she'd done was against the law and fire department regulations, it was a mandatory fire exit. Finally we got the nails unfastened and opened it; the wind could rush through again now to clear lingering odors from our section of the building. On hot sultry nights, a little gust from that window felt delightful.

Yasue and I lived in apartment 505, where the fragrance of pot and incense was common. An elderly British actor, Nelson Welch, was right across the hall; he cooked fresh kidney pie almost daily. Smelly fried fish was the usual aroma from Anna's. One night, Mr. Welch was rehearsing for a role, I just happened to open our door for some fresh air and there he was completely naked except for a silk scarf around his neck. The tall figure slithered into his place rather quickly without saying a word.

The reason Anna moved into the El Prado was because her own children couldn't stand her, they told Ginny when she first arrived that she was an eccentric. Maybe she was even crazy, but during her lifetime she managed to collect many valuable things. She always wore a lot of gold jewelry and her apartment was nicely furnished by her family, but wherever she went, the fool carried all her valuables in a black cloth bag. She toted around bankbooks, cash, checks and a number of expensive trinkets. This busy bee never worried about living in a dangerous neighborhood, yet she claimed to fear our harmless cats. We tried to be friends, though we didn't appreciate the nonsense she constantly babbled. If we were having tea with cake or sweets, we'd offer her some, she even shared a few Filipino treats with us; however, the annoying feud over the hall window would continue.

No matter what the season, California can get very hot during the day, but it always seems to cool down after sunset, unlike the east, where the humidity stays oppressive all night long throughout the summer.

One June evening we came home from work around seven and the house was scorching, so we turned the fans on, changed into lighter clothes and opened the front door for a refreshing breeze. Lo and behold, Anna had nailed the hall window shut again; this time Yasue was really furious.

I went right to her door and pounded very hard, but she wasn't home. A short time later we heard the fire door open and it was

Anna. Just as she walked past our place, I ambushed her and pulled her into the apartment. She was absolutely flabbergasted as I grabbed her bony shoulders and gently lowered her tiny body onto the floor, as I wrapped my large hands around her throat and spoke very clearly. "Anna, you don't know how close to death you are, if you ever nail that window down again, I will send my killer cats into your house to finish the job."

She just got up, dusted herself off and casually declared, "You must tell your cats to stop stealing from me, then I won't close it down anymore." Afterwards, we took the nails out and camped on the airy fire escape until nearly midnight.

Within a week of liberating the hall window, I received a letter from the District Attorney's office. They said I had to make a personal court appearance on a certain date. This was a criminal action suit filed against me by Anna, and the charge was attempted murder. We took the day off to go to court and my mother came along. The young female ADA was very gracious until I sat down, then she read me my rights, which was scary. Anna caused everyone to laugh upon disclosing her cat and window fable. I told the lawyer that she carted her valuables all around town and the case was dismissed immediately. Issues regarding my threats or dropping her to the floor were never brought up.

After the court hearing, Anna had the gall to ask for a ride home and even suggested that the four of us have lunch somewhere, her treat. We just gawked at each other for a moment, said we'd made other plans, but we thanked her for the generous offer. In spite of her delusions, we actually felt sorry for the lonely old woman, yet she wasn't the least bit sensitive. From then on, if we happened to meet at the elevator or in the front hall, I would simply act charming. When my next novena began, I prayed hard to find an inexpensive apartment close to the shop, and a peaceful place to live.

Now that Dad was gone, Yasue and I had literally outgrown the El Prado, we seemed to have a lot more belongings, and the one closet we shared was bursting at the seams. Someone once told me that if you ever need anything, speak to everyone you meet; they might have what you want in their garage. It was time to move out of the big brick house, so we informed our customers that we were looking for a modest place in the area. Sure enough, one of our new clients, Jan Holden, said she had a vacant apartment and offered to rent it to us. The address, 1915 Mayview Drive, sounded so idyllic.

I am a lucky little rabbit. Her house sat on a hill in a very pleasant location with a large backyard for the cats and plenty of gardening for Yasue to enjoy. It was small, one-bedroom, cheery, and with lots of light; we just needed to furnish it. In a short time, we turned an old hippy pad into a graceful home. The rent was four hundred and fifty dollars monthly, much more than the ninety-five we had been paying. Now we'd have to bring in some extra business and work on a few more dogs and cats. Together, our power of positive thinking was awesome and I knew we could really make this change happen.

Thanks and Blessed Be.

Carole,
A Lucky Little Rabbit

Part Four

*"The first time I experienced a strong earthquake,
I thought it was the end of the world.
It's sudden violent destruction terrified me, but now I realize if
we were lucky enough to survive a huge disaster, people would
launch a constructive renaissance of rebuilding.
I've nearly conquered my naïve fear of doomsday."*

Originally Jan Holden's house was a single family residence, but she converted it into two separate apartments. The wiring was rather faulty and the baffling maze of bad plumbing was done by a heavyset woman who used the 'Mickey Mouse' method. There were sixty-two narrow steps from the street up to our door, so we chose to use the rear entrance because voices echoed in those halls and we didn't want to disturb anyone while filing past Jan's windows. I usually parked on the road above, that way we could walk down the back stairs and through the craggy backyard to our quarters.

Our new landlady had a lover named Jean, and they seemed to have one thing in common, money. While the rent was four hundred and fifty monthly, we were also required to pay half the gas, water and power bills for the entire property. We agreed to stay there one year, but paying for their utilities was a huge rub to Yasue, who counted all our pennies. On the first day of each month she would go downstairs, sit around a large pine table, arguing about who should be paying what bills. I chose not to get involved with finances and felt blessed to be distanced from Third Street.

We bought a California king-size bed even though the boudoir was fairly small; it was a definite improvement over the antiquated Murphy bunk that came out of the wall. Without thinking, we got an all-white sofa bed and the cats began to scratch it at once, the dirt they carried on their tiny feet became quite noticeable on our chic white couch. A division of shelves based between the kitchen and dining area housed our shiny crystal glasses, which flashed multicolored prisms at certain times. The bonus room was a slopped narrow sun porch surrounded by jalousie windows, so I turned it into a cozy study, highlighting a beloved relic, Dad's old writing desk. I placed my freshly painted lavender altar in the eastern corner of the bedroom with a comfortable matching straw chair.

When Jan first came to K-9 with her wonderful Cockapoo, Buffy, she demanded the perfect haircut and told us she used to groom dogs at a fancy salon, therefore she knew everything. Yasue gave her dog an excellent hairstyle; hence they became regular clients. Buffy began to visit us upstairs for hours and became bosom buddies with our five cats after we moved into their house. If Jan had to go away, she depended on us to care for the pooch and furthermore, we didn't even charge her.

Ms. Holden was a shrewd Gemini who was extremely concerned about money since she didn't really have a paying job, she boasted about writing a very compelling and controversial play involving women. Jean had a good position with the Board of Education, yet she did all the menial chores for their household while Jan drove a big and boxy classic Volvo, an apparent dyke status symbol.

Many diverse female acquaintances came to visit with Jan, and they all seemed to be connected with the NOW organization. Later we found out they were attempting to get a lesbian sister out of jail. The person they were trying to help was a woman named Ginny Foats, recently arrested for bludgeoning an old man on the East Coast that allegedly occurred when she was much younger. Old warrants were circulated for her arrest, but she'd remained discreet until the day she went on live television to defend battered women, she was a celebrated advocate behind several issues, but altruism got her busted.

Whenever this group of female defenders got together, we

heard loud conversations from downstairs; the boisterous lesbians probably thought no one could hear them, while we could care less about their secret dramas. Ginny pleaded not guilty in spite of the serious evidence against her from twenty years ago, but a kindly judge sentenced her to a short probation and community service anyway.

Jan tried to cover some very deep pockmarks on her face by using a lot of pancake makeup, she wouldn't leave the house until her complexion looked all right, causing her to run behind schedule regularly. She was medium height, slightly pudgy and rather cute in an Irish way. Jan tried to look womanly though her attire was quasi-butch, basic khaki pants and starched shirts. Jean was feminine, average-looking and clearly the schoolteacher type, she reminded me of a bygone Girl Scout leader.

I've always been sensitive to insult, and Jan could ridicule or belittle a person in a friendly way. She asked about the altar and my practice of intermittent novenas. I explained that many religions call for some type of sacrifice; abstinence from alcohol for nine whole days was my personal offering. I defined this ritual warily, as she grinned and said, "Oh I see; you're actually just a controlled drunk."

Our new digs seemed like a million miles away from the El Prado, which made us feel somewhat classy. We didn't have much company up there besides my mother and one periodic caller, Sidra, who was dating a nasty woman named Susan. They came to our place on a Saturday night and brought along Sidra's mother, Dunno, who was in the early stages of Alzheimer's disease. Before they even got to the back gate, we could hear Susan talking loudly, using terrible language in front of that poor old lady, our neighbors must have been shocked, considering how quiet Yasue and I usually were.

Inside and outside, Susan was an ugly person; she was very angry and displayed it to everyone. I don't know why Sidra was so fascinated with her, maybe because she came from northern California and her wealthy family owned a huge Christmas tree ranch, or she was clever enough to bamboozle my artful pal with love. That evening was a nightmare, yet I had to brave driving the monster home.

When they first arrived at our peaceful little home, Susan

smugly introduced herself and went on to say, "It's a pleasure to meet you; I've never called on midgets before." Fortunately Jan and Jean were out that night because the later it got, the more Sidra and Susan fought. It was nearly eleven o'clock when they began to use their fists on each other, I jumped in between the two tall women and pleaded with them to stop or leave. Sidra suggested that I drive Susan home, for obvious reasons, besides, her Ghia was only a two-seater and Dunno was a bit hefty. I prayed for patience as I went beyond exasperation, ready to blow. How dare this repulsive woman disturb our serenity?

Susan was a bourgeois alcoholic but downplayed it; she believed that was the way true aristocrats behaved. I sensed she would even carry bad vibrations to my car, the White Witch, but I drove her anyway. Since it was Saturday night, I asked if she minded stopping by the Jungle Bar on Sunset for a nightcap, she said fine. I got us a drink at the bar and proceeded to the dance floor bustling with young Latino ladies. My frustrations were easing as I danced up and down the walls like a maniac. Later a princely dyke asked me how old I was in a very earnest way, I admitted to being eighty-five. She scratched her head and remarked that I had better moves than a twenty-year-old. By this time, I couldn't handle any more abuse from Susan, so I called a cab and paid the driver to take her home.

We lived in Jan's house for a year and appreciated a few amicable neighbors like Paul, who played the flute at night from his deck; the music was so soothing we thought it was heaven sent. Paul was a cute redhead with an adorable girlfriend whom he used to take on skiing trips. They went away for one week and our cat Lady Bug was locked in his garage by accident. Paul finally came home and let her out; she looked emaciated but okay. Subsequently he became a producer on *The X Files*.

Mrs. Wong, our neighbor in the house above, frequently gifted us with Chinese fruit preserves. Her husband wasn't long for this world, but they had a wonderful son who took good care of the family and gradually cleared a path between our yards by cutting away clusters of dense bamboo. The elderly woman liked me, and I enjoyed her company, she used words sparingly, and got right to the core of a conversation. Though she never applied color, her hair was jet black, shaped like a bowl, and as straight as a poker. I brazenly asked her age once and she gently responded, "I am old enough to collect Social Security." Estimating from her background, the cultured Asian lady was more than a century old.

*****

Andy Warhol always congregated with 'the beautiful people', while they had to compensate for the pleasure of his celebrity. When he invited an attractive group out to dinner, each person was expected to pay their own fare. I too enjoy being around artistic individuals, but when I chose to entertain someone, it should be on my nickel. Before we moved to Mayview Drive, a strikingly beautiful young lady walked into our shop on President's Day of 1981. Her name was Diane, and she owned two little mixed poodles, Peppy and Abby, and this refined client became a friend for life.

Diane breezed into K-9 carefully holding a dog in each hand, she was an Aries, and moved very quickly. I began to stare at this lean lady with a classic Victorian face and the body of a dancer. She was the most attractive woman I'd ever seen in this neighborhood. At first Yasue and I thought she was an actress or model, but her real occupation was writing. Diane left us instructions for the dogs, and rushed off. As she got into her older burnt orange, spacious Mercedes Benz, she winked at me, which may have triggered my endless obsession with her. That day she forgot a classy leather checkbook so we phoned right away. I felt very uneasy when Yasue decided to look at the huge balance.

I was very much in love with Yasue then, and I still am, yet the moment Diane looked at me, I developed a crush and felt young again. She was twenty-nine, three months pregnant, and radiant; I was forty-one, and spirited. The genteel woman intrigued me, and by way of astrology, I knew she was feeling Saturn return. Her husband, Andy, was a terrific guy and had a good job in the television industry. They were well matched and deeply in love. From the outset, the loving couple brought their little dogs to us every two weeks, while some customers only came in once a year.

I've always had insomnia, but when my fascination with her started, falling asleep was hopeless. Diane brought out feelings that I hadn't dealt with since cruising gay bars in search of the most convenient beautiful woman. She was the definitive 'Up Town Girl', the kind you always hoped to land but never got close enough. My charming friend wasn't aware that she subliminally encouraged me to stand taller, look sharper, and use my mind more. In time I became a better person for knowing her, only we never really discussed how much her extraordinary presence affected my life.

Diane and I were chitchatting in front of my shop one afternoon when she mentioned she'd just been to lunch with people she didn't especially care for. We enjoyed conversing, and had good rapport, eventually I got up the nerve to ask her out, and to my surprise she said yes. Yasue thought it was awesome that we'd made a date; we used to joke about bringing pretty women home to share. She was free on Friday so I made a reservation for lunch at the New York Company, a trendy bar and grill. We met at the shop, and sped off in her big orange Mercedes. I didn't fasten the seatbelt, and she got adamant about why I didn't value my life more, I was foolish enough to say that seatbelts were only necessary for long distances. From then on I tried to be politically correct about everything.

I dressed casually in a hound's tooth tweed jacket, brown pants, blue oxford shirt and penny loafers, Diane wore a basic black outfit, accessorized by dainty European antique jewelry. Perhaps she thought I had clout when the waiter took us directly into an elite dining room called Wall Street, but I actually knew this sweet gay man and arranged everything ahead. My first faux pas was the seatbelt hang-up; the next mistake was whipping out a cigarette from a fancy box once we were seated. Eventually it dawned on me that smart people didn't smoke, and she was very intelligent so I put the imported cigarettes away. My third indiscretion was ordering a vodka tonic instead of an ordinary white wine, but I really needed a heavy-duty drink that day because she made me very nervous.

One night I dreamed I was making love to Diane, which turned out to be a lesbian's cruelest nightmare. She laughed in my face when I failed to satisfy her. A sexual liaison with her would never happen, and I couldn't bear to be rejected. She invited me to her beautiful home on Waverly Drive one afternoon, we drank a little wine, and I began to compliment her in an amorous way. Diane made it perfectly clear that even though she genuinely liked me, and would always be my friend, she could never reciprocate my romantic feelings for her. I didn't intend to make a fool of myself, just going out with her once in a while would be gratifying enough; therefore, I never made an advance.

Yasue wasn't the least bit jealous or disturbed about my sudden interest in someone new, and she enjoyed the idea of me being happy. Diane was like a stimulating intoxicant to me, a challenge to my creativity, but Yasue was the air I needed to breathe, and it was impossible to imagine living without my lifetime partner. Diane and Andy will always be a loving couple, committed to love, marriage, a fine, blessed newborn son named Joseph, and continuing to evolve spiritually.

Diane was born during the year of the dragon, filled with impassioned opinions; she actually listened to the Oliver North hearings and supported various deserving causes. She was the first person I ever knew with a computer, and while her new house was being remodeled, she rented an office space on Hillhurst, even though the building seemed creepy. Yasue and I gave her three inexpensive bookcases we weren't using, and my pal Bill, owner of The Boy Next Door, carried them up to her suite.

Diane joined me one day to taste some of my freshly made spicy chicken curry when we lived on Mayview Drive. Our furniture was new except for the large baroque dining room set, given to us by a woman named Inez. We had a new stereo, but many of my favorite tunes were still on vinyl records. I asked what kind of music she enjoyed. She said her taste was eclectic, which kept me guessing. Should I play Beatles' albums, or stick to a selection of classical pieces? She thought our apartment was nice, and was curious as to how we got the bathroom floor so white. I was very self-conscious, while attempting to make everyday conversations; I didn't know her very well then.

My friend and I went to a lot of colorful places, and sometimes we tooled around Melrose Av. In that area we could have a marvelous lunch and still find fun things to do. There were stylish boutiques, fine restaurants, and many chic art galleries. Yasue's friend Suzie, from grooming school, opened a modern art business on Melrose funded by Japanese backers. She carried contemporary art, sneakers, hats, and even accessories to match, so we stopped in to congratulate her pal.

Diane was around five feet eight, and I was five one, yet it never mattered. It felt great just to make the scene with her; certain people actually thought we looked attractive and cool together. I never knew anyone who walked faster, but somehow I kept up. After each carefree luncheon rendezvous I floated on clouds.

On July 16th, 1981, Diane gave birth to her son Joseph, a blessed event. While she was pregnant, I prayed for the baby and secretly hoped I could be his godmother. Yasue understood how I felt about Diane, she told me to buy a baby gift at the Broadway. I didn't know anything about newborns, but once I got to the infants' department, I noticed a pretty cool item. It was a large mobile to hang above his crib, garnished with colorful hot air balloons, and it played *Fly Me to the Moon* when turned on.

I charged it on my gold card, had it wrapped nicely, and called Diane's house. Her sweet mother answered the phone, I told her I just wanted to drop off a gift, and she invited me over. When the door opened, I was amazed to see a tall beautiful redhead standing there; she was a stunning woman who seemed quite cheerful. Diane was upstairs resting so I left the present and hurried off.

Shortly after Joseph's birth, Peppy and Abby changed, they acted jealous, and even attacked the baby while he was in the crib. This became a serious concern for Diane; should she keep the dogs hoping in time they might accept their new rival, or should she try to place them in a good home? She told me it was difficult to make such a heart-wrenching decision, but now Joseph was the most important family member. Eventually she asked us to help her find them a kind and loving owner.

As luck would have it, one of our regular clients, named Laurie, was looking for a small dog to keep her single mother company. We told her a friend needed a good home for two small dogs, but they had to stay together, and I described their concerns for Joseph. Laurie talked to her mom, and she wanted the pair right away. We asked Diane and Andy to bring the dogs to K-9 for an adoption ceremony. Later we all had champagne, knowing that Peppy and Abby would really be loved by these people.

*****

An entire year had passed; it really was time to move out of Jan Holden's house. Yasue continued to agonize over the way Jean juggled the utility bills in their favor and the scene was becoming ugly. I didn't want to run right out and look for a place while the planet Mercury was in retrograde, as this wasn't a good time to make important decisions, but by fluke one day, I drove down Cumberland instead of taking Mayview and noticed a rental sign in front of a strikingly well-kept house. Later I called the number indicated and quickly made an appointment with the owner to look at the apartment.

Herb Winters, the gay landlord, used to be a part-time actor on many old television comedy shows like Laverne and Shirley, he never had a speaking part, just walk on roles. He was a Virgo, good-looking, and dressed smartly. His birthday fell late in August and was fifteen years older than I, yet he always maintained a good sense of humor. The idea of two competent gay women living in this lovely flat amused him; he was rather impressed because we owned a successful local business.

This hillside house had three apartments, Herb lived in the beautiful upper residence and there was a tiny single unit on the bottom level, and the one for rent was in the middle. We talked for a while, and at last he took me to see it. I was knocked out by the view of the city and he claimed that on a clear day you could see Catalina Island. The place was small, but we could probably shift our furnishings around to make it very attractive. There was no backyard, only a narrow area on the side to create a miniature garden. Herb placed mirrors everywhere, lending the impression of a more spacious interior. Its tiny kitchen had a lengthy bar counter and a large wooden deck sat right outside the sliding glass doors, the bedroom barely had room for our king-size bed. Herb said the rent was five hundred and fifty a month, more than we were paying; regardless, I couldn't wait to tell Yasue all about it.

I went to check out the apartment on a Saturday while Yasue was having a very busy day at the shop. The place was great, it had wonderful ambience, I described it to her as best I could and she was anxious to see it for herself. That evening I called Herb back to ask if we could both come over to look at it on the following day, and he said certainly. On Sunday morning we got all dressed up and only had to walk a half a block up the hill to get there. The quiet narrow street was downright picturesque.

Before we arrived, he made a fresh pot of coffee and seemed like he really enjoyed having company. Herb's apartment was much larger than the one downstairs, with more amenities like a hot tub, fireplace and air-conditioning. Yasue looked everything over and decided she wanted to live in this charming house right away. She was even excited about planting a garden in the little side yard. We went back to Jan's to sit down and figure out finances for the first month's rent the last and a security deposit. Each time we moved the rent went up, but we always upgraded to finer surroundings.

After putting our heads together, we agreed that if we simply groomed a few more dogs, we could well afford to live there, so we gave Jan and Jean our notice at once. They said they would miss us, but they were never sincere about anything. I asked all our friends if they would help us, I told people it was going to be a Coke and Pizza moving party. During the early eighties, everyone, including Yasue and me, used small amounts of cocaine, which may have been a catalyst for the birth of AIDS. The one block procession would take place on the following Sunday, our crew consisted of several friends, and I don't know how many strangers, but most of these folks were flying after a few toots.

Sam and Shimko owned an art gallery above our shop and were quite helpful. Dennis and Noburo from San Francisco also pitched in, and within a few short hours we were completely moved.

We did a good job of arranging furniture, the king-size bed and even my lavender altar fitted in the tiny bedroom, and everything looked really nice when we were done. It was always fun having good friends visit us on Cumberland, we enjoyed a lot of music, a great view of the city, and an occasional hit of cocaine, the marijuana smoke, however, drifted directly up to Herb's place. He was polite and dropped a few subtle hints about our drug use, but he never really complained since our rent was paid on time.

*****

March 23rd was Diane's birthday, and I suggested we have a party to celebrate the event, she thought it was a fine idea so we planned a soiree for Friday at eight o'clock. I asked whether she would mind if we invited a few friends over; she said the more the merrier. I served plenty of finger foods, in addition to a full bar on the counter. Guests showed up we weren't expecting, but somehow everyone seemed to ballet around everyone else in a small area. Diane had a flying lesson at the Van Nuys Airport that night, her flight ran behind schedule, and the guest of honor finally arrived two hours late. She brought her husband Andy, and they were still wearing stylish leather bomber jackets.

Herb invested in a tiny apartment many years ago at The Castle Green, a well-known Pasadena landmark. When he took us to see it, we thought the building itself was very impressive, but his unit was quite ordinary, it just didn't have any ambience or character. When the lease expired with one of his tenants, he would simply decorate the place with more mirrors, and fresh paint. His tenants never lasted long there; it was only big enough for a single person. Each time he visited the Castle he liked it more, and when he ran out of things to do around the house, or got bored with his friends, he talked about moving back to 99 Raymond Avenue.

We were happy on the second floor for a year, then one day he shocked us by asking if we'd like to move upstairs into his spacious apartment.

We suspected what he was planning, but we tried to act coy. I asked him what was going on, and he said he really wanted to move back to his apartment at the Castle fairly soon, remember he was a Virgo and his every whim seemed urgent. He hoped we would stay on as managers to look after the house and take care of things. Of course our rent would go up, nevertheless, we would gain a large hot tub poised on a covered patio, the freestanding red fireplace, a bigger deck with an extraordinary view, and much more space than we had downstairs. Considering those additional amenities, his modest terms seemed well worth it, besides, we were lucky to just live in a spectacular place like that.

The next question was who could we get to move into our old place? It would have to be folks who weren't afraid to dwell in small quarters, and someone we felt comfortable having around. Sam and Shimko were literally living in their art gallery above K-9 Tubs. They scheduled regular art showings and when the spectators left, the boys laid out several blankets on the floor to make a comfortable bed. Their suites didn't have showers or a place to cook; yet they managed because rents were very high in that area. These guys freely helped us move into the same apartment, so I approached them about becoming the new tenants, they were ecstatic, couldn't believe it, and said yes right away.

Sam, a good-looking Libra man from New Mexico, was medium height, dark, had a round face and a warm smile. Shimko, a tall Capricorn from Nebraska, was nice-looking, but always tried to promote his far-out concepts. The couple first met outside the Mayfair market one Sunday. Shimko was rummaging through a dumpster for food when Sam noticed him and out of compassion asked if he would like to go out for breakfast. They fell madly in love at the Crest Restaurant and remained faithful domestic partners. Soon they rented two office spaces in our building, voilà, the art gallery.

Shimko collected a hefty, monthly government check ever since he served with the army in Viet Nam. He claimed to suffer from Agent Orange and no one could prove otherwise, and he constantly walked around without a shirt in spite of his unsightly back, which was covered with nasty abscessed boils. After the military, he turned into a real derelict, yet somehow befriended a woman in Atwater Village who took him in as a boarder for a while and gave him the opportunity to paint. For many years, Sam held an excellent job with the DMV, he was reliable, saved money and well liked by everyone.

It didn't take Herb much time to make his move back to the Castle Green; he'd done it before. I can appreciate how he felt about that splendid place; the architecture was awesome and as you walked through the basilica type entry, you might be overwhelmed by an enormous sunroom on the right. White wicker furniture was positioned in front of the huge, floor to ceiling cut glass windows; the carpeting was a rich oriental pattern. An old-fashioned hand-carved mahogany front desk was the focal point. This citadel was originally built as an elegant hotel, but converted to condos in the seventies.

All we had to do was move upstairs and once more it went very well with Sam and Shimko's help. Herb left us his kitchen table and even a microwave, which we'd never owned before. The living room would be in the front, using part of its space for the dining area. Our new front bedroom had a great view and a marvelous red fireplace. When we finished organizing things, the boys moved into our old apartment, which hardly took any time because they didn't have many belongings. Once we were settled upstairs, I asked Herb for permission to install a washer and dryer in the small storage part of the basement, and he said it was okay. I hired a vagabond plumber to do the cumbersome job in that dirty confined area, but soon, everyone in the house was able to do their personal laundry downstairs.

*****

For the first year or so at K-9 Tubs, the two of us worked harder than anyone can imagine, slinging big dirty dogs around and trying to keep the noisy ones quiet were rigorous duties and my patience was beginning to dwindle. We took additional appointments on Saturdays; many working people designate that day for doing errands and having their dogs groomed. Each week the shop grew more popular and our establishment flourished, but one particular Saturday, I was at my wit's end and lost it with a rowdy sheepdog. I literally lifted that heavy mutt right off the table and found the strength to cradle him above my waist, and in that anxious moment, I decided to sell the business and end this misery.

It was the ninth day of my novena and I couldn't drink alcohol till midnight, which might explain why I was in such a terrible mood that day. I decided to call our landlord Bob C. who was in Palm Springs for the weekend. He always left an emergency number, and this crisis was very important, so I called him.

"Hi, Bob, this is Carole of K-9, how are you? I need to know what we have to do first, because I absolutely want to sell this company, it's driving me crazy."

He was calm and simply commented, "First, you should get drunk, then think about what you might be throwing away, when you go back to work on Tuesday, hire someone right away, let the business work for you." Yasue was happy, she really didn't want to sell this busy little shop; so later on I got drunk and felt much better.

After my conversation with Bob, I put a help-wanted sign in the window and began hiring young men to bathe and brush dogs. I made up my mind to just employ American workers, everyone else in business took advantage of poor Mexicans, and I didn't want to operate that way. The first guy we hired, Tom, was a good-looking blond and resembled Brad Pitt, but he was the sloppiest worker we ever saw. Tom had bigger things on his mind; at night he starred in professional porno movies.

We called the golden boy 'Bicycle Tom'; he lived in Hollywood with an older gent and rode a bike to work every day. His sneakers were always unlaced and he wore dirty-looking white jeans with grungy T-shirts. This twenty-year-old sprayed water everywhere; he couldn't control the dogs and aimed the hose wildly. The floor was always drenched around the tub and he tracked all the muddy water up front. After two weeks I had to let him go or there might have been a river in the cellar.

Cats were indeed my specialty at school; therefore, we catered to many feline-loving clients. Bathing one can be difficult, but I had it down to a science. First I would hypnotize them with an ethereal touch, then get a firm grip around their neck, if they thought about escaping, I turned their heads, when they looked left, I'd shift them right, it was all in the control and timing. I bathed them quickly with confidence and without sedation; cats were a good portion of our business in the beginning.

The next beauty we hired was a gay guy named Douglas who looked like the Marlboro Man. He was a likeable chap in the morning, but by three p.m. he grew tired and grumpy. When the sun came over the front of the shop, it got very warm, I noticed him sweating, so I told him to take a break. But instead he became even more hostile with one of the poodles. I heard him say to the dog under his breath, "Behave, you son of a bitch."

My heart stopped and I commanded him to take a break right away, he needed to come with me to the bar down the street and have a cold beer. When we got there, I ordered him a brew and a coke for myself. After he let out a big sigh of relief, I began a serious conversation. "Douglas, we like you, but you can't direct your negative feelings toward a client's pet. It's okay if you call me a son of a bitch, but precious animals in our care must never be exposed to bad vibrations. I hope you've learned something positive from us, you are definitely fired, and so have a nice life."

Being a boss really didn't appeal me, I could never give an employee orders, and through the years we engaged many diverse workers. When I tried to explain something to the staff, I always said please and sugarcoated the directive. Early on Yasue was quite self-conscious about her broken English, and I had to do all the communicating. She was very shy with new customers and people usually assumed she couldn't speak the language. Nowadays she has no problem reading someone the riot act.

We were having a chaotic day and could have really used an extra hand when suddenly another gay guy walked in looking for a job. He even had some experience, which was unusual. Although he could really sling a groomers' brush, the man acted like a genuine sissy. His name was Tom, his hair was flaming red, and hence we christened him 'Redheaded Tom'. He was a brooding Pisces and hard to read, in the morning we'd say: "Hi Tom, how are you?" From the blank look on his chalky face, you could only see despair, but he would flail his hands about and tell us he was marvelous, absolutely marvelous. This hapless fellow worked at K-9 for a month and still couldn't focus on the work. One Saturday I caught him lifting a poodle's leg way too high and when the dog yipped, I fired him on the spot.

One of the most regal employees we ever had was a gay man named Rhiner Von Fleck the third, a Leo. He walked in just like everyone else looking for work, but this one had a certain air about him. Rhiner was staying with friends of the family up on Moreno Drive, a delightful street. Two older gay men rented their basement to him, which wasn't quite an apartment, but he had a bed and a fancy armoire that he brought down from his former home in San Francisco. From the moment he spoke, we knew he was educated and I hired him without hesitation. The guy appeared somewhat nervous, he sucked his teeth constantly and his body always seemed to be jerking to odd dance moves.

Cocaine was rampant throughout the early eighties and gay men acted more promiscuous than ever, group sex was a daily activity with the hipper guys. Bill and Richard, who owned The Boy Next Door, persuaded me to go with them on an important crusade one evening. This was to be the first AIDS march in L.A. They handed me a big plastic cup full of wine and off we went to the Federal Building in Westwood. I had to admit my ignorance and finally ask what AIDS really was. They described the disease with abbreviated answers and I sobered up fast. Every gay man in our community could have been infected without knowing it and sadly, we may lose a lot of friends.

Our lives intermingled with certain customers and I became close buddies with a new client named Mark Thomas Jones. He had a Wire-haired Fox Terrier called Spanky and always booked a Saturday, leaving him free to carouse in saloons all day. Mark Thomas was the headmaster of an exclusive boys' prep school in the valley, he made a huge salary and confessed that he might have seduced a few affluent teenage adolescents.

One Saturday he called the shop to say he couldn't keep Spanky's appointment because he lost his truck somewhere, I volunteered to pick him up so we could go out to look for it. He had a blackout and couldn't remember where he parked, we drove all around the county, but the cops finally found it in Hollywood, a block away from his favorite watering hole.

Mark owned a charming house in Atwater Village; he was an impeccable Virgo, which the cottage reflected. He emanated great sexual energy and craved erotic encounters daily, yet he was a former priest. We began to hit clubs together on Saturdays, which was fine with Yasue until the day I lost track of time; she closed the shop and waited for me at home for hours. We lunched at the Greenery, hit the Gold Coast and every other bar on Sunset, until we finally closed at the Detour.

My friend was short, well-groomed but balding and sported a mustache. I insulated my negative thoughts concerning his sexual compulsions because he was a wonderful man with a heart of gold. One Saturday, instead of making our usual rounds at the bars, we went to his house, he wanted to take some canned goods to AIDS Project Los Angeles; they recently established a food distribution center for people with HIV. These disabled lads didn't have insurance or any means other than welfare assistance. It broke my heart to observe young adults who might be damned, the men who awaited this food were skinny, partly covered with lesions and only a handful would survive this atrocity.

The original food project was called Necessities of Life, which started in a small dank warehouse on Sunset. It was like a supermarket with shelves and freezers, but they really didn't have enough provisions. I glanced at sick-looking guys moving through a line with large brown paper bags, and they crammed those sacks with as much as they could carry off. Canned goods, paper products and grooming articles were badly needed; Mark Thomas believed that I might acquire a few items from our clients. Everyone who came to K-9 cherished a dog or cat; therefore, all my patrons had heart.

Accumulating food for a worthwhile cause left me with a good feeling and I became obsessed with helping the APLA group. I started shaking people's pockets the moment they walked into our shop. "Good Morning, have you ever heard of a humanitarian organization called Necessities of Life? Surely you must have a few things in the pantry that those poor people might find useful. Peanut butter is good; perhaps you can spare a can of beans as well, or even some spaghetti sauce." I didn't work hard to promote this drive; people simply heard about it through the grapevine and passed the word. In a short time, K-9 Tubs collected tons of packaged groceries etc., which were indeed appreciated.

*****

Our little White Witch finally went to Toyota heaven because too many major parts were going bad. I shopped around, but we didn't have much of a credit rating since we always paid cash for things. Someone suggested that we lease a car; we could own it someday if we kept it long enough, and once again I got lucky. We leased a silver sedan with low payments from a young man who looked like he snorted a lot of coke; no one else would even consider giving us a loan.

Within a short time, we collected enough groceries from clients, to load up our first brand-new car, a 1983 Toyota Corolla.

Mark Thomas was probably the most promiscuous guy I ever knew, but I told him from the start that I had no interest in the details of his sexual activities. He dressed in smart black Levi's and generally wore a bright white T-shirt, and his face was always very red, perhaps from booze. We drank a lot then, but I couldn't keep up with him. When we dropped an anchor at a local gay club, we'd dish the hopeless bar flies thinking that we were superior. Aside from being Virgos, we had other things in common. We both happened to be ring-around-the-collar Catholics, who constantly analyzed religious dogmas.

Spending more money than we earned was another trait we shared, but we were very giving. Mark Thomas flew to San Francisco often to visit his dearest friends. One compatriot was the famous artist William Gatewood, and his partner's name was Beau. They owned a large mansion on Page Street, an absorbing place, it was a three-story wooden Victorian structure, but when you stepped inside, you realized this home was a beautiful temple. Except for the kitchen, the entire first floor was a maze of fantasy rooms used to perform gay marriage ceremonies and other rites. Beau was a hard-working minister and William spent most of his time in the attic smoking dope and painting, while he was being guarded by two enormous brown Standard Poodles. These exquisite dogs were trained to attack intruders.

William and Beau decided to drive to L.A. one weekend. They planned to stay with Mark Thomas and come to our place for an impromptu hot-tub party. The dogs were at home with a house sitter to free up their limited holiday. Before they arrived, I cleaned the patio area, fixed some wonderful appetizers and chilled plenty of champagne. I assumed these guys were very spiritual and priestly, so I was a bit surprised when they all got naked and jumped into the hot tub; I just wore a T-shirt and shorts.

In trying to make this party very special for them, I foolishly put a box of bubble bath in the sauna, which was not cool. Yasue was congenial, though she never understood their infatuations with sex. I splashed around with them, listened to some great anecdotes and kept everyone's glass full, but at one point I thought I was going to pass out, maybe it was the hot water, cold bubbly or sheer excitement; anyway, it was a happy day for us, we bonded as friends and very soon I would visit them in San Francisco. They said they really enjoyed being with us and before they left William gifted me with one of his elite lithographs called 'Skyfan'; later on he mailed me a signed print entitled 'Kimono'.

Whenever Mark Thomas and I went anywhere, Tina Turner's song *What's Love Got to Do With It* was the tune that played most often and we belted it out loudly with feeling. We frequented a bar on Los Feliz called Mr. Mike's, local gay ones enjoyed the place, the bartenders were sweet and even allowed me to sing *Lilly Marlene* while sitting on the piano, I was usually the only woman there.

Our singing turned into heavy conversations about AIDS as time slipped by. APLA was growing fast and had moved across town. We stopped collecting food when the agency got some big donors involved, like food chains, produce farms, dairies and wealthy benefactors from the entertainment industry.

Our shop was doing well with Rhiner's competent help, but the neighboring stores were not. The Boy Next Door seemed to be putting the profits up their noses and couldn't pay major bills, such as Levi's distributors etc. Richard saw the writing on the wall and decided to return to his career in education. Bill was a die-hard and stayed in that dark back room juggling books until all financial hope was lost, and ultimately they had to close. Bill advertised the store, but no one offered to buy it. This was a bleak time, but a very ambitious man was about to turn their chic place into a contemporary video store.

A Piece of Class was also in trouble, only not because of coke. Everyone noticed how well they lived; Ed and Jay went to their favorite getaway in Palm Springs every weekend, so we assumed things were fine. Meanwhile, their bill collectors were anxious for payments, the Sheriff's Department soon arrived with official documents and two lawmen sat behind their cash register every day to collect all the money from sales. Our pals finally abandoned the glass boutique, but didn't seem very chagrined about losing their beautiful shop; Ed began to teach again and Jay went back to work as a bookkeeper.

Fred Chriss was the guy who launched the new store named Videoactive; he was smart, sharp and Jewish. He was a recovering cocaine addict and had a wonderful family. While he was still using, he lived in an old building near the Fairfax district. Fred was an electronics genius and way ahead of his time; even his circular bed was remote-controlled. Paranoia set in after a while, so he built an electronic corrugated door to enter this trendy suite. One very hot day the air conditioner shut off abruptly and the power in his apartment was completely out. Fred phoned the electric company, but they said he had to pay the current bill before they would turn it back on. How could he get out of there to clear the debt? Alas, he invited the fire department to chop the metal portal down with hatchets.

His mother's name was Rene, and I always enjoyed seeing her.

She was a Libra, very attractive and lively for her age. Sam Strang became Fred's lover and partner, the instant they met; he was a striking man from a wealthy Texas family and made huge contributions to get the business started. Fred had one brother, Chuck, who actually surveyed our block before they rented the place. He spoke with every resident in the area and concluded this was the perfect location for a business with so much potential.

He wasn't ashamed of his Pittsburgh roots, though he often joked about it. Fred added panache to every project, he had great taste in clothes, and his mother told me that Freddy always had to have the best of everything. When we first met, his favorite musician was Bruce Springsteen, he drove an aquamarine Fiat convertible and loved art galleries, he fell for Sam at a ritzy west side exhibition.

When he first got clean and sober, West Hollywood is where he learned all about the video business, he used to work for two gay women, only that's not exactly what he called them. He was a very smart Gemini and quickly determined how to work within that industry while conspiring to bring about his own company. Those lesbians were making easy money just from renting tapes, Fred also recognized the infinite possibilities of video cassette recorders, and Beta programs would soon become obsolete.

Yasue and I held the first free lifetime membership at Videoactive and would never have to pay for a movie, only now we needed to buy a VCR player. Fred advised us to get one with high fidelity sound, not a contraption put together with rubber bands and paper clips, so we bought a good machine.

The store was coming together nicely; he built a modern desk top out of smooth sheet metal and used tall wooden horses for legs. The countless shelves were of his design, well constructed and lustrous.

*****

Diane's son, Joseph, reached his third birthday on July 16th, 1984, the first day of my traditional novena. At sunrise during that particular ritual, I chose to abstain from cocaine forever, it was expensive, and caused paranoia. My life wasn't making sense. I couldn't think straight. We were always invited to parties that flaunted coke, and I couldn't resist; it was definitely time quit. Yasue and I vowed to each other that morning that we would never use the provocative drug again, and kept our word.

A huge and meaningful event took place when the 1984 Summer Olympics arrived in L.A. The universal torch would be carried down Hyperion Avenue, passing directly in front of our shop. It was late July on a Friday afternoon and the news spread like wild fire. We were told the procession would arrive on our block shortly after six p.m. Crowds started showing up around five, and by seven, the street was bursting with all kinds of people, rooftops became balconies, there were even baby buggies filled with libations. It was thrilling to see many strangers gathered together for an experience which made all Angelinos, and especially Silverlake residents, proud to be Olympic fans in America.

It was dusk when we saw numerous police motorcycles coming closer, we got excited, but not as much as the boys from the gym. They enjoyed making crude remarks about cops on bikes wearing squeaky leather accessories. Basically, we kept a relay going from Bogie's liquor store to our shop. Rhiner hauled a great deal of champagne and beer, which we passed out to whoever smiled or simply wanted a drink. Finally, as the torchbearer came to our block, we were able to get close to the adorable young athletic woman. She clung to that beacon with remarkable pride, wearing a beautiful smile, and everyone felt high-spirited as she displayed the famous trophy. It very was appropriate for committee organizers to route a patriotic black lesbian down our street through a very gay neighborhood.

Most people watched the spectacular opening of the summer Olympics on television, and during the games we oozed with pride each time the USA won a gold medal. Carl Lewis streaked to victory in the 100-meter dash and Mary Lou Retton dominated the women's gymnastics events. The closing ceremony was the most exciting part of the collective experience and Lionel Richie dazzled everyone with the song *All Night Long*; that uplifting melody lingered in my head for quite a while after.

Despite our pleasure from the Olympics, 1984 was a cruel year; we lost many friends to AIDS, and saw little hope for a quick cure, yet partying remained a constant way of life. One client tried to lure us to a bash with an invitation containing a razor blade and a plastic bag filled with baking soda. There were many funerals to attend at the time and our sick brothers needed encouragement. I delivered a dog once to Douglas, the owner of a nearby bathhouse known as Mac's, and noticed some contoured hollows in the wall. I asked the attendant what they were for and he answered with a devilish grin, "Those are glory holes, my little naïve one; too bad you don't have the right equipment." The horrible HIV epidemic was growing fast, people should have been more careful but they just weren't.

The Latin guy who occupied the basement apartment at Herb's was moving out and coincidently, our chief employee needed to change his residence as soon as possible. Raccoons and skunks interfered with his need to sleep, so he moved into the small place when it became empty. Rhiner Von Fleck practiced celibacy for several years; hence we didn't worry too much about him acquiring the virus. He had a huge cat named Boris, and they seemed content sharing mutual affections. Rhiner played his music loudly at times but Sam and Shimko, who lived above him, didn't mind, and I no longer had to fear the scent of my marijuana wafting all over the house with an outsider living downstairs.

Silverlake had become a small gay Mecca thanks to trailblazers like Herb and a few other closet-case actors who chose to make this carefree community their home. K-9 did a thriving business and most of our clientele was gay, but I felt awkward about taking money when someone offered a tip. I told them to put it in their church's poor box, and Yasue would glare at me, making a profit was important. We advertised K-9 Tubs only once when we first opened, which was a tiny piece in the Lithuanian church paper. The ad said we performed painless pet grooming and carried out our work with cookies and love. In all this time, we've served exactly two Lithuanian customers, so much for advertising.

Bobby Leone and Mark Barker were the original bitch sisters from the gym next door. Once in a while they'd visit our shop just to rank or insult us, and they always belittled our shabby multicolored tile floor. I felt bad when Bobby said, "This place has lots of class, fourth class." Then they would laugh. These two men were genuine bodybuilders, they had health, youth and energy, but that image was about to change. Jim stayed active taking care of business by holding court privately for new members, while Bobby worked on his oil paintings and took care of the house. Their risqué lifestyle became a public curiosity when, without discrimination, they began to bring strangers home for group sex.

A couple of years later we saw much less of Bobby, Jim kept making excuses for his apparent absence on the block, though several close neighbors assumed he was sick. One morning as I walked up the driveway from my car, Bobby was hobbling down; he faltered and seemed awfully weak. Earlier he looked like a pumped-up Adonis, but he quickly became a very skinny older person, he had been stricken with the merciless AIDS virus. Because of Jim's ridiculous Leo pride, Bobby's disease was kept secret until they finally had to hospitalize him; no one was allowed to visit other than his own family.

Finally the pneumocystis set in and Bobby died at the age of thirty-six; Jim, and Bobby's younger brother Denny were at his side. Their Catholic family wouldn't allow gay people to attend the funeral, but Jim held a private service for friends anyway. Soon after, Mark Barker moved back to Pennsylvania and continued to fight about some of Bobby's paintings; he said that he was promised certain pieces, but Jim would never give up any of that unique artwork and they quarreled for some time. After Bobby passed away, Jim bought a plush place in the hills of Los Feliz and vacated their old house quickly.

In the early days, we were the new kids on the block and the owners of Body Builders' Gym gave us plenty of attitude. Bobby and Al Beal were former chorus line dancers in Las Vegas, then Al met Bob Cameron, and soon after Bobby became lovers with Jim, who worked at Bob Cs. hair dressing salon. When Bob decided to sell the beauty shop, Jim and Bobby took over that space and turned it into a small local gym which never ceased to grow. Bobby always kept his body svelte and having a gym was perfect. Jim knew it was time to give up coiffing hair when he began to hit testy little old blue-haired ladies over the head with his brush. There should have been a twelve-step program for stylists.

Jim dictated with great authority and I admired his many leadership qualities. One morning we were outside sweeping our sidewalks before the street cleaner came, I asked him how he kept up with all the obligations concerning the business. He answered with one word, 'prioritize', an appropriate lesson for me to learn.

A huge big-finned Chrysler convertible is what Jim drove and every Sunday he and Bobby rode around looking at beautiful homes for sale. They lived like upscale folks until the partying with heavy-duty drugs began and started picking up big black guys right off street corners. Our neighbors fancied men who sported enormous penises for the ultimate primal experience.

I invited Fred Chriss and his boyfriend Sam to join us for dinner one evening while we were still nesting in the middle floor at Herb's. We weren't quite sure of Sam's status, but Fred was definitely on the AA and NA twelve-step programs, so we didn't dare to offer or display any alcohol. I cooked a superior chicken curry dinner which we enjoyed in the dining room. Later we all went out on the deck for desert. On that peaceful night the city lights were dazzling and the universe seemed very close.

After a few quiet moments, Fred piped up and said with command, "I want it."

"What is it that you want?"

"I want this apartment."

"Well, you can't have this place, but as it happens, there is a vacancy in the house next door with an identical view."

Felix Schauzer, a gruff building contractor from Austria, was the landlord and lived around the corner with his Korean wife, June, a practicing Catholic. The robust man wasn't religious and Herb frequently alleged that Felix was an actual Nazi, yet they remained friends for many years. Between Herb's and my persuasion, Fred easily leased the place.

Sam was the only person that Fred had a relationship with since he'd become clean and sober, and they were very much in love. Fred moved in right away and soon felt the need to have a cat. A good friend just happened to have two little kittens that needed a home, so Fred took both felines and named them Noodles and Gator. We never knew a better parent, he really loved those two, he fed them only the healthiest food and had both examined regularly. Whenever he left his sliding glass doors open, our cats would sneak into his place and eat all the gourmet cat food, but Fred never complained. When it was time to give Noodles and Gator their first bath, Yasue dispensed a few lessons and taught him how to do it himself; he was a quick study. He endowed his new apartment with fine paintings, computers, all kinds of wiring and electronic apparatus; he was a very savvy and contemporary guy.

Later on when he mentioned living next door to us, Fred always referred to those good old happy days. He identified Cumberland Avenue as 'Cucumberland', perhaps because a lot of gay men resided on our charming narrow street. We shared some fine meals together in the beginning, but from then on, our brief camaraderie declined. He tried hard to cover it up, but the truth was that Sam developed the virus and needed to visit various doctors all the time. This sudden AIDS-related condition was grave and unless he received an immediate bone marrow transplant, he would die. Sam was barely twenty-eight.

When they first met at the art gallery, Sam wasn't shy about flaunting his wealth and Fred was never reluctant to accept it. One time they took a long ride to Sedona Arizona in a big van equipped for camping and brought along Sam's old cat, Midnight. By a fluke, the cat got out of the vehicle and took off. They searched the entire area but couldn't find him, so Fred gave his phone number to every person he met and offered a huge reward to whoever found him. They drove back to L.A. feeling very depressed, but three days later a guy who owned a gas station in the desert called to say he was taking care of him. Without hesitation they chartered a private plane just to reclaim Sam's beloved sidekick, Midnight.

Sam entered a costly hospital in Houston and had to live in a bubble for a while, the donor was ready, but everything had to be decontaminated before this delicate transplant took place. Fred was totally devastated, so he flew to Texas before the risky procedure. Sam only survived the surgery for two days, then his entire system shut down, and he passed away peacefully with Fred hunkered by his bedside. This was the worst ordeal Fred had ever lived through; he stayed in seclusion for a long time until he realized that life goes on. Soon he bought a spectacular house in the upper hills of Los Feliz and poured all his grief into modernizing the place. We rarely saw him after he moved away from 'Cucumberland'.

*****

I was always big on sending Christmas and birthday cards; one person whose address I kept and regularly sent cards to was Angela

Calomiris. Regardless of our sometimes-stormy relationship, I cared a great deal about her and knew she was delighted to hear from me any time. After the winter holidays, she sent me a heartwarming note to say that she'd be coming to L.A. in the spring. She was traveling south to her newly acquired hacienda in Mexico and decided to visit us for a while, her longtime friend, Hilda, would also be eager to show Angela her beautiful new condo in Marina Del Rey.

Hilda was the widow of Gabriel Miorca, the refined man who hand-painted all those wonderful hobbyhorses at Angels' Landing in Provincetown. Ever since they attended grade school in New York City, Hilda seemed to have an endless infatuation with Angela in spite of her happy marriage. Scott was Hilda and Gabby's son, a successful Beverly Hills lawyer and the real reason she moved out here.

It was late March before we knew it; our spacious home was clean from top to bottom, and when I picked Angela up at the airport, we were rather glad to see each other. She insisted we stop at a nearby liquor store to buy a big bottle of cheap wine at her expense, which was the start of a totally inebriated week. We still had the white sofa bed from Jan's house, so her bunk was directly in front of the TV, and thanks to Fred we purchased a great VCR player to enjoy all the free movies he supplied.

Angela was beyond impressed with our apartment and said we lived like movie stars. She enjoyed the hot tub and watched a lot of videos; her favorite flick was *Prizzi's Honor*. We did plenty of fun things during that week and even had a classy meal at the Getty Museum in Malibu. Yasue suspected Angela had a hidden agenda throughout this cheery visit but continued to be patient with the little dictator.

We all went to dinner at a local gay restaurant the night before she left for San Miguel, and as usual, Yasue's intuition was right, Angela made a whopper of a proposition. She wanted me to work at the Cape in mid-May. This was a very special season, it would be the twenty-fifth anniversary of Angels' Landing; she even had red T-shirts printed up for her special clients. Angela offered me one thousand dollars to prepare all twenty-two units in time for a dynamic Memorial Day opening, she didn't even bother asking for my lover's approval, when I spoke to Yasue she said it was fine.

While Angela questioned how our shop was doing, I said business was great and boasted that we easily made one hundred thousand yearly, with a bit of resentment she claimed she never earned that much money annually in her life.

Rhiner was very competent and I trusted that he could look after things and stay close to the princess while I was away. I booked a reservation with American Airlines, and began to pack. Angela said I was very insecure because of the many trappings I usually traveled with. This project should only take a few weeks, yet I filled three suitcases and an additional box of shoes.

The plan was for me to fly to La Guardia Airport, and take a taxi to her small cave on Horatio Street. I arrived in New York early on Friday, but we wouldn't be leaving for the Cape until Sunday morning, so I made arrangements to meet my good friend Samantha Sloane that Saturday night. Sam became my pal through a guy named Ralph Cioffi when Bill and Richard had their store. Ralph formerly served in the Peace Corp, he was a schoolteacher when we first met and Samantha worked as a model for various magazines. Almost everyone we knew then partied, but these two had more savvy and condemned cocaine. My association with Sam evolved at once; we were both ardent believers in the occult. She was a tall stunning Libra with a classic face and a joy to be with whenever possible.

Sam moved to New York after her obsession with Dwight Yokam came to a halt. Without knowing him she went to his home in L.A. and caused an awkward scene. Feeling very chagrined, she decided to move far away, hoping to forget about him, that's when she opted to pursue a different type of career in the Big Apple. When she lived in L.A., she came to a few parties at our place on Cumberland, she was indeed beautiful and all my gay boyfriends adored her. We shared astrological information often and discussed infinite esoteric subjects, she was a good friend and I missed her after she relocated.

She kept her word, got an excellent job with the BMI Music Corporation, and found an amazing apartment in Harlem. Just before I left for New York, I called to say that I was coming and she was ecstatic to think we could be with each other for a special night on the town. We preplanned a route for the evening because Angela lived in Greenwich Village. When I told Angela about my date, she went into a rage. I assured that her Sam and I were not lovers, just good friends and that she was certainly welcome to come along, but her anger persisted. We would be side by side at the Cape for weeks, so what was the big deal about me having one casual rendezvous? Rivalry was her usual hang-up.

All my stylish clothing was packed neatly in a suitcase for convenience, so I borrowed a classic tweed jacket from the boss. Along with the sports coat, I wore plain Levi's and a black cashmere turtleneck, perfect for May weather. Sam knew her way around the city, so we met on Christopher Street in the East Village. From there we walked several blocks toward the Hudson River, lingering on different stoops to have a few tokes from a joint and laughing all the way. Sam was craving Mexican food and knew of a trendy spot on West Street. When we reached the bistro, it was packed; we drank Dos Equis beer while waiting for a table, caught up on the L.A. gossip and really had a marvelous time.

She took my mind off the AIDS crisis, which had brought about some depression at the time. I appreciated Samantha like a breath of sweet air, and didn't want our night to end. After dinner I escorted her all the way up to Harlem via the subway, but she insisted I only go as far as the station at 110th Street, then cross over to head back to the Village. We said farewell at the station, I regret not visiting her artistic apartment, and though I'm sure it was beautiful. In all the years we'd known each other, Sam and I never actually kissed, yet for one split second that evening, we came close. Sam and Diane were the only women to ever attract me since I bonded with Yasue. These two ladies will always be very special, but my partnership is much more meaningful than any conscience-stricken affair.

It was four a.m. when I got back to Horatio Street, but Angela was still up. She was wearing her little granny glasses, smoking a Lark cigarette, and poking through a bunch of stuff that was going to the Cape. If looks could kill, I'd be dead, she was furious because we were supposed to scurry out of town in her yellow convertible by seven. I apologized for coming in late, but assured her I could drive well anyway. After a shower, I packed the car, and we took off right on schedule. Her conversation was sarcastic, but I overlooked the jealous anger to reflect on the fun I had with Sam. Whenever I needed to escape Angela's moods, I'd simply think of a cheerful friend who made me feel happy.

New York was sunny when we started out, but as we got closer to the ocean a thick fog set in. We stopped for lunch at a seaside restaurant in Rhode Island famous for delicious lobster sandwiches. Angela ordered the seafood special with a Bloody Mary, while I had the Portuguese soup, hot French bread, and a glass of white wine. To me there is something comforting about New England food, even the boss turned into an amicable Chatty Kathy after our hearty meal, or maybe it was just the booze.

It was drizzling when I drove her coupe over the hill with the panoramic view of the tip of Cape Cod, but the fog was so thick we couldn't see anything, which might have been a sign of things to come. As we breezed through town, the place didn't seem the same compared to other pre-seasons; it was lifeless. We'd be staying in the cottage of Xanadu, a sort of warehouse for bed linens and kitchen stuff. Prior to this trip she bought several gallons of cheap wine, and after the car was unloaded we had a glass then walked down to the diner on the pier to have some dinner and make plans for the next day.

When Angela said she'd lined up some people for work, I was naïve enough to think someone else would be helping me with the labor. Early in the morning, after coffee, I took a summary tour of those twenty-two apartments and drew a diagram of each unit, listing what had to be repaired or refreshed. She probably scrambled to close the place at the end of last season because everything was in disarray. Only one woman came down the path for a job, her name was Judy, she was gay, and around twenty-five, but she didn't look very healthy. After a brief chat about her astrological sign, I concluded she wasn't exactly ambitious, but took her to every apartment anyway and asked her to take the trash out first.

The heavyset woman didn't satisfy my ambitious criteria, so I informed Angela right away. Everything I asked her to do, I ended up doing myself, then it dawned on me that I was now fifty years old, and no longer the energetic kid who took speed to fix up that broken-down landing. The boss conned me into thinking she hired other helpers, yet Judy was the only one who showed up, meaning I was stuck with her until someone else came along. I expected employees to work from eight a.m. until five, but this character was totally exhausted by two. Perhaps if I hit all the local bars, I might be able to find an ambitious young recruit, however, a real townie would never work for Angela once they became aware of her attitude. Most bar patrons without jobs just wanted to sit around and drink all day.

Though we didn't always agree, Angela was my mentor, a major figure in my life, I tried to analyze how she became such a difficult person, her grandmother was a mean-spirited woman and maybe some of it rubbed off. The Captain was born in Greece, lost both parents to a fatal illness when she was a baby, then raised by the tyrannical matriarch along with her retarded sister who was a bit older. She was quite secretive about her life before Provincetown, but if she got drunk enough, a smattering of truisms would spill out; my butch boss never once mentioned having a relationship with a man.

Granny moved them to New York City and found out through the local Greek community that the two young sisters were required to attend school at once. Angela was five years old when she enrolled in public school and couldn't speak a word of English; her sister was placed in an institution for special kids. Embarrassment became her motivation to learn the language, so eventually she mastered it and the immigrant youngster would never be ashamed to raise her hand and ask questions again.

There were twenty-two apartments to prepare for guests with Memorial Day reservations, but the weather wasn't on my side. During the first week it rained nearly every day and I felt a serious cold looming. Angela constantly made excuses for being somewhere else while the work was going on, this time she had to go to New York for a couple of days on business; I would appreciate the solitude.

After sundown I'd make my usual phone call to Yasue, then paddle around town and talk to people, nonetheless, I still missed my wonderfully understanding partner and the easy California lifestyle. The more I socialized in P. Town, the more I recognized the AIDS epidemic. Certain prosperous gay women took advantage of that awful situation and accumulated the best shoreline properties by way of haggling with men who were virtually wasting away; those greedy predators were worse than vultures.

Judy showed up daily reeking of booze and I usually directed her to the basic job of painting an entire unit. Once she got started, I'd walk to Land's End Hardware store for more paints and cleaning supplies, charging it to the landing. All the curtains had to be washed, stoves required scouring, mattresses had to be shuffled and all the plumbing needed to be checked for leaks. Each day I made a priority list of things to do, but I knew we were running out of time; after two weeks only eight apartments were completely finished, leaving us barely ten days to beautify the other fourteen.

Angela returned from the city after a couple of days, but first she went shopping on Fourteenth Street to buy more sheets and bedspreads. In an odd way she was very giving, she brought me back a couple of pairs of distasteful chintzy jeans and though I'd never complain, I wouldn't be caught dead in them. She depended on me for breakfast, lunches and especially haircuts; she insisted that I did a better job than anyone else, considering what thin, extra-fine hair she had. The chore I resented most was shinning her shoes, which she left outside my bedroom door to be polished whenever I had time.

The town would never be the same, no one seemed to be having fun anymore, the backdrop was almost complacent, and while I worked my butt off, Angela spent a great deal of time on the phone with those swindling gay business women. I practically begged her to hire more help, but somehow she believed the three of us could get the whole place finished in time for her approaching anniversary party.

Day after day my contempt grew, she left all the strenuous details to me and I was annoyed with being her personal servant. We were having dinner at Ciro and Sal's when I told her I didn't want to be there any longer.

"What about your earnings for completing the job?"

I explained that no amount of money was worth the aggravation, and I wouldn't take a penny for the work I'd already done.

Running up and down stairs so many times a day and dashing in and out of drafty apartments caused the harsh wind and chilly rain to worsen my cold, I thought I had pneumonia. When our chores were done, I asked Angela to join me for a brandy so I could tell her that I wanted to leave. I was sorry for disappointing her, but if I stayed for the milestone event, we would surely

268

become enemies, and I'd much rather part as friends. She apologized for making me unhappy with her boorish ways, and she realized how much I missed my adorable partner. Angela wished me the best and invited us to visit her beloved domain, the Casa Del Angel in San Miguel Mexico, during the coming winter months.

Yasue was thrilled to hear I was coming home, even if I didn't make any money for the unfinished project. I gave the boss two days to find additional help, and quickly booked a direct flight from Logan Airport to LAX. She was more shocked than angry and paid my return airfare to save face. I was merely a lackey to Angela, yet very much appreciated by my friends in L.A. The whole sky brightened up the day I breezed out of there on a rickety bus, and that was the last time I ever visited Provincetown.

Prior to the unpleasantness there, the flamboyant little town embodied my fondest old memories, being with Niki, frolicking at the A House, joking with Ronny and Freda, or simply admiring the sun rise and set over the vast ocean. This journey reminded me of how much I'd grown since I stopped using, it proved there was no returning to the past; I must now stay focused on my beautiful life and future.

Angela endured frequent confrontations brought on by her, and the reason she came to me for help was because she didn't have many real friends. She lived by the notion that she was a Greek monarch, when she back was turned folks laughed and called her a jerk. Never again would I walk behind her apologizing for her insensitive deeds or the audacity which drove so many nice people away.

Before I left the landing I gifted Judy with a pound of homegrown marijuana, I didn't get to enjoy it very much, Angela wouldn't have approved.

Yasue and Rhiner were waiting for me at the luggage carousel inside LAX, and I was never so happy to see anyone. When we finally gathered my heavy suitcases with all the sharp clothes I didn't wear, I got to drive my own little car to our place.

It was great to be home, but since I still had a bad cold, I decided to stay in for a couple of days to get some rest and clear my head of any negativity. I've been an insomniac for most of my life, resulting from an obsessive-compulsive disorder, therefore each unfinished detail frustrated me, and I couldn't complete all the apartments in time for paying guests who expected a charming nautical ambience. Nights at Xanadu meant total sleeplessness, so I'd stay awake to review every aspect of work for the next day. Though I was only in Provincetown for two and a half weeks, it seemed much longer.

I was anxious to get back to K-9, I could see the many beautiful dogs and talk to people who weren't just customers, and they were friends. If Angela ran her business affairs the old-fashioned way with honesty and fairness, she wouldn't have so many problems. It was apparent that controversies and confrontations would always be on her agenda, and I realized she wasn't very ethical regarding local real estate deals.

*****

The first person I called was my pal Mark Thomas, he was glad I'd returned and wanted to party right away. He picked me up on Cumberland and surprised me with what he was driving; my wild friend had traded in his little butch Ford truck for a brand-new black Chrysler. He said it might better his image at the Preppie School where he loved being a headmaster. We hit all the usual saloons and had a wonderful time, but during a drunken moment he let it slip that he was sick. In the next instant, he was cruising a good-looking guy across the bar, hoping to take him home. Would they really be safe?

At the time it seemed like I was living in the eye of a storm called AIDS, surrounded by hopeless gay friends who wore a jaded look of death, the epidemic really depressed me. Since there were no drugs for the illness then, I saw countless unwilling young men en route to heaven; it was heart wrenching. I'd just entered the early stages of menopause and cried over everything, even if a leaf fell off a tree. *Girls just want to have fun*, but I couldn't enjoy myself, so I appeased my daily sadness with booze.

I was napping on the sofa trying to get rid of a huge hangover after being out with Mark Thomas the night before, when the phone rang and startled me. Our landlord, Herb, was on the other end and spoke in a grim tone. "It's time for you to find another apartment, I know you're happy there, but I'm really bored with

Pasadena and want to move back into my hillside home. Will you start looking for other quarters right away?"

To say I was shocked was an understatement, but somehow I perked up and replied cheerfully, "We'll move out as soon as we can find another place willing to accept pets, when we do, your abode will be left clean and in perfect condition." Following his surprising news, I thought I might have a breakdown; change terrifies me, and I also worried about Yasue's response.

From the outset he never guaranteed we could stay forever, while it was a great niche, our blissful interval on Cumberland was over. After we lampooned Herb for taking back what was rightfully his, we decided to tell everyone; perhaps a client or neighbor knew of a pet-friendly place. I began to spend more time at K-9 and drank much less as I needed to be around ordinary folks to communicate our urgent situation.

A longtime patron named Ines, who gave us the dining room set, managed a large apartment house on Los Feliz Boulevard and cared for a few personal pets. She had one vacancy in the building and seemed very eager to rent to us, even though we had six cats. We set up a meeting to check out the unit on Sunday, and it rained unusually hard throughout the day, was it an omen?

We parked around the corner from a very busy intersection and hurried to the front door to get out of the rain. Ines met us in the entry and took us to see her apartment first. Everything was nicely decorated in arid shades of red, the furniture, carpeting, even the accessories. She said everyone in the building enjoyed having a pet or two and Ines herself had three well-behaved, perfectly groomed dogs. An elderly woman who lived next door to the place we might be renting actually had fifteen cats.

Ines was a strange Virgo, but really loved animals; she literally climbed over fences to rescue a crying dog on someone's private property. She was thirty-eight and kind of cute, only we couldn't quite tell if she was all white, mixed Caucasian, or perhaps a mulatto. Jazz was the music of her choice, and over a glass of wine she hinted about having a gay liaison once; she'd been alone for a long time.

We left her place and went to look at the vacant apartment, it was quiet enough to hold a séance on a wet afternoon, and the spaciousness was awesome. There were two bedrooms, two baths, a huge living room, a balcony for the cats and an outside swimming pool. One nuisance would be driving through heavy traffic just to get to the underground garage and the long walk to a dinky elevator for a slow ride upstairs, which could be annoying since I took several trips from home to our shop every day.

A lease wasn't required, the price was right and our pets were welcome, so rather than have Herb on my conscience tapping his foot, we decided to take the place at once. Ines would be happy to have amicable people like us living there, while the Chateau Los Feliz seemed largely occupied with grumpy old negative characters. We agreed on a specific moving date and shortly after I went to the bar to arrange for a crew of friends to help. My buddies were great on moving day, they laughed about everything; most of them were loaded beforehand, but they had a good time in spite of being exhausted.

The move was flawless and we left Herb's house immaculate with a little help from Yasue's Japanese friends. Every window and mirror shined, the bathroom and kitchen were clean, as were all the floors, which I hope he appreciated. Moving is an expense no matter how many people offer to help you for free. There is always the first and last months' rents, a security deposit, the movers, gas, phone etc. Regardless, this abrupt transition was necessary. I didn't presume it would be our permanent residence, just a quick solution to the immediate problem. Within one week we had everything in its place.

Having six cats meant shopping for a lot of cat food and litter, as well as everyday household items, but coming home from the market was no picnic. I had to brave a busy Griffith Park Boulevard to the driveway, park in the back of the garage, and walk down a shadowy area hoping to find a shopping basket to haul the goods, push a wobbly cart from the elevator onto the third floor, while passing by everyone's open doors and windows. I resented that trek yet it was necessary. A tiny den became the prayer room, my lavender altar fit nicely and soon I would begin a fresh novena, which I really looked forward to.

We rented the place on a quiet day, but once all the windows were open, the constant street noise became unbearable to me. Early in the morning the kids who attended Marshall High jumped on and off buses toting ghetto blasters, the bus stop was downstairs right by the front door. After three p.m. when the schools let out, the disturbances grew worse. Car crashes caused some ruckuses which usually woke us up after two a.m. when the bars closed; it was a dangerous corner. I've always hated noise, and even the birds on that block were too loud; they chirped all day and all night. I tried to meditate before sunrise, but the roar of the traffic distracted me, in fact I attempted to pray at three a.m., which was futile, the racket from hundreds of chaotic crows blew my concentration. Yasue wasn't quite as sensitive about these issues; she just waltzed around the plants on the balcony and kept our cats well groomed.

Yasue and I started to argue a lot then because of my constant complaining about living there. I began to drink champagne in water glasses like it was Coca-Cola and wanted to move right away. My logical Sagittarius partner knew it would be another huge expense and believed we could tough it out for a while, she also feared losing Ines as a regular customer, but I just didn't care. Once again I told everyone we knew that we were looking for a place, except this time I really wanted to find a house.

Someone else was making a big move; Mark Thomas suddenly decided to sell his home and everything in it because he planned to live out the rest of his days in San Francisco. This came as a total shock to me since we were pretty close, but his disease was making him weaker and he wanted to be around William and Beau Gatewood for some peace of mind. His cottage sold immediately, then he held a huge yard sale which was a charming farewell party; I bought a few things to remember him by.

One of the many people I told my tale of noise to was our friend Fred Chriss, owner of Videoactive. We had a special bond from 'Cucumberland' and he really liked us. One morning he popped into the shop and seemed excited to tell us that he discovered a house for rent on De Longpre Avenue, just one block away from Herb's. Yasue was still reluctant about moving anywhere, but I pressed her to go with me just to see the place and meet the landlord, whose name was Marty. He was a nice guy, his father owned a big business in Irvine, and Marty bought, sold or rented different properties for a living.

The cozy two-story house was awfully small, the living room was only eight by twenty-two feet long, and our broad bed might not even fit in the bedroom. Downstairs had a small living room section, a complete bathroom, a large walk-in closet and sliding glass doors which led to a cemented patio area. Originally it was to be a separate rental for a single person, but who could ever live in that tiny place?

The small house was on a hill, and we had to walk down several steps to get to it. The slopes on the side were covered with weeds and the lower section of the yard was completely overgrown. Marty refinished the interior thoroughly with fresh paint, new carpeting and a good air conditioner, but he hadn't done anything about the grounds. Yasue noticed a few half-dead rose bushes by the front door and thought it might be nice to do some outdoor gardening as opposed to working on the noisy pulsating balcony. After the tour we went home to discuss the possibilities of nesting there.

I kept telling Yasue the structure of the building vibrated from all the heavy street traffic, which made me nervous, she said she didn't notice at first, but now admitted that it shook slightly at certain times. She also acknowledged that most of the tenants in the building were eccentric, and mingling with them was impossible, they were angry people, not very friendly and broadcasted negative viewpoints, whereas Yasue was a cheerful optimist. The idea of tending to her own garden was all the incentive she needed, so we called Marty to say we wanted to rent the house, and he said he'd be delighted to have us.

We'd barely lived at the Chateau for two months and dreaded having to tell Ines that we were planning to move out; she was a natural cynic, just like those elderly tenants who'd been there forever. At first she was very cordial and tried to convince us we were making a mistake. The she began to raise her voice in anger about how much we'd disappointed her. During our agonizing tête-à-tête she implied that she would never take her dogs to K-9 for grooming again; as usual Yasue's hunch was accurate.

We enjoyed the big old dining room set that she gave us on Mayview Drive, but now we would take it right back to where it came from. The table alone would have taken up the entire living room in that small house, so we carried it down to her dusty basement. Ines was furious with us for leaving.

Around the time we abandoned Los Feliz for De Longpre, we

became good friends with a couple of gay guys who came to our shop with their Scottish Terrier Seamus. James MacDonald, a.k.a. April, was a strong-minded Aries and his partner Victor, a.k.a. Vicki, was an opinionated Leo; they were both from Massachusetts, so we bonded right away. They'd been partners for the about the same amount of time as Yasue and me and owned a gracious home at the top of an elevated hill in Glassell Park which overlooked half the city. April was vice president of a company that made products for space vehicles, and Victor was an uptight accountant for a currency exchange firm. I started hobnobbing with them at the Toy Tiger Bar, which was great fun. April had an excellent sense of humor and Victor liked to converse; they were kind, sweet, generous and loving men, I trusted them with my life like family.

I didn't have the nerve to ask for anyone's help with this move, my friends already thought we were crazy, so we hired a professional moving company and let them do all the heavy work. We had one sofa, two end tables with a few lamps, and fortunately our king-size bed fit in the tiny bedroom. Next we needed to get a small dining room set. I was seduced by a furniture store at the Glendale Galeria called This End Up. Mainly they sold pine furnishings, which were fashioned after the old orange crates hippies used in the sixties; their articles were very well constructed but not cheap. We bought our first new furniture there and through the years acquired other pine pieces; it was nearly cat proof.

K-9 was having a good year, so we decided to buy a bigger television. I browsed everywhere and finally bought a twenty-eight-inch Sony with an incredible surround sound system. Our living room was only eight by twenty-two feet, which left very little space in between the coffee table and the new TV. The dining table and four chairs went right in front of a six-foot bay window with a view of two noisy tire shops; whenever they changed a tire, we heard the constant rat-tat-tat sounds.

Felix, the Austrian contractor, and his Korean wife, June, were adjacent neighbors and the girl next door, Mary Applegate, was a quiet, nerdy schoolteacher. At the beginning of summer, some awful music started wafting up the hill from Fernwood, the street below us. If you heard RAP limericks at that time, you might have thought black people were behind it, but this was not the case, the brazen guys who played that reprehensible gibberish were all young white males who indeed lived on the block. They played that racket for over a month and it was really getting to us, especially while all the windows were open.

On July 15th of 1987, I attended a funeral for a friend, who died of AIDS, when I got home I built a huge martini to kill my sorrow. It was a very hot day and even though I turned the air conditioner on, I couldn't escape those nasty and violent lyrics. The more I drank, the angrier I became, so I phoned Yasue at the shop and said I was going to Fernwood Street to stop the noise once and for all. She begged me not to go, but my diluted mind was already made up.

I drove down the hill wearing Levi's, a designer cat T-shirt, a pair of thin moccasins and brought along a two-by-four. I was altogether surprised to see six white teenage boys enjoying this Rap bravado. They blasted it from five large speakers mounted on the back of a pick-up truck. I pulled into their driveway and appealed to them, please lower the volume, or shut the damn stuff off. The group of dullards grinned when I argued that it wasn't music; it was only two beats with some depraved lyrics. They asked what I was into, when I said I liked the Beatles, they laughed harder. While they were still giggling, I gunned my engine and steered straight into their tacky house, they got serious at once.

My car seemed to be embedded in the house foundation, so I got out carrying the big wooden stick and defied them to catch me. I hiked one block when the cops nabbed me and carted me off to jail.

They handcuffed me, threw me in the police car, and drove to the Northwest division on San Fernando. The officers were overly abusive to me, but I was drunk, which made it easy to tell them what I really thought about cops. When I mentioned that no one read me my rights, they told me I didn't have any. Finally, I made my one phone call to Yasue, and told her I would be a guest at Sybil Brand Institute until she could bail me out. She paid Heidi's girlfriend, Darcy, to drive my car back to our house.

Landing in jail on a Friday night was devastating; finding someone able to bail me out was a problem. Our longtime friend and customer Cheri Marino actually talked her father into putting up his house for collateral, but I had to stay there until the paperwork was finished on Saturday. I don't think I ever felt as sick, I vomited all night, and the inmate in the bunk above me said she would kill me if I didn't stop moving around. Cheri picked me up and brought a cold coke, but I needed a stronger drink.

A court date was set, and the charge was property destruction with a lethal weapon, my car. Yasue had to work, but my good friend Diane came with me to lend support. They didn't hear my case during the morning session, and I had to go back in the afternoon. Diane couldn't make it so I drove her home. Aware of the time, I stopped at my house for a stiff cocktail before my trial resumed.

I took a seat in the back row until I spotted the creep who filed the suit, and then I got directly behind him and whispered, "If I ever hear that Rap coming from your place again, I will blow up the whole house."

He was shaken, and told an officer I threatened him, but no one said a word. The judge sentenced me to thirty days, with a restraining order to stay off their street and make full restitution for damages. Jail was a horrible experience, the only sounds the inmates played was the same violent stuff that got me busted. Somehow my threat worked, when it was all over they actually stopped playing music altogether.

*****

The era of dishy queens and hostile dykes was coming to an end as the AIDS outbreak reared its ugly head, men and women relaxed their shallow differences to develop brother and sister kinships. By the close of the eighties there was an abundance of love between gay men and lesbians, which is when many gay people stopped using unkind offensive labels. We all needed to become more altruistic, straight, gay or otherwise. This disease affected and touched everyone with a sick family member or a casual friend. I admired April and Victor for being in a monogamous relationship, I didn't have to worry about them courting the illness; they were bright enough to realize the grim consequences.

I named their abode the 'Ponderosa' because it was a large property with lots of land. To get to this remote place, you had to drive up many winding, narrow, and congested streets. The first time we went to visit them, I followed April's diagram quite well, but the ride back home was a nightmare. We had several cocktails and I hadn't eaten anything; I was pretty loaded. Yasue didn't know how to drive, so when it was time to leave, we thanked them for a good time and got into our car. It was dusk as we started down the steep hill, and I forgot to take my regular glasses, I was still wearing sunglasses. We got very lost, I thought we were in Tijuana, but then I saw a freeway and drove right toward it.

As it happens, I was driving on the wrong side of the highway; heavy traffic was coming at us fast from the next lane. Yasue was terrified and wanted to jump out, but she couldn't bolt because the car was moving rapidly, she just kept screaming. Suddenly I noticed a black vehicle driving very close to us, I thought that we'd sideswiped each other, but I wasn't sure. By the time we reached Chinatown, I was happy to see the city lights and when we finally got home, Yasue really admonished me for frightening her so much. The next day a cute macho kind of guy came to our door and demanded fifteen hundred dollars for damage to his pickup. He ran my number plates through DMV to find our address.

The nice young man's name was Joe, he was a real fast talker and I couldn't argue about my involvement. Yasue wrote him a check without hesitation. He seemed honest, so we didn't bother looking for damages on his truck, but one of us really should have checked. He left in a big hurry and I assumed our payment was the final restitution. Two whole years had passed before Joe showed up at our house unexpectedly claiming that he'd received a back injury from that quasi accident which I'm not even sure happened. He was using a cane and asked for monetary compensation, this time I literally balked at his audacity. I nearly threw the guy out bodily and advised him to prove it or file a lawsuit. What a nerve he had to come back for an additional payoff, he must have thought we were foolish.

Our little house was delightful, and I loved having my own budding marijuana garden. When the plants grew more than ten feet high, I gifted all my smoking friends with big trash bags full of pot.

April and Victor were always cleaning out their place and gave us many worthwhile things. They bought a new refrigerator and delivered their old one right to our door. There was an ugly avocado green icebox in the kitchen, so we took it downstairs to provide cold drinks for guests. Angela camped there for a week en route to Mexico and Mark Thomas showed up whenever he chose to play in L.A.

After my 'wrong way Jose' fiasco, I decided to quit drinking. From our bay window, we could hear the people at Alcoholics Anonymous applauding and oozing with gratitude for the blessing of sobriety. The drab tacky hall, known as the AT Center, sat on a hill diagonally across from us; Alcoholics Together was a predominantly gay group. I joined up and went through all the motions, but I didn't talk to anyone, I was self-conscious around all those strangers, perhaps it was anxiety from smoking weed. Before work I attended a morning meeting, which meant I had to get up very early, I even got there when it was cold and rainy. In a curious way, I felt free and absolved after each gathering.

Unlimited energy kicked in after I got sober and I needed to find something constructive to keep my overactive mind busy. At the time, people all around were talking about computers, it was IBM this, or Commodore that, and I didn't want to be left out of the loop so I enrolled in a computer science class at LACC. My teacher's name was Mrs. Nayle. Her wimpy dull blond hair was parted from the back and combed forward. She was six feet tall and her huge dated shoes resembled boats, she wore one-piece shoulder to toe jump suits covered in blackboard chalk from wiping her big hands on the outfits. The most profound thing she said was that a computer is only a cold hard stupid machine and if a project didn't come out right, it was our fault; we should have given it better information.

The first day left me wondering, but by the second class I had no doubts that she was really a man. My instructor was in her late fifties and often mentioned her wonderful husband. One Saturday he came to pick her up and as they walked down the hall together holding hands, it was like watching a *Mutt and Jeff* cartoon, her mild-mannered spouse was barely five feet tall.

Mrs. Nayle acquainted our class with basic word programs, but to gain real hands-on experience, there was a room with many computers available for students to practice homework. At this point I began to measure our tiny living room, figuring out where to place a large electronic contraption with the essential components.

My friend Ron owned a successful insurance business in the office above our shop; he used several computers for his work and knew a great deal of current information pertaining to them. When I could afford one and it was time to get my own, Ron drove me out to the valley and hooked me up with a Chinese man who sold basic computers, it didn't matter that my machine was a clone of the IBM. This was a very exciting evolution considering I couldn't type, but I bought a dot matrix printer anyway. I sent my eccentric teacher a note of thanks for a pleasing B+ average, also for defining the future.

*****

I was more competent and responsible now and Yasue decided she wanted a dog, so she began to tell everyone. A canine-loving client told her that someone she knew owned a Shih Tzu who was about to give birth to a lot of puppies and there would be no charge. Yasue said she would love to have one of them, so she called the lady to ask her to hold on to a female. When the seven little shavers became eight weeks old, the woman chose to put an expensive price tag on them; this really turned Yasue off. We didn't believe in paying for a pet while there were so many at the pound with tags on their toes.

It was ironic that we owned a pet grooming shop and didn't have a dog. I never really had one, other than Johnson, who belonged to my wicked stepfather. Yasue enjoyed having a mutt when she was a kid in Okinawa, but my only knowledge of canines came from my old boss Dr. Goodman. Our customers educated us with the intimacies of their pets, and we really needed to have our own dog.

The lady with all the puppies finally phoned and said she sold six of them, would we like to buy the last one? Yasue became adamant; originally they were supposed to be free. By the end of the day, the woman called back and we became the proud owners of an eight-week-old Shih Tzu whom we named Megan. She was born in the Year of the Rabbit, just like me, which automatically made her a very sweet, sociable and home-loving creature; words cannot describe the happiness she brought.

I raised Megan while Yasue was at work, every morning I massaged her gums to make her teeth straighter; she had a few crooked ones in front. In the beginning she chewed up everything, especially my leather shoes, she even got into the hamper and dragged our underwear around the house. Throughout the first year, I thought I needed an analyst, she tested my patience daily with all her bad habits; nonetheless, I came to love her and the adorable puppy became a big part of our family.

I wasn't patient enough to teach her, but Yasue finally learned to drive. She took several lessons from a Korean driving school and got her license without any problems. During that time our family car was the 1983 Toyota, which was built like a compact tank. Every day she got better behind the wheel and drove us back and forth to work, but she still needed more practice with parking and backing up.

For Japanese people, New Year's is the most important and high holiday of the year. Yasue decided to drive down to the Fujiya market by herself to pick up some special cultural foods. While traveling south on Virgil, she was suddenly rear- ended by some drunken gay guy wearing cowboy boots, which forced her to plow into the car ahead which was stopped at the red light, luckily no one was injured. The boozer didn't have any insurance, he claimed he just bought that brand-new truck, but the paperwork with the dealership wasn't complete. He apologized and blamed his flashy new boots for slipping. They exchanged the usual amount of information, and when Yasue called to tell me, she was hysterical.

I didn't really know what shape the car was in, but I didn't want her to drive home with frazzled nerves, so I took a cab to where she was waiting. The accident occurred only two blocks away from the Japanese market and she hadn't done her shopping yet. I checked the car all over and I realized it could still be driven, so I insisted upon going to the Fujiya to pick up whatever she needed for the New Year. Our invincible little Toyota was completely totaled; it was badly damaged in the front and rear.

Thank God she wasn't hurt; we aren't really the suing type. I reported the accident and when the holiday was over, I took it to an insurance claims adjuster, and they said they would give us four thousand dollars, which sounded like a healthy down payment for a new one. Our trusty car was seven years old with forty thousand miles, paid for, and I used to think we could keep it for ten years.

Each year early in January, the L.A. Convention Center hosted a giant auto show, and I needed to find a new car. I asked Sidra to come along, I would pay the expenses, and she thought it was a fine idea so we went on a Friday afternoon.

The place was awesome, it featured every new car and prototype on the market, along with many cheap-looking bimbos who pranced around smiling, hoping to motivate sales. A maze of rooms filled with exciting sports cars, luxury types and trucks displayed price tags ranging from $3000 to $300,000. I didn't know what I was looking for, but I enjoyed the pursuit.

It felt like we'd walked for miles; we were getting tired and decided to sit down, catch our breath and have something to eat. Sidra appreciated the adventure because her Gemini mind was hard at work critiquing every vehicle. She ordered a cold beer with her meal, but I wasn't drinking so I had a coke. After our refreshing break, I felt energized and anxious to walk through a few more showrooms.

Just beyond the cafeteria I noticed a red sports car, the color spoke volumes and I thought about Yasue right away. Sidra rambled on about the others, yet I couldn't take my eyes off this beauty. The car was the first model of the Eclipse that Mitsubishi ever built, and I fell in love with it. There were a lot of people hovering around, but I slithered in close enough to look at the sticker price and realized we could own it for $11,000, even though Yasue had set a $10,000 limit to purchase a new one.

The Napa Red Metallic color was captivating, the body was very sleek and it brought to mind those thrilling days of driving my sporty old MGs. I really coveted this flashy car; maybe something weird happened after I turned fifty. Bob Smith's Mitsubishi located one for me; there were only twelve cars like it in the whole state then. With four thousand from my insurance we had a deal, however, by now the computed price went up to $15,000, so my sweet mother arranged to lend us a thousand.

With a little financial juggling, this lucky little rabbit got the car of her dreams, but I needed to park it in a decent place. There was a wide patch of ground above the house, big enough to hold one car. I called Marty, the landlord, and offered to put up a nice redwood fence all around the front if he would pave that ugly dirt area with asphalt, he said he'd be glad to. My carpenter, Bob Jolly, finished the fence, a gate enclosure, and he even built in a fancy mail slot. Marty's crew paved the entire top section, and I placed a couple of four by fours in the gutter to make a driveway access. Yasue lost the courage to drive because of that surprise accident, she'd only driven the new Eclipse a few times, but when she got hung up one day trying to get out of a tight parking space, she stopped driving altogether.

*****

Let me recap a moment how we got our five original cats; Habib, Lady Bug, Sebastian and Tama came from Bark N' Purr, and Mello Boy was a gift to my father from Rita the redhead, but I didn't mention our sixth. While we were living at Herb's house, Drew, the guy who occupied the downstairs apartment, found an undernourished kitten outside the restaurant where he worked in Pasadena and brought it home. This was really a wild animal that didn't trust anyone, and Drew just couldn't handle him. He begged us to take the little tyke, and after a brief discussion we said yes. We named him Tiger, he was a gray-striped tabby with the greenest eyes and longest legs I'd ever seen, and he could run like a deer.

We asked my mother to stay at our house so we could get away to a charming motel in Malibu for a romantic weekend. Mom eagerly said yes, she always wanted us to be happy, but could she indeed take care of six cats and a puppy? I made a huge list for her regarding what they ate, their feeding times etc. It was marvelous to be away, yet I called home often to check on the pets. Everything went smoothly until Habib brought a huge lizard into the house, then my mother freaked right out. She took a broom and beat that poor little creature to death. I didn't know if she would ever sit for us again.

Felix Schauzer was a stubborn Taurus and his wife June was a fragile Libra going through menopause. Every evening after dinner he would take out his frustrations with her on a roaring buzz saw. At times it sounded as though he cut enough wood to build an entire house, we could always tell when he was extremely upset, by the hours he spent sawing lumber. June worked a lot around their yard and it was always manicured to perfection.

She came over to visit us once in a while just to complain about hot flashes or mood swings, so we gave her herbal teas, held her hand while she cried and encouraged her to see a doctor. I was smoking a joint one day when June walked in, she was sweating bullets, I offered her a puff and she took it without hesitation. In minutes she stopped perspiring and began to laugh.

Mark Thomas called to say he would be coming down from San Francisco in a day or two, and would we please leave the downstairs door unlocked; he usually arrived in the wee hours. There were times we thought he picked up a stray trick and brought him to our house, but we never really saw anybody. One afternoon Mark and I hit the bars, and he had to cruise everyone in sight while I sat next to a guy he'd dated recently. Without thinking, I mentioned that Mark had a doctor's appointment on Monday and the brunette man wanted to know exactly what for. I realized at that moment that he wasn't aware of Mark's condition and I changed the dialogue fast, although in his mind, he already perceived that he might be sick.

The next day I had a serious talk with my friend. I told him it wasn't fair to avoid explaining his illness to sexual partners, he could pass the disease on to others without their knowledge. Mark really blew up at me and told me to mind my own business; he went back home and we never spoke again. Mark Thomas Jones, died in March of 1989, and if my neighbor's Ken and Lloyd hadn't told me, I never would have known. He advised William and Beau not to notify me about a service, the ex-priest went to his grave hating me for speaking the truth, and I surely regret the way our friendship ended.

Angela called to ask if she could stay downstairs at our house while she took care of some important business with Silverlake's most well-known real estate figure, Karen Weiss. I introduced them during Angela's last visit with us on Cumberland and they really hit it off. I assumed their secretive deal had something to do with selling the illustrious Angels' Landing in P. Town. Furthermore she made references about calling on Hilda's son Scott, the Beverly Hills lawyer, to revise her old will.

Before she arrived, we cleaned up the downstairs studio, installed a soft reading lamp over the small bed, stocked the refrigerator and turned the bathroom into an attractive nook. Angela recently went through surgery to remove some cancer in her throat caused by years of heavy smoking, which was probably the reason for getting her affairs in order. Yasue and I were still smoking, but we soon found out how adamant she felt about smokers now, so we limited our habit and tried to cover it up. It was a shame that she didn't feel as resolute about booze, the first thing she wanted was a jug of wine to keep by her nightstand, without thinking I became vulnerable and blew my sobriety to drink with her.

She was especially impressed with our red sports car and expected to go someplace different every day. Karen invited us to join them in Palm Springs for the biggest weekend of the year, the Dinah Shore golf tournament, which meant that many well-to-do lesbians would be in attendance. Karen and her sweet Libra lover Lois were happy we came to visit and share their charming ranch-type home, which had a pool and all the amenities. Yasue couldn't make it because she had to work that day.

It was a Saturday night and they took us to some trendy women's gay bars, however, one embarrassing incident occurred when Angela tried to pick up a beautiful woman. She told the young maiden she was quite rich and just wanted to have fun; the girl said she was also rich, but didn't need a floorshow.

After we closed the bars, we went back to their house and had a bite to eat; I took two aspirins with a lot of water before going to sleep. They had three bedrooms and gave Angela and I separate rooms. I woke up first and muddled around the kitchen looking for some coffee, but there didn't seem to be any, so I jumped in my car and drove to a store. Since no one else there smoked, this would be a good time to enjoy a cigarette. I came back with the *Sunday L.A. Times* and a tin of Maxwell House.

Early that morning we went to the country club which held the annual Dinah Shore golf tournament. Angela took a lot of pictures; we all looked great because everyone was dressed in fine white clothing. There were signs posted everywhere instructing people not to take photos within the complex, yet Angela ignored all the warnings; she was a big shot professional photographer. Though this event was held in early April, Palm Springs still got very hot, so I bought the boss a Ping golf cap to keep her little head cool.

Along the main path we were able to buy beer, but she argued that I shouldn't have any. While she was guzzling, I drank a cold one anyway; I couldn't take any more orders from her.

Angela snapped photos of everything but was soon admonished by a very polite security guard. Her conversations were noisy and she got busted again for talking loud while some famous players were trying to concentrate on this crucial competition. Those were just a few examples of how she always embarrassed me, but these classy gals just fluffed off her ignorance.

Later we went back to their house and packed our stuff, I wanted to hit the road early and get home to my sweet Yasue. The freeway seemed wide open, and there wasn't much traffic in either direction so I pushed my Eclipse up to 120 mph. As we got closer to home, Angela asked me to stop at the Mayfair market to pick up some wine and while I was at the store, I bought some beautiful flowers for Yasue. I appreciated that she made an effort to understand the boundless and compelling love/hate relationship between Angela and myself.

Before Angela opened the landing for the summer season, she would head down to Mexico for a while. She wanted us to join her there for the next Easter holiday, a huge and widespread celebration. When her legal business was finished in L.A., she arranged to have Karen and Lois as her guests for the most exciting week of the year, the annual 4th of July celebration in P. Town, and they would be staying in her finest apartment.

When they got back from the Cape, Karen called me to rave about what a great time they had, the Captain was on her best behavior as she wined and dined them. The girls said I was lucky to have lived in such a wonderful place, but they really didn't know Angela darling all that well.

*****

Nearly a whole year had flown by when she reminded us about taking a trip to her citadel in Mexico. Somehow Angela had grown very fond of Yasue, she saw her as my strength, but my partner couldn't take time off during the week before Easter, our shop was usually too busy. "When the lady goes for a hairdo, the dog does too." I received Yasue's approval and blessings for this vacation, so I booked a flight to Mexico City, from there I would have to take a long bus ride to this historical landmark, San Miguel de Allende. I had no idea how congested the place would be throughout that holiday.

After the plane landed, I was instructed to take a taxi to the main bus station in Mexico City. Next I hopped into a very old empty cab, but it didn't take long for the driver to cram in four more riders. He drove through red lights, turned corners on two wheels and came so close to traffic, I nearly lost my arm, which was dangling outside the window. As we approached the bus depot, it was so crowded the cabby had to let his passengers out one whole block away.

Since I never learned to speak Spanish, it was hard for me to converse; however, I did understand that all the coaches were reserved until the following day. I was literally stuck; the only alternative was to locate another taxi to take me up that mountain to the Casa Del Angel, as soon as I could retain a friendly and accommodating driver.

I carried one bulky suitcase and wore heavy Wolverine boots, so I didn't want to walk far. The buses waiting to roll hauled everything from chickens to television sets; people were packed in like sardines. Luckily I discovered a neat-looking taxi driver who could speak English. His name was Roberto and I explained that someone important was expecting me in San Miguel de Allende, he knew exactly where it was and said the trip would take about three hours, but suggested we stop at a store to pick up cold drinks or snacks before we started up the steep hill. Corona beer and packaged donuts turned into my staples of choice and the smiling driver made charming conversation as we proceeded.

Roberto set his price for my ride, which happened to be two hundred dollars plus gas and tolls, but it was well worth it. We arrived in town at sunset and he seemed familiar with every street, pointing out many interesting places.

There was a huge ornate entry door large enough for a car to drive through in front of Angela's old villa, yet vehicles never used it. The place was otherwise surrounded by a high wall crowned on top with broken glass, making it difficult for anyone to trespass or try to rob her.

Angela came down from her ivory tower to greet us when we

rang a very loud bell from the street. Roberto carried my bag into the courtyard and I introduced them. As I paid the nice taxi driver his rightful fare, I kissed him on the cheek with gratitude for getting me there safely. This was my first big mistake from her standpoint, she said women in this country didn't kiss men in public as it handicapped their macho egos, but I rather thought he appreciated the friendly little peck. My second indiscretion was overpaying and tipping, all this baloney before she even said hello.

As we walked upstairs to the kitchen area I felt dizzy, it was probably the combination of high altitude and beer, and nevertheless I sat down in the breakfast nook, opened another beer and lit up a Marlboro. She screamed and pointed to my quarters, "This is the only place you can smoke, now hurry up and change clothes for dinner."

My room was small, but had a view of the street below and I could hear every sound. When the sun went down, it got quite chilly, so I put on a warm sweater and after savoring a cigarette, I went back to the tiny kitchen. Just before I left L.A. she promised to have some hot chicken soup and chilled white wine ready when I got there. There was a large pot of cold chicken soup on the stove and she asked me to strain the grease off the top, then set the table, the boss also cautioned me not to cook things too long since it was bottled gas and very expensive. I thought a guest didn't have to serve the hostess.

When we finished the oily soup and a glass of cheap white wine, she insisted on showing me the town. There were many plazas, churches and an awesome cathedral in the main square, the hilly streets were cobblestones and there wasn't a neon sign anywhere. Ordinances in San Miguel were strict because they wanted to keep this historical city exactly the way it looked forever. Once again it appeared that Angela was blazing a gay trail in an artist's community, just like she'd done earlier in Provincetown.

Good Friday was the next day, the moon was full in Libra and the sun was in Aries, typical for Easter dramas. We ambled into a chic bar; the Mexican version of the Atlantic House in P. Town. The music was different, but the same well-heeled American status seekers gathered there for margaritas. Some were artists or writers boasting of their prosperity, and planned to develop this artistic hamlet.

Angela said I was only to have one cocktail, maybe the full moon added to my hostility, but suddenly I began to resent her telling me what to drink or how many I was capable of drinking. We drifted back to her house through some very dark alleys, at one point I was tempted to punch her out, yet I held my tongue and fists since I had to keep the peace until next week. She arranged to do several errands on Saturday, while I looked forward to just taking great photos of the local residents in true daylight.

We said good night and I went to my room, free to smoke a cigarette and drink a bottle of warm beer. The town was very noisy, and I was relaxing on the bed when all of a sudden I heard the most ungodly sounds from somewhere on the block. I imagined those screams were coming from a sacrificial goat in the name of some obscure religion. I dashed to Angela's room, but she must have passed out. In the morning she explained the ghastly ritual and said they only performed it on holidays, she'd heard this frenzy before and was used to it. I thought it was sickening and couldn't wait to go out for breakfast to down a Bloody Mary. As we were about to leave, I noticed a pair of shoes outside my door along with some shoe polish. She was doing it again, trying to use me as a valet and I hated her for that.

I relaxed once we got to the Cantina; it was a great location to catch the action and snap photos of striking people. There were tourists like me, devout Catholics from everywhere and beautiful natives enjoying their families. Angela made her usual petty scene over the check, so I paid our bill, and took off to go shopping. The boss was having a party on Monday, April Fools' Day, and she invited every local person of affluence or influence, plus a handful of starving au courant artists and writers.

Soon after she left, a very smooth-talking handsome Latin guy asked me politely if he could sit down. The place was crowded and he looked cultured, so I said he could join me. Raphael was his name, but he was no angel. It didn't take long to figure out that he was into cocaine, and I really had to watch my back. We had a couple of friendly drinks and I managed to get rid of him in a short time.

I walked around for a while and ended up back at the villa; I took a nap, showered and dressed up rather nicely. Angela wanted to go to a very hip bar which only played American music. Shortly after we arrived there, I boldly asked a beautiful young senorita to dance with me and Angela went nuts.

She signaled me to get off the dance floor immediately, and I couldn't imagine what was wrong. The girl I was dancing with was half my age, very sharp and beautiful; we were really having a great time. Angela dragged me away from her quasi-intellectual friends to tell me the young lady was Mexican. "That woman is a native, if you do anything off color here; she is liable to send for her macho brothers who would love to kill you." That was the last straw! It was bad enough when she put a limit on my drinks, but she ruined the only real fun I was having. We left right after that ludicrous scene.

The full moon affected my rage and as we walked down a dark alley toward her place, I went off like a firecracker. I reminded her that I was close to fifty-two years old and could no longer take her crap. It wasn't right for me to strain fat from chicken soup, or for her to presume that I would shine her shoes; I was a guest, not a servant. She didn't seem to think these issues mattered, which caused me to become even angrier. We yelled and screamed at each other enough to wake up the whole neighborhood, while I lowered her body to the ground like the harmless maneuver I used on Anna, the crazy Filipino. "You don't know how close to death you are, you ugly little tyrant."

She said she was going to take me right out of her will, I laughed since I didn't know I was in it. Her money never made a difference to me before, why should I worry about an inheritance now? After we parted, I went back to the same bar.

When I got to my room that night, there was a note on the table. The scrap of paper read: "Carole, I heard that a lot of people will be leaving San Miguel tomorrow. There are vacancies all over town, The San Francisco facing the square, rents single rooms from $20.00 up. The place is cheap, central and clean. I want you to disappear early, just tell any taxi driver to take you to this well-known hotel. Your beer is outside the kitchen door, take it with you."

I went to sleep, woke up at dawn and packed all my things, but my plane reservation was booked for the following day and I had to stay somewhere.

I had no choice but to get a room at the hotel, and I needed to call Yasue. There were no outside telephones in the whole town, if you had enough money you could wait in line at a small dinky office where an operator would put your call through for a hefty fee. As I waited, the sweat just poured off of me, I was really hung over. Finally a cheerful lady got Yasue on the line, but she didn't seem very happy to hear from me. Angela had called her earlier to say that I was a complete mess, and when I got home she should get me to a shrink ASAP. I assured her this was only Angela's paranoid rendition, she shouldn't be too hard on me, and after all there were two sides to this unpleasant story.

   By now I was down to about two hundred bucks and checked into The Hotel San Francisco, right next door to the police station. My room was small, it had a picture on the wall of Jesus kneeling down, there was also a large portrait of Our Lady of Guadalupe, but otherwise the abode was simple and clean.

   A huge religious procession was happening down the street, so I went there to take some photos. It was a spectacular scene as hundreds of children marched carrying statues of Christ and sacred banners. Groups played daunting music, while one guy literally seemed to be nailed to a cross, men flagged his torso with thick bamboo sticks and real blood spurted from every orifice of the Lord's body.

   After that reality show, I needed to sit down, relax and have a drink. I ended up at the Cantina where I met Raphael previously, and there he was at the same table. He beckoned me to join him and I did, I didn't have another soul to talk to as I anguished in the unfamiliar town, so I bought us a drink and uttered my tale of woe. "I came here to be with a friend, she treated me very badly, now I can't wait to go home." He sympathized and suggested that he walk me back to the hotel because I looked weary, but first we stopped at a store to buy a good bottle of Tequila with the worm at the bottom.

   Raphael escorted me up to my convent-type room; I gave him a shot of Tequila and sent him on his way. I went to bed fully dressed wearing Levi's, a sweater and shirt; the only money I had left was tucked in my boot on the floor covered by a pair of socks. After I took a big gulp of the wormy booze, I fell fast asleep.

   The windows were covered with paper-thin curtains and when

the sun rose, I was blinded by the light. I felt happy until I noticed the door was open, then I picked up my boot and realized the money was gone, fortunately I still had my plane ticket, so I ran down the winding flight of stairs to find the desk clerk and announce I'd been robbed, he was standing outside talking to a cop.

When I told them about Raphael, they didn't seem too surprised or sympathetic, but when I mentioned I was Angela's houseguest they appeared to get angry. One young policeman told me they always had problems with her, he said if anyone parked in front of her entrance gate, she would come out in the middle of the night and slash all their tires. My informal police report was futile; the reality of being totally broke meant I had to swallow my pride and go directly to ask her for traveling money.

I carried a full sack of quarters in a purple velvet whiskey bag which I intended to pass out to poor people but never took the opportunity. Her villa was about eight blocks from the hotel, so I clutched my things and hoofed right down there. When I rang the bell, she opened the ornate door and jumped back on her feet when she saw me, I told her I needed to talk, and that she could at least be civil enough to hear me out. It was difficult for me to ask for anything, especially after telling her how much I disliked her, but I really needed to borrow my bus fare home. Naturally she said I was stupid, but since she wanted me out of town in a hurry, she lent me one hundred dollars. I gave her the pouch of coins, and that was the last time we ever saw each other. I would never again be criticized by that self-ordained Leo king. As I boarded the colorful Fletcher Amarillo bus, I felt relieved and peaceful.

Along the route to Mexico City many picturesque sights within this very poor country amazed me. Hearty people held onto their limited possessions, everything was valuable, waste not: want not. There were plenty of Volkswagens on the highway and tiny stone shrines poised on either side of the road designated for praying. Everyday passengers on this bus were genuine art forms in lovely tan bodies, most seemed happy just to be alive. If an outsider looked directly at a native, they quickly turned their heads. When a tourist snapped their picture, they believed that person was trying to steal their soul.

The crowded coach arrived at the depot after a long ride down the mountain; suddenly I felt sick and couldn't breathe so I rested a while. When I finally caught my breath, I took a taxi to the airport, went through customs easily with my opened bottle of Tequila, and boarded the plane to L.A. Thank God I would be home soon. It was a smooth flight and they even served beverages in real glass tumblers, not the plastic type. I ordered a vodka tonic instead of a margarita; I missed ordinary cocktails. After a couple of drinks I fell sound asleep but didn't wake up until the stewardess gestured to me.

During my nap, reflections of this miserable excursion flashed through my heavy head. From the moment I arrived, Angela seemed embittered, I hoped that she'd become somewhat spiritual while living down there, but instead she'd grown meaner. She called me a punk and I guess I was she said I reeked and I probably did. Whatever she or I had become, we could never be close friends again. In the old days when I was young, good-looking and her constant minion, she flaunted me like a poster child in front of her wealthy lesbian associates; it is conceivable now that she resented me for being older. The April Fools' party was to be in my honor, but later she told her guests I had to leave abruptly due to an emergency at home. Angela's disabled sister died long ago, and Hilda and Scott were her only friends at the time. Shortly after we relinquished our thirty-year bond, she became a total recluse.

I was the last passenger to get off the plane, and just as I entered the LAX terminal four young airport police hovered around me and insisted they had grounds to conduct a body search. Three men and one woman began to hassle me, they probably noticed that I was a little tipsy, or perhaps they were verbally abusive because I was gay, I'll never know. They forced me into an obscure restroom-type area, the guys turned their backs while the female made me take off my boots and drop my pants, then she inspected every crevice of my body, but she didn't find anything. It was a humiliating ordeal.

Before I took this trip, I decided not to carry any dope whatsoever into Mexico. In the first place, Angela would have been angry; secondly I was advised to be very cautious around foreign cops. After belittling me with that contrived illegal search, they tossed my suitcase. I was told in Mexico City that my opened tequila bottle was all right providing it stayed in my luggage. The kid cop bullies were infuriated and disappointed because they didn't find any contraband and had to set me free.

It was about two in the morning when I called to say I got in okay, and could Yasue please be waiting with some cab fare when I got home. Throughout our considerable time together, Yasue must have figured that I was above reproach, she always allowed me to go places alone, but from now we would only travel together and limit our vacations to Hawaii. She was indeed my earthly guardian angel.

*****

Sitting on our couch surrounded by six cats and a young dog was a rich and loving experience that could never be measured by money. I stayed drunk during most of my trip south of the border, I felt completely isolated, hurt, empty and often depressed in San Miguel. Being at home with my family had now become the most meaningful thing in my life. I developed a whole new outlook on gratitude, booze was off-limits again and I gave away the wormy liquor that I worked so hard to keep.

Life was back to normal on De Longpre, the computer kept my mind busy, and we had fun going places in our bright red car. Meanwhile, our crazy neighbor June bought a small Yorkshire terrier to amuse herself while Felix got off on his buzz saw. Her high voice carried everywhere and we could hear her screaming at the poor little puppy. She told the pet where to pee, if he didn't go exactly where she pointed, there was a smack and the dog yelped. I peeked over the fence to see what was going on and saw June holding a broomstick. She glanced at me and chuckled, she claimed it was only a training exercise to teach him where to urinate. I begged her to never hit him, but she denied that she had.

We felt awful when we heard the Yorkie crying constantly, it was agonizing, we treated all pets like children, and hers shouldn't be any different. I recorded a bit of her cruel discipline to document the dog's abuse and eventually called the Department of Animal Regulations, they told us an audiotape wouldn't do, they said it had to be caught on video, but we didn't have a camera. I leaned over the fence to yell at her several times, but she would just scurry off to the other side of the house. When I approached Felix about this problem, he said he wasn't aware of her cold-hearted behavior, but agreed to speak with her. He recognized that June was menopausal and should never have adopted an animal.

I was having recurring nightmares about how to murder June, and I couldn't even stand to look at her. Felix practically built their house with his own two hands; we reckoned they would be there forever, so we began to think about moving rather than wage a war with a respected neighbor, I tried to be a peaceful little rabbit. We lived there for five years and literally outgrew the tiny dwelling, so once again I began to ask people if they knew of a decent place for rent in the area. Our good friend Joyce, who was in fact Felix's tenant on Cumberland, surprised us one day when she mentioned there was a rental on Sanborn Avenue. The house was on a hill with a panoramic city view, and only two blocks away.

As it happens, we used to deliver a cute dog little named Lucy to the same address. We brought her home a few times when Steve, her owner couldn't pick her up at K-9 on time, we extended the same courtesy to a nice gay man named John Baker who lived directly across the street; we groomed his beautiful longhaired white Persian cat, Bagoas, regularly. Each time we drove up the rustic hill to take a pet home, a twinge of envy came over me and I wished we could live on that block someday.

Kedrin Jones was about to become our new landlady. She was a competitive person who worked in the television industry. After buying Steve's house, she only lived there for a brief time. Kedrin decided to move into her boyfriend's home in Bel-Air. Her fiancé, Peter Werner, was a successful television director. Kedrin's busy schedule forced her to hire a real estate agent named Vernita Mason to handle the details of our rental contract. We breezed through the appropriate credit checks etc. but the lease was only for twenty months which was the kicker, we were promptly told to take it or leave it. Kedrin had a bad reputation around the neighborhood; people rarely saw her, and anyone who actually spoke with her said she was an arrogant bitch who bickered with neighbors about boundaries and community esthetics.

We upgraded to better surroundings each time we moved, but now our rent would be an additional five hundred a month, though if you saw this incredible place, you'd understand why we had to take it. Several huge pine trees grew on each side of the Sanborn hill and converged together above the road to screen a section of the peaceful street. A lush green lawn covered the front of the bungalow and there was a brick path to the door with banana trees in each corner. All the front windows were designed in stained glass. Steve was an artist as well as a great contractor. In between the living room and den, he crafted a breathtaking wall of stained glass which was the focal point of the interior; he also built an enormous field stone fireplace in the living room with lots of hidden cubbyholes for storage.

Except for the kitchen and bathrooms, the entire inside of the house was paneled in natural knotty pine. Steve used a lot of Malibu tiles, the floor and lower walls of the master bath were tiled in a stunning cobalt blue, and the room also had an old tub with clawed feet and antique fixtures. A tiny airplane-sized shower room was dressed up with some very unique tiles. This property was in fact two city lots, which gave the place an endless back yard and even a few hidden paths to stroll. Outside the rustic kitchen windows several fragrant Hawaiian Plumeria trees stretched beyond the fruit-bearing cactus plants.

A spacious brick courtyard area accommodated a large picnic table and chairs for having parties, barbecues, or friendly gatherings. From there you could see the Hollywood sign and the Griffith Park Observatory. Our new bedroom had two sets of French doors, one led to the side garden, and the other went to the deck. The large wooden deck housed an antiquated hot tub, which never really worked. Steve built an awesome bar between the kitchen and living room, and even installed a brass foot rail with room for stools. He created another beautiful stained-glass design above the bar counter. Thick Berber carpeting covered the living room nicely and the compact kitchen had three skylights.

Vernita had the keys to the place, and without telling Kedrin, she permitted us to move in before the arranged date of May 1st. The L.A. riots began on April 29th 1992. As we stood on the deck, we heard endless sirens blaring and eerie black smoke appeared everywhere. News programs showed details of looting and damage. I still couldn't believe how a court decision could turn half the City of Angels into a discontented war zone. I saw the video just like everyone else, but violence could never change what happened. Fifty-five people died, 2,300 were injured and countless buildings were burned to the ground. Firemen were still trying to put out fires after three chaotic days, and Rodney King went on live television to say: "Can we all get along?" Our first day in that house was very unsettling.

It was a very rainy day the first time I saw Kedrin face to face. I called her office to say we had a major leak in the kitchen ceiling, and she rushed right over from Beverly Hills. Neighbors provided me with a slight profile, but I was surprised to see that she was black. Our new landlady was a tall graceful woman, attractive in a frigid way, dressed from head to toe in Armani and wore a classic Burberry raincoat. We discussed the leaks and I mentioned the broken hot tub. Maintaining a pleasant dialogue was awkward; she seemed to resent having any obligations for that old house, though she did agree to fix the leaky roof. The hot tub became a moot subject so we paid someone to check it out later.

When the sun passed over, the open skylights made the kitchen so hot you couldn't cook; I soon had custom-made shades installed at our expense, which was futile since that was where the leaks came from. In spite of all the wonderful characteristics that old house embodied, there were always problems.

For the short time we resided there, it was one hassle after another. Vernita no longer liked her client and refused to be the go-between concerning any problems with the house on Sanborn, so Kedrin called us late one night to say she wanted everything out of the garage as soon as possible. She had already hired a maverick crew to rip out the old concrete, align the garage floor with a new cement driveway and rebuild the structure. The rickety enclosure was filled with junk and old gardening stuff which needed to be cleaned out anyway. This filthy job caused a great disruption to our lives with the noise and dirt. Weeks passed before they finished, at last then we thought we could enjoy some peace and quiet.

Her next unwelcome phone call was to let us know that someone else was coming to take the shingles off the roof and replace them with new ones. The roofing job went on for days, the racket was awful and our cats hid under the bed with the dog until it was over, we were also sickened by the smell of tar.

Soon after that terrible imposition, Kedrin called again to say she was having the entire house painted. The woman never once apologized for causing us those inconveniences; she was the big shot landlady. I began drinking again and not just socially. Yasue and I both felt very unhappy about living there with so many noisy workers around all the time. For a while we couldn't entertain company or enjoy a party, the place was always in chaos from one project or another. Ms. Jones had her own agenda and didn't care about ours. She intended to list it on the market as soon as our lease was up; meanwhile everything in and around the bungalow was being repaired, which cost us much privacy and tranquility.

When the workmen began to paint, they covered all the windows with heavy brown paper and we were literally sealed in for about a week. This was the last straw, my nerves were shot and I really wanted to exterminate Kedrin. Rather than watch me go completely nuts, Yasue suggested that I take a little trip to Hawaii to chill out, so I booked a four-day package with the Outrigger Hotel in Waikiki.

My inner anger caused some bad karma during that holiday. For spiritual reasons I never drank when I went to Hawaii with Yasue, but this time was different. I was sitting at the bar of the hotel and befriended a congenial Caucasian girl who was waiting for her husband, a local fisherman. When he arrived, we went to my place, ordered room service and watched a current movie. This comical guy only spoke pigeon English, and I could barely understand what he said. After a few drinks and some laughs, I started to feel better. The couple was gone by morning, so was my good camera and cash.

Yasue was terrific to let me to go on a trip which we probably couldn't afford, yet I continued to be in a bad place, it didn't matter that I'd gone to paradise. Those petty thieves simply disillusioned me, but I still felt agitated about our home life. The worst period of our lives emerged from a charming house.

During those twenty intense months, another huge intrusion engulfed us simultaneously from a new structure next door. An Armenian guy named Misak Tebelekian was building condos and employed several foreign laborers at the site every day, including Sundays. This construction work was even noisier than what we had just endured. His ragtag crew had their wives bringing daily lunches, when the clan ate together; they cackled uproariously right underneath our windows. Mello Boy, our young scavenger cat, managed to find his way to their food and helped himself to some uncooked chicken. Yasue confiscated a couple of breasts from him, not knowing whether the meat was good or not.

The condos were being developed on the lot below us, though numerous trees obstructed a clear view of the place, listening to all that commotion drove me crazy. One Sunday morning I had a wicked hangover and some folks were having a loud conversation in Armenian, I began screaming obscenities from our deck, but they just carried on. The next day I went downtown to buy a powerful BB gun, then practiced shooting with it in our yard. One afternoon while the group was having a leisurely meal, they became hysterical over an asinine joke. I wasn't able to see anything, but I fired the gun aggressively until it was empty. Everyone became silent and I figured if anyone had really been shot, they'd all be screaming. I found out afterward that I'd only shot out two very thick broad bay windows.

I didn't know what sort of damage I'd done, and I was too chicken to go over there right away; however, I did hear glass breaking. The owner was probably afraid to come and see me, and I couldn't blame him.

Two weeks passed before my curiosity and conscience got the better of me, so I walked around the corner to the contemporary building hoping to speak with someone about offering restitution; there he was, planting flowers in the courtyard. Misak was a short middle-aged man who appeared educated. Once in a while I noticed him as I drove up Sanborn, he was usually screaming at his workers.

Misak buzzed me in when he saw me standing at the security gate and probably wondered why I was there. I introduced myself and said we needed to talk about the damage I'd done, but he asked me to look at his elegant condos first. It was a three-level building with an underground parking garage. Number five was the first apartment he showed me, a rear townhouse partly separated from the others, and it had two broken bay windows in the living room. Basically the nine luxury units were finished, but he needed to sell two of them quickly to make bank payments. I was impressed with his overall achievements and guessed his incentive for being so amicable that day was because he wanted to sell me a condominium, under the circumstances it was hard to imagine that the man could be so gracious.

We toured three apartments, but after I compared them to number five, the others seemed inadequate. Each unit had a balcony or two, the place I liked didn't, but it was much larger. I could see portions of our formerly leased house, the deck where I shot BBs from, and the artistic landscaping we planted on the side. We were supposed to be out of there in one month, but then the Sanborn property would go up for sale. Kedrin was asking $450,000 for the tiny bungalow, but since we couldn't come up with a down payment, we had to think about relocating. Moving next door seemed like a wonderful solution.

Misak only had one unit rented to five Armenian college students at the time, but assured me they were nice guys. After he took me around the well-manicured grounds, we finally discussed the broken glass. He said each double window cost three hundred dollars, so I wrote him a check on the spot. When he noticed the name Markarian, he asked if I was Armenian, I lied and said I was half, when in fact I'm barely twenty-five percent. He seemed grateful that I went there to see him, and after our breezy chat, I set up an appointment for my partner to look at the place.

Yasue and I ambled down the hill to check out the spacious townhouse, and were astonished by the abundance of modern conveniences.

We didn't want to buy a condo so Misak offered us unit number five for thirteen hundred a month, precisely what we were paying Kedrin, and he didn't mind us having all those cats and a dog. This dwelling had three bedrooms, a huge bathroom upstairs, a guest powder room on the first floor, and also two bonus rooms. We admired the central heat and air-conditioning, in addition to a stylish marble fireplace bordering the bijou wet bar, which was the focal point of this forty-foot living room. There was an intercom to talk to other tenants or buzz visitors in, and the carpeting throughout was muted beige.

Yasue loved it and wanted to move right in, our friend Karen Weiss just happened to be Misak's broker for the building. We were sold on the place by the owner; nevertheless, Karen had issues. Eventually she did all the paperwork relating to our lease and still earned half her usual rental fee. I called Kedrin to tell her we were moving, and she sounded congenial for the first time. The bitch insisted that we stay there on a month-to-month basis. We'd be miserable again once the house went up for sale, herds of nosey lookers would impose on our privacy, and when it sold we'd have to relocate anyway.

Our proud move to The Sunset Villa took place on Thanksgiving Day of 1993. The house on Sanborn was always cold, the windows were drafty, the antiquated furnace barely kept the living room warm and sounded like a B29; we had to use portable heaters regularly. It felt splendid to be warm and toasty in our new apartment, the heater worked well and the gas fireplace was likewise a comfort. From then on I wouldn't have to carry heavy logs from outside or clean out the hearth very much. Our cats even had a private chamber downstairs for their litter business. Closets and storage areas were plentiful, and my Eclipse seemed secure in the lower garage. There was a built-in dishwasher; the only essential we needed to buy was a stack-type washer and dryer. Most of our furniture came from This End Up, although it was a contemporary apartment, our rustic accessories complimented the surroundings.

Misak was a constructional engineer with several degrees from the old country. He bought a rundown property on Sunset Drive which had four aging cottages. Rumor has it that he allowed those tiny houses to deteriorate until the appalling conditions finally forced the old tenants out, and bulldozed the site to build condos. His first plan was to erect a seven-story apartment complex, but several neighbors, including Kedrin, went to City Hall to protest the obstruction of their view. The locals won, and the city officials said he could only develop a three-story manor. He drew up new blueprints for nine large units hoping to sell four places and rent out five. His brother was a wealthy doctor and a collaborator in this project; initially they had a third partner, a distant relative who stole an unspecified quantity construction funds.

Their traditional Christmas was on January 6th, so I went with him to an Armenian service the night before. He wanted me to look at that specific church because he built the whole thing; I remember the beautiful and exquisite details. After the ceremony, which was similar to a Catholic mass, he drove me to his home in Glendale, his wife and sister-in-law were busy preparing wonderful edibles in the kitchen. He presented his two sons then gave me a drink; it was the Armenian version of brandy and tasted like paint thinner. The man seemed miserable, but I tried to make him laugh and cheer him up.

Though I went by the name of Markarian, I didn't know anything about this nationality. Friends in the east seemed to think all Armenians had money, I found out that wasn't true. They were incredibly clannish about friendships and marriage, rarely accepting strangers, which is why so many stayed oblivious to American decorum. I learned not to ask how they felt; it would only start up a conversation about the Turkish genocide. These people were always depressed about something, and they only seemed to be happy when attending a party.

We lived at The Sunset Villa for seven years and experienced great frustration while struggling to understand a few people from crude, ill-mannered backgrounds.

*****

Shortly after we settled in, Karen Weiss called to tell me Angela had just passed away. She suffered a massive heart attack at her home in Mexico and died all alone. Karen thought it was a shame that she left all her money to The Metropolitan Opera and not to me. I was sorry about the way she departed; yet really glad she didn't leave me anything. I'd always feel like I had to shine her shoes. As an employee I could get away from her when my work was done, as her beneficiary I'd be haunted forever.

We had a wonderful Mexican gardener on Sanborn named Kennedy, who was given the Irish name by his grandfather; the old man once met JFK face to face and came to adore him. Yasue bossed his crew around to keep the yard perfect, while I gave them lunch with a beer when they worked. I decided not to shoot my BB gun after we moved so I gave it to Kennedy. From now on we'd have Ed Kuwahara, a Japanese gardener, every Monday I served him Henry Weinhard's beer with macadamia nuts.

It was awesome living there at first, we scarcely saw the college students from the front unit, and only a few looky-loos came through the property on weekends. I had a marvelous video camera to tape this chic apartment along with our superstar dog, Megan; I even filmed the cats romping with skunks.

Early on Monday morning, January 17th, 1994, a huge

earthquake struck in Northridge causing colossal loss. Our only visible damage appeared to be the big television set, which dropped on the floor in the master bedroom and landed on its remote control. The Sony was fine, but we had to replace the remote. I wasn't drinking much then, however, when the quake hit, I craved a strong beverage.

Our crazy neighbor Sydney from across the street came over in a panic. She wanted to know if I had any brandy, but I didn't. It was still dark and we all felt very anxious. When daylight finally arrived I couldn't drive out of the locked garage because the power was out, so I hoofed way down to Bogie's liquor store.

As I made my way down Hyperion Avenue, there was a lot of damage along the footpath. Sidewalks had buckled, many windows were broken, palm tree branches lay everywhere and I could still feel the earth shaking. This was really the scariest day of my life. My first stop was to check for damage at our shop. The door was off balance a bit, but everything on my altar was still standing; only a few insignificant plastic bottles had fallen over. When I got to Bogie's, Sam and Suzie were sweeping up the glass from the inside and outside, all the plate glass windows were broken or cracked and there were numerous busted booze bottles on the floor; the place reeked. I wasn't the only customer there, some people needed cigarettes, others bought batteries, but liquor was the main item. They sold things through the open windows because you couldn't walk in the store without boots; the deck was drenched in wine.

I bought a big bottle of brandy and some smokes for everyone, but before I headed home, I walked east to look at the Mayfair market. It was closed due to extensive damage, I even noticed that a whole wall had collapsed and you could see right through the building. There used to be an aerobic studio upstairs, but that place was now on the ground. A sick feeling stayed with me for quite a while afterward.

A guy I knew drove by and asked if I wanted a ride, I said definitely and jumped right in his car. He was in shock just like me, so I suggested that he come to our house and for a drink. The guy refused, he had to go somewhere to check on his mother. Earlier when I called my mom around five a.m., she said she hardly noticed the quake and didn't have any damage.

My trip to Bogie's seemed endless to Sydney, but she was

happy when I finally brought the liquor back. Mother Nature's wrath scared a lot of people. My friend Fred Chriss actually talked about it to a shrink every day. Yasue was pretty cool about the whole thing; she said tremors were common in Japan. I thought it was the end of the world, but she saw it as a time for adjustment. I began to drink a great deal of brandy to calm my nerves.

The next day I wanted to see if my favorite occult store, The House of Hermetic, was still standing so I drove around the hardest hit area in Hollywood and videotaped parts of the devastation. Almost every building on that boulevard was critically damaged and red taped. Upper verandas and balconies within large structures had been shaken to the ground. I looked right through homes without walls, and I'm sure the majority of people were asleep when the quake hit. My video exposed much ruin, and it was difficult to control emotions after that virtual tour. I wasn't afraid to die, I'd come close to death before; all the same, my greatest fear was not knowing if a catastrophe like this would happen again.

Hollywood is a well-known Armenian community, and many of these people would have to find other places to live now. Misak's church was at the hub of the disaster, yet hardly damaged at all. Though we didn't know any details, we knew that he offered his glamorous apartments to the newly forsaken homeless. Within one week four migrant families moved to our building, and not very quietly. We began to hear sounds in the middle of the night, so we'd look out the windows and observe strangers carrying suitcases through the courtyard. Some nervy tenants were bringing in their unregistered relatives.

A family called Ghaldazian moved into unit four next to us. Acrid smells from the food they cooked came into our apartment, as well as brawling conversations and strange music. At first the mother tried to seem cheerful, but the father always looked angry; their two teenage sons were into kickboxing. They hooked up with the other families and began to play soccer in the beautiful grassy area below us. All the men drank some kind of liquor and shouted throughout the games. It was more than we could bear when they started to play in the garage. They knew they weren't supposed to do this, yet they defied everyone. I brought my video camera down to prove what they were doing and exhibit the commotion. One tough guy saw me recording and kicked a soccer ball right into my stomach.

From then on we lived in a hostile environment. The males hovered around the front entrance smoking cigarettes and interacting to heated political discussions while the women cooked their food. I stopped going outside to the mailbox to avoid getting dirty looks, either they disliked the idea that we were gay, or they just hated us because we were different. Out of those four Armenian households, only two guys seemed to have regular jobs, the others just mulled around all day. We did our best to avoid conflicts until their noisy parties started. Unit number four received the most visitors, and everyone brought food, some even carted musical instruments. These gatherings always started after ten p.m., our walls began to vibrate. Women screamed bizarre chants, the men played drums, and everybody danced wildly. We called the police regularly, but they only restrained themselves until the following weekend.

After the earthquake I got hooked on brandy; the new neighbors were driving me crazy as my anger grew worse. Finally I couldn't stand to drink any more so I called AA to declare I needed help. They sent a woman named Catherine right over to talk to me. She stayed for a few hours and watched me finish the last of my booze, then came back in the morning and drove me to a straight AA meeting across town. I gladly raised my hand to say, "I am an alcoholic and I really want to quit." I sobbed and made a serious commitment in front of total strangers. That was on February 25th, 1994 and I didn't touch alcohol for nearly seven years, I stopped going to meetings after one year, but I still didn't drink. People started to get on my nerves, they were consuming me with their depressing lives, and I needed privacy.

I had a lot more energy once I became sober. There was an area which I dubbed 'No man's land' just above the eight-foot wall surrounding the property. The overgrown weedy patch of earth became my personal haven. I cleared away trees, dense vegetation growth, and left a lot of small lizards homeless. To get to this oasis, I had to climb a ladder. If I didn't want anyone to go there, I took the ladder away.

It took more than a year for Kedrin to sell the house on Sanborn, but she finally sold it to a young married couple. An actress named Ana Gasteyer and her computer-active husband,

Charlie McKittrick, got to be the new owners. They bought the place for $229,000, a big drop from the $450,000 she anticipated. The twosome didn't have much, but borrowed the down payment from their parents. Ana was appearing with a small theater group on Melrose when a producer from Saturday Night Live discovered her and signed her up for a job on the show straightaway. She headed to New York with a hefty contract and performed on that program for several years. Charlie traveled back and forth for a while, so decided to lease their house to Elisabeth Röhm, the actress, who later starred on the TV show *Law and Order*.

Liz was loud while speaking on her cell phone. Sometimes she'd pace around the deck holding a drink shouting at people, while always schmoozing her well-paid agent. We even heard Liz arguing on the telephone with her mother about why she deserved a new Mercedes. She claimed it wasn't as costly as a fancy Ford, and well worth the image. I found it curious that Kedrin, Ana and Liz were all Taurus women.

One rainy day Liz found a tiny black female kitten on the street, brought it home and named her 'West'. The plucky feline came to our yard to visit us often. Once she felt a little more secure, she learned how to use our living room window and came into the house, she liked our cats' food which was always on the counter. Rescued at only six weeks old, she probably missed her mother, the double-pawed small kitten liked to suck on Yasue's fingers. Liz went away sometimes and would let her stay at our place; West enjoyed dominating the other pets. We became quite attached to her in two years, but Liz got an esteemed job on Law and Order and moved to New York. We would really miss that sable-colored, darling of a maniac. Though we thought of her as our own, she was always loyal to her first master. Before leaving, Liz adopted a young male feline named Gould as a mate for her.

West was my constant companion when I worked on the hill, she hunted for everything and enjoyed our fun time. After clearing the land, I planted wild flowers, made footpaths with tiles and arranged a small grassy area using blocks of sod. I couldn't drag a lawn mower up there, so when the grass began to grow I kept it trim by cutting it with scissors on my hands and knees. There was a hole in the cyclone fence which West used as a pet door. I broadened it and placed a piece of linoleum around the opening so she wouldn't get scratched coming or going. Every day I left sunflower seeds along the wall for squirrels, and other creatures like skunks, possums and raccoons also used the custom-made access.

We saw the beautiful terrain from every window and watched the birds and squirrels tease our cats. I began painting with oils, my first canvass was of the picturesque hill, and I called it 'Wilson's Park'. Our gardener, Ed, said he could pitch a tent and live up there in peace. That's when he was having problems with the old man he took care of. Sometime later Ed brought about a godsend to us.

When I completed the hillside above, I planted another section with some sod and made an attractive lawn outside our windows. One morning I looked out and noticed the sod was all over the place, this mystery continued until I stayed up late one night and saw a raccoon digging for worms, the rascal was the size of a cocker spaniel. I went to an animal regulation office the next day and rented a trapping cage. They said to use pet food for bait. At daybreak we discovered a terrified neighborhood cat in the back of the crate. The following night I caught a hefty skunk, when I went aloft to look at it, the beast let off strong fumes which made me sick and stank to high heaven. I climbed into the house naked, my clothes had to go, I took a shower at once, but couldn't get that horrible stench out of my head. We called an animal control officer to take it away; before I returned the contraption at the end of the week, I captured two more possums. After all my efforts the cunning raccoon never came back again.

Wilson was a frequent guest who spent a great deal of time at our house during that time. Like all the others he came in through the window. Chris Cassidy was his owner, a nice guy who lived next door to our old place on Sanborn just a half block away. He was a busy man; Chris owned a contemporary tile business and had several girlfriends. Wilson's dad was spending less time with him, so he came to call on us more often. I believed the orange tabby was somewhat depressed; nearly every day he went to sleep in a cold terracotta flower pot outside our apartment, hibernating in the same position for hours. Eventually the sad kitty came to live with us; he slept in our bed, and was very affectionate.

One Saturday morning in late November we were getting ready for a busy day at the shop, so I opened the window to let Wilson out at the usual time. Yasue walked our dog Megan, up to the cul de sac regularly, but on that fateful day she scolded poor Wilson for playing in the street. When she strolled back down the hill, the crestfallen cat was lying bloody and lifeless in the gutter. It was a quiet dawn, yet no one heard a sound. Wilson had apparently been killed by a hit and run driver who never stopped.

Our good neighbor, Elton, was leaving for work and saw what happened, he couldn't identify the vehicle or driver, but noticed Yasue crying over Wilson's body, he insisted on driving her to the nearest vet. She came back with Megan first, seemed frantic, and couldn't stop weeping. I gathered the five-year-old was dead, but I wasn't quite dressed so I met them at the clinic. Yasue was hysterical; how would she explain the atrocity to Wilson's owner?

She called Chris from the doctor's office and said nervously: "I killed your cat." That's not what she really meant to say; her translation was cryptic. He appeared to have hard feelings until he learned what actually happened, and understood it wasn't her fault. Subsequently we were able to exchange photos and stories with Chris; we all shared Wilson's love.

Lady Bug was twenty-three years old when she departed for heaven on Sanborn, and Habib succumbed to cancer after we moved. Tama died of natural causes, Sebastian followed her, and Mello Boy passed away silently. We had John Baker's cat Bagoas for a while longer, then he united with his master. Habib was always my favorite, she was my first pet in L.A. Tiger was likewise very dear to me, but he kept sneaking back to his earlier stomping grounds on De Longpre Avenue.

He hid out down in the weeds for more than three months; we went there every day hoping to bring him home. Pioneer Chicken was placed regularly on the back porch of the old house, we knew he was still around and called him repeatedly, he just wouldn't come to us. We carried an electric can opener back and forth which plugged into the patio, all our cats were familiar with the sound, but even that didn't tempt the wild one. I felt heartbroken and missed him terribly; I told Yasue the only gift I wanted was to get my Tiger back. She went down there again on that chilly Christmas Eve with a cotton laundry bag, and magically lured him into the sack. When they appeared, I laughed and cried with joy at the same time, it was the best present I could ever have received; now he would be grounded permanently.

When he first lost his appetite, we took him to the Los Feliz animal clinic and had him checked by Doctor Liz Friedman. She found a massive growth in his intestines which turned out to be cancer. It wouldn't help to open him up, he was getting sicker by the minute so we set a date to put him to sleep, and I wanted to keep him with me for one more weekend. We tried to feed him special treats while Sashimi went for thirty dollars a pound, but it was hopeless. On a clear Monday in March of 1996, Doctor Friedman gave him the euthanasia shot as I held him close. He didn't feel any pain; he simply stared at me with those beautiful green eyes, I saw them change colors, then he was gone. I got in my car and released primal screams all the way home. Later we sent Liz flowers for being kind to him.

*****

A tiny building a few doors away from our shop always fascinated me; originally it was a child's playhouse moved here from an awesome mansion in Pasadena. When we started our business, the place was called Hats on Hyperion, and was owned by a sweet man named Alex, a great hat designer during the time when people enjoyed wearing them. He operated a big factory downtown which supplied his other stores. Hats on Third, was probably his best-known company. Alex drove a hot-looking Corvette, but his face showed a great deal of pain. He acquired the dreaded virus, and quickly drafted his last will and testament. He provided for all the loyal workers at his factory, who were mostly illegal aliens.

After he passed away, it became various thrift shops, the last person to have such a boutique was a crazy woman named Boops. Each time I walked past her store on the way to Bogie's; I grew more attached to the quaint little shanty. The lady wasn't at all pathetic; she was a dynamic Aries with an enthusiastic attitude, yet she usually attracted a large cast of unsavory characters. Boops was into drugs, but I liked her anyway. When the rent was due, her naughty behavior intensified. Friends saw her climbing in and out of trailer trucks on the street; she'd kiss the driver, and lower her blond head into his lap.

She paid the rent directly to Jerry Lippert, usually a month late. He didn't like her and couldn't wait to get her off the property. Boops would hire boys from the drug and alcohol recovery house right next to the bar and compensate them with wine or crack in exchange for work. It was clear that she'd really gotten out of control, so I began to think about leasing that spot to start a different type of business. My expense for this place would be two hundred a fifty dollars a month, which shouldn't be hard to come up with. The store itself was only about twelve by twenty feet, but had a basement downstairs with additional space, and an elevated cement area where Boops slept sometimes. Not having water was the only kicker, but if I needed to use a bathroom, I could simply walk a few steps to my shop.

Jerry liked me, he stayed in our downstairs apartment for a while when we lived on De Longpre, and controlled several properties for Gene Mileiu, the self-made millionaire. Gene owned a stretch on Hyperion which included the Toy Tiger Bar/Restaurant, and the little playhouse was just to its right.

I befriended a guy named Kenny, the manager of the bar, who gave me a tour of the entire establishment. The owners of the saloon lived and entertained in a large enigmatic apartment upstairs, and there was even a hot tub. Kenny told me stories about this fairytale gay bar; he said it was built with Mafia money, intended as a discreet watering hole for Hollywood movie stars to come out of their closets. Rock Hudson, the Toy Tiger's most famous gay patron, often arrived there in a chauffeured limo.

It was official when Jerry gave Boops a specific time to abandon the building, but she resisted like crazy. Boops really loved the little place and felt comfortable on our idyllic street. I asked Jerry if I could be his next tenant, and he thought it would be great to have me in there. Before she took all her rags away, I meandered by each day to bless that door handle with frankincense and activate good vibrations.

Every morning I sat at my altar surrounded by spirit friends and asked them what my new business should embody. I believe in angels, they are always close, and the candles I burn are instruments of ethereal contacts. Incenses blazing to heaven in brass braziers are sacrificial offerings, and rainbows indicate a peaceful gay society. **A**ngels, **R**ainbows and **C**andles brought about

'The Arc'.

We paid the first month's rent for the Arc on April 1st, 1996, but the place needed a great deal of repair. I hired a man named Richard who turned out to be a wimp; he could only work during certain hours. Inside and outside of the tiny building had to be painted, and it needed a new tile floor badly. Bob Jolly, an amazing handyman, took over the job and finished in time for our grand opening on May 1st.

Yasue was fine with the idea of owning a second business. K-9 Tubs was doing very well and employed two full-time workers; my credit cards were in good shape so there was no reason not to take a chance. For the store interior I chose soft paint colors in pinks, blues, and lavenders which enhanced the lovely background. One wall was for special gifts and novelties like crystal angels. We kept a large stock of attractive receptacles to go with the many beautiful candles. Another wall displayed a complete line of gay pride and rainbow items, which were in great demand at the time. My favorite section embraced an abundance of religious paraphernalia such as spiritual oils, candles, brass incense holders etc.

'Sanctuary' is what I named the downstairs space. We painted every inch, put in a couple of new steps, and built a complete altar on the counter to demonstrate how one could meditate within the universe. I placed a large mat on the concrete where Boops took her naps and used it to practice yoga. Astrology played a big role in my new business; people always needed to hear positive things about their lives. Black lights throughout my peaceful Sanctuary produced the illusion of a cozy hippy retreat.

During the day I'd run back and forth to K-9, then head downtown to popular outlets and shop for unique gifts to sell at night. I generally went to a wholesale warehouse in south central L.A. for occult articles, candles, incense and oils. When Yasue finished work at the shop, she'd go home, take a hot shower, grab a bite, and join me at the Arc to collect cash from customers. It was awkward for me to charge anyone sales tax, but my partner seemed to enjoy that detail. New clients came into our alluring store each day; my astrology service made the most profits and I didn't have to tax people.

I made simple brochures to define this curious business. The first column applied to Astrology Plus. *'Astrological Charts, Tarot*

Card Readings, Meditation Techniques, and Spiritual Tools.'

The center column discussed the Arc's array of Angels, Rainbows, and Candles. *'Contemporary gift items, Rainbow Flags, Stickers and Jewelry. Free Monogamy Certificates and Arrangements for Gay Marriages.'* In the third article I defined: *'Your Personal Altar Setup, How to Join our Round Table and Consultations on Getting to Know Yourself.'* This tiny little place attracted numerous people, and I made acquaintances with a lot of fine folks, some of whom I am still close with. During busy nights the store was wall-to-wall characters, four customers made the compact room seem crowded.

One Friday as the sun was setting, a middle-aged African-American guy came into the store and I thought he seemed angry. I smiled, said good evening and asked if he was looking for something in particular. He demanded to know why I sold rainbow flags, so I explained they represented the gay community, that's when he bristled. "Jessie Jackson created 'The Rainbow Push Coalition', so therefore it belongs to the RPC group."

"Begging your pardon, sir, but the first rainbow flag was introduced at a gay pride parade in San Francisco in 1978. Mr. Jackson's celebrated movement for peace, civil rights, gender equality, and economic and social justice was not formed until 1984. You of all people should understand minority oppressions, so please try to remember that God created the rainbow for everybody to enjoy." This triggered a smile, and then he bought a heart-shaped rainbow sticker for fifty cents.

The Arc was in fact dedicated to my exquisite cat Tiger. When you walked through the door, you could see an awesome picture of him with a caption that read: 'All you need is Love.' Shortly after Tiger passed, our good friend Fred Chriss succumbed to pneumonia. Everyone at Videoactive was in denial when he couldn't come down to the store. They claimed he just kept getting sicker from the flu, but no one really believed that. In my opinion he was the smartest guy on our block, and I would miss him. Fred's loving memory communiqué embraced the words, 'Like a bridge over troubled waters.'

*****

Yasue and I took our first Hawaiian holiday together in 1989 when we lived on De Longpre. A sweet gay man named Robert Mount became our faithful house sitter. He was wonderful with the pets, and a very reliable person. Bob made future vacations easier; we could relax while he cared for our home. Pernell's travel agency was a block from the shop. They were good neighbors and worked out an affordable package plan for us. Seven nights at a hotel in Waikiki, roundtrip airfare, plus transportation to and from the airport only cost $399 per person. Our agent, Elsa, said no matter where we stayed in Waikiki, most resorts were within one block of the beach, and the bed sheets were always clean.

The plane ride took five and a half hours from L.A. and the moment we glided over Oahu. I could smell tropical flowers in the air. I thought I was having a heart attack when we stepped off the aircraft, the heat overwhelmed me; I was a heavy smoker and found it difficult to breathe. A pretty native girl gave us fresh orchid lei at the airport and let us know that our transport van waiting outside. Several people rode in the same mini bus, but were going to different hotels. Some checked in at the elegant Hilton. That picturesque oasis must have cost a bundle, but the background was breathtaking. Our beefy Hawaiian driver had a terrific sense of humor, as he made everyone laugh en route to Waikiki.

We were booked at the Hibiscus Hotel on Lewers Street. This congested location was bustling with bars, restaurants, and young redneck tourists looking for a party. After checking in we were given a room on the far side of the building. My first hang-up was about the awful view; all we could see was a large rooftop next door which housed several loud air-conditioning units. Another daunting problem was a mysterious beeping sound which engulfed our room. I called the desk and said we needed to change accommodation; the noise was driving us crazy. They apologized, and upgraded us to a deluxe suite with an ocean view for no extra charge. Our first vacation in paradise was off to an amusing start.

An employee took us up to our new room on the street side. If we stuck our heads out the window, we could see the ocean, which were a few blocks away. When the maid left, I could still hear the beeping so I began to unpack things and soon discovered my tiny clock. The alarm was probably turned on from being bounced around, regardless; the elusive noise got us better accommodation.

From then on I'd always travel with that little timepiece in case we checked into an unattractive hotel room again.

We didn't follow the usual tourist itineraries during our first vacation in Hawaii; we simply traveled around Oahu using 'THE BUS'. The entire island was only forty miles across so I'd study the map at night and pick places of interest to visit the next day. Yasue was no stranger to the area; she'd lived there for quite a while before moving to L.A. It was completely new to me, the constant smell of flowers, happy local people who smiled all the time, and a feeling of timelessness. Like everything else I ever enjoyed, I got hooked on this enchanting island instantly, and began to plan our next holiday.

The following year we went back and I obsessed on the idea of living on Oahu. I advertised that our shop was for sale when we came home. The Lesbian News ad aroused a couple of gay women who seemed interested, so we disclosed our earnings and let them hang out at K-9 Tubs to get the idea. They were ecstatic about the business, but couldn't come up with $100,000. After wrangling a bit, they agreed to pay us $85,000 in cash. One of the ladies was a Taurus named Diana, the difficult partner.

Diana looked very tired when she strolled in one busy Saturday. I could see she was losing patience with a rowdy dog, I knew then that she was not the right person for this place. I told her to take a break, and informed her one must maintain the same level of patience from eight a.m. until five p.m. As much as I wanted to pack it up for Hawaii, I could never trust her to handle pets with love the way we did.

I canceled the deal unequivocally. It seems those women were only interested in our place because of the profits, they didn't know what we were all about, or how much we loved the business. Some customers were scared off when they found out we might be selling K-9; people are fickle and afraid of change. A few steady clients even shopped for other groomers to work on their precious pets, but we hung in there and continued to be the best, most loving pet grooming shop in L.A. Our business did well and we were able to take regular vacations in paradise, but we couldn't afford to live in Hawaii.

My mother was happy that we stayed here, she was getting old fast and I knew it. I phoned her twice a day, and if I missed a call, she started to worry. All I could say was, "Hi, Ma, how are you?" She was hard to entertain and could never relax at our charming townhouse on Sunset Drive.

One Mother's Day we took her to the Hilton Hotel for lunch, and she complained incessantly. She said her meal was cold, the waitress was a bitch, and the bill was too high. An inexpensive local gay-friendly restaurant called the Crest was the only place she enjoyed. I questioned why she wore the same old clothes when she had a closet full of new duds that we bought her; she said she just wanted to be comfortable.

Yasue went to Hawaii without me for a family gathering in July of 1996. I couldn't go because I was worried about Mom's health, and my obligations at the Arc. When Yasue left, I took Mom to the Crest for breakfast, and she agreed to stay at our house for a while. The next day when she came downstairs she was coughing hard, but she still reached for a cigarette on the coffee table. After lighting up she began to choke and sweat a lot; the cough became relentless. It was the 4th of July, and my mother could have died before an ambulance arrived. So I carried her down to my car and rushed her right to the emergency room at Hollywood Presbyterian Hospital. They gave her oxygen at once, and told me she had barely survived a major heart attack, it was too soon to tell if she had any real brain damage.

It was the worst nightmare I could ever imagine; I really believed she was going to die that morning. As I paced the floor waiting for test results, my entire life flashed before me. Mom struggled through some tough situations trying to keep us all together, I will forever be grateful for her protection and love. At times I yelled at her for silly things, now I wished I could take it all back. She was a good woman and did the best she could with what she had, her kindness and devotion were constant.

I called Yasue in Hawaii to tell her what happened. She wanted to cut her vacation short, but I said that wasn't necessary. My mother was completely out of it in the intensive care unit; I just sat there staring at her, praying for hours at a time. For days they had her hooked up to all kinds of wires, and she could only breathe through a respirator. My mind was playing tricks on me, so I took some depressing photos when she was at her worst. I wanted to show my brother how close to death she came. We hadn't spoken in years, but I called Earl to inform him about her heart attack, he didn't seem too upset and never mentioned coming out here to see her, I came to realize then what a cold person he really is.

The physicians kept her at the hospital for more than a week, then Yasue and I took her to our house, and she resented being there. We didn't allow her to smoke so she quickly went back to her own place where she was content and could puff freely. Meals on Wheels delivered most of her food, a nurse came in to take care of her three times a week and I brought her some homemade entrees whenever I could. We got her a decent microwave oven which she was afraid to use at first, but later she couldn't live without it.

Within a year Mom had another serious heart attack, only now she needed a triple bypass. This operation would take a lot out of her, the doctor said she should go into a nursing home following the surgery, but she wouldn't hear of it. Her delicate condition scared me because there would be a huge void in my life without my mother's presence. From then on we would be much more attentive.

When my mother got sick I couldn't work regular hours at the Arc, but the business never made much of a profit anyway, and not charging taxes meant the lost revenue had to come from K-9 Tubs income. There was one conspicuous problem that bothered me about the little shop; a huge dumpster was parked three feet away from my storefront which the landlord refused to move. It reeked of rotten garbage from the restaurant and I begged Jerry to discuss this nauseating problem with Gene Milieu. The little tyrant said moving it would inconvenience the trash men, and therefore it couldn't be taken from that spot.

Each evening when I arrived at the Arc, I'd bless the place wall to wall with frankincense oil, then go outside to light charcoal in a brass burner for the strong smoky resin incense. As people walked by my charismatic store, they appreciated a cathedral like fragrance wafting above the raunchy dumpster. Some folks said these essences reminded them of church and felt comforted by the ancient aromas.

A gay guy named Cal Meeder lived around the corner on Griffith Park Boulevard, and turned out to be one of my best customers. He usually ordered long-lasting two-week white glass candles, as well as seven-day colored candles for special purposes. In the past we'd shopped at The House of Hermetic for occult supplies but had never met. When that store moved from Hollywood to Eagle Rock, they lost clients like Cal, who was delighted to discover the Arc on his way to the gym one night. We swapped amusing stories about Matthew, the negative man who spat on candles if he didn't like someone.

My astute patron was an energetic, hyperactive Virgo, who was born in the year of the Rooster. While astrology was our main interest, we also participated in mystical practices like burning Bayberry candles for luck. I regretted the day that Cal moved to San Francisco, yet we remain great friends. I send him an astrological calendar each year, and he visits us whenever he's in L.A. for a new Da Vinci tattoo.

I always woke before sunrise if I got to bed early, but the Arc had me staying up late to oblige patrons who chose to shop at night. A lovable character named Tom enjoyed slinking around the dark streets after frolicking at the bar next door and became a regular visitor once he found my store. Tom was a good-looking Irishman. He drove a delivery truck for the L.A. Times during the day and cruised for tricks all night. The first time we met I was impressed with his sweet face and courteous demeanor. When I looked down, I noticed he was wearing a pair of bright red patent leather stiletto high heels.

'High-Heel Tom' was a Pisces, and not very interested in my goods, he simply dropped by to chat. Except for two lovely gold hoop earrings, a hint of makeup, and those large snappy red shoes, the guy looked normal. Butch plaid shirts and neatly pressed Levi's were his standard outer clothes, but underneath he wore silk ladies underwear. Once in a while I listened patiently to his drunken drivel about his failures with an estranged ex-wife, and how he felt about his only son, who was in trouble with the law. I liked Tom in spite of his kooky attire, and we continued our friendship long after the Arc closed.

I was an honest astrologer, and my client list grew quickly, but I'm not sure if my career entailed listening to chilling confessions from troubled people. An attractive Aquarius gentleman paid me well to do his chart; we then set up a time to address every aspect of his destiny. He knew a great deal about himself, but expected that our consultation might help to change his sexual obsessions. This sort of perversion baffled me; I became speechless. The guy had no control over sudden urges and needed to pick up several men a day for relief. It was easy to contact AIDS then; therefore, I couldn't understand why total strangers would risk their lives for fleeting erotic pleasure. After calculating an accurate profile, I knew he lacked spirituality and couldn't be encouraged to meditate, or even learn how to burn candles for instant peace. I provided him with positive astrological insight, but I never wanted to see him again.

Most of the time the Arc was busy, but occasionally it got quiet. I made the store cozy for myself with a portable radio/tape player to hear the latest music. My clientele could also listen to the best of the Beatles or sassy Alanis Morissette tunes. Although I didn't drink alcohol at the time, Bogies' liquor store was handy for beverages or snacks. A small basic floor heater kept me warm on cold nights. I had a cooler for soft drinks, and a five-inch black and white television which enabled me to watch *Ellen* on Thursday evenings. While the celebrity lesbian delighted an entire society of gay ones, she may have helped to increase sales on the rainbow items I carried.

The Arc was a serendipitous place, a delightful experience; I had a lot of fun there. It made me grateful for the opportunity to mingle with many extraordinary strangers. A few of my artistic clients became long-lasting and cherished friends.

Moving that filthy dumpster away from the store became my obsession; it just wasn't fair. I mailed Gene Milieu, the landlord, a registered letter, but he never responded. Meanwhile Yasue booked a two-week vacation for us in Hawaii, we needed to relax and take our minds off the Arc and K-9. When we got back from our carefree holiday, I decided to close my utopian business for good. The only uncertainty was about what to do next, should I try to sell the place or simply hold a great big sale?

I became a mail order minister to perform gay marriages for extra money before I opened the Arc, but mainly our limited income came from astrological readings etc. No one in their right mind would want to buy a company that didn't show a profit, so I gave up the idea of selling it. Several locals were interested in the building, one man hoped to sell makeup there, and another thought it was the perfect block to merchandise health food. Everyone wanted to change the store into something else. My friends were upset, they said I should confront Gene face to face and make a last ditch appeal. Gerry told him I wanted to have a meeting, but Milieu wouldn't hear of it, perhaps my butch attitude scared him.

Sidra had opinions about the Arc's finale and wanted to know how large this movement might be. "Will it be a one, two, or a three-ring circus?" We planned to march, from the Arc up to the Victory Bridge and back again. A date to close the store was decided, so I sent press releases to every paper and TV news station to announce that we were having a peaceful demonstration on the night of June 20th, 1997, all because of a dumpster. The happening drew a huge crowd, but no one from the press showed.

It was indeed a 'Love in'; I was amazed at all the wonderful people who came to support us. We passed out incense and peppermints while the group sang *Give Peace a Chance*. Everything was for sale, the prices were cheap, and anything left over could be stored in the garage of our townhouse. We closed the celestial little place with great respect and dignity, though I felt very sad when I returned the keys.

*****

Ten years before the Arc was even a twinkle in my eye, a man named Michael Tucci came to K-9 with his dogs for the first time. He was married to a lovely woman named Kathie and lived in Silverlake. Michael wasn't shy about telling us that he was an actor, in fact he played a funny guy in the original movie *Grease*, with John Travolta. He was a regular on the TV show *Diagnosis Murder* with Dick Van Dyke, but after five seasons the producers canceled his character. Fortunately his well-paid manager offered him a leading role as Amos Hart, in the acclaimed stage production of *Chicago*.

When he first brought his dogs in, we had a lengthy chat which led us to drive around the hills overlooking Silverlake. Our talks were enjoyable. I spoke to his Aunt ZiZi once, as well as his father, Nick, in New York. We drove back to K-9, danced a few steps on Hyperion Avenue and amused some passersby. Tucci was an animated Aries; he wore glasses and was light on his feet. We were at ease discussing life or simply exchanging mundane information. I felt very comfortable around him, and he appreciated having me for a friend. Michael and I bonded at once, and he became part of our family.

I never asked for details, I just assumed the Tuccis couldn't have children. They adopted a beautiful young child named Kate, and shortly after that they adopted another baby girl and named her Kelly. This was a righteous Catholic family, and although I didn't go to church, we shared the same faith.

Kathie had an excellent job with NBC, and the children were well cared for by a devoted nanny. Michael went on the road with *Chicago* the musical, and we talked regularly, starting with his first gig in Toronto. The ensemble toured more than fifty cities, but we finally got to see this famous production in Costa Mesa, California. Yasue and I took our friends April and Victor to see it, and we were all riveted by the show. I couldn't believe the marvelous performance from Jasmine Guy, whom I always had a crush on. Tucci was outstanding as Amos Hart. When he sang *Mr. Cellophane*, it brought tears to my eyes. Afterward he took us to an Italian restaurant, attracted a crowd, and paid for our meal.

The year I turned sixty, Yasue suggested we go to Las Vegas and celebrate. Tucci was still there doing *Chicago*, so I got to see the entire show again and Jasmine Guy looked even more spectacular. Michael took me backstage to meet her, but she'd left early because she wasn't feeling well. Later on he told the star that I wanted to do her chart and gave her my phone number. It was a big surprise when she actually called; I was shocked, nervous, and began to stutter. After analyzing all the statistics, I promptly mailed her a large package of astrological data in exchange for an eight-by-ten glossy.

Tucci had a suite at the Luxor, which is where we booked a room. Yasue decided to gamble rather than see the show again; when he finished working we joined her in Olive's at the Bellagio. They seated us on the balcony overlooking that incredible water extravaganza. Michael and I danced to the rousing music, while the waiter kept serving us fabulous refreshments; this was an unforgettable birthday.

*****

Following my mother's first heart attack, we noticed that she seemed off key. Sometimes when I called, I'd let the phone ring for a long time, but she wouldn't pick it up. If she didn't answer right away I began to worry, then I'd drive right over to her place, use my key, and find her sound asleep. We didn't know she was using Valium prescribed by her regular physician, Dr. Kumar. She got really adamant when I asked if she was taking pills and promptly told me to mind my own business.

When she recuperated from the triple bypass, I had to give her an ultimatum. She could have her own room at our house, or check into a nursing home, but she would not be able to live alone. Mom just couldn't take care of herself. Dr. Kumar urged her to go into a convalescent home and finding the right place was up to me. L.A. had no shortage of drab institutions, so eventually I landed in Glendale at the Golden Haven, which had charming ambience. The staff seemed friendly and the dwelling was clean. While I filled out the papers, they arranged for an ambulance to take her there from the hospital. There were problems from the outset with her assigned roommate, an old Armenian woman who couldn't speak English. My mother was very outspoken, and I knew she wouldn't be staying long.

The next thing we had to do was get all the stuff out of her apartment before the rent came due. Yasue worked side by side with me since we had a deadline to meet. While rummaging through her dresser, we found several bottles of Valium, which could explain why she was always sleeping. We filled countless trash bags with junk, but left all the good dishes, pots, pans and kitchen stuff in the main hallway for the needy Latinos living there. I packed up her best outfits, and some necessary cosmetics, the only things I kept for myself were a few religious relics. Her neighbors were grateful to receive what we threw out, and they promised to pray for her. Even though we brought many of her finest belongings to the rest home, she grew angrier about not having her own apartment, and I felt terribly guilty.

My mother was negative about everything, she hated the beach, the sun was too bright, and movies gave her a headache, the music was too loud. She did enjoy watching baseball, but she could never root for the L.A. Dodgers as she despised the manager, Tommy

Lasorda. There were certain men she disliked instantly, one of whom was Ronald Reagan. She watched the news constantly, and each time someone she disapproved of came on, she turned into Archie Bunker. Much of her conversation was spent on criticizing ethnic persons. If she went to MacDonald's, she'd bitch about those bourgeois Korean ladies who ate there. She claimed they all overdressed and took advantage of our assistance programs.

I cast her into a foreign environment surrounded by Armenians, and therefore her cantankerous bigotry would be aimed at them now. She complained the food was terrible, they lost some of her things in the laundry, and her roommate moaned all night. To cheer her up I visited every day, and sometimes in the evening with Yasue. We brought her things she liked, especially ice cream. A nurse told us she was delightful around the staff, but belligerent to the other patients, and even combative. The director finally called to warn us that she must learn to behave or soon we would have to find another convalescent home.

Mom stayed depressed for four weeks, and asked, "Is this dreadful place where I'll be spending my final days on earth?"

Her concern made me feel ashamed of myself, but if she couldn't take proper care of herself, where else could she go? For some odd reason she didn't want to be at our house, and placing her in another rest home would only provoke the same problems. I sat at her bedside and said, "Ma, you have three choices. You can live with us, you can move in with my brother in Georgia, or we can simply call the firing squad."

It surprised us when she indicated that she wouldn't mind living with Earl and his family, so I called him right away. He affirmed that he'd love to have her, and that she wouldn't be a problem. We put her on a plane forthwith, and sent her there with our blessings.

We sent her to Georgia on October 2nd 1997. Before she got on the plane, we gave her a small amount of Valium for the long trip, and acquainted the stewardess with her health problems. She flew from LAX to Atlanta, where Earl picked her up. He lived in Carrollton, a small town forty miles from Atlanta. Their modest three-bedroom house was in a rustic area, and Pat's son C.J. lived with them.

I couldn't visit her before our busy Christmas season, but I flew there shortly after with many gifts. Mom seemed happy, which amazed me. Pat took good care of her like a nurse while working a full-time job at Wal-Mart, but eventually they hired a caretaker three days a week. Just as soon as Pat retained a good helper, my mother would fire the person. She said one aid was too rough while bathing her, and constantly criticized their southern accents. Earl finally put his foot down and said she had to be pleasant to the next attendant or else move into a rest home. My brother was strict, but she seemed hardy.

During my visit we shared quite a few laughs, and I think it was the first time I ever really bonded with my brother. He wanted me to move there, and he showed me some huge properties that were incredibly cheap. A broken-down abandoned place which used to be a gas station and car dealership was for sale on a small highway. There was a great house in front with two fireplaces, a three-car garage, two storefront rentals, and a separate showroom building for new vehicles. This country bastion sat on three and a half acres with a tiny lake in the middle; the price for the complete parcel was only $175,000.

I thought about the possibility of having such an empire, but then I noticed some good old boys riding down the road in a pick-up truck with a shotgun rack on the back window. The redneck population of that locale would never approve if I hoisted a rainbow flag, nor would I be able to bring any flamboyant gay friends around to help us decorate. We were emancipated in L.A. and I appreciated that liberty.

I only stayed three nights, but gave Mom plenty of loving attention. She went to bed right after dinner and the nightly news, but I'd tuck her in and tell her how very much I loved her. The tiny room was crowded with some of their things, the bed was small, and I didn't sleep well, as I braced her thin hand all night, while anguishing over how frail she'd become.

During one of our familiar evening dialogues she apologized for not being a good mother. "Ma, you did the best you could with what you had, you managed to keep our little family together when others doubted that you could. I will forever be grateful for your tenacity, and appreciate you for overlooking all the wrongs I've done."

My brother was a control freak, and insisted we eat every day at Ryan's, a huge family-styled cafeteria. He would deliberately park his car in the back of the parking lot, far away from the place, he said the more Mom walked and exercised, the healthier she would be. The frail old lady just clenched my hand while huffing and puffing to get there. She'd make awful faces at him behind his back, but she never really complained. After he directed us where to sit, he'd bolt to the hot steam tables and prepare her plate. The menu never changed, he always brought her back the same food; he knew everything she liked. While riding home, Mom whispered she was sick of looking at those monotonous pine trees. They often drove for miles on boring country roads looking for cheap restaurants. Pat didn't cook much.

She seemed to be in the right hands, but underneath the smiles I felt she really missed Yasue and me. My brother and his family were fine people, yet we lived in two different worlds, and always would. As kids, I denied we were related; he acted like a jerk then, and hadn't really changed much. Mom stayed home when they drove me to the airport, but she slipped me three one-hundred-dollar bills before I departed. En route, we criticized her inflexibility in a comical way. Our mother was a headstrong difficult woman with a heart of gold. I thanked them and expressed my appreciation for taking good care of her.

It was great to be home, yet I couldn't shake the agonizing feeling that my wonderful mother's life would soon be over. Since death is inevitable for everyone, I prayed she would go in peace, and made every effort to keep her spirits high until I could get back to Georgia again.

Carole,
A Lucky Little Rabbit

Part Five

*"I was fusing my peaceful soul within a brilliant golden sunset
When several delicate pink and purple clouds approached.
They gently nudged my dreamy visions far beyond the rooftops.
Everything is temporary, and nothing is perfect."*

Since I didn't have the Arc to spend my energy on, I decided to write a lighthearted newsletter, and called it 'The Good News'. It was intended to be given free to our clients at K-9, but soon I got a few local folks to post copies in their store windows. I felt great when I saw someone stop and take time to read my humble one-page publication. Just below the title, the second line underscored 'Silverlake Scuttlebutt, volume #', and season. I wrote breezy articles crammed with information. My column on astrology was very popular. It stimulated the believers with positivity and inspiration.

Sometimes I had to write an obituary piece. Our best wishes were sent to friends who passed, and when the Chairman retired, I drafted a special tribute to Frank Sinatra. *The Good News* discussed mentors like Milton S. Hershey, who brought the richness of chocolate from France, built an empire in Hershey Pennsylvania, and cared about his workers. Colonel Harland Sanders earned fame for his Kentucky Fried Chicken industry. Other figures on my forerunner list included John Johnson, the creator of *Ebony Magazine*. Sam Walton was acknowledged for starting Wal-Mart, the working person's store. In addition I offered advice to pet owners, and reviewed classic four-star movies.

My editorials were current and meaningful. I believed that we should show more patience with foreigners who took their time shopping in large stores. Some could barely read English, and might be delayed by examining labels on products. Everyday customers needed to be more considerate of newcomers. I explained that civility should be a basic requirement for all supermarket shoppers.

I paid for the paper, ink, and copies of *The Good News*; it was a form of enjoyment. The people who appreciated reading it compensated for my efforts. At the end of each story I used fanciful names for authors. For instance, movie reviews were penned by I. M. Passe. There was a piece, called *Downtown is Grand*, by Mary Da Mop. An eye-opening series on etiquette and punctuality began with Mrs. Nudge, and Madam Gozonga took credit for *Astrology Plus*. *Give Peace a Chance* was a column by X. Hippie, and *Good Advice* was offered by Penny Royal. *Life Is Like Poker* was composed by A. Savant, *Easy Recipes* came from Auntie Em, and Carly Mark commented on pet care. *Ben Franklin, an Illustrious Citizen*, was outlined by Rod Lightning. The Arc was once my church, but *The Good News* became my pulpit for two fulfilling years.

A few smart community-minded people who took an interest in the area began some fun activities. The theme was called 'Summer in Silverlake', and one of the first scheduled events was the doggie pageant. It was held on a Sunday so more neighbors could attend, naturally Yasue and I had to show off our beautiful little Shih Tzu, Megan. The grassy park was next to the reservoir, an ideal place. Hundreds of folks came out of their hillside homes with all kinds of dogs, hoping to win a prize for different contests. Even the Channel Eleven television news crew was there, and the master, or mistress, of ceremonies was Christina Gonzalez, a butch woman and popular news anchor.

Yasue and I were dressed in colorful island summer clothes, and Megan wore a Hawaiian hat. After all the contestants ran through hoops, barrels, and did their tricks, Christina announced the winners and handed out ribbons. Megan won first prize in a novel category; 'Dog and owner who most looked alike'. Later on the news Yasue was shown holding her, and they really did look alike.

The Silverlake Summer Committee also sponsored art shows,

poetry readings, and plays. Our local Doggie Pageant was different the following year; the founders turned it into a money atomic number 4 event, and didn't even broadcast news coverage. Free samples of food were passed out, vaccination shots were available, and Darla's Dog Wash booked an entire booth, yet I was too shy to hand out our business cards. We talked to several good customers at the competition, and they assured us that K-9 would always be the best. Other shops come and go, but ours will outlast many of them.

Megan wasn't very ambitious, if Yasue walked her too long, she'd just sit right down on the grass or in the middle of the street whenever she felt like it. I brought along my new video camera and shot some wonderful moments of her with other dogs. She was a sociable Libra, though a bit lazy. The final contest was for the pet that could eat the fastest, and when it came to food Megan was no slouch, she actually came in second place. Our client, a big Austie named Ranger, took first prize.

Throughout the years K-9 Tubs has probably hired hundreds of employees, and some stayed longer than others. A Polish woman named Grace used to push a shopping cart around to recycle bottles, so I asked if she wanted an indoor job and she jumped at the chance. We knew Grace for a while, and liked her, but later we found out that she had a heroin addiction, which meant we couldn't trust her.

At the time Rhiner was the manager of the shop and should have been aware of her problem, but instead he felt sorry for her. Grace was in her mid-thirties, not very bright, but very gentle to our dogs. She hung around with an older black man who always looked sick. One day she just took off with him without telling us. When she came back loaded I held Rhiner responsible and fired them both.

One more time I put the help-wanted sign in the window hoping to get someone willing to work, and lo and behold, a tall handsome gay man named Cary Bobier, who looked like Errol Flynn, walked in, introduced himself, and told us he was a professional groomer. He had a regular job on weekdays, but after a brief conversation we hired him to work for us on Saturdays. It seems Cary used to travel around the pet grooming circuit with his tools cutting dog's hair, and made a good living by entering grooming contests in places like Las Vegas. The prize money was often more than $1000 per clip, after watching him work; we determined he was well worth one hundred dollars a day.

Yasue and I trained at Bark N' Purr, but only learned the basics, Cary was able to show us easier ways to groom since he was so competent. He taught Yasue all about fancy scissor cuts, and instructed the boys who washed and brushed pets on how to do their jobs better. He'd say: "I want the comb to flow through every single hair, and you guys will keep brushing until I say its right." As a true Gemini, he was easy to get along with, and his dialogue was never a bore. Cary told us that he was a careless person when it came to affairs in the park, he admitted being much too wild at a time when many people were dying of AIDS. The artistic young man simply could not abstain.

Our prima donna hair cutter occupied a huge apartment in Hollywood, and eventually we gifted him with that bulky dining room set we inherited from Ines. He worked with us every Saturday for nearly two years, but then he began to show signs of getting sick. Everyone loved Cary; he was an amazing guy. When he told us he had come down with the deadly virus, we felt really sad and were powerless to help. By now he had reunited with a devoted former boyfriend who would be moving him to Santa Barbara for his final days. We went up there to visit Cary twice and shortly after he passed away.

While I'm on the subject of memorable former K-9 employees, I must tell you about Rachman Ross, a.k.a. Rocky. One summer day he walked into the shop looking for a down-to-earth job and told us he'd just graduated from John Marshall High School. He aspired to become a drummer in a band and didn't use drugs except for some occasional pot. Though he was straight, he was very sensitive. Rocky's dad was a Jewish doctor with his own practice in Seattle, and his Irish mother taught school. She was an artistic lesbian living with her longtime lover, which didn't seem to faze him.

Rocky had a beautiful smile, golden chestnut hair, and girls came by simply to admire his ponytail. He could have dated any number of desirable women, but he led a quiet life except for the drums. After working with us for a while, he found an apartment in Silverlake; constant quarrels with his mother were more than he could bear. He practically lived on TV dinners so we bought him a microwave. At eighteen, the guy had a great deal of common sense, loved the Beatles, and even practiced yoga.

When it came to working on dogs, Rocky was more than gentle, I never wanted to lose him, but his Libra sun always caused indecision and ambivalence. He assisted us for several months while trying to find a gig with a local rock band. It turned out that L.A. was a cruel, competitive place for a young musician to find that type of job so he promptly decided to move to Seattle where the cool music was happening. We loved him, and it broke our hearts to let him go, but we wished him the best.

Things didn't work out between Rocky and his dad, so he moved to a tiny island off the coast of Oregon with an uncle. He stayed there for a short while, grew bored, and returned to L.A. It was just a matter of time before he went on another soul-searching journey, but we always took him back.

At the end of April in1998, I took another trip to see Mom, and took the family some little gifts. The soft pair of Italian loafers from Cole Hahn made her feel great, but she would have fainted if she knew I paid three hundred dollars for them, she always bought cheap shoes. I also charmed her with a delicate sand dollar on a gold chain. She appreciated the way I cut her hair, so I took my time and gave her the best bob ever. When we went to eat at Ryan's, I advised Earl to park closer, I asked him to be more accommodating, Mom didn't understand his discipline, she simply needed love.

Mom never stayed awake past seven p.m. and there wasn't much to do in the boondocks other than eating and renting movies from Blockbusters. During the day we shared some funny stories, I made her laugh a lot. They all got a kick out of it when I told them about my first trip to Las Vegas with her, though Yasue. Mom had been there many times. They used to take the Greyhound bus; until I found out we could go for five dollars each by way of a turn-around trip. The deal was to get on the tour bus by five a.m. and pay the driver five bucks. We jumped on and off the coach at different hotels to keep their twenty-four-hour Vegas schedule, then we had to ride back home in the morning.

Before we took that turn-around trip, I filled my pockets with special religious articles. I really believed I could win if I carried all these things. Mom and Yasue stuck together and played slot machines, while I became absorbed in a poker game. At first my luck was awesome, I had a lot of money in front of me, but at the stroke of midnight a waitress asked me what I wanted to drink, so I ordered a scotch on the rocks. After one drink I began to lose, my mother alleged the alcohol did me in. At five a.m. we had to be back on the bus to L.A. Yasue and Mom won a little, I lost everything except three pennies, and whimpered all the way home, I never expected to lose.

Earl seemed to be doing well with the extra money from Mom, and asked me again if we'd consider moving there. He pointed out that you could buy five loaves of bread for one dollar, and knew where they sold cheap gas for $1.00 per gallon. His house was far from the beaten path, and you had to drive a long distance to access commercial stores. The first few miles were endless rows of pine trees, and old cemeteries off the highway, with a large array of tacky trailer parks everywhere.

Mom's nurse told Pat to get a special chair so Mom could sit down in the tub while showering. Old age often causes people to protest bathing, and this was a dreaded task for her. We located a medical supply company where I was able to get her a sturdy plastic seat. She didn't want to shop, walking through big stores exhausted her, so Pat and I took a ride to Wal-Mart while she napped.

It was the first time I'd ever been to that chain store, and I was amazed when several blue-haired chubby little old ladies greeted us at the front entry. They evangelized The Good Lord and even gave us their blessings. Pat mentioned that her feet hurt, and one of those fine women literally prayed over her, then directed her to the shoe department to find something more appropriate for standing. I ended up buying Mom some cozy pajamas, a warm robe, and a comfortable pair of slippers.

My mother was now eighty-one but seemed older than some folks her age. She didn't stop smoking until after her heart surgery at seventy-nine. The last time I was in Georgia she asked me for a cigarette, but I refused, this time she didn't mention a smoke even though I had an occasional puff out on the back porch. Her condition was very fragile, and I could see that Mom appeared debilitated. I believed the end was near, so I disclosed my love to her by evoking our happiest memories.

My plane reservation to go home was for May 5th, I needed to get back to a coherent life in L.A. Yasue couldn't close the shop to be with me to Georgia, she would have absolutely hated it anyway. For some reason she had a bad impression of the south, perhaps it originated from movies which maligned the place, or else she could never understand what southern people were saying.

When our wonderful landlord, Al Beal, was still alive, I maintained the Hyperion Center grounds for an extra seventy-five dollars a month. I kept it all neat and clean by sweeping and hosing down the parking lot, front sidewalks, and driveways, this was our business place, it had to look respectable.

On Saturday, May 30th, I left for the shop very early to tidy up the parking lot. When I finished, I went back to the house to get cleaned up and dressed for a busy day. Just as we were about to leave for work the phone rang at 7:30 a.m. It was my sister-in-law Pat calling to say my mother had passed away earlier that morning. She said Mom had her coffee and toast as usual, and curled up on the sofa for a short nap. After a few minutes Pat looked over at her and realized she was dead. Earl promptly called 911, and when the medical examiner came, he said she simply died of natural causes.

I screamed out loud several times, handed the phone to Yasue, and went into complete shock. Yasue had to go to work that day because we were busy, but I was glad to be home alone. All day long I just sat on the couch crying, and reflecting on our last visit together, which was meaningful.

Later, Earl wanted to know what to do about her meager bank account, I said I didn't want anything, and they should inherit whatever was left for taking care of her. I told Pat to keep the little gold sand dollar, but I asked her to please mail me those expensive loafers since they were my size.

It was my mother's wish to be cremated, so Earl and Pat had it done right away. They brought her ashes to The Neptune Society in Savannah, where the remains would be scattered off the Coast of Tybee Island in Georgia. My parents were never meant to be together. Mom was now drifting in the Atlantic Ocean, and my father disappeared within the Pacific from Malibu. They both died peacefully while sleeping. I would be grateful if Yasue and I could expire the same way. Earl sent us a colorful T-shirt from Tybee

Island, but I didn't appreciate it or even try to wear it, so I gave it away. Everywhere I went; I thought about Mom and never knew I could miss her so much.

*****

When my energy returned I went back to work on Wilson's Park, the area I called 'No man's land'. Liz's black cat, West, would be leaving soon, Wilson was dead, and for the first time in ages, I was a cat lover without a cat. In mid-February of 1999, I took a ride to the Humane Society in Glendale to get my very own kitten. The pound didn't seem to have many choices, except for a few really old felines, so I asked the keeper why that was. She said if I wanted a very young one to come back in late April or early May, there were always plenty of kittens after the winter mating season.

As I strolled through the small room full of empty cages, I passed an all black kitten like West. When I approached his cage, he seemed calm, and didn't move, but he stared at me in a seductive way. After I'd roamed around the Lair Du Chat a couple of times, I looked at him again; he was eating dry food so I asked the attendant why he was the youngest one there. She told me that he'd been rejected twice by two different ladies who were willing to adopt and love him, but they brought him back very soon because he was shy and hid all the time. One woman alleged that he stayed under her tub for a week, and she thought he might starve. The other one said he was too frightened and spooked.

With my limited patience, there was no way I could wait a month or two for a fresh selection of kittens. I drove to the shop and spoke with Yasue about the black one; she said to go back there if I was certain about adopting him. The woman who ran the place seemed to think I would make an excellent mom, so I filled out all the papers. They gave him shots, and I wrote a check to pay for vaccinations plus neutering. According to their records he was about five months old, therefore he was an apprehensive Scorpio. A staff guy put him in a fresh carrier, and once we were in the car my young cat looked up at the sky as though this flight was exactly what he wished for. We stopped at K-9 first; Yasue cut his nails, and checked for fleas before the little tyke came home for good.

I thought about christening him with Dad's name, Harry, but somehow the word 'Magic' popped up, and this became his new identity. He wasn't the most handsome cat I ever owned, for a male his head was small, he had an extra long tail, and his eyes were rather dull. I always tried to assure him that he was a handsome prince. The first day he came home with us I smoked a celebration joint at the coffee table, which really attracted him. Afterward we ordered take-out dinners from Louise's. I got the pappardelle and sausage, and Yasue had a seafood pasta dish. Apparently Magic got the munchies; without hesitation he hopped up on the table, dove into the food, and sampled everything.

Magic was very athletic, I used to throw soft cat toys down the stairs to the basement, and he'd run like the wind chasing them. We didn't let him out for the first month so he would recognize the scent of our home if he ever wandered off. When we did allow him to go in the yard, he seemed to be in heaven. In the beginning he enjoyed rolling around in the grass, until West became his playmate. He absolutely adored her, but she just kept pushing him around, and he didn't seem to mind.

Six months after I adopted Magic, we went to Hawaii for our regular two-week vacation. Robert, our dear and trusted friend house sat for us again. We told him that Magic was grounded until we got home. He had become a real killer outdoors because once I counted ten dead birds on the lawn. There was a huge orange cat from the neighborhood that used to beat him up all the time, so he was better off inside until we returned. Our dog, Megan, got along great with Magic, they slept together back to back, yet he always hid when strangers came. I told the woman at the pound I'd make a man out of this weird little cat, but it never happened, he was still shy, and even hid from Robert.

Previously, during the summer of 1995, we took our usual summer vacation in Hawaii. When we got home, I bought a small ten-gallon fish tank at K-Mart, which Yasue put in her bedroom to remind her of Oahu. She bought a fashionable sea life bedspread, and a few other accessories pertaining to the tropics or ocean. We discovered a place called The Fish Tale, the owners, Stan and Fran, who were husband and wife, taught us how to keep the water fresh and clean, they also advised us on which species would get along. Yasue was in her glory with this new pastime, and ultimately ended up with six tanks.

Beyond the living area we had an additional bonus room. I bought a professional poker table with matching chairs, poker chips, ashtrays, and bowls for snacks. Del knew quite a few people who enjoyed playing cards so we invited some of them over. When I thought of poker, I reflected on the good times that Walshie and I had in Massachusetts while we were snowbound, but no one ever took our casual games seriously. We were just having fun on winter nights. These strangers who came to play cards in our home turned into monsters if they lost. Their faces and dispositions got ugly so I promptly sold the poker furnishings and made more room for good-natured fish.

Meanwhile, our misery at the Sunset Villa intensified. Those four Armenian families became louder, bolder, and more aggressive in their behavior. Misak gave three couples a notice to pay their own water bills, there were too many guests, but they strongly objected and took him to court. We didn't pay for water because our lease said it was included. One day he knocked on the door and asked if I would do him a big favor. He begged me to go with him to testify against the unruly tenants, so I agreed to be his witness. Why not? Those brazen people daunted our lives and despised us.

I wasn't thrilled about helping him; after all, he never defended us when they drove us crazy with endless wild parties. Perhaps if I told the judge about the trouble they caused us, he might order them to move out of the building. I met Misak at the courthouse, three husbands and three wives sat on the other side of the room scowling at us, but I ignored them. When the motion against Mr. Tebelekian got started, the judge was extremely courteous to the plaintiffs, he commented on how well dressed they were. His honor even gave a speech about good citizenship in America.

Finally I heard the astonishing news that they were living there through a grant from Section Eight, meaning they only had to pay one third of the average rent, and water bills were included in the monthly payments. The case was closed, Misak was dead wrong, and I was furious. In all the time we lived there, he never once mentioned they rented those luxurious apartments for just four hundred dollars a month while we were paying thirteen hundred. After the big earthquake they were displaced, which is why our government helped them out to begin with. I couldn't have gotten my own mother into such a grand place, even if she could afford it. Three of those boisterous families moved out of the villa right away, and we were ecstatic each time a moving truck left the place.

The Galdazian's were the last Armenian's to leave, and they moved away soon after the others. They didn't qualify for Section Eight because the father had a job. Their two teenage sons went to school, and the mother worked. This clan wasn't related to the three families on welfare, yet they shared the same culture and enjoyed having loud parties. When those spiteful tenants moved out, there were broken stoves and refrigerators, filthy carpeting had to be replaced in all three units, and they even poured some kind of lard or grease into the toilet bowls. Misak had to deal with a huge mess.

Karen Weiss sold three of his townhouses. Walter Woo was the first owner. Then Helen Miller, a lovely black lady, bought a place with her mother, and the third was purchased by a young Korean family. Meanwhile, Maggie and Oscar Mansilla from Guatemala accepted a rental, while a pretty black woman named Gail Butler moved into a front apartment. When unit four became available, Misak called on me to ask if I would help him to find some acceptable gay tenants as opposed to renting to more of his own people. I liked that idea, so I made nice signs describing the Sunset Villa, so I posted the ads all around my store where there was plenty of gay foot traffic.

Several people came to our shop inquiring about those amazing three bedroom apartments, but only two guys made a good impression on us. Both of them were called Michael. One was a Sagittarius who worked in the medical field, and the other chap was an Aquarius studying to be a lawyer. They were longtime domestic partners and owned an energetic Dalmatian. Every day they rode their bicycles and appeared to be healthy. They'd just sold a house because the area was full of Latinos who were unfriendly to them, and they needed to find a place before escrow closed. I introduced them to Misak; they signed a lease, and would soon be living next door to us in the Galdazian's old unit.

During our many years of friendship, Michael and Kathy Tucci were more than generous to us. They graced us with L.A. Dodger VIP tickets, and even a pair of crystal candlesticks from Tiffany's.

If you turned things upside down in our house, many objects would say, 'With love from the Tuccis.' Kathie knew I liked the classics, and Mahler was being performed by the L.A. Philharmonic. Four tickets to this sold out Hollywood Bowl Concert was a most unforgettable gift from them.

I invited two gay friends to join us; one was a handsome guy named Tony Cannella, and the other was a nice man named John Dotson who had a crush on Tony. I agreed to provide a fine picnic meal if John would drive us there, my little Eclipse wasn't really built for four people. These costly tickets included VIP parking, and box seats in the fifth row. I loved the amphitheater. The setting made me feel elegant, and we actually rubbed elbows with some famous people. It was a rare night at the bowl; they put up big screen television monitors for this exclusive program, which wasn't usually done.

My knowledge of classical music was limited. I wasn't at all familiar with Ms. Helene Grimaud. The brilliant young lady opening the show was a world-famous classical pianist accomplished in Paris at twelve. She wasn't only talented, but breathtakingly beautiful, I fell in love with her the moment she walked on stage. Dressed plainly, she brought incredible glamour to the piano. I got chills when she began to play. Her body swayed to Schuman's music as though she fused inside the piece. Two obnoxious drunken older men were seated directly below us with their younger dates. Helene performed with amazing passion, while one of them shouted, "When is she going to come?"

I leaned over to hush the jerk, but he didn't pay any attention, he just carried on making obscene remarks about this gifted virtuoso. We tried to ignore him, but everyone around us was annoyed.

We looked outstanding for the occasion. I wore black pants, a purple silk jacket with a breezy Hawaiian shirt, and Yasue dressed, in a long colorful Jam's World dress. John wore basic black, while Tony went with a natural beige cotton look.

After the show we were herded back to the parking lot, and I noticed a door which seemed to be an entrance for the stars, so I wondered how one might get invited there. The next day I mentioned my curiosity to one of our good customers, Michele Zukovsky, who was a principal clarinet player with the L.A.

Philharmonic. She told me to call her when Helene performed in L.A., my name would be put on a guest list, and since they were friends, I could go backstage to meet her. The following year I met Ms. Grimaud face to face.

I soon began to check the Internet for information about this elegant piano maestro and was amazed to learn about her other accomplishments. Helene's home was located in Connecticut; she actually raised wolves, and was deeply involved with trying to save these nearly extinct animals. Her many acres of pristine property were created as a natural environment for them. She even held huge fundraisers to acquire money for the wolves by playing her incredible music to private wealthy groups. Although she wasn't tall, modeling chic fashions for charities was another thing she did skillfully.

Art and artists have always attracted me, so I decided to practice painting for a hobby. I bought everything needed to start with, small canvasses, good brushes, oils, and an easel. My studio would exist in the bonus room where all the peaceful fish lived. The first piece I did was on a 12"/15" canvass board, and I called it *Wilson's Park*. It was a picture of our back yard and hillside. There were trees, flowers, squirrels, a patio, and even my black cat, Magic. Everyone who saw my first masterpiece appreciated this very simple but happy landscape. A lavender orchid was my next composition.

Another regular customer at K-9, Gloria Martin, was an acclaimed artist in her own right. She'd received several awards for her designs on huge floats featured in the Rose Bowl Parade. Gloria taught a beginner's art class at Los Angeles City College so I signed up for Saturdays. During the first class she asked the students to pick up some glue from her desk, along with different pieces of colored tissue paper. We were instructed to create something original by pasting these scraps artistically to a poster board. When we finished, everyone set their art down on the hallway floor to be observed, then she would comment on our work. After glancing at mine she said it was too symmetric or perhaps too plain. I felt a little hurt when she claimed my flawless piece showed no imagination.

She had me pegged as a person who didn't like variations, and wasn't willing to take risks, she was probably right. I am a creature of habit who never liked moving furniture around, if something looked all right where it was, I wouldn't change it. I attended nine classes, but didn't learn very much so I continued doing simple compositions at a leisurely pace in the peaceful aquarium room.

*****

We went on vacation to Hawaii the year that Michael and Michael moved next door to us. Robert took good care of the fish; he walked our dog, Megan, but he almost never saw my spooky cat, Magic. He would only come out to eat when Robert went to bed. We spent two wonderful weeks on Oahu, then halfway home our plane developed engine trouble. First the jet took a dive straight down, and started to shake. Everyone panicked except me. I was only upset because we had to turn around and go all the way back to the airport. This was big news when we reached Honolulu, there were television news crews with cameras all around, I really didn't care to be filmed, I just wanted to smoke a joint and relax. After a long frustrating wait we boarded a different plane to fly home.

While the first plane was bouncing around, a woman and her daughter seated across from us were sobbing hysterically. They thought they were going to die and prayed as they held each other. Yasue was simply concerned about the new clothes she just bought, if she died, she couldn't wear them, and I resented the cowardly pilot who didn't get us to L.A. The two frightened women overheard me bitching about their intense personal drama, and knew I was irritated with their cynical behavior. When we arrived at LAX, they looked angry with me, ironically we all had to ride home on the same shuttle bus. The wisecracks I expressed on that terrifying flight were rude, yet I didn't feel guilty.

Quite a while before Mom got sick; Yasue treated her to a round-trip airline ticket to Las Vegas. Flying there only took fifty-five minutes compared to a six-hour bus ride. After being seated on the plane, Mom became desperate to have a smoke, but Yasue begged her to wait until the plane landed. She slipped into the restroom anyway, lit up a cigarette and got busted because the smoke detector went off. Yasue was mortified when the stewardess said she could have been arrested, but let her off with a gentle warning because of her age. My mother was the epitome of a dragon lady; she was brazen, stubborn, and never took orders from anyone, which might explain why she married four different husbands within one lifetime. In a funny way, once in a while I admired her courage.

*****

Wars often begin because of real estate. For instance, if one leader decides he wants broader more widespread properties, he usually ends up fighting with bordering neighbors. This theory manifested when I drew a line in the sand with Michael and Michael. I explained how much work I put into the yard outside our apartment and asked them to keep their dog off the lawn. At first they agreed, but eventually they allowed their annoying Dalmatian to destroy all the lush green grass with her urine.

When the boys moved in, they suggested we join them for a glass of wine sometime, but I wasn't drinking then, and it was better if we didn't socialize. An ugly feud began when we came home from Hawaii in the summer of 2000. I phoned them about their dog ruining our lawn, the student lawyer argued that they had every right to walk anywhere on the property. At the outset we agreed to respect each other's boundaries, but now they were saying we had no business making that cheerful area our personal domain, and the dog could do whatever she wanted to as long as Misak got his rent. Fortunately our privacy was acknowledged by the other tenants, who were never discourteous.

The morning after I complained about the grass, Yasue took her usual stroll around the garden and discovered the nozzle to the water hose was missing. Later when I fed the squirrels on the hill, I saw the spout in the next yard. Evidently one of the Michaels took it off and threw it there. Several of our lovely plants were uprooted and tossed everywhere. The little pricks must have skulked around in the middle of the night to do all this damage; yet we never heard a thing.

I knew they were home so I knocked on their door to talk about the existing destruction, but the cowards didn't answer. Then I wrote a polite letter regarding the situation outside and inserted a memo about playing their loud music at all hours, which also annoyed nearby residents. I left the note on their windshield, and the next day I found it torn in little pieces all over my garage floor.

Our peaceful home turned into a daunting place. One or both of them smoked marijuana every morning, first we could hear someone coughing, and their music got louder. If they were potheads, it was hard to imagine how they lived with such anger, or why they had become so antagonistic.

We called Misak several times to complain, I even took photos of the damage for proof, he said it was our own fault for bringing them into the building; therefore, it was up to us to dispute boundaries. When he finally came to check out the yard, it looked better that day, and he didn't see anything wrong because they rearranged things nicely before his visit. Misak really thought these young men were great and went along with all their whims. Our longtime landlord treated us like the outsiders.

After living there for seven years, it was time to think about moving; we couldn't secure our privacy or ever feel happy, so I read all the local classified newspaper ads looking for a rental. I admit the Sunset Villa was attractive, but the walls were made of paper, and sometimes our spacious apartment lacked a cozy, homey feeling. It was discouraging to ride around every day looking at outrageously priced shanties. The city was inundated with foreign people and short of decent housing. I drove further out into the suburbs of Glendale hoping to locate a small house. Once again I decided it would be best if I talked to everyone we knew about helping us to find a nice little home.

Ed, the Japanese gardener, showed up at the usual time on a Monday; I had a cold bottle of Henry Weinhard's beer ready for him and a fresh can of macadamia nuts. While we sat out on the patio chatting, I mentioned that we were trying to move because of aggravation from the new tenants, but now we'd like to rent a house. Ed said, without hesitation, "I have one for you." The old man who he'd taken care of for six years was failing and had been placed in a nursing home, so Ed had to relocate. A professor named Kenji was the ageing man's nephew and was in charge of the property. He told Ed the cottage would be for rent as soon as everything was moved out, but he didn't want to deal with fixing up the place. I got directions to the Los Feliz abode and dashed over to check it out immediately.

The charming house was one of ten on a quiet cul de sac street built in 1937 by an architect named Anderson. Each window was covered with tattered curtains or shades so I couldn't see the inside. I walked around the residence and realized it was a good-sized property. The old-fashioned home had a fireplace, large front and back yard, with a two-car garage and bars on the windows for security. I was really impressed with this older house.

It had a great deal of character. I drove back to the shop to tell Yasue with confidence that our new address would be 4411 Ambrose Terrace. We went to look at it together when she finished work, and she fell in love with the scenic landscape and the quiet little road on which it sat. The next step was to call Kenji Matsumoto, the current owner, and apply for the place. Yasue spoke with him in Japanese while I held my breath. They talked for a long time, he asked her what we could afford, and she told him we were paying fourteen hundred monthly for the townhouse. After some dickering, he agreed to let us have the house for fifteen hundred and gave us free rent for the month of November because there was a huge redecorating project ahead.

Kenji lived in Orange County; he was adopted in Japan by the old man Carlos, who was also a professor of languages. We never met him, everything was done by phone; rent payments and the informal two-year lease was mailed back and forth. The idea of an absentee landlord felt liberating.

Early one morning while Ed was still living there, he showed us the inside of the house we couldn't believe it. The living room was enormous; it had a good-sized dining room, two bedrooms, one and a half baths, a small kitchen, a breakfast nook, plus a laundry area. There was a double enclosure on the back wall for the milkman's goods, and mail came in through a quaint letterbox on the porch.

The first thing I did was change all the locks, then I carted over a folding table and chairs to use in the small room as a makeshift office. I brought a small refrigerator, a five-inch black and white TV for the news, and a portable radio to hear classical music. November brings about dramatic weather, and the year 2000 was no exception. Our new house had a huge furnace that sounded like a B29 when it started up, but it comforted me on those cold days. I went there each morning to make lists of things to do or buy. At sunrise I studied sample paint colors in the changing light of every room.

To say the place was a mess would be an understatement. We took down heavy wooden valances wrapped in yards of blinding crimson cloth, and most of the floors were covered with red shag carpeting. When the rugs were removed, the hardwood underneath seemed to be in very good shape. Each room had a distinct chandelier, but they were hung very low so I assumed Carlos was short. The one in the breakfast nook was imitation crystal, the dining room featured a monstrosity with Chinese dancing girls, but we soon replaced those fixtures. Yasue insisted that we get two new toilets installed, so the Home Depot became a necessity. Both bathrooms reeked of old men's urine and required a great deal of cleaning. Now we had to find an inexpensive painter so I called Rick.

He was my marijuana connection, and in between regular jobs he worked as a handyman. After studying countless colors, I decided on certain tones for each room. We didn't want to look at all white walls anymore. I laid out cans of paint with notes attached to explain exactly where each color belonged. The kitchen was to be done in various shades of country greens, and I wanted the unique arched ceiling to have an emerald look, like a diner. Rick could only work for us at night, he took up all the ugly red shag carpeting right away, then began to paint the kitchen overhead the next evening.

I arrived at the house in the morning to look at Rick's accomplishments and went into shock when I discovered the kitchen ceiling had fallen down. Evidently he painted over some old wallpaper and the wet paint loosened it up, causing the buffer to collapse. He wasn't aware of what happened until I called to chew him out. He didn't realize it was paper and soaked it so he wouldn't have to paint it twice. The distinctive green paint cost more than thirty dollars a gallon, and now it was all over the floor. Rick the stoner was fired, but we still had to get the interior done before moving in.

One of our good customers, Cathy Shultz, contracted remodeling work so I called to ask if she had any leads on a good housepainter. Fortunately she knew a guy named Jose who said he could do the whole place reasonably, but he and his crew worked on a narrow time frame. We agreed to pay fifteen hundred dollars for the job which didn't include the breakfast nook. I bought all the paint, supplied every brush and tool, yet they complained the job was going slowly because I gave them too many different colors to apply. They were supposed to have the place ready by Saturday, but when I checked, they had a lot more work to finish. Jose said the job was complete, but it wasn't, and he refused to finish the work on Sunday. We paid him for Cathy's sake, but I had to cleanup many unfinished details.

On Sunday, November 19th, we had a pizza and beer party, several friends and clients came to help us move. They carried a hundred cartons, most of which could be temporarily stored in the garage at the new house. Everyone took a few boxes, and before we knew it a ton of stuff was transferred. On Monday, November 26th, Phil's Moving Company came for the heaviest furniture etc. The only real problem they had to deal with was our huge refrigerator. It took them two hours to get it into the kitchen. From that day on, we have been living in peace at 4411 Ambrose Terrace.

Before we ever considered moving, I bought a brand-new Toyota Camry LE in January of 2000. Those popular SUVs bothered me because I couldn't see over or around them in my little Eclipse. Another reason to buy a new car was to have enough room to take friends out to places like the Hollywood Bowl. When I talked to Tucci about selling the Eclipse, he said his housekeeper was shopping for a small car. He sent a woman named Elie over to check it out and she loved it at first sight. After discussing the figure with her husband, they came right up with three thousand dollars, which was a good value for a flawless ten-year-old car with forty thousand miles on the odometer.

I felt awkward driving the Camry at first, this was the biggest automobile I'd ever owned, but I got used to it. The roomy car was a godsend while we were moving; we carted many things back and forth, including all our fish tanks. For six nights we emptied one tank at a time, then carried the fish carefully in buckets to the new house and placed them in clean tanks. We began putting things into the car around three a.m., but it was usually foggy; at times I couldn't even see across the road. Moving the fish was a difficult job, coordinating their environment was done with great care.

As soon as he finished throwing all the junk away, Ed moved into a boarding house off Virgil owned by an elderly Japanese woman. Evidently he and Kenji didn't part as friends; Ed said he was screwed out of many things that were promised to him. He came around to visit us once in a while, and I always had a cold Henry Weinhard's with a can of macadamia nuts. I asked him if he wanted to become our new gardener, but he claimed he was too busy. We concluded that he wasn't very ambitious, and although he didn't show it, Ed was more than sixty-five years old. Eventually he moved back to his estranged wealthy family on the big island of Hawaii and we lost touch.

Angela Shelton became the owner of the house we used to live in next door on Sanborn. She paid Ana Gasteyer and Charlie McKittrick $349,000. Karen Weiss brokered the deal and called to tell us all about our famous new neighbor. Angela co-wrote the acclaimed Academy Award nominated film *Tumbleweeds* with her ex husband Gavin O' Conner, who directed it. Their movie generated a big profit which was how she paid for the cottage, and soon married a guy named Ryan.

I noticed Angela walking around the yard with her German Pointer, Norma, but before I could muster up the nerve to introduce myself, or share a brief dialogue, I should at least see her film, so I promptly rented it on video. Yasue and I were impressed with the simplicity of this charming picture. It was indeed Angela's personal story which cleverly chronicled her adolescent years.

One Sunday afternoon she was moseying around the yard with her big dog, and I figured this might be a good time to approach her. I climbed up the ladder to No Man's Land with a chilled bottle of champagne in hand and started a conversation over the fence. Angela was tall, and her personality was pleasant, cheerful, and dynamic. Yasue came to join us and we all got acquainted, I said the champagne was a gift for doing such good work on *Tumbleweeds*; we'd really enjoyed it. She told us she was feeling a bit depressed that day, and said she wanted to drink it right away.

Angela was concerned about our contemptible neighbors Michael and Michael, and it amused us when she asked if we needed her to hire a hit man. This was the beginning of an interesting friendship. In a short time she came over for chitchats. We also met her lovely mother while she was visiting from North Carolina. When we moved to Ambrose Terrace, she stopped by more often.

We lived in the Sunset Villa for exactly seven years, and I stayed sober for six and a half of those tumultuous years. In mid-November, before we moved, the creeps next door exasperated us with more of their petty abuse. One Sunday they played loud music until my head throbbed; I had a terrible cold, but decided not to fight with them any more so I drove down to Bogie's to buy a choice bottle of brandy. I sipped from a crystal glass until I passed out, and that was the best night's sleep I'd had in a long time. My sobriety was breached, but I didn't care, I simply drank to calm down.

After we moved to Ambrose, I didn't want to drink again, there was too much to do. It felt good to be alive, and it was great to give our old-fashioned house a new image. This relocation was a very costly project; I'm ashamed to say I had to borrow five hundred dollars from my poor brother, who was usually broke. Yasue acquired two thousand more from her brother-in-law Allan. There were many expenses starting with the movers, painters, plumbers, phones, cable, etc. In addition to the essentials, we had to buy new window shades for each room, carpeting throughout, and two toilets. It took a while, but we soon began to enjoy the comfortable ambience. I believed we would pay rent until something serendipitous happened, then maybe this peaceful home could be ours forever.

I threw the capture on the master bedroom because my bed was a California king; Yasue had a regular size. The computer and printer fit in the room snugly, as did my mother's old TV, but I didn't know where to put the altar. There were other priorities so it took two months to finally set one up in my room. When I started making novenas again, I increased my standard practice from once to twice a month, which gave me a total of eighteen days abstaining from booze. My faith evolved during this period, each time we faced difficulties, I sat at my altar and prayed for a miracle.

We slept together for twenty years, but now we opted to have separate bedrooms. If one of us were restless, or coughed aloud, the other would wake up. After sleeping with five cats and a dog, we should enjoy having more space. Megan slept with Yasue, and Magic was my bed buddy.

The last room to be completed was the tiny breakfast nook, and since those bungling painters refused to come back, I did it myself with a few leftover colors. We arranged the living room furniture to accentuate the large fireplace, then cleaned and polished every charming French window.

Two of our workers from K-9 hauled over more than a hundred stepping-stones from the old place. Originally I lugged each of them from the Home Depot to build the patio that started a war, and I wasn't about to let Misak benefit from our creativity or expense. When I finished the details inside our new house, I began to work on the back yard. The junk outside my room had to be taken away in truckloads, it was like the city dump, and the cluttered garage was next on the list to reorganize.

Yasue brought over, two additional truckloads of plants, which our boys also helped to move. While she worked around the foliage, I built a path to the side garden and used the round stepping-stones which once graced Wilson's Park, one of our few fond memories from the previous seven years.

Our good friends April and Victor gifted us with an unusual housewarming present, a new lawnmower. It was the kind you had to push around, but first it needed to be assembled. Yasue insisted she could manage, but somehow the rubber piece for the handle broke apart. After I taped it we both tried to march it up the hilly lawn and realized what hard work this was. We had to get a gardener.

Angela came to visit often once we got settled. She was a talky Sagittarius and extremely open about her life. At this time she was divorcing her second husband, Ryan, which was the same reason for breaking up with hubby number one, irreconcilable differences. He was a cute guy, but much shorter than his tall bride. Ryan was a standup comic at different clubs in L.A., only his act never took off, in my opinion he had no real sense of humor or timing. For their honeymoon she took him to London, then they traveled around Africa, but it just couldn't work out between them. His Jewish mother contributed ten thousand dollars when Angela bought the house, and now she wanted it back. My new friend was twenty-nine years old and freaked out, she wasn't aware of the Saturn return.

I didn't have money to buy pot, there were other priorities, and so I used my stash of roaches to get over it. Most conversations with Angela were about astrology. She paid me one hundred dollars to interpret her astrological chart, which is when I introduced her to my ingenious 'System of Seven'. The young writer was really impressed with my detailed information and began to hook me up with close friends. They paid the same amount for a similar package; now I could buy some fresh marijuana. Her pals were all beautiful, sharp, smart, and really liked my work. We always had great times together, I fed them well, we drank plenty of wine, and smoked a lot of grass; these attractive ladies were treated like royalty. They appreciated the warmth of our home, as well as my spiritual guidance.

Chantal Moore, a true Gemini, was Angela's closest buddy, she was very attractive, but came with a lot of baggage. The second most important person in her life was actress/model Heidi Schranz, a magnetic Aries. It was no secret that she was dating Angela's ex, Gavin O' Conner. Heidi got pregnant at once, and Gavin gave her a divine antique sapphire ring as an engagement present.

Angela felt a bit jealous, she'd never scored a beautiful present like that from him, but the ring wouldn't change her friendship with Heidi. There wasn't much money when they worked on *Tumbleweeds*, and giving elaborate gifts wasn't typical of Gavin anyway, he was a prudent Capricorn.

They needed to get insured as a couple before the baby arrived so Heidi asked me to perform their wedding ceremony. As an ordained minister, I wrote a simple exchange of classic vows. We chose the ideal Saturday night, and Susan and Brian Wakil would be witnesses at this marriage. Our home became a romantic chapel for their happy event; the lovers drank from brass chalices as I joined them together in holy matrimony. I signed their license with red ink by mistake, and City Hall sent it back to be endorsed again, other than that small hitch their nuptials were legally binding.

During our first year on Ambrose Terrace we entertained company almost every night. Angela's friends became regular guests, as did John, Tony, and Michael Tucci. I was drinking too much then, and began to wake up shaking in the middle of the night. I'd get up quietly and pour myself a glass of Cabernet to cure my sickness. Yasue had a sixth sense about these things; one night she caught me red-handed and calmly asked if I was turning into an alcoholic, naturally I denied it.

At that moment I became conscience-stricken and decided to slow it down for a while. The problem was I never learned the fine art of drinking in moderation. I had no self-discipline or rules about when or where to pour, but it was time to change. For instance, I would not drink before five p.m., or after bedtime. From then on I would try not to drink alcoholically; I must sip slower, savor the taste, and never consume a whole bottle by myself. I made up my mind to become a controlled drunk.

I taught Astrology and my 'System of Seven to a few beginners, but Angela was always my best student, she really got it. Her pals were only in it to take advantage of their fortunate periods, or how to succeed in love or business.

One night I gathered a group to take part in a full moon ritual. My awareness of White Witchcraft demonstrated the marvels of drawing upon natural forces. Everyone was given a folder containing several proven petitions to evoke prosperity and other desires. Later on I was annoyed to learn those smart young women really didn't take much of it seriously.

Other than Yasue, everyone in my clique smoked grass, and we enjoyed many creative pipedreams. My fantasy was to buy this wonderful house or perhaps move to Hawaii if we won the lottery, Angela was constantly elevated to bigger goals. The girl was full of brilliant ideas; she planned to write a novel assaulting plastic surgery, and at the same time sell a movie to HBO about a white family in the south who came to inherit a black baby by a fluke. One night while Googling the net, Angela Shelton discovered that countless other women had the same name. First she made a long list of these women to canvass, and concluded they were all very different characters. She e-mailed some of her namesakes to arrange phone interviews, and mapped out where they lived.

One flighty pipedream turned into a reality when she decided to make a full-length documentary called *Searching for Angela Shelton*. She would lead an expert crew all across America in a forty-four-foot recreation vehicle. Gallo was hired as the cameraman, Giovanni, the sound engineer, and Sylvia became the production assistant, her good friend Chantal was a producer. Angela used money from her movie residuals, and accumulated additional capital whenever she pitched the premise to independent backers. What began as a low-budget journey turned into a very expensive venture At one time or another she'd worked with all these handpicked professionals, now she had to figure out if the same gentle people could get along while sharing close quarters in the RV, and would they remain friends under pressure through endless miles across America? Before they went on the road to call upon the first Angela Shelton, she paid me to do astrological charts for her entire team.

Gallo was a self-absorbed Sagittarius but said to be an excellent cameraman, Giovanni, the negative Capricorn, was a great sound engineer, and when Sylvia wasn't crying or depressed, she seemed like a cheerful Capricorn. Chantal, the stylish Gemini had a talent for turning men on then walking away. I gave the crew discrete consultations to explain their good qualities, which were outlined in the charts, and tried to raise their spirits by addressing only the positive traits. They were grateful for the insight and promised to call me via cell phones if they had any questions. I inflated them with plenty of courage, ego, and enough enthusiasm to perform an exceptional job on this unusual project.

Her first interview was in northern California, so they headed to Seattle for the second liaison. Angela Sheltons were quizzed about their lives in Chicago, New York City, Saint Augustine Florida, and other places. This documentary was far more complicated than the apparent similarity of names. The movie was literally intended to show how many of these strangers had been molested, Angela graciously coerced several subjects into admitting they had previously been assaulted or battered.

By her own father's hands, Angela was sexually abused through part of her childhood, which was real the basis of this film. The past weighed heavy, she cried when she spoke of her daddy's evils. Near the end of the journey, she satisfied her greatest obsession, confronting him with the truth.

I took photos of Angela's group departing from Sanborn in the huge RV and felt sad because they would be gone for months. She hired a house sitter named Nancy to take care of her dog, then asked me to do the woman's chart. The mellow fifty-eight-year-old was staying with her daughter across the street while going through a painful divorce. Nancy felt at ease confiding in me, and told me that she'd recently discovered her spouse of thirty-two years was gay. Even though they had a child, her husband had carried on as a closet case throughout their entire marriage. I asked why it took her so long to figure out, she said she just didn't want to acknowledge or admit it. Norma was being well taken care of, and the nice lady even managed to organize Angela's household bills. Channeling positivity to a cynical Capricorn wasn't one of my virtues. I read her chart and quickly said goodbye.

My phone began to ring off the wall. Giovanni called when he was upset with Gallo, and Angela phoned in daily reports on how the film was going. This trip was hard on everyone; once in a while they would stay at a motel for a good night's sleep. The toilet in the RV had to be cleaned out regularly and could only be serviced in certain areas. They battled stormy weather on the road, the RV broke down a few times, and they had picayune fights amongst each other. In spite of all the challenges, Angela continued the expedition in harmony with courageous confidence. The interviews were going well.

The crew arrived in Asheville, North Carolina just in time for Father's Day. Beforehand, Angela made arrangements to meet with her dad at his home. They parked the RV at a distance, and Gallo zoomed in with the camera. Though she felt anxious, Angela marched up to the house and rang the bell. He opened the door, gave her a hug, and invited her inside; she refused so they talked on the porch. Giovanni couldn't pick up much sound, but she had a tiny tape recorder hidden in her pocket.

Gallo discretely shot close ups when he came to the door beaming at the sight of her. To look at this predator, you'd think he was a respectable preacher, yet the well-dressed old creep was responsible for tarnishing Angela's life, as well as her siblings. Her sister Lisa had been abused repeatedly, but avoided talking about it, and after being molested by their dad, their kid brother eventually turned gay.

The father and daughter hadn't seen each other for many years. She didn't want to go into the house out of camera range so they sat on the front steps, after exchanging salutations; she got right to the point. Angela demanded to know how he could have done all those depraved things to his own children. With an innocent poker face, he swore he had no idea what she was talking about and claimed the fantasies she'd just described were merely figments of her adolescent imagination. He emphatically denied acting inappropriately with her or the other kids, which wasn't what she hoped to hear, a simple apology or an admission of guilt might have eased some of her hidden anguish. At that moment she ran back to the RV hysterical and lapsed into an exhaustive emotional breakdown.

The crew came home with countless tapes from this amazing expedition. Now the big job ahead was to edit and format the footage into a poignant and marketable documentary. She hired an Italian film editor, and my friend Andre Miripolski would illustrate the credits. Finishing the composition seemed endless and became more expensive each day. Her ability to entice backers for investing fresh capital in this risky venture was amazing. Angela lit up every occasion with southern charm and openness, she was irresistible, intelligent, cheerful, optimistic, beautiful, and didn't have a mean bone in her body. Before she married Gavin, she worked as an actress and fashion model in Paris. I believe she was a star at twelve years old when she boldly played the role of Romeo in school.

She threw a who's who fundraising party, and sold *Searching for Angela Shelton* T-shirts. Yasue and I applauded her project, but didn't have money to contribute; nevertheless, she gave us a free copy of the first video when it was available. We were impressed with the sound and photography; however, Ms. Shelton flaunted herself in almost every frame and became absorbed in an ego trip. Her in-your-face star presence overshadowed the basic story; therefore the earlier version needed changes. The finished product eventually turned into a compelling opus. Her friends Chantal and Heidi were also victims of abuse and identified with the degradation of certain characters in this film. Angela is now a harbinger for different sexually abused and battered women's groups.

*****

Tucci's manager got him a small role in the movie *Blow*, starring Johnny Depp and Penelope Cruz. A short time later he asked me to go with him to the world premiere at Groman's Chinese Theater. As a cast member they sent him fancy invitation etched on a glass mirror, comparable to the type used for cutting or dividing cocaine. When we reached Hollywood Boulevard, the traffic stood still because of all the media coverage. I really enjoyed the picture, and when it was over, a huge crowd gathered around the luminaries under the marquis. We were standing right next to Johnny Depp and Paul Ruebens, yet I couldn't say a word. I had the chance to shake hands with these movie stars, but I didn't because I couldn't breathe. The crowd knocked the wind out of me, and I felt overwhelmed.

*****

I heard a radio commercial about a research program for people my age with respiratory problems. If a person qualified, they could get free drugs and be paid for their input so I called right away. After not hearing anything for a while, I phoned again. This time they got back to me the same day. I was interviewed and agreed to a ninety-day study, after that I participated for three more years.

In Mid-August of 2001, I decided to write my autobiography. Angela thought it was a fine idea and encouraged it because she was familiar with some amusing anecdotes from my colorful past. She gifted me with a wonderful paperback called *Bird by Bird* by Anne Lamott. It was simple reading and taught me a little about using too many words or cluttering up sentences. I began to draft my story though I could barely type, and my grammar was, and still is terrible. Our young friend said she generally wrote about twenty-five pages a day while I struggled to finish one or two.

Yasue and I used to wash our shop towels at a Laundromat. The dirty ones were laundered, then brought back to K-9 warm and fluffy to dry the pets. Just before six a.m. on Tuesday morning September 11th, 2001, we went to the shop for the soiled linen. I was listening to the news on the car radio when I heard the announcer say that one of the Twin Towers in New York City had been struck by a plane. The report was startling, and I just couldn't believe it. While our things were in the washers, Yasue stayed to finish up the towels, and I drove back to clean up the breakfast dishes. By the time I got home to turn on the TV, both prominent skyscrapers had been attacked.

They flashed early footage of each jet as it flew into the buildings. Those extraordinary scenes played repeatedly, the whole world watched the buildings collapse, and saw human figures jumping from windows to their death. Enormous clouds of dust coming toward people were like backdrops from a science-fiction movie. Panic-stricken New Yorkers were in total disbelief, and I felt sickened in a way I never experienced before. I couldn't figure out why the terrorists hated us so much, or how they could argue it was done in the name of religion. For days everyone stayed glued to their TVs, the 9/11 catastrophe anaesthetized America, causing our mighty nation to shed many, many tears.

After 9/11 I began drinking again, and drinking hard. My birthday was on September 15th and the Saturn period I was going through would be coming to an end, but until then I was psychotic. Things often seem worse than they really are during that phase, and I couldn't have felt more depressed. Fifty-two days prior to everybody's birthday, the Saturn influence arouses a person's melancholy and self-pity; hidden anger then surfaces and manifests the dark side of a person's inner soul.

Details aren't clear because I was very drunk, but when Yasue got home from work on Thursday night I complained about everything that ever bothered me about her. She spent more time with the fish and in the garden than she did with me. I ranted about how badly she was running the shop, and said she could be replaced by another groomer so I really didn't need her. Somehow we started to fight physically, and she scratched my arms with her nails, which bloodied my nice summer shirt. Magic got freaked out and couldn't relax for quite a while. After Yasue phoned Angela, I called a cab to go to the bar. The taxi took too long so when Angela drove up, and I asked her for a ride.

I was a real mess when I got to the bar, yet Angela didn't leave, she patiently listened to me ramble about things that bothered me. Pedro, the bartender, was shocked when he overheard me mention I could end this agonizing depression by driving my car off a canyon road somewhere in Malibu. While I was busy commiserating with some local drunks, Yasue went to April and Victor's to stay at their house overnight.

I felt horrible the next day when I thought about really losing her, besides the love we'd shared for more than twenty years. If we separated for good, suicide seemed to be my only option, so I called John Dotson to ask if he would consider adopting my cat

Magic, he said no right away. Perhaps my nervous breakdown began earlier and simply came to a head on 9/11.

Saturday was my birthday, and I was supposed to start a novena on Sunday the 16th, which meant I had to snap out of it, fast. I drank more during that week than any other time. Booze wasn't the only reason I was sick. I really felt awful about putting poor Yasue through those disgusting scenes caused by my madness. My pal Del gave me some Valium to calm my nerves, and since I couldn't go to K-9 with liquor on my breath, I had another belt of vodka and called her at the shop. It wasn't easy, but I persuaded her to come over to the house after work and talk about our ridiculous issues.

She got a ride home from one of our workers and walked in carrying Megan. This was an awkward moment. We sat down to discuss what was really bothering us and began to cry, then we cried some more. Yasue promised to pay more attention to me, and I committed to stop drinking for a while. This was our fiercest fight ever, but I think we both really knew in our hearts that one could not survive or be happy without the other. Before sunrise I went to the altar and prayed that my insane reactions would never be repeated. Forgiveness is the key to any successful relationship.

People often brought up the painful subject of the Twin Tower disasters, which added to my constant anxiety. Happiness seemed to disappear, I couldn't write a pleasant word and thought America might never be safe again. K-9 was an escape when I needed to take my mind off the daunting news reports. No matter how busy I stayed, a black hole of feeling uneasy just wouldn't leave me. The sins of a few radicals led our nation to question the entire Muslim race. I asked God to help me let it go, but this atrocity would take time to ignore. Nowadays the world is a scary place so I play it safe and rarely travel more than a mile from home. Fortunately our pets were immune to the catastrophe and never knew about hatred, they simply provided us with unconditional love.

My breathing problem grew worse, if I just took the trash out I had to sit down and catch my breath; I thought I was going to die of a heart attack. At last I got to speak with someone from the research program, The Southern California Institute for Respiratory Diseases. Their offices were on Third Street in the Cedar Sinai doctors' building. Daniel, the egotistical coordinator, liked me and signed me up at once. He worked directly with the physicians, and

Patti Isaacson was his new assistant.

Two weeks before the interview I felt uneasy about my recent pot use and expected them to test for drugs so I stopped smoking it. A local head shop carried products to cleanse the system, but it takes a whole month to remove all the marijuana from one's bloodstream. I doubled the dosage of a de-tox elixir, drank tons of water, and ate lots of fruits and vegetables to purify my body quickly.

During our first meeting in October of 2001, Daniel made inquiries regarding my medical history, like whether I had allergies to drugs etc. His final question was absurd: "Are you pregnant?" We giggled because I was sixty-two and obviously gay. The fuss I made about smoking grass was pointless. They didn't take a blood or urine test and never acknowledged my old track marks.

The preliminary appointment was to determine if I qualified, and they eagerly accepted me; each time I went for a study they would pay me sixty-five dollars. On the first visit I was given an EKG to make sure my heart could survive a pulmonary breathing test, then a nurses' aid took an x-ray of my chest. Their computer analyzed my lung capacity, which was only functioning at about 25%. Patti instructed me to take two puffs from an inhaler and tested me thirty minutes later. I could breathe much better, in addition to that miracle they sent me home with plenty of free drugs.

Just one of those brand name inhalers cost forty-eight dollars, and they gave me three six packs of Ventolin and Combivent; I was indeed a lucky little rabbit to have this opportunity. Their diagnosis confirmed that I had COPD, Chronic Obstructive Pulmonary Disease, my condition wasn't asthma or emphysema as first suggested. I was expected to quit smoking cigarettes at some point, but the drugs helped me to smoke more. What if random tobacco firms were involved in a conspiracy?

Each time I went they gave me a sequence of questions to answer for a pharmaceutical company called Glaxo, Smith and Kline. I had to keep a diary to disclose any health problems, headaches and insomnia were the only complications, but I didn't blame the medications entirely. My first study contract was for three months, after that I signed up for three more years. The cost of those free inhalers came to several hundred dollars monthly, another divine gift to my preservation.

One of the breathing aids was a placebo, it was alleged to be Advair, but Daniel told me it wasn't. He was an active Leo who enjoyed gambling on sporting events, but he seemed a bit on the shady side. Patti, who was a Pisces, reported something unethical about him to the head doctor and eventually he was fired. Afterwards she inherited his job and gained a big pay raise, she was more generous to me with the corporation's drugs. She doesn't work there anymore, but we still keep in touch.

I've never been a pension planner because I didn't think I'd ever live this long. Neither of us had health insurance, to get Medicare one must be sixty-five, and I wasn't quite there, meanwhile Yasue and I hoped to stay healthy. Those inhalers were godsends, they eased my breathing, and each day I felt better. It always embarrassed me to be around people when I became breathless or wheezy.

*****

Yasue wasn't overly fond of classical music, but she knew how much it meant to me.

Helene Grimaud was to perform a solo concert at the Dorothy Chandler Pavilion, and when the tickets went on sale I chose front and center seats. I'd raved about Ms. Grimaud from the moment I first saw her, and I really wanted to hear her play again. Angela was free that Sunday afternoon and said she'd love to join me. She wanted her boyfriend, Jason, to come along, but I'd only bought two tickets. Magically she was able to get him a seat right next to us. It's nice to be chauffeured once in a while so I let Jason drive my shiny car downtown, then we enjoyed a lovely lunch on the Pavilion patio before the show.

After Helene's brilliant performance we were escorted backstage to join Michele Zukovsky. A large gathering of sophisticated people waited to approach Helene, but Michele pushed forward and we were introduced right away. I'd been carrying two orchids around since noon, one for Michele, and the other for Ms. Grimaud. When I finally came face to face with this spectacular woman, I handed her the beautiful flower, then we exchanged a few pleasant words. She was petite, and even shorter than I imagined. My knees buckled, I was awestruck and could barely speak; meeting her was thrilling. My companions were busy fondling each other and overlooked the enormity of her greatness.

Angela met Jason while living the good life in Paris as a model. He was an emotional, charismatic Cancer. They each enjoyed agonizing about being molested as children. This smart couple would get along for a while, but soon separate for absurd reasons, they had a longtime off-again on-again connection. Jason Lewis was a beautiful guy who was around her age and worked as a fashion model; he also did some acting and wrote movie scripts. The Adonis owned a house in Tujunga, but one day he just decided to sell everything and hit the road like Jack Kerouac. His departure was a real bombshell to Angela.

Yasue and I thought of Angela as a daughter, we embraced her every move while she was making the film, and when it was finished she had a lot of time on her hands. After Jason left she became very promiscuous, she made booty calls whenever or wherever; we only hoped she was having safe sex. One day she screamed loudly while walking up the front lawn. "I am a lesbian now, I have a great girlfriend, and I'm in love." Her voice bellowed throughout our tiny, quiet cul de sac. That affair lasted a month, when she hooked up with her former boyfriend, Tutor, from New York City.

The woman was exceptionally bright; she remembered important things I taught her about my System of Seven. For instance if I said we were approaching the Mercury hour, she knew exactly what I meant. At the outset I didn't understand why she needed to see a shrink, she seemed normal except for the erotic behavior. She came to our house one evening, and we shared a joint and drank some wine as usual. Before we finished the first glass, she got a faraway look in her eyes and astonished me when she asked why we were being so nice to her. Angela was direct; she wanted to know if we were expecting any money from her. My eyes welled up with tears, I told her money never entered our minds, and that she was surrounded by people who cared simply because she was special.

She said her mother always hustled her, and she assumed anyone who was decent wanted something from her. We adored Angela, she'd become part of our family, and I tried to explain that our motives were pure. Yasue didn't hear any of this conversation because she went to bed early and had no idea what was said until I told her in the morning. After Yasue called to admonish her, Angela came right over to apologize. I was more hurt than angry, but I finally admitted to myself that Angela Shelton really needed a shrink. We lost respect for her, and our friendship would never be the same.

*****

Nicole Conn was one of K-9 Tubs' first customers, and it was always a joy to see her. She had a pretty face, and clear eyes which seemed to look right through a person's soul. Ms. Parker, her lovable little dog, came to us regularly for grooming. We were surprised to find out that she wrote, produced, and directed the highly controversial lesbian film *Claire of the Moon*. After that she created another romantic woman's movie called *Cynara*, and we were given a free video. Nicole wrote several books and sent us an invitation to the L.A. book signing of her current novel. *She Walks in Beauty* was a charismatic story which appealed to gay women worldwide. Loyal fans converged on the West Hollywood bookstore hoping to meet the revered author and get an autographed first edition.

We spoke on the phone once in a while, and I mentioned I was drafting my autobiography, Nicole said she'd like to read it. When part one was complete, I left a copy with her secretary at her house. Her life was always hectic, but she gave up valuable time to review my work, six months later I received a wonderful letter. She thought I'd led a remarkable life, and she advised me to continue documenting my experiences no matter how long it took, but I needed to improve my grammar. Before her note came, I felt discouraged, ready to quit writing, but she restored my confidence, and I was grateful.

Nicole's domestic partner, Gwen Baba, was a sharp, smart, and pretty woman. Her father was an honorable statesman so she came from a good background. Having a mind of her own, Gwen worked as an activist for several gay rights organizations. We had profound conversations whenever she came to pick up Ms. Parker, or when we ran into each other at the market. She shocked us one day by boasting she was pregnant. The happy couple decided to share their beautiful lives with a child of their own. Through artificial insemination, Gwen was impregnated with Nicole's fertilized eggs.

Gwen gave birth to a beautiful healthy baby girl, and they named her Gabrielle. She was a bright Gemini, the light of their life. Ms. Parker had to be placed elsewhere when they noticed her acting aggressively around the new baby. They took her out of town to live with Nicole's family where she would be treated like a true princess. We were fond of the sweet little dog, and we were sad to lose her, but the new parents were being cautious with their newborn daughter which justified the sacrifice.

They were the greatest parents we ever saw. When Gabrielle turned two years old, Nicole insisted on providing her with a companion sibling. Gwen didn't have an easy time with her first pregnancy, after serious discussions they decided to find the perfect surrogate mother to give birth to their next child. Through ambitious research they chose a woman presumed to be in good health. For a steep price the young lady signed a legal document agreeing to carry their baby for nine months, when the infant was born she would hand it over to them at once. Nicole's fertile eggs were used again.

Mary, the surrogate, wasn't truthful about her health. She had a defect which caused the baby to arrive prematurely. Nicole bought a video camera to film the delivery whenever it took place, but never imagined their son's birth would happen so soon. Nicholas James Baba Conn was born at Cedar Sinai Hospital in March of 2002, a hundred days before the due date, and weighed less than one pound. Expert doctors said Nicolas had less than a one-percent chance of surviving; he was extremely under developed.

Nicole refused to take their word and believed she could will him to live through intense love. She actually camped in the ICU at Cedars for 158 days and stood over the incubator every day breathing prayers into him. The hospital gave her full access to film the development of her preemie son.

An ultrasound had confirmed the fetus was developing too slowly, and doctors warned the surrogate to abort, Gwen agreed but Nicole refused. They finally removed the baby by means of an emergency C-section. Nicole obsessed on keeping him alive; she really believed this entity needed to be here. Nicholas endured a respirator with tubes connected all over his tiny body to monitor vital signs. The infant was smaller than his mother's hand, with a heart the size of a peanut, and lived in an incubator for months. As Nicolas fought for his life, Nicole comforted him twenty-four/seven with selfless love and dedication, aware that her newborn son would confront endless life-threatening setbacks.

Constant physical breakdowns followed when he came home, my altruistic friends had to make many exhausting trips to the emergency room at all hours. Nicole's desire to save him caused Gwen to question if preserving his life was worth alienating their relationship. The couple's relaxation and fun were now obsolete. Nicholas consumed every waking moment, leaving them little quality time, eventually both weary parents adjusted to sacrificing worldly pleasures for their God-given family.

Nicole's brother Brian recorded the baby's progress from birth, but the staff didn't always appreciate her taking charge or ordering them around in the ICU. At the time Nicolas was the smallest baby ever born at Cedars. Nicole and her people shot countless videos, which turned into a huge award-winning documentary. After editing endless tapes, a private screening was then shown at the American Film Institute, and we were her guests. I've always admired Nicole's work, but I was even more impressed when we saw *Little Man*. Yasue and I wept through much of it, we only dried our eyes long enough to laugh when we saw Nicolas wearing his little eyeglasses and a hearing aid. This film was intensely touching, but his angelic smile made her tireless crusade seem worthwhile.

During the first part of the film I thought she was a little crazy to sacrifice so much for Nicolas, not to mention almost losing Gwen, her steadfast domestic partner of many years. In time I came to understand why Nicole really wanted this baby, I couldn't imagine my selfish ego ever yearning for a child even if someone guaranteed it would turn out perfect. Some women choose to be moms, but I never did. Nicole was the most committed parent I ever knew, and I admired her greatly.

I left a phone message at Nicole's, but she didn't return my call, instead she sent a lovely note with some brochures to advertise her overwhelming film *Little Man*, which would soon be playing at the Laemmle Music Hall in Beverly Hills. She said Nicolas had been hospitalized twice recently but was doing much better now. When the film festivals started up late last spring and summer, my friend earned every coveted award for her intimate personal adaptation. It was the foremost winner in all the documentary categories. Her movie won first place in Los Angeles, New York, San Diego, Chicago, Miami, Philadelphia, and other venues. With all my heart I respected Nicole's selfless devotion to a child when all the odds were against him, I'm glad she documented this extraordinary story, however, I don't think Yasue or I could watch it again, it was incredibly heart wrenching.

*****

We acquired some great friends through K-9 Tubs. It was the Mecca of our universe. That special neighborhood attracted artists, poets, writers, actors, and directors; after all, it was Hollywood Land. Our little shop appealed to the same types of down-to-earth people I dealt with while working at Angels' Landing in Provincetown, but my life was seasonal then. Many celebrated people came to trust us with their pets, we did an excellent job, and they appreciated us for treating their little darlings as though they were our own.

The walls at K-9 embraced photos which included numerous distinguished clients, and acquaintances that we have been proud to know and care for. This is a partial list: Tim Curry, John Glover, John C. Reilly, Bill Condon, Joan Rivers, Bud Cort, Judge Judy, Steve Kmetko, Greg Louganis, Amy Hill, Phillip Charles Mackenzie, Judge Joe Brown, Gillian Anderson, Jasmine Guy, Liz Rohm, Michael Tucci, Adam Bitterman, Angela Shelton, Chantele Moore, Heidi Scranz, Bob Jacobs, Kim Chase, Dale Thompson, Jennifer Lewis, Rodney Kagayama, Gedde Watanabe, Sab Shimono, Mark Espinoza, Richard Frank, Lawrence Jacob Hilton, Elizabeth Mouton, Loann Bishop, and Katherine Joosten. Presently Eva Longoria, Roma Maffia, Catherine Haun, and Lesley Jordan have agreed to mail us an 8/10 glossy. We have an old photo from the *Northern Exposure* show thanks to Diane and Andy, who are writing the final season of *The Sopranos*. They even sent us an autographed print of the original actors.

Yasue agreed when I decided to sell K-9 again in the spring of

2002. Why would we let go of a good business with such an amazing client list? We were getting old and began to worry about the lease for our home on Ambrose Terrace which expired on December 1st. Where would we go if we had to leave? This time I really wanted to sell the shop and make our final move to Hawaii.

It was 2002, the Year of the Horse, an active Gemini communication period, I began to advertise the shop for sale at $100,000, lock stock and barrel. We didn't have very good luck with the ladies who found our 1990 ad in the *Lesbian News* so this time I decided to try other options. I placed an ad with the *Korea Times*, also *Rafu Shimpo*, a Japanese paper, and *Frontiers*, a gay men's publication. The *Recycler* brought countless inquiries, but most were just window-shopping.

Ads in the *L.A. Times* yielded several out-of-town folks who didn't have a clue about our colorful area. One afternoon a dapper man drove up to K-9 in a huge black Lexus with New York license plates. He stated he was an Arab Jew from Iran who wanted to buy a business, he wouldn't need us to stay and teach his people the work, and money was no object. When I mentioned that we had a basement, he wanted to see it immediately. The guy asked twice how far we were from downtown, which made me curious. I didn't get good vibes, and my clientele wouldn't appreciate his superior attitude. He implied that he would come back again, but I told him no deal, I just changed my mind. After 9/11, I could only imagine burly men making bombs in our cellar to blow up City Hall.

Several Koreans came to check out the place, but their English was very poor, and they didn't know anything about pet grooming, they only considered our profits. A few even offered to go to school and learn, but we couldn't leave our clients with inexperienced people. One grumpy and cynical customer said he would never trust his dog with an Asian who might anticipate having it for dinner. We agonized over who could carry on with the fine work we did, and do it with unconditional love. Until we found the right person to run the business our way, we couldn't abandon K-9. The costly advertising seemed futile. As a last resort I opted to give the *Lesbian News* another whirl.

A gay woman named Pat telephoned the same day my ad appeared in the '*Lesbian News*. As it happened, she and her girlfriend, Evelyn, were regular customers of ours. They had a very old fragile dog that we always took good care of, and this devoted gay couple admired us. Pat had a good job with a doctor who specialized in treating AIDS patients, while her partner did some kind of social work.

Pat, the butch one, instinctively knew that the grooming shop for sale was ours and got very excited over the idea of owning a comfortable business for the first time in her life. She and Evelyn had been sober members of AA for several years and were quite proud of it. They'd recently purchased a nice house in East L.A. Evelyn, the feminine partner had two teenage children from an earlier marriage, but Pat was happy to act like the good dad and always referred to Evelyn as her wife.

When Pat called to ask if it was true that we were selling the shop, she'd already made up her mind to have it. In early June they said they would love to buy our business, even before we showed them the books or an inventory list. Their main concern was finding enough capital. We were asking the same price as before and required 50% for a minimum down payment. They both came in on a busy Saturday and promised to come up with the money ASAP. Astrologically this was the perfect time to sell.

From then on, Pat called with constant excuses. First their accountant wanted to go over our books, following that she asked for loans from several different banks. Time was quickly fleeting by so I brought her to see Marisa, the VP of our bank. It seems their home wasn't worth the amount they expected to borrow on it. While Pat was observing us on Saturdays, we told some of our customers that she might be the new owner; I believed she was the right person to take our place then.

In July while Pat was trying desperately to come up with the down payment, I hired a company called Fussy Painting to beautify the shop. I bought all the paint and chose light blue, lavender, and pink to brighten the place up, so I checked out local supermarkets to find out who maintained their shopping carts. They all used a firm named Peggs Inc. and got them to recondition our shabby cages.

After everything looked fresh and clean, I took our Gloria Martin art collection of pets from the living room wall and arranged the eight pieces front and center at K-9, where they belonged.

Back in June my initial plan was to take the fifty thousand, find a reasonable place in Hawaii, then move there by December. Yasue could continue working at K-9 for a while to help them out. She would draw a paycheck, and stay with her cousin Christine while I set up housekeeping on Oahu.

Evelyn's son came to work for us. He learned the basics about washing dogs carefully, cleaning ears, and the unpleasant task of expressing anal glands. Weeks flew by, but they didn't seem any closer to buy the shop. She came to us in late August, and promised to have the cash within three weeks. By then we were frustrated, her delays had already caused us too much anxiety.

Pat had her heart set on owning our place and was apologetic for each holdup, but by mid-September she'd missed her chance. I said we really wanted her and Evelyn to have the place, only now it was too late. The planets had regrouped, and my courage for change vanished. They were angry and disappointed, yet I actually did them a favor by changing my mind. During the next several months, business got very slow, and the ladies would have seen a sharp decline in profits. After we disclosed to clients we were selling K-9, some were appalled and had taken their pets elsewhere for a while.

I really felt awful about disappointing those wonderful people, but it just wasn't meant to be. Pat was driving a new BMW which belonged to the doctor, if she quit the job she would have to buy another car right away since they lived out in East L.A.

She claimed to earn one hundred thousand a year for that stressful job, which may have been an exaggeration, but she said she would be much happier working at K-9. How could they survive when the business slowed down after summer? They would have to pay Yasue a healthy salary, take care of two teenagers, make mortgage payments, and Pat would need transportation. What would happen if we really moved to Hawaii, and they couldn't make the final payments? Things worked out in our favor, K-9 looked great, and we were back.

Staying on Ambrose Terrace was our foremost worry. Yasue finally called Kenji Matsumoto to ask the absentee landlord if he would consider renewing our lease for two more years. The man we only saw once said yes right away because we were excellent tenants. We took good care of the place, paid the rent on time, never bothered him with incidental problems, and genuinely loved the house.

The idea of selling K-9 began with my insecurities about moving. At least we could stay for a couple of years without worrying about how to find a decent place close to the shop. It took time to get comfortable here, but after a while everything went into place, and there was a place for everything. Now when seasons change I know exactly where the sun will rise, and in November I look forward to dramatic sunsets from my tiny art room. Lastly, our neighbors have accepted us and indicated approval, however, I'm still not in a hurry to hoist the gay flag. I never referred to Yasue as my wife, we aren't married, but we are legal domestic partners. Our home on the tiny cul de sac is enjoyable, it reminds me of Pakachoag Street, in a way we even resemble my Aunt Emily and Uncle Leo.

*****

Painting with oil was my favorite pastime when we moved from the Sunset Villa. And once we got settled here, I started my hobby again. We were blessed with customers who were also close friends; one such couple was Susan and Brian Wakil, the same folks who witnessed Heidi and Gavin's marriage. They had seven dogs of various breeds and sizes, but these beautiful people cared a great deal about each of them. We bonded long ago at K-9 and continued a delightful friendship.

Susan, a Taurus, taught art at a private Catholic girls' school, while Brian, the innovative Aquarius, worked in real estate. He had an uncanny gift for eying a house, buying it cheap, and modernized the place. They own a wonderful home by Silverlake, where Susan has a separate art studio and where all the pets hang out. This couple is completely vegetarian; we were not, although we shared many meals. They'd come over here, or vice versa, and occasionally we went out for some authentic Indian food.

Susan mentioned she would be on vacation from teaching and offered to give me free art lessons. I was thrilled. My classes with Gloria Martin were futile, but maybe I could grasp more from my pal. She told me to get a sketchpad and some oils, which I already had. When she came over here on a Sunday morning, my art table appeared to be well equipped, and I was eager to be her student.

The first figure she painted was an egg, and I was to render one simultaneously, I didn't know a plain egg could be this complicated or have so much shadow and depth. It's hard for me to practice in front of an expert; consequently the first egg I painted came out terrible. My assignment during the week was to improve on it, and I must have sketched a hundred. When Susan returned to look at my homework, I completed one egg which almost looked perfect; next we'd try a Calla Lilly.

Susan was brilliant. Her art depicted beauty with detail. We were invited to her first major show at the 'O' Gallery in Pasadena. Yasue's cousin Christine drove us there in the rain. Her paintings were priced out of our league, but a few shrewd collectors bought up nearly every piece. The artist looked beautiful, yet she was modest and didn't really enjoy being at the center of attention.

Brian's mother was an English woman, his dad was Iranian, and Canada was their home. Susan hailed from Minnesota, her background was mostly Irish, and they were a stunning couple. The innovative Aquarian husband dressed in trendy clothing, whereas Susan's attire was conservative, yet cosmopolitan. I smoked plenty of weed with Brian, but she never objected. He used to get great pot from his brother in Quebec, and I always contributed my share of mediocre stuff. I stopped painting when I decided to write this book, but Susan encouraged me to start up again when I finish it.

As I mentioned before, we were blessed to serve the finest pets and clients in our neighborhood, and Bill Condon was a local patron. He had two dogs when he first started coming to K-9, in time they died of old age. One day he came to pick up his kids, and I asked him what he did for a living. In a very modest tone he said that he worked in film. Everyone from our area fared in the movie industry; for all we knew, this adorable clean-cut guy with an old BMW could have been a set decorator.

It turned out that Bill was a well-known writer/director, and producer of several films. He accepted an Academy Award for his well-written screenplay *Gods and Monsters*, and the man also received numerous honors for his amazing movie version of *Chicago*, my personal favorite. After that he went on to write and direct *Kinsey*, a film called *Dream Girls,* with Beyoncé Knowles.

When we first became acquainted with Bill, his significant

other was a good-looking guy named Ryan Murphy, who sometimes picked up the dogs. Ryan was the serious type, and wasn't easy to have a conversation with. On the other hand, Bill was a lot of fun, he loved zany chitchat, and it was a pleasure to laugh with him. When the relationship ended, they remained good friends.

Ryan conceived the short-lived television show *Popular*, which wasn't very absorbing. Now he's the executive creator of the TV series *Nip Tuck*, which he wrote, directed, and produced from the beginning. In spite of much success, Ryan is currently drafting fresh screenplays. We haven't seen him lately, but he sends Tim, a darling assistant, with his two small black dogs, Fancy and Moes.

Jack Morrissey a charming Irish American guy began to show up with Bill after his split from Ryan. They seemed very happy as mates, and complimented each other's potential. Jack took care of the pets, household chores, and accounts, while Bill carried on with his writing. I always enjoyed seeing them side-by-side at the shop. We generally shared plenty of chuckles and a great deal of fun.

Jack brought their dogs in one morning and asked for my e-mail address. He said we'd be getting an invitation to a private screening of Bill's new movie, *Chicago*, before it opened in theaters. His note stated the event would be held on a weekday, and Yasue couldn't make it. He knew my partner was busy, but sent two tickets anyway, he said I could bring anyone I wanted. Michael Tucci came to mind immediately. He performed in the road production of *Chicago* for nearly three years, and he felt a profound connection to the show. Tucci was delighted when I asked him to join me; after all, he'd taken me to an exclusive screening of the film *Blow* where I saw many celebrities.

Chicago was to be shown at a huge movie complex in Century City on December 19th 2002. Michael picked me up in his shiny black Lexus. I'm not used to driving at night. We parked, and took three escalators up to the cinema lobby. It was exciting, we were surrounded by famous actors, and one such name was John C. Reilly, another K-9 client. He played Amos Hart, which was Michael's role when he performed in the road show. I didn't recognize the renowned leading lady, Helen Hunt, maybe because she wasn't wearing any makeup. Tucci noticed her instantly. She was seated next to me dressed in plain jeans and a sweatshirt. It would be disrespectful to strike up a casual conversation with a star that big so we just glanced at her from the corner of our eyes.

When the show was over, Bill got an awesome standing ovation; the film was better than we anticipated. Wine and hors d'oeuvres were served in the lobby later, but we passed on the libations. Tucci chatted with Bill about the road adaptation he worked on, while I couldn't say enough about John C. Reilly, who brought tears to my eyes portraying Amos. Bob Fosse would have been proud of Rob Marshall's beautiful direction. Renée Zellweger, Queen Latifah, Richard Gere, and Catherine Zeta Jones were amazing. This delightful picture made the entire audience happy.

It began to rain hard as we got on the escalator, yet no one cared. I think my friend Tim Curry was a little tipsy when he shouted to me, "Hello, my tiny dancer." Folks were leaving the theater with genuine smiles and couldn't stop snapping their fingers or singing *All That Jazz*. Bill's production easily garnered six Academy Awards. Catherine Zeta Jones won for Best Supporting Actress, and *Chicago* got Oscars for Best Art Direction, Costumes, Sound, and Film Editing. We proudly watched Bill on television as he anxiously walked on stage to receive the coveted Best Picture Award.

Two years later I received another e-mail from Jack Morrissey. He invited us to a private screening of Bill's latest movie *Kinsey*. Yasue couldn't make it again. She had a busy schedule the following day. Tucci was the first one I asked, but he couldn't stay out late on a weeknight. He'd taken a position at an exclusive school in Burbank as a drama consultant. After chatting with a few available buddies, Chris Cristoff, a regular customer, said he'd be happy to join me and wouldn't mind driving.

Chris worked in the movie industry as a costume expert, my young friend chose the outfits on several big films, and I liked him a lot. He came to pick me up early, had time for a beer, and conversed with Yasue for a while. We left the house and ran into a huge traffic jam on Los Feliz, which made us late for the theater in Studio City. We had to park in the back of the lot and endure a long hike to the escalator on a very chilly evening. An Aries walks faster than anyone else, and Chris was no exception. I tried to keep up, but literally lost my breath, I wasn't used to walking distances.

By the time we got to the first level I was really exhausted, but I managed to buy a bottle of cold water from a Baskin Robbins store in that mall. I told Chris to ignore me and just go upstairs; I'd be fine.

It took all my strength to get on those escalators. Chris was upstairs already, but if my breathing got much worse, I'd have to ask a stranger to call 911. It was the first time I felt this afraid. My fingers were tingling, and I assumed it was a heart attack, God knows I didn't want to die in the valley.

Eventually I made it up to the lounge, and Jack shouted, "Glad you could make it. How are you?"

He laughed when I said I didn't feel well, and asserted I'd be sicker after watching Bill's film. His nervous rebuttal was a reaction from opening-night stress. Sweat poured from my every orifice once we sat down, yet I was freezing, I had to wrap my skimpy wool blazer around myself for warmth.

Chris was very cool about my breathing difficulty, but I think underneath it made him a bit nervous. In time I began to breathe normally, and didn't want to miss one frame of this riveting film, which we enjoyed immensely. It ended with comical film clips of different animals mating, which delighted the audience. After that Bill went on stage to receive an enormous standing ovation, and a great deal of cheering, as he began the Q&A.

Bill greeted me like a long time friend. Someone asked how he came to choose Liam Neeson. He answered with a big smile. "When my script was finished, I knew he would be perfect as the main character. Liam and I met to discuss the picture, shared some wine, and felt much enthusiasm for Kinsey's story."

It would be simple for me to get down to street level now; Chris discovered an elevator, which could have made life much easier earlier on. We were quiet throughout the ride home, but my mind seemed remarkably clear. I realized it was finally time to quit smoking, and it also occurred to me that I didn't have any kind of health insurance. If I had to go into a hospital, how could we pay for my visit or any kind of treatment? Chris walked me to my door, he hoped I felt better soon and said good night. He was a considerate friend, and I was grateful he didn't turn my humiliation into a drama.

That night was the worst breathing episode I'd ever

experienced, I puffed on a Ventolin inhaler several times, but it didn't help. I was still attending the research program at Cedar's, so on my next visit I told Patti about my terrifying experience at the theater. She reminded me I have a progressive disease called COPD and should really limit my activities. For instance, if I lost my breath while doing chores like taking out the big trashcans, I should sit down to rest in between. Patti knew how I felt about being powerless. She had asthma, and compensated me with extra inhalers. I decided to make a real effort to live longer. Besides my beautiful partner, many good friends wanted me around.

Recently I'd seen a brief section on the *Entertainment Tonight* show about Peter Falk, the actor. They claimed he attended sessions with a hypnotherapist and was cured of a long addiction after only two visits, but his therapist's name wasn't mentioned. I made up my mind then to pursue a respectable professional who could end my expensive filthy habit. After studying the yellow pages, I decided to check out an institute called Holmes Center for Hypnotherapy; Dr. Wanita Holmes was the director. Her daunting advertisement featured skull and crossbones holding a cigarette, but the serendipitous headline really tempted me: 'Walk in a smoker, walk out a non-smoker.'

I phoned about rates, and the secretary said it cost $699 for a complete hypnosis procedure, credit cards were accepted. She asked what type of service I required, and how I heard about them. "My smoking is out of control, I can barely breathe, and I hoped your method could help. It was the ghastly skull and crossbones ad which prompted me to call." The office was nearby so I booked an appointment.

Previously her secretary specified that I had to stay all day for my first appointment with Dr. Holmes, which was early on a Friday. There would be an initial briefing before the hypnosis since the doctor and I needed to get acquainted. Wanita was late, and I wanted to smoke. When she finally arrived, I saw a heavy regal-looking blond woman with a pretty face, dressed well, and quite friendly.

Her office was nicely decorated, cluttered, yet warm and cozy. She tried to make me feel at ease by telling me she'd been married four times but was single now. Two daughters worked as her assistants while they practiced holistic healing in the same complex. I told her I was gay, and blessed to share a wonderful life with my domestic partner, Yasue, whom I'd been with for many years.

While exchanging personal information, she shared more about herself than I cared to know. When I asked her birth sign, she replied, "I'm a Leo, the mighty lion." Then we focused on smoking habits, and my favorite brand of cigarettes. They'd instructed me to bring along my last pack, but I felt ambivalent and left them home. She'd amassed many partly used packs from people who quit. NOW cigarettes were my preference, which she never heard of, but every other type was on a table, including a couple of joints. I never intended to give up pot so I let her assume I didn't smoke it.

Wanita also showed me graphic images of damaged lungs and grotesque pictures of people on respirators caused by smoking. It alarmed me when she explained how many chemicals were added to one cigarette. She took a partly filled glass of water, and dropped a few broken butts in. After stirring the water, it resembled strong brownish tea, when she asked if I wanted to drink some. Believe it or not, I was tempted to put that stinking glass to my lips; I was so craving a cigarette. The contents of that tumbler actually turned into poison, nicotine is fatal under certain conditions.

Before I got on the couch to be hypnotized, the chatty doctor gave me directions to follow when I got home. I had to drink plenty of water to get rid of the toxins, eat three oranges or pink grapefruits per day for vitamin C, and take Tums for extra calcium. Three tablets of vitamin B 100 complex had to be taken for the next ten days, which helped nervousness. Besides the non-smoking addendum, she gave me various papers to read and study. There was even a timetable for physical problems to improve during intervals. A frightening photo from the American Cancer Society depicted a woman holding a cigarette with a totally blackened face. The caption read: 'If what happened to the inside of your body, happened on your outside, would you still smoke?' Her tactics were arousing.

She was a strong likeable character. She directed me to position myself comfortably on a soft leather sofa, except it was never easy for me to relax. Our session was being recorded while ethereal music played in the background. In a gentle breathy voice she told me to inhale deeply, hold it, exhale, and relax. This was the same procedure I experienced with John O'Brien at the hospital when I was there trying to give up heroin, even then I couldn't go into a complete trance.

This woman enunciated perfectly and explained it is easier to learn something when you are fully relaxed, you can abandon bad ideas or habits if you allow your conscious mind to just let go. I was like a pebble which moved slowly from the surface to the bottom after being dropped into a well. "You are going down, down, and further down, drifting effortlessly beneath the water." Wanita said something about spokes in a wheel turning, and I relaxed more. "You are quite calm and comfortable as you let go. Counting backwards from ten to one, you are willing to let go and feel at peace with yourself. You are determined to do whatever it takes; you are confident and eager to quit smoking."

The hypnosis took about forty-five minutes, I certainly felt relaxed, but I'm not sure if I went into a trance. John O'Brien's treatment failed because I was aware of things and wouldn't give up control. While I was supposed to be under her spell, I couldn't let go completely, it just didn't happen. She gave me a cassette from our session to be played every night, and I had to get rid of my cigarettes in front of Yasue. I broke up the last pack, and dropped the butts in a glass of water to show her the visible toxin in nicotine. I poured the stirred contents over an anthill and watched them scramble for their lives. We had another meeting in one week for my final session, which would also be recorded. She instructed me to call in every night and say "I'm still a non-smoker."

I spoke to the answering machine for about two weeks, but I only lasted as an honest non-smoker for a couple of months, therefore I couldn't endorse the Holmes method to anyone still addicted. Yasue continued smoking her favorite brand, NOW menthol, so I began to sneak one here and there, gradually I went right back to cigarettes and really disappointed her. I'd squandered a lot of hard-earned money in vain. The first day I quit, we promised to never smoke inside the house again, when I relapsed into that old dirty habit, the porch became the only acceptable area to light up.

This chronic breathing difficulty escalated, and my state of health wasn't very good. Before I turned sixty-two, and became eligible to collect Social Security, a friend advised me to apply for

SSI disability so I promptly went to the nearest office to fill out an application. Patti from the research group could vouch for my debilitating COPD condition. In a short time the SSI office sent a letter with a date for me to see their respiratory doctor. I kept my appointment at a tiny office in a tacky-looking mini mall on Sunset Boulevard. The personnel were all foreigners, but quite accommodating.

A nurse checked my height, weight and blood pressure while I waited to see a doctor. I told him I was on a study program, and he asked if I brought any medication. He would be giving me a breathing test like the kind I had to do for Patti, but first I had to dash across the parking lot to fetch my Ventolin from the car. When I returned, the doctor noticed I could barely catch my breath. He told me to breathe deeply into the apparatus, hold it for as long as I could, then exhale. They would test me again in fifteen minutes to compare the results following two puffs from my inhaler. His report to Social Security qualified me for disability payments. American senior citizens should be entitled to assistance if they have health problems, and soon I began to get a monthly check.

*****

We had two pets when we moved to Ambrose Terrace, our aging Shih Tzu, Megan, and Magic, my spooky Scorpio black cat. In late August of 2002, a large skinny-looking tabby smeared with sticky stuff introduced herself at our back door. Yasue liked her right away and named her 'Necco' which is the word for cat in Japanese. This one was bold, yet very affectionate; I just couldn't handle her until she was clean and had to confront major doubts about accepting another pet.

Necco wouldn't take one step into our house at first, perhaps she sensed Magic's curious presence; he always seemed to intimidate other cats. We left plenty of food and water outside and made her a comfortable bed on the back porch. A large storage container from the garage, tilted sideways, sheltered her from the elements, so we padded it with soft towels because she chose to be outdoors. Her calloused feet indicated that she'd been traveling over hot sidewalks for a long time and had probably endured a hard life with much hunger along the way. Within a month Necco grew much heavier, her appetite was insatiable. Yasue groomed her regularly and I kept her fed.

When the autumn chill arrived, we tried everything to get her inside our warm house, but this elderly cat was very stubborn, we guessed she was more than twelve years old, her rotten teeth said it all. I bought a larger container for her new bunk at the Home Depot one Sunday and placed additional bedding in it. The expanded sides would protect her much better from wind and rain. When the temperature hovered around thirty degrees, she finally surrendered and came inside one night. She slept on Yasue's chair until she graduated to the bed. Necco became Yasue's constant companion while assisting with the yard work. I took some wonderful photos of this brawny feline covered in a huge pile of autumn leaves; she was a pretty one and enjoyed being photographed.

Megan was an enjoyable little dog. She was good-natured with our cats, sociable around other pooches, and charming to people. All her life she suffered with annoying skin problems common to that breed. Fortunately she had only one major surgery, which was to remove a damaged spleen. The vet at Los Feliz recommended we take her to a choice surgeon over in West L.A. She recovered quickly and stayed in good health for a long time after. Then acute arthritis set in and simple walks became very difficult for her. We think it was related to her years of being on prednisone.

Our dog was getting old; during her last two visits at the Los Feliz Small Animal Clinic she wanted to bite everyone who came near her. Her usual sweet, lovable attitude changed when she got close to the place, I had to drag her in from the car. It occurred to me that the assistants were probably rough with her when they took her in the back out of my sight, and maybe even mean. I asked the secretary what happened to Dr. Liz Friedman. She said Liz worked part-time at a pet hospital in Glendale, but also made house calls. Her business card was a godsend; no more taking our elderly pet out of her comfortable home, a veterinarian we trusted and admired would be coming here now.

Jay Shafer was a peculiar guy who owned the house next to us. He wore a ponytail, stayed unshaven most of the time, and didn't work. When we first moved here he was very cordial, but he turned out to be a compulsive talker. Sometimes I had to walk backwards trying to escape his lengthy repetitive conversations. The man slept all day and stayed up all night watching black and white TV. He kept vodka in his refrigerator freezer, and drank a lot of it. There was much tragic history within his Jewish family. Jay's younger brother was murdered and the parents died fairly young. They left their house to him in a trust fund. He also inherited monthly checks for the everyday needs in his life.

Other than his only living relative, Barbara Kaufman, Jay didn't have many visitors. His attractive cousin drove him to lunch once a week in her older white Jaguar. I don't think the man was completely psychotic, but the fifty-nine-year-old Taurus still wasn't quite right. His prize possession was a very old, and tiny, longhaired white cat named Samantha, who needed grooming badly. Foolishly he smeared her all over with Vaseline to kill fleas. Once he asked Yasue to groom her, but he never followed through with a commitment. On warm nights we heard crickets chirping constantly, Jay told us he raised them in his living room, furthermore he didn't mind the skunks living underneath his house. This crackpot guy had a huge heart, and loved all creatures, great and small.

Sometime during Friday, October 10th 2003, Jay died of a heart attack sitting on a gossip bench, holding the phone. If not for his loyal friend, John, he might not have been discovered for a long while. They already planned to have a party that night with lots of food and booze to celebrate John's 40th birthday. He kept getting busy phone signals so he drove over and began screaming to Jay from the porch. Every neighbor within earshot wondered what the commotion was all about.

John called 911 at eight p.m., when there was no response the cops broke down Jay's front door. A black female detective found his collapsed body and called the coroner. By nine p.m. Jay's lawn was crowded with curious people, some knew him well, others not at all. We asked the policewoman what might happen to Jay's cat now; she said someone from the pound would be here once the body was removed. It broke my heart to think Jay's sweet companion may soon have a tag on her toe. I told the officer his ageing cat should be with us to live out her final days and begged to keep her. Barbara couldn't be reached so they gave us permission to take her home when the inquest concluded.

Yasue was leery when I offered to take Samantha, perhaps

because I'd drunk some beer earlier. She recognized a twenty-year-old cat might have serious medical problems, but I really didn't care, I only knew that Jay would appreciate her going to a loving home. Barbara owned a pair of large Borzois and had two young sons; she wouldn't know what to do with a frail old feline. The following Monday she dropped by to appraise Jay's things and to say that she was grateful we accepted Samantha. With a very busy agenda, Barbara would have been forced to put her to sleep.

After they took Jay's body out, I was there waiting to rush Samantha over to our house. We never saw a smaller, skinnier cat. There was a thick brown scab covering her nose, it seemed like she'd rubbed up against something hard while hunting for food, God knows how long she'd gone hungry. We carried her into the kitchen for a fresh bowl of cat food and some water; she dove in like it was her first nourishing meal in ages. Yasue weighed her in the morning, and she was barely four pounds. Jay's beloved pal was emaciated; she only had five broken teeth so I fed her soft foods.

Liz Friedman made a house call to give Megan a check up, and we asked her to do a complete exam on Samantha. Every blood test was taken right to the lab, she even took a urine sample, but she couldn't find anything wrong other than old-age traits. Diarrhea was her most apparent defect, which was tough on Magic since they shared the same litter box. While she lived with us, the tiny cat grew lively and seemed quite happy at times. Before sunrise I would close the doors to meditate, and she was always content to lie on my bed while the braziers of frankincense filled the room with smoke; I believe she found peace here. Jay must have been delighted to glimpse at her from above once she turned frisky again. Magic, Necco, and Megan would now be Samantha's new roommates.

*****

In August of 1988, Bruce and Regina Joi Drucker brought their brown poodle PJ to K-9 Tubs; we had no idea at the time that they would become our most benevolent friends. Bruce was a smart Jewish lawyer who speculated in real estate investments, and did very well; he sported a big black Cadillac. His wife, Regina, was a beautiful Mexican-American transgender person, had exquisite taste in clothing, patronized only the finest establishments, and was a genuine authority on authentic antiques. Yasue recognized that Regina, was very different, but I needed to look at her again since I had the urge to cruise Regina when they first came in.

RJ went to heaven due to old age. In 1991 the well-off couple bought Ruby and Rumsey, a pair of gorgeous King Charles Spaniels. Their new puppies began to come in for grooming once a week and felt a strong bond toward us. Through the years we became good friends with their owners, we are closer than ever because they literally enabled us to buy the fine house, we own now.

While there was still one more year to go on our lease, we got an alarming letter from our landlord in January 2004. Matsumoto was a language professor at a college in Orange County. One day he took a terrible spill on his bicycle and saw his life flash before his eyes. The man we'd only met once had inherited this place from his estranged uncle and didn't seem to need the money, nevertheless, he intended to sell the house we loved and had taken care of for the past three years. We argued about the remaining time on the lease, but he showed no compassion, Kenji just wanted to free himself up from responsibilities. Yasue was wise enough to save the original note stating he was willing to sell it to us for $450,000. If the going rate for a down payment was 20%, Yasue and I were screwed. Where would we get $90.000? Once again I began to look at overpriced rentals feeling very forlorn.

Bruce and Regina came here for dinner several times. They adored my cooking. One night Regina said she'd like to buy the house, dress up the place as an investment and we could still rent from them. When Matsumoto's note came, I considered what she said. First I checked out several disgusting rentals, but then decided to ask if she was serious about buying this house. Bruce asked what our goals were, I told him we were doing well at K-9, nothing else seemed important. He hinted that it was possible for Yasue and me, to buy our little dream home if we really chose to.

They gave us hope when our world seemed to be collapsing. Bruce's father had passed away recently and willed him considerable assets. There was also a pension fund at his disposal for the future. He told us he would put up the down payment money from his retirement savings if we promised to make these higher mortgage payments on time. Words cannot express the relief and joy we felt.

The first thing we had to do was inform the landlord that we wanted to buy the property. Yasue always spoke with him in Japanese, but I noticed some frustration while talking to him about the price. Matsumoto talked to several local real estate people, and his price was now $550,000. We called Bruce at once. He asked Yasue if she saved the valuable letter stating that Kenji would sell it to us for $450,000. His note had only arrived twenty-one days before, yet he said he didn't recall writing to us.

Our friend confronted him like a concerned relative, then like a sharp lawyer. Ultimately Kenji agreed to abide by his original figure. We got in touch with Bruce's broker whom did business with and were on our way to signing a million papers at an escrow office in Glendale. We acquired our first home when I was sixty-four years old, further proof that I'm still a lucky little rabbit.

I rode along with Bruce to his main bank in the valley on a rainy afternoon in that big black Cadillac. He took care of business then handed me a cashier's check from his pension fund. Five thousand dollars was earmarked for our closing costs, and $90,000 would apply to the down payment on the house. How many people would lend friends $95,000 just to keep them from parting with the place they loved? Bruce and Regina was extremely benevolent people. We are blessed to know them.

Bruce drew up a contract regarding how we'd pay this money back; the terms involved little interest, and gave us ample time to compensate him for the loan. This document was called 'THE PLAN'. On February 27th, 2004 we closed escrow and became the proud owners of 4411 Ambrose Terrace. People began to ask, "How does it feel to be a homeowner?" I'd smile and say, "The only thing that's different is our landlord."

We'd have to send bigger payments to a bank, pay the property taxes, and be committed to maintaining the property. I had to pinch myself at times and still couldn't believe we owned a house. Our rent to Matsumoto was only $1,600 a month, now the mortgage would cost more than $2,600 monthly, which included taxes and insurance. We tightened our belts, ruled out vacations and took every bedraggled dog into K-9 for grooming.

Our devoted friends Bruce and Regina had changed addresses several times since we'd known them. Early on they bought an apartment house in Beverly Hills as an investment but couldn't live there. Aggressive homeless folks constantly prowled around their property. Then they moved to a Pasadena chateau on four acres above the Arroyo, next to the famous mansion shown in the *Batman* films. Regina turned the home into a museum, yet for all its grandeur we never felt comfortable there.

Bruce was the tenacious workaholic, he tended to business deals while Regina bought and sold prime real estate. She once owned an elegant antique shop, and even sold their Spanish-style home in Los Feliz to Madonna personally.

Our friend Regina collected many elegant and valuable pieces. She was passionate about antiques in the same way Josephine Baker felt when she adopted orphans. Bruce made plenty of money, and his wife knew how to spend it, yet they were a very loving couple. Later he got involved as a consultant in The United Arab Emirates. They pay him well to bring about energy-saving windmills for new resorts. His patents were on the cutting edge of success.

Shortly before we bought this house, their female dog, Ruby, died of heart failure. They both took it hard, but our pretty friend Regina was beside herself with grief for quite a while. Later the couple had to go to New York for an important family gathering, and they asked us if we could take care of Rumsey for a few days. Their lovable dog knew us from the shop, and was always happy to visit; we liked him very much. He arrived with an elegant pillow, a blanket, toys, and special food.

The first night he was here, he ate every doggie treat we handed him and seemed to be having a good time with our Megan. The next day he was listless and didn't look well; he refused to eat anything. They left the name of their veterinarian so I rushed their pet, to The Larchmont Pet Clinic; the doctor had Bruce's credit card number on file. Little Rumsey had many health problems, but the exact cause of this sudden illness was because he'd been on too many drugs, which did more harm than good. We called Bruce and Regina in New York right away to let them know. I never prayed so hard over a pet before. Rumsey was their only baby now, if anything happened to him in our care we'd feel guilty forever.

Fortunately he was back to normal before they returned.

We went through many changes during 2004. Buying this house was an unexpected turning point, but they say it takes both rain and sunshine to make a rainbow. Samantha gave up eating and began to act strangely. In the seven months since Jay passed, she never attempted to go outside, but she'd glance over at her old house next door from the side window. Then she began standing by the back door crying loudly so I decided to let her go into the enclosed yard.

Samantha went outdoors for the first time ever and sat at the base of the tall pear tree for hours just staring up at the sky. Since she wasn't eating, I thought she might be experiencing a sort of dementia. Her diarrhea was out of control when I called Liz Friedman to make an appointment for a house call. Liz said she was close to death due to old age; she was more than twenty years old. We didn't want to witness her passing so our considerate veterinarian took her back to the Arden clinic and put her to sleep there. I knew in my heart that when the tiny cat sat lifelessly beneath the tree she was calling Jay to receive her in heaven. Nesting with us simply extended her life for seven happy months.

Liz came here a lot throughout that active year and now Megan was having problems. Her arthritis was so bad she could hardly walk. When she went outside to do her business, we had to hold her up at times with a brace. I was ready to let our daughter ascend to heaven with the other pets, but Yasue couldn't let her go. She'd be at work while I watched her suffer more every day, and it made me feel like crying. The one habitual thing about our dog was that her appetite was rarely affected by an illness. Ultimately Yasue had to face the fact that Megan was really in pain, and there was no remedy for our seventeen-year-old dog. We asked Liz to put her to sleep and chose the following Saturday afternoon of July 24th. At least we would have the weekend to grieve.

The day before Megan left us, I cooked the finest veal from Gelson's market. On her final day, I fed her several spoonfuls of vanilla ice cream throughout the morning, and for lunch she feasted on tiny pieces of filet mignons. Yasue finished work early to be with her for the last time and couldn't stop crying, she didn't want to watch her die. Liz arrived on time, and explained that she would give her a strong tranquilizer to relax first, but took her back to the clinic for the ensuing euthanasia. Yasue held her after the shot, and before Megan passed out, she kissed her on the lips. Her belly was bulging when I wrapped her in a fluffy towel and carried her to Liz's car.

Yasue cried constantly for a week while I held back tears, I truly loved our very first dog. I raised this Shi Tzu since she was a pup, but I was home more than Yasue. Our customers were most sympathetic, many of them had lost pets and they understood the sorrow. This was our only dog, and I doubt if we'd ever get another. Megan lived with the same two devoted owners all her life; she was well cared for, and certainly loved by us. Everything reminded us of her. She could never be forgotten.

Subsequently Necco grew closer to Yasue, and she slept with her every night, which was a good thing. One day we noticed a big lump around her middle so I took her directly to the Arden clinic. Liz tended to our adopted feline, the staff x-rayed, and took ultrasounds to check the growth. It turned out this stray cat had cancer which was beyond treatment. They advised us to just wait and see. She seemed healthy because her appetite was still fine. On Friday night, August 13th, we were admiring the opening ceremonies of the Olympics in Greece on TV. Suddenly, we heard Necco crying loudly. She was in great pain right outside our window and dying. We went out and watched her convulsing on the lawn for a long time until she finally gave up. There was nothing anyone could do.

That night I promptly wrapped her in a towel, placed the corpse inside a cat carrier and left her in the cold garage until the clinic opened in the morning. For a small fee they would cremate her.

After I took Yasue to work, I went back home for Necco. The pet hospital was a few miles away, which gave me plenty of time to reflect on our estranged relationship with this happy wanderer.

Yasue was really fond of her; she was a cheerful hobo who just walked in and stayed two years. Necco was a pretty cat, but pushy with a mind of her own. I liked her, but whenever I paid attention to her, she'd be all over me. At one point I believe she was more than twenty pounds, and she always looked grimy. Once in a while she would pounce on my bed just to intimidate Magic.

Three of our pets went to the hereafter within three months could there be something to the old cliché about death happening in threes? Now we only had Magic, the spooky one who never comes out from under the covers when people are around, a cat who Yasue still can't take a shine to; he hisses at her. He is a one-person creature, what he lacks in social skills, he makes up for with loyalty and affection to me. Habib was allegiant, but she also loved Yasue and our friends.

During the summer of 2004, we were annoyed constantly by our neighbor's boisterous parties; every madcap sound carried over to us. The man was an unemployed actor named Saverio Guerra, a short Puerto Rican with plenty of anger management hang-ups. It was almost comical to hear screaming matches between him and his wife, Kim, when they were outdoors, but she seemed to hold her own and usually argued back. If we didn't hear them fighting for a few days, we thought perhaps he'd murdered her. Then they'd have another loud party with the usual obnoxious guests.

Their house was just around the corner, one lot away, yet we could still hear their colorful dialogues from the moment we stepped onto the back porch. Our yard was supposed to be a peaceful place to relax, instead all we heard was a big-mouth guy who cursed all the time using words most people in our area wouldn't even know. On television he always played the role of a jerk, in real life he was the consummate asshole. Each time I thought about sitting in our yard to enjoy the beauty, I was daunted by their frequent noisy parties. Yasue told me to ignore them, but I couldn't. We assumed he was using cocaine then; we recognized the characteristics from back in the day.

They partied throughout that entire summer, causing much misery; finally I decided to write a letter to the inconsiderate neighbors. I tried to explain how upset we were, and I also mentioned that their every graphic word could be overheard clearly by the whole neighborhood. "Do you honestly want everyone to know your personal business?" My one-page letter was mailed on Monday, the day after another loud party. It was cordial and even kind considering the aggravation we put up with.

Shortly after 2 p.m. on Tuesday, September 21st, 2004, Saverio stormed over here and pounded on our front door. When I opened it, he was holding the letter I wrote; his face revealed his rage. The tiny man freaked out, he was crazed, as he tore the note up in my face and threw pieces around the hallway. The short guy started yelling loudly. "You are a fucking ugly old dyke, how dare you say these things to me. You don't know who you are screwing with. I'll kill you if you ever come near our home."

I assured him he didn't know who he was dealing with either. Fortunately Yasue was home early that day to witness his threats. Uri, the woman next door, heard every word, as did Rosemarie from across the street. He ranted, raved, and cursed for quite a while before he left in a huff.

I wrote him the letter because I was aware of his explosive personality. He and his wife had been inside our house once when they wanted to know who to contact about Jay's place. They were thinking of buying it for Kim's mom, who might be moving here from Texas, but thank God they didn't. We gave them the information, but from our brief conversation we sensed Saverio had a short fuse. Kim was censured for everything she said, and he hurried her through all the discussions.

After the fight I went over to talk with Rosemarie and Uri since they'd overheard the bitter quarrel. I showed them a copy of the letter I sent, and they agreed it was a polite note considering the annoyances we put up with. Then I called Bruce Drucker, who was an attorney with a vested interest in our house. He said I should report this to the police right away.

A nice policeman took my call at the local Rampart division, and I explained why Saverio threatened my life. He asked if I wanted to send the detectives over to explain the ramifications of browbeating someone, but I refused. We just wanted this on record in case things got worse; then we'd be delighted if the cops were to arrest him.

He's been keeping a low profile since the confrontation. Our yard is once again a peaceful retreat, and their parties have subsided. Lately they entertain in the front of their house, and we can't hear a thing. Perhaps he cleaned up. I'd like to be everyone's friend, but that's not always possible.

How can anyone expect to achieve peace on earth if they can't get along with neighbors on the same block? He enjoyed the adulation of companions; I considered underneath his loutish Brooklyn ways there was a good man. Maybe we'll have a reason to speak someday, but till then, he isn't my friend. They own a mixed pit bull named Maisy, if these folks can love a dog, they can't be all bad.

*****

Los Angeles received huge amounts of rain in 2004, from early autumn until spring of 2005. It was the second heaviest rainy season on record. Our living room sprang a few ceiling leaks when the big downpours came. We put plastic over exposed furniture, and kept some pails handy, now that we are actual homeowners, we couldn't complain to the landlord. Bruce had an investment in this house, and our contract stated he would pay half for any major repairs, including a new roof.

Bruce did business with Rubin Lomelli on other properties and said he was honest. I called Rubin when we decided to fix the roof before another wet season. To rip out the old one, cover it with plywood, do the shingles, and install new gutters, his price was $10,578. I'm a cautious shopper so I arranged several appointments with other firms to compare estimates. Bids ranged from $3,550, to $14,000; some didn't include replacing the decrepit rain gutters built in 1937.

I was reluctant to commit to Rubin at first; the cute young Gemini sported fancy tattoos, and drove a big brand-new Dodge Ram truck, leading me to believe he might be more expensive than the rest. It turned out Rubin was very reputable, he quoted us the best price, and his able crew did excellent work, so we took the deal. The noisy job lasted a whole week, and the filth was unbearable. Bruce took care of his share, while we practically emptied our bank account for the balance.

When the roof was done, a tall nice-looking guy named Federico rang the doorbell on my birthday. He said he was a location scout for a television show called *The Shield* and would like to use our place to film part of an episode. I told him another guy was here before, took photos, and said the same thing but never came back. Federico was more charming, so I allowed him to photograph.

He said he had to go back to the studio and show his boss the digital photos, then he called later to ask if it would be okay to bring the director, set dressers, and producers, back here. Three huge white vans drove up, and about twenty people ambled up the path. Our house really appealed to them, and they were sure about using it for a couple of scenes. Federico told us they paid $2,500 for a one-day shoot. Five hundred dollars to prep, (take our stuff away), $1,500 for the actual filming, and $500 to strike (put everything back). Yasue agreed to let them; she was delighted with the offer of money.

We had a new roof now, but the living room ceiling was still a mess. I called the Fussy Painters because they did a great job at our shop. Scott Johnson, the hearing-impaired owner, looked over the large space and quoted $1,500 to scrape the ceiling, plaster, paint it, and touch up all the other bad areas in the room. I told him we needed the job done quickly. A crew would be here next week to film. The painters were on time and worked furiously. It was a filthy job, but we cleaned the entire house after they finished. We packed all the delicate pieces, and got rid of some frilly things they wouldn't be using. Regrettably the bulk of the money we received would go to Scott.

On Wednesday, September 28th, they prepped the house and put our things in the garage. They used many locations in our area since the studio was just down the street on Prospect. Thursday the crew wrapped up filming at a house nearby and arrived at our place late. Our tiny cul de sac had several parking monitors and cops; it was an incredible sight when those huge trucks pulled up. The amount of equipment to be used was amazing. There was even a big truck to get free food. Federico wanted me to eat, but I was too excited.

We were prepared to stay out of the house until they finished shooting, which might be around eleven. Yasue went to work as usual that day, but I didn't leave until the moment the trucks started to drive up. She gave me the key to her cousin Christine's apartment close by. Instead of hanging around the noisy shop all afternoon I decided to go over, and wait for Yasue to call when she was done.

There were six remote controls on the table for one television, and a DVD player. Each was marked with a memo. 'Turn on TV only'. 'Change the Channels'. Etc. Within five minutes everything went wrong; somehow I screwed up all the programming, and could only wish for Yasue to call. I felt very uncomfortable, perhaps even a bit claustrophobic. This cramped bachelorette pad was like a neat mini warehouse. Her aloof Siamese cat, Peekaboo, hid all day, which made me feel worse.

When Yasue finally called, I picked her up and drove her there, Chris would return after six. We made plans to have dinner at Palermo's, around the corner. By the time Yasue got cleaned up, Chris arrived home. We walked to the restaurant and were seated promptly. Yasue drank ice tea while her cousin and I shared a carafe of red wine. The food was mediocre at best, but Chris took all the leftovers anyway. After dessert, I got in my car and headed back to our neighborhood.

Around eight, I parked on Commonwealth and walked over to be near the action. Our usually quiet lane was bustling with hundreds of people and bright lights. A young lady named Katrina, whom I just met recently, saw me standing around, and asked me up to her apartment for a glass of wine. The French windows exposed a panoramic view of the animated cul de sac. While I was getting acquainted with my charming new gay friend, Chris and Yasue found a parking space on the corner.

During my fleeting visit to the Berkshire, I learned that Katrina was an actress, her lover, Tamara, was also an actress; they had a terrific relationship. Tamara was returning from a job in Florida later, and Katrina had to pick her up at LAX. This was the first time I'd ever chatted with her. She had very light skin, yet I saw a person of color. Her black father was a career army man, and her white mother was a schoolteacher from New Zealand. Tamara happened to be a stunning Caucasian from Newport Beach. Sometimes I'd see them getting in or out of their cars; they were never shy to display feelings toward each another. That lively evening gave me a chance to befriend them.

I thanked her for the fine hospitality, wished her safe trip to the airport, and went over to sit in Christine's new sedan. As soon as someone shouted, "CUT!" we got out of the car, maybe we could meet the actors. Federico took us directly to Forrest Whitaker, who turned out to be one of the nicest men on earth. He was warm and approachable; he even gave me permission to take photos of him embracing Yasue and Christine. We returned to our house when the crew began packing it up.

This episode of *The Shield* was about a cop getting busted by Mr. Whitaker, the troubled detective from internal affairs. The man being arrested happened to live here; Lemonhead was his character, played by Kenneth Johnson. Lemonhead was a macho type, good-looking, but very sloppy. Our decor was too ornate for his personality, so a dirty old surfboard replaced the lovely mirror and table in the hall. Graceful art pieces were switched to tacky posters comparable to dogs playing poker. Federico said they might use our place again to shoot Lemonhead's return from jail, but the writers didn't have a script completed yet. We said okay, providing they didn't film any wild or violent scenes. Our home is a quiet, serene, and sacred place; we only want to attract good vibrations.

We arranged the furniture just the way it was, our living room looked fresh, but there was still a blank wall above the fish tanks. I'd taken Gloria Martin's delightful animal prints to hang in the shop after painting the place. The cheerful drawings really dressed up K-9. We embraced two celebrated lithographs at home signed by William Gatewood, and I hoped to locate more of his work.

Social Security granted me a small amount of money, we didn't seem to be struggling with the mortgage, and my credit cards were clear. I began to surf on the net, and one biography said he was an incredibly talented man, whom I recognized, but I wasn't aware of his death in 1994. When Mark Thomas passed away in 1989, my bridge to William and Beau collapsed. They all succumbed to AIDS.

There were thousands of art sites on the web, but when I typed in his name, I came up with many reputable art galleries who carried some of his work. I looked at countless lithographs, but the same uninteresting posters kept showing up. We had two excellent compositions; his best work was either sold or impossible to find. The pieces I considered were only sold in England, and very expensive. One gallery had a composition titled *North Country*, which I fell in love with; it cost $3,000 American dollars. Prices for his acclaimed gold foil artistry ranged from $100 to $10,000.

I bought four William Gatewood lithographs for several hundred dollars, excluding the frames; our living room walls were now complete. We could forever admire *Sky Fan*, *The Kimono*, *Olan sun*, *Spring Kite*, along with the *Wisteria Screens One* and *Two*. My friend was a godly man. I feel spiritual whenever I see his omnipotent art and appreciate having it. We only spent a short amount of time together, but I experienced the presence of greatness. He finally returned to the planet 'Olan'.

We closed the shop from Thursday until the following Tuesday to take a mini vacation over the long Thanksgiving weekend. Yasue made plans earlier to fly out to Las Vegas and join her sister Toshie and her husband, Allen. The couple from Hawaii enjoyed auto racing, and often attended major NASCAR events, Yasue preferred to make the rounds with slot machines. Before she left for the airport, I predicted my mother's spirit would chaperon her and bring about good luck.

When she came home, her facial expression said it all. "I won a lot, but had to report my winnings to the IRS." She hit a jackpot for twenty-five hundred dollars. She proceeded to win several smaller pots which paid for her air fare, hotel, and a seven-course family dinner at a chic restaurant.

Yasue was exhausted from the trip, which is when I decided she needed some help with the housework. It was difficult for me to do certain things lately; just bending down took my breath away. I had to limit myself to easy chores like washing dishes, taking out the trash, or grocery shopping. Our neighbor Uri had employed the same housekeeper for years, her name was Eugenia, and came from Guatemala. She was a single mom with a little girl; evidently she was good with children. Uri told me Eugenia was slow at times, but steady and completely trustworthy, which was a concern.

We asked Uri to send her over to discuss whether or not she could work for us. The young woman was a pretty Virgo, quite pleasant, a bit pudgy, but didn't speak English very well. She could only be here on Mondays. If the girl worked every single week, she would get sixty-five dollars, if she came every other week, we'd have to pay eighty dollars. Eugenia accepted the job instantly. Yasue's day off was always on Monday, and she could designate basic cleaning chores every other week.

We were both neat, and there was never much heavy-duty cleaning to do, just basic stuff. Yasue worked hard at the shop five days a week, and took care of the endless yard work, besides cleaning the house. A domestic was a blessing to her, and she'd only have to be here every other week. Uri said Eugenia refused to do litter boxes or fireplaces. She didn't have to clean the fish tanks or touch laundry. Eugenia was forward and independent, which is probably why she didn't have a husband.

I bought a large plastic carrier and filled it with every kind of cleaning product available. She arrived at nine on the first morning, but said she could only work until two. We asked our neighbor if Eugenia brought her own lunch or should we supply it. Uri said she usually fed her with whatever leftovers were around, but we didn't have any so I went to a Carl's Junior drive through to get her a chicken sandwich meal. Yasue ate a fish combo while they chatted gleefully in the dining room.

Recently her new car had been stolen from an underground parking space at her apartment house. She had to take a bus to work and pick up her daughter at school after work. I drove her to the bus stop the first time because we pitied her and was grateful to have our very first housekeeper. Yasue said the woman really knew how to clean, but I had my doubts. She could get hung up staring at things, especially family photos; she seemed to take more time polishing pictures than doing other jobs.

My altar was off limits in the future. I told her not to clean it again. Everything she touched went back in the wrong place, not even close to the way they were. Maybe she dusted places that showed, but the floors were never really clean to me, she barely passed a mop over the hardwood, and the mirrors were streaky. The same huge cobweb on my wall was there four weeks ago.

The next time she worked, we provided her a fine lunch, some fruit, and plenty of Coca-Cola for pep. We were going shopping at the Galeria, but left a portable radio, perhaps some music would keep her moving. Mexican hip-hop was her choice. When we returned just after two, she was gone.

After the third day, I made a list of things she didn't do, and Yasue agreed it wasn't worth the considerable money we paid her. If you did the math, Eugenia was earning about sixteen dollars per hour, more than I paid my boys who worked so hard at K-9. In addition to supplying lunch, I resented having to drive her to a bus stop. One morning she was on her way to work next door at Uri's and rang our doorbell just to say hello. It was the holiday season; nevertheless, I had to explain why we no longer needed her services. I made up a story about my brother in Georgia, I claimed we had to help him out with money and could no longer afford a housekeeper. The headstrong woman was shocked, and she asked if her work was bad. "Your work is fine, but we're having other problems." Before she walked off in a huff, I gave her a Christmas card with money and wished her well.

*****

Jay's house remained empty for nearly two years, which gave us privacy, and the creatures living under the place were also happy. Finally the real estate broker sent painters there to make the interior look good. When Jay passed away, his cousin Barbara really expected to buy it for $450,000; she was related and thought she could get it for the same price we paid for ours. The property sold on the first day they had an open house. A nice Filipino family bought it 'as is', and paid $800,000 for the small abode on a busy street corner. It had three tiny bedrooms, needed much work, and there was hardly any backyard. Pong Castro became the new owner, and his wife's name was Beth. They had two lovely young daughters who attended a Catholic school and wore little plaid uniforms.

We didn't close for our regular vacation after Christmas. We needed to keep ahead of mortgage payments, and now I required periodic prescriptions. When I turned sixty-five, I joined the Kaiser Permanente plan for seniors and Medicare proved to be a blessing.

Traditionally January is a slow business month, most of our customers have their dogs groomed before the holidays, and they weren't expected to come in for a while. Stormy winter weather could also bring about unforeseen losses in revenue.

When we needed help, my prayers were always answered. One chilly day in January, Federico called to ask if we would let them use our house again to film *The Shield*. I was pleased and said yes right away. He came over to discuss the schedule, and the $2,500 compensation would be the same. I wasn't sure if I wanted to go shoulder-to-shoulder trying to help a crew of rugged movers, but the money affected my decision so I signed a new contract. Last time I exerted myself from carrying things, but their routine seemed familiar now so I intended to do less bull work.

The next day he marched in with an army, a director, a few producers, and technicians. I established a good rapport with Dena Allen, the set decorator. We'd had a lovely chat when she was here earlier. This time they'd be shooting a major scene in my bedroom, suddenly I realized what bad shape it was in. One wall had blackened from five years of blazing charcoal and frankincense.

Through the magic of Hollywood, they could still use my room by camouflaging the darkened walls with bourgeois art. I befriended a nice guy, Jim, who came from my area of Massachusetts, and we talked about different things. He asked why I had a huge California king-sized bed, when I was such a tiny person. "Yasue and I used to sleep together; we had five cats who also shared this bed."

When they were here last time, I told them not to even think about moving the fish tanks or our new 36" HD TV. The wiring behind that set was awfully complicated. Our aquariums stayed, although they did take our television out, certain scenes with the manly cop required an enormous 60" TV. This time I worried when someone mentioned removing the computer, I objected because of all the connections, but finally agreed, providing they stored it inside, and not out in the garage.

This episode was filmed during the day, and we got to come back inside our house early; a technician even left the big TV connected so I could watch a Lakers game that night. The day after shooting, an alert crew put everything back exactly the way it was except for the bedroom furniture, which would remain in the garage, until Fussy Painters renovated my boudoir and bathroom. A large part of our revenue went to Scott Johnson, who earned twelve hundred dollars just to paint that area.

The studio movers were happy to hear they didn't have to cart all that heavy furniture back. This crew was an eclectic bunch. One guy wrote science-fiction stories in his spare time, another man was strictly into health food, and another chap considered himself as a contemporary city farmer. Federico had actually written a script about Tom Cruise. "What if he'd been late for his first major movie audition?" He rambled on about Tom's disappointments and the setbacks which might follow.

I wrote my annual paper relating to the Chinese New Year prior to January 26th, 2006, the day they filmed. The Year of the Dog was about to begin on the 29th. I gave a copy to Dena since the dog represents a Libra, and she was a true Libra, perhaps this sign would bring her good luck. Then I invited her to celebrate the event with a few good friends here on Sunday, January 29th.

Bruce and Regina stopped by early but were expected elsewhere and only stayed a short time. Susan and Brian came over carrying a choice bottle of champagne. We had lots of finger food, plenty of bubbly and red wine. Our neighbor Katrina brought her sister Diana just in from Chicago, along with her partner, Tamara. I was surprised when Dena showed up with a sweet little statue of a green dog for the occasion. Her angelic daughter, Luna, was here briefly while her mom was working, but this soiree might get bawdy, so I'm glad she didn't bring her. The teen attended Immaculate Heart, an excellent school nearby. Tucci showed up later with a delicious chocolate cake, and everyone had great fun. Dena wanted to read the finished parts of my book so I promptly lent it to her.

The drama filmed here, Lemonhead's place, finally aired on television in mid-March, and the episode was entitled *Of mice and Lem*. Steinbeck would roll over in his grave if he only knew how twisted it was. Dena asked one of her assistants to press over a whole new set of king-sized sheets for Lem's bed. We were bound to watch the tasteless show just to see how our house looked.

Lem jumped up, ran to the bathroom in a hurry, and vomited blood. The relentless internal affair's cop (Forrest Whitaker) was at the front door with a muffin in a sack. While Lem (Kenneth Johnson) was trying desperately to get rid of him, he continued heaving into a wastebasket by the living room. They swapped a few words then Kavanaugh (Forrest Whitaker) left. We were disappointed, they filmed here for many hours, but it took less than a minute and a half to see on TV, I'm sure a lot of it ended up on the cutting room floor. I noticed personnel standing around a great deal. The cost to produce a major show like that must be colossal. Studio managers should do something about idle crews, and try to use fewer locations per show, now I realize why some film companies leave L.A. to cut costs.

Steaming wrinkles out of sheets seemed like a futile task, but their most frivolous project was removing all the bars from the front windows. Six men struggled to pry off those ancient bolts, while painters arrived to touch up the exterior woodwork. Their cameraperson moved very fast, and didn't focus on the disheveled character's tidy new bed sheets. I thought one scene might take place on our front lawn or path, but they never showed the grate-free windows. They eliminated the iron enclosures because Lem might have a problem looking at bars now that he was out of jail.

Scott Johnson's crew came over to paint my bedroom the day after our Chinese New Year party. They scraped and patched the ceiling, then applied two layers of primer on the blackened walls. I chose bright white for doors and windows, antique white to cover the walls, and the trim would be clay beige. A color called 'man on the moon' went on my bathroom walls, which matched the tile; the trim was also bright white. When they finished, I wasn't very happy with the color I chose for the border. After they left, I bought a quart of Aquamarine semi-gloss at the hardware store and painted it myself. His men carted all the heavy furniture in from the garage and arranged everything. I tipped them generously for a job well done, while Scott grossed twelve hundred dollars.

The Shield probably won't be using our place for a location again. They killed off poor Lem in the following episode. It was an exciting time which gave me the opportunity to make friends with some creative people. I enjoyed Dena; she had a keen sense of humor and was a total perfectionist at work. She sent me an e-mail which said she was back from a hiatus, and would call soon. I literally laughed out loud when she mentioned that my book was equal to three copies of Doctor Zhivago. Her honesty was refreshing.

*****

February 5th, 2006 marked the 25th anniversary of K-9 Tubs. We felt proud for hanging in there. Through happy times, and an assortment of sad events, this caring little shop has thrived as the best grooming establishment in town. Yasue works hard, she cuts hair incredibly well, and our patrons are always satisfied. Most dogs are anxious to come in. These creatures of habit generally anticipate treats while enjoying a painless beauty treatment. We understood the client's needs and problems; we tended to our own wonderful Shih Tzu, Megan, for seventeen years, and it was a constant learning process.

My outside sign above the Arc came from Lacey's Art Service so I went to see my friend Ricardo. I wanted him to make an eight-foot-by-four-foot banner that said, 'K-9 Tubs - 25th Anniversary', and asked him to place a large rainbow in the center of the purple lettering. He did a great job, it was ready in three days, and he sent two workers over to put it up. I was happy when we hung the banner. It would let folks see exactly how long we'd been here. Friends stopped by to congratulate us, some sent flowers, while others brought wine.

Yasue worried about someone tearing it down, other rainbow flags had gone missing at the Arc. But I wasn't worried, we are grateful for the past twenty-five years, which were very good to us.

Presently we have an outstanding assistant called Jefferson McCarty, an Aquarius from Alabama. He's a good worker, our most conscientious employee to date, and he's been with us for more than a year. It was clear that Jeff came from good stock, the guy is sharp and smart, and we don't have to tell him twice, he gets it right away. Cruz worked with us for six years, yet every day we had to repeat the same instructions. Throughout this period, we've hired hundreds of workers. It is, and always will be, hard, dirty work. Anyone can wash a dog, but not everyone has the patience or the stomach for this job. Our personnel at K-9 are required to be kind, gentle, and handle each pet with love.

All things considered, "This is as good as it gets." I'm blessed with more than I ever dreamed, and grateful for the wonderful friends we've come to know through K-9. Susan Wakil is now an acclaimed artist, and Brian is building a spectacular retreat for them in the desert of Palm Springs. We are fortunate to work on their seven well-behaved dogs. They bring us a tidy source of income.

Michael Tucci gave up acting, it was too hard on the family, and now teaches at a Catholic school. Recently his wife, Kathie, had a series of heart attacks and needed to slow down. Their two beautiful adopted daughters have grown up, Kelly entered high school, and Kate chose to attend college at Cornell University. The family plans to spend a summer vacation in the east, mainly on Cape Cod, they will also visit Tucci's lovely sister Maria, and likable father, Nick, on Long Island.

Diane and Andy have two wonderful Maltese, Titus and Lilly. These tiny adorable dogs gave Diane a new source of parenthood. The pair have enjoyed coming to K-9 since they were puppies. Recently my writer friends are braving life in New York City, Titus and Lilly stayed with them until the bitter cold set in, then were flown home to L.A. Betty, their housekeeper, takes very good care of the pets and brings them to us regularly for grooming. Joseph, their handsome son, once worked a crafty magician, at the illustrious Magic Castle, and later married his charming girlfriend, Anna.

Diane and Andy were chosen to write for *The Sopranos*, one of my favorite programs, the only hang-up was traveling back and forth to New York. That would be the final season of the colorful drama, but my creative friends were sure to come up with a stylistic ending. They've earned Emmys, for previous shows, in addition to Peabody awards. I'm proud to see their names on major credits.

Whenever I watch Sasha Cohen ice skating, I see a youthful Diane; there is a stunning likeness. My friend is beautiful, very smart, an outstanding Tango dancer, and I still think of her as my uptown girl. She traveled to India a while back to research Meher Baba, an avatar whose basic philosophy teaches one to be happy and not worry. Diane doesn't say much about religion, though she is gifted with infinite wisdom. One day at lunch when I made a reckless remark referring to the Iraqis as 'THOSE PEOPLE', she reminded me we are all one. The woman is like adrenaline, but I was never tempted by forbidden inklings. We will always honor and respect a healthy friendship.

My old chum Sidra vanished from our lives in 2001. The last time we saw each other was when she had her eyelids lifted at Brotman Hospital. She needed a ride out of there and a place to rest until she could see more clearly. Someone else was expected to do her this favor but canceled at the last minute, as usual she counted on me in the middle of a busy day.

Angela Shelton generally brought her attractive friends here on Friday night to discuss their astrological charts. I'd just started to cook a delicious Osso Buco dinner when Sidra called and begged me to pick her up at a medical center in Culver City. She cried like a baby, how could I say no? Her family had cut her loose long ago, others avoided Sidra, I didn't have the heart, and she really was insane. Taking me away from dinner with friends was bad enough, but the real frustration was driving through rush-hour traffic on a busy night. It took more than an hour to get there, which gave me a chance to reflect on our estranged relationship. The more I thought about her selfish ways and mighty ego, the more my secret animosities intensified.

It was bedlam when I finally reached her hospital room. She was hysterical and appeared crazed. "I'm not ready, you don't have to wait, and I'll get home somehow."

Sidra probably sensed my frustration, though I'm sure her frenzy was caused from the drugs that hadn't worn off. They wouldn't discharge her until someone showed up, the agitated nurse was about to commit her to a psychiatric ward before I arrived. We kept her calm long enough to get her dressed, pack a few belongings, and sign the paperwork. She draped a flamboyant scarf around her head until you could barely see her huge black sunglasses. Melodramatic scenes were fun for Sidra.

When we got to my car she began to cry and apologized repeatedly for bothering me. I couldn't listen to any more nonsense during the long ride home, and this was a chance to tell her how I felt. "Sidra, my anger today is an accumulation of all the malarkey you put me through in the past. Yasue is courteous, she tolerates you, but my mother couldn't bear to be around you at all. Your narcissistic attitude intimidates everyone. You boast of superior intelligence, yet you never learned the true definition of humility. I am really tired of serving you, and furthermore, I don't really like you."

The US Navy gave her a medical discharge on the grounds of mental incompetence, which allowed her to get disability benefits for the rest of her life. She never felt guilty about accepting money from the government or anyone else. Sidra survived like a common bag lady, yet was still able to vacation in Europe, while also having plastic surgery. I expressed much disdain during that drive home.

Our lives were not all about Sidra, and friends were here when we arrived. Yasue was not pleased, but politely suggested she might try resting in the bedroom. We offered food and drinks, instead she chose to pace wildly and rave absurdities, finally I rushed her back to her own place; this was my last courtesy. We didn't hear anything after that and assumed she moved up north with family.

We hadn't heard loud celebrations from our neighbor Saverio's place since he threatened my life. I really thought the ill-tempered guy should have attended anger-management classes. Lately we hear harsh blows to a punching bag, an apparent outlet for his rage; he also plays the drums indoors, but not often. The man tries hard to be accepted, and maybe there is a good person beneath that rowdy facade. During previous parties, we listened to bitter discussions about his father, implying that Saverio's defiance started early. Recently they had a baby.

If only they were more considerate about noise, we might have been friends. I confronted the couple with our grievances in a letter to avoid a verbal clash, yet he chose to argue the allegations. Ultimately they got the message, and nowadays our area is peaceful.

*****

I don't have many regrets about the past, yet there are things I wonder about. What if my sister Anne had lived? She was a Taurus, born a couple of years before me and died too young. Would a sister have influenced my life? Whenever I'm near siblings who are truly loving and close, I feel a twinge of envy. Though I can't see her, I know Anne is always around; she is one of my guardian angels.

'Neither a borrower, nor a lender be.' William Shakespeare was also a Taurus whose words make more sense to me today. Money was tight when we moved to this house. I swallowed my pride and borrowed five hundred dollars from Earl before his illness, then paid it back with interest in a short time. My brother suffered a stroke, his finances plunge, and he needed money for essentials. We lent him a large sum to save his car. Sometimes we spoke on weekends, but they completely avoided the subject of paying us. The next year Yasue had to leave suddenly for Japan as her father was dying. I wrote a polite note to ask if Earl and Pat could somehow pay back part of the loan. They didn't reply, nor have we heard from them since. I regret not speak with my brother.

When we bought this house, we didn't have the down payment, Bruce and Regina eagerly lent us $95,000. What I didn't know back then was that our backers got to own fifty percent. After paying on time for two years, the bank sent us a notice saying the percentage rate had just been raised making our new mortgage excessive. We tried to get the rate lowered, and finally asked Bruce if the property could be refinanced for less through his broker.

It took my breath away when Bruce mentioned he would get

fifty percent after we sold the place. That was the first time I realized that we only owned half of this property. In my haste to borrow, I never actually read what I was signing; I figured we simply had to pay back the original $95,000 along with some interest. No wonder our lawyer, Frank Peck, said it was a bad idea. Yasue grasped the whole concept of a third party ownership; she believed I understood it as well. Bruce is a businessman, in retrospect I think the deal was a bit unfair, but we don't dwell on it.

His name was removed from the first deed until our loan application was accepted. 'THE PLAN' was revised. An appraiser from the bank told me the value of this house had doubled since it was purchased. Ron said our credit was good, and since we were never late with a payment there was no reason to turn us down. The only misrepresentation was not divulging our contract with Bruce, which I think was all about taxes. World Savings approved refinancing, and 'THE PLAN' was extended three more years, at least we could stay here until then. He expected us to sell the shop and put the house on the market as soon as possible. His investment of $95,000 was paid off with the new mortgage; nonetheless, he still owns fifty percent.

Our deal seemed to work in his favor, we aren't disappointed; things always turn out fine, but in the future I must pay attention to reading a document before signing. I was in a hurry, and foolish enough to think we could own a house without considering the existence of a pay back.

Please don't get me wrong, Bruce and Regina are two of the greatest people we know, if not for their generosity, we couldn't possibly have come up with a down payment for this place. We'll always be grateful, their friendship is cherished, and we love them. They own an elegant chateau in a pastoral area of Pasadena, recently their focus has been on remodeling a beach cottage north of L.A. Bruce closed a huge deal recently in The United Arab Emirates, and I say bravo.

We are aging, and eager to sell the shop, but K-9 Tubs will only be available to the right people. Yasue can't work as hard as she used to, basically her enjoyment comes from puttering around the yard for hours. After twenty-seven years of experience, we are altogether committed to faithful clients and their beloved pets. When the business is sold, my enduring faith in God will lead us to our ultimate destination in Hawaii. 'If at first you don't succeed, try, try, and try again.'

The state of California recognizes us as domestic partners. Nothing will change; K-9 was founded on high standards. It's hard for me to be there lately. I don't breathe well around the hair.

Lately my activities have slowed down, if I don't feel like cooking, we pick up a healthy take-out dinner locally. I get some money from Social Security, my car has a handy disability placard and I don't have to serve on jury duty. The timing was perfect when I joined the Kaiser Permanente Program for seniors, since I never imagined I would live this long.

The executors of our wills, April and Victor have been our closest friends for many years. The two guys from Massachusetts are family and have been very good to us. Victor is three weeks older than I am. Before he retired to collect Social Security and Medicare, he considered many healthcare organizations, but chose the senior plan at Kaiser Permanente. It seemed to satisfy my picky friend, which is why I opted for the same provider. April had a tummy tuck recently at Kaiser in San Diego. Within six months he successfully lost more than one hundred pounds and feels great.

On the first visit to Kaiser in the spring of 2005 they assigned me to a primary physician, who noticed my breathing difficulty right away and scheduled respiratory tests. Later the exam proved just how badly my lungs were functioning and she put me on the appropriate inhalers. The nurse took my blood pressure, which was very high, so my new physician prescribed a pill to lower it. After one week my pressure still hadn't gone down; I needed stronger medication. Since then I have fired two doctors.

I was scanned for osteoporosis, my bones had shrunken enough to change my height, but I could take a pill once a week for that. When the results of my blood tests came back, another doctor was surprised to learn I had hepatitis C, a serious liver problem. I was aware of contracting it while shooting dope intravenously in the sixties and there was no cure. An internal specialist told me a drug called Interferon could make it all vanish but the arduous treatment would take from twenty-four to forty-eight weeks. In addition there might be drastic side effects like constant flu symptoms, insomnia, constant fatigue, a loss of appetite, nausea, diarrhea, as well as chronic depression.

My dear sweet Indian doctor, Amandeep Sahota needed to find out how badly my liver is damaged and asked me to have a CT scan. One thing I know is that I hate being sick for one day, let alone endure forty-eight weeks of awful side effects caused by a precarious drug which may or may not be a cure. Part of my condition could be hereditary. Dad's mother died of jaundice in her late thirties, and never drank. Both my parents were alcoholics, my father had cirrhosis when he was young, yet continued to drink. Mom quit when she reached sixty, I'm sure her liver was also flawed, in spite of which she lived to be eighty-one.

We lasted at the Sunset Villa seven years, and I stayed sober then for more than six years. I started drinking again when those two psychotic gay guys began to taunt us there. Wine became an accepted staple after we moved here. Friends usually brought a bottle of wine over and I would pick up extras when certain brands were on sale. Party time was limited since I made two nine-day novenas a month, but during the past year my hangovers got worse, so now I only drink a toast on occasion. It's not in my character to complain, I always tell people I'm fine regardless, but I'm not young anymore. Yasue understands and never nags me about anything. I just can't do what I used to.

I pray that the right people will buy our shop v soon so we can finally move to Hawaii. In spite of my usual resistance to change, now is the time. This marvelous old house in a great location should go quickly. When it is sold, the bank gets paid first and Bruce takes an easy fifty-percent. If there is any money left, maybe we can still afford a small place on the north shore of Oahu.

We've learned it is easier to pay rent than worry about fixing up an ageing house; we could simply lease a cozy two-bedroom place near the ocean. I thought of trading in my Camry for a small BMW, but now I'll wait. We'll need to get rid of many things. It's not the time to buy anything new. Our gardener, Jesus, is happy to accept extra clothing and discards. He sends it to poor people in Mexico. Most of the furniture can be sold through *Recycler* ads. My lovable cat, Magic, will have to stay in a quarantine area for a while. We will only be taking some breezy attire, religious accessories, the computer, TV, also a few basic art supplies. I plan to start painting after I set up a proper altar in Hawaii.

There is only one major move left in me, and this will be it.

Some say I could get cabin fever, but I don't think so. It scares me to consider leaving L.A. I've been the 'Mayor of Hyperion' for ages. Today our whole existence takes place within one mile of this house. Shopping, preparing food, and visiting K-9, is my daily routine. Later I pick Yasue up from work, serve dinner, and watch some television. Everyday life won't change much, only our zip code. Yasue doesn't wish to look for work right away, but she'll find a great deal to do anyway. She is ready to adopt a dog now, and grow orchids as a hobby. It's important to find a gay-friendly community on or close to the north shore. I imagine a peaceful environment which includes carefree artists, hip galleries, and country stores.

Soon Yasue will fly to Okinawa to visit her ailing elderly mother. She is ecstatic about seeing her relatives and old friends again. Perhaps she'll get a chance to reflect on how hard she works just to pay our mortgage, which is a mere fifty percent of the final selling price. I hope she returns with a strong urge to live on Oahu forever. Life is simpler there. I must pray hard for help.

Before Nicole Conn got busy filming her incredible adopted preemie son, Nicholas, she wanted to produce a different type of documentary. The concept entailed long-term lesbian partnerships and she intended to interview various female couples. Nicole hoped to feature Yasue and me as contented lesbian role models. We were expected to comment on how our amazing relationship had survived. My partner bristled at the idea of being in front of a camera to declare her bond with me for eternity. Yasue was never able to admit that she was gay. "I am not GAY, though I love you with all my heart, I could never be close with another woman." We vowed to cherish each other forever, so why worry about a three-letter word after all these years?

Recently I saw Nicole at the local market, and she told me she was going through an ugly separation with her long-time companion Gwen. My friend was happy that I asked her to visit with us. She needs someone who understands what hell she's going through as a single parent caring for two adopted kids.

It bothers me to some extent that Yasue has not yet glanced at this book. She claims to know the story and might find it boring. After all my time and effort in writing this, she said that I was not to use her real name since our relationship might embarrass her family. She was adamant about hiding her real identity until I persuaded her that this book had to be a completely truthful account, and she is the best part of my life.

During the early eighties a new amnesty law offered a plan. Eventually we struggled through it, and Yasue got a permanent green card. She is not yet a United States citizen because she avoids the hassle of paperwork and doesn't make an effort to study our laws. I scold her when she glances at gossip media, but I can't order her to finalize the citizenship documents. Though she doesn't care much for reading, I never dictate a timetable or tell her what to do. After all, we are equals.

For years we've shared a fulfilling existence, we are still deeply in love and happy. Yasue is the very air I breathe, and it's apparent she needs me just as much. I believe we would literally cease to exist without each other. My lovely Sagittarius has been a great inspiration, and an extraordinary source of light to me. I've endured considerable anguish during my life, but it's hard to stay depressed around Yasue, her cheerfulness and optimism always carried me through a mixture of turbulent times. She now owns the business and drives a new Toyota Yaris.

While there are never guarantees, I might have extended my life if I didn't drink or smoke so much. Now I rarely smoke or tip a glass just for celebrations. I'm practically a vegetarian. Today I realize the best you can be is honest and the most one should expect is contentment through happiness. I need to slow down, unplug negativity, clear my mind through meditation, get back to nature, relax, and always remember to breathe. Being angry is wrong and against my nature, wrath is one of the seven deadly sins.

Despite the fact that I am doubtful about reincarnation, I will continue to study various religions. The Sikhs believe in only one God and I agree. They are taught to love all humanity without prejudice, but they also say wealth must be protected by the sword. I'm glad we are not rich. The Amish, whom I find admirable, isolate themselves to keep out the modern world and have faith in heaven or hell.

I like a simple existence and do my best each day to sleep without fears or uncertainties. My standard novenas will continue as long as there are candles and time.

God willing if the right person comes along, we hope to sell our business and move to Hawaii permanently. You may think the end of my story seems anticlimactic, compared to the beginning so I hope you are not too judgmental or disappointed. when this manuscript is ready I expect to complete a short book of prose, practice Tai Chi and paint with oils again. I thought that *this was as good as it gets,* but maybe it will get better.

Peace and Love,

Carole, a Lucky Little Rabbit.

www.ingramcontent.com/pod-product-compliance
Lightning Source LLC
Chambersburg PA
CBHW021956160426
43197CB00007B/154